D1553567

Islam and Democracy after the Arab Spring

Islam
and
Democracy
after the
Arab Spring

JOHN L. ESPOSITO,

TAMARA SONN,

AND

JOHN O. VOLL

OXFORD
UNIVERSITY PRESS

OXFORD
UNIVERSITY PRESS

Oxford University Press is a department of the University of
Oxford. It furthers the University's objective of excellence in research,
scholarship, and education by publishing worldwide.

Oxford   New York
Auckland   Cape Town   Dar es Salaam   Hong Kong   Karachi
Kuala Lumpur   Madrid   Melbourne   Mexico City   Nairobi
New Delhi   Shanghai   Taipei   Toronto

With offices in
Argentina   Austria   Brazil   Chile   Czech Republic   France   Greece
Guatemala   Hungary   Italy   Japan   Poland   Portugal   Singapore
South Korea   Switzerland   Thailand   Turkey   Ukraine   Vietnam

Oxford is a registered trademark of Oxford University Press
in the UK and certain other countries.

Published in the United States of America by
Oxford University Press
198 Madison Avenue, New York, NY 10016

Library of Congress Cataloging-in-Publication Data
Esposito, John L.
Islam and democracy after the Arab Spring / John L. Esposito, Tamara Sonn,
and John O. Voll.
pages cm
Includes bibliographical references and index.
ISBN 978–0–19–514798–8 (hardback : alk. paper)
1. Arab Spring, 2010–   2. Democracy–Arab countries.   3. Democracy—Islamic
countries.   4. Democracy—Religious aspects—Islam.   I. Sonn, Tamara, 1949–
II. Voll, John Obert, 1936–   III. Title.
JQ1850.A91E86 2016
320.917'67—dc23
2015007381

1 3 5 7 9 8 6 4 2
Printed in the United States of America
on acid-free paper

For those who continue to struggle for justice, equality,
and democracy

Contents

Acknowledgments

THE AUTHORS WISH to express their deep gratitude to Cynthia Read, Senior Editor, and to Gina Chung, Editorial Assistant at Oxford University Press, for supporting and encouraging us through the long process of tracking and analyzing the impact of the Arab Spring. John Esposito also wishes to acknowledge and thank Nathan Lean, his former Senior Research Assistant, and John Voll wishes to thank Shazia Kamal Farook, Gurbet Sayilgan, and Tasi Perkins for their invaluable assistance in the research and writing of chapters of this book. Tamara Sonn wishes to thank her students for always asking the right questions. We would also like to thank our spouses for their patience and support as the ever-changing events connected with the Arab Spring commanded our attention.

*Islam and Democracy after the
Arab Spring*

I

Introduction

MANY WESTERN OBSERVERS were shocked when Arabs began open rebellions against their governments in December 2010. Authoritarian rule had been the reality for so long that some considered it to be, if not the preferred form of government among Arabs, at least the expected and accepted reality. That many political scientists were utterly unprepared for these developments was acknowledged by Gregory Gause in an article in *Foreign Affairs* in the summer of 2011 titled "Why Middle East Studies Missed the Arab Spring."[1] Secretary of State Hillary Clinton, presumably recipient of expert advice from the nation's top experts, stated simply, "We're facing an Arab awakening that nobody could have imagined and few predicted just a few years ago. And it's sweeping aside a lot of old preconceptions."[2] Political scientist Jacqueline Stevens put it more bluntly in a June 2012 *New York Times* op-ed piece titled "Political Scientists Are Lousy Forecasters." After reviewing political scientists' failure to foresee the demise of the Soviet Union, the rise and potential impact of al-Qaeda, and the Arab Spring, Stevens concluded, "Chimps randomly throwing darts at the possible outcomes would have done almost as well as the experts."[3]

Some analysts suggested that the seemingly spontaneous uprisings were the unpredicted effect of the confluence of the "youth bulge"— majorities of populations being under the age of 30, unemployed, and usually better educated than their parents—and their facility with the new public cyber-sphere. Muslim-majority countries share with many other developing countries the fact that the majority of the population is under 30. Reflecting success in reducing infant mortality and improving healthcare overall, this phenomenon causes enormous social pressure in countries unable to provide employment opportunities for their restive youth. Unemployed youth in authoritarian regimes can become a potent force, especially in the context of the new social media technologies most commonly associated with younger generations. Digital social media have allowed the creation of a new, virtual public sphere that allows activists to bypass authoritarian governments' prohibition of freedom of speech, press, and association. As the work of Jon Anderson and Dale Eickleman demonstrates, the virtual public sphere neutralizes class, gender, and even sectarian distinctions, allowing for the creation of a new kind of social activism, one that does not require a charismatic leader or vanguard, just numbers. In the first decade of the 21st century, participation in this virtual public sphere was approaching critical mass. All that was needed to see the effectiveness of online social/community organizing was a "tipping point"—to borrow Malcolm Gladwell's term. Just what would serve as that tipping point was the only aspect of the Arab Spring that was unpredictable. In the case of Tunisia, it was fruit vendor Mohamed Bouazizi's self-immolation; for Egypt, it was the killing of computer programmer Khaled Said in Alexandria. For Libya and Yemen, it was Tunisia and Egypt. For Syria, it was the torture of teenage antigovernment graffiti artists in Daraa. One way or another, the new cyber social sphere was going to be the means to release pent-up demand for democracy, especially among the "cognoscenti youth bulge."

Others suggested, more traditionally, that Muslim countries were at last catching up to the rest of the world. In 1991, the year that the Soviet Union imploded, political scientist Samuel Huntington had described the history of democratic transitions since the American and French revolutions as a series of "waves."[4] The first wave, lasting from 1828 to 1926, saw the United States, Argentina, Chile, Britain, France, Switzerland, Italy, and Spain extending democratic participation beyond the elites who dominated earlier governments. The results were not perfect, but at least half of the adult males achieved the right to participate in competitive elections. By Huntington's count, this "long" wave involved perhaps thirty countries. Military coups and the rise of fascist governments in Latin America and Europe ended that wave and resulted in World War II. The defeat of the fascists in that war then gave rise to the second wave of democratization. It lasted from 1943 to 1962 and comprised the restoration of democracies destroyed by fascists and the addition of a few more countries to the roster of democracies, thanks to decolonization. But by the late 1950s authoritarianism was on the rise again in Latin America, Asia, Greece, and Portugal. What had been a democratic Portuguese republic, for example, was replaced by the authoritarian Estado Novo in

1933. Repressive and unpopular, it was overthrown in a popularly sup-ported and nonviolent military coup in 1974 (known as the "Carnation Revolution" because its supporters filled the streets and placed red car-nations in the barrels of the soldiers' guns). This transition marks the beginning of Huntington's third wave of democratization, which would include countries in South America, the former Soviet Union, Europe, and Africa. It involved generally nonviolent populist movements and was spurred by an array of factors, including economic and military failures, increased urbanization, rising levels of education, and resultant surges in people's desires for freedom and abilities to express those desires. The Arab Spring's mass popular protests that resulted in toppling some of the Arab world's long-standing authoritarian regimes led some to speak of a "fourth wave of democratization."[5]

But by summer 2013, it had become evident that the Arab Spring uprisings had failed to produce democracy everywhere except where they began, in Tunisia. Egypt's first democratic government had been over-thrown in a military coup that was ostensibly popularly supported. Syria had descended into a protracted and brutal civil war that has, as of this writing, brought the United States and other European powers back into combat in the Middle East, along with other regional powers. And Libya has simply fragmented; it has two mutually hostile elected governments, one in Tripoli and one in Tobruk, while various militias control different sectors of the country.

These developments demonstrate, to begin with, that there is no inev-itable transition from a popular uprising—youth bulge and new social media or not—to a sustainable social or political movement. In order for an uprising to become a sustained movement, as Sidney Tarrow has argued, there are a number of prerequisites, including diffuse social networks, familiar forms of collective action, cultural frames shared broadly across a population, and political opportunity. As the re-emergence of military control indicates, in Egypt and Syria, at any rate, political opportunity was lacking. In Libya, it is questionable whether any of Tarrow's social move-ment elements existed. In any case, there are arguably as many youth involved in protests against the elected Egyptian President, Mohammad Morsi as in demonstrations supporting him, and in Syria's and Libya's militias. Pew surveys conducted in 2012 indicate that nearly two-thirds of Egyptians preferred the Saudi model of governance over Turkey's secu-lar model.[6] And, as the queue of ISIS videos indicates, not all tech-savvy youth are pro-democracy.

But what about the "fourth wave" hypothesis? Was it overly optimistic? Is the overall failure of the Arab Spring uprisings evidence that the "fourth wave" hypothesis was ill founded? As Ahmet T. Kuru points out, in the wake of the apparently failed Arab Spring, there is a temptation to revive the hypothesis that there will be no "wave" in Muslim-majority countries because Islam is indeed the insurmountable object in the way of democratization.[7] That hypothesis is associated with the same Samuel Huntington who came up with the wave theory of democratization but also claimed that Muslim countries would never have their own wave because of inherent contradictions between Islam and democracy. In 1996, John L. Esposito and John O. Voll tackled these issues in *Islam and Democracy* (Oxford University Press). Based on six case studies—Algeria, Egypt, Iran, Malaysia, Pakistan, and Sudan—they demonstrated that Islam and democratic governance are far from incompatible but that different sociocultural and historical experiences result in diverse approaches to democratization and its relationship to Islamic ideologies. In light of the Arab Spring uprisings and their apparent failures, we will revisit the question of Islamic approaches to democracy. In case studies—including Arab-majority and non-Arab states, we will trace the trajectory of struggles for good governance. We will examine the current state of democratization efforts in the subject states, taking into consideration critical factors such as the impact of colonialism, the Cold War, and changing demographics. We will argue that the Arab Spring uprisings represent only the most recent developments in struggles—ongoing for well over a century— for good governance and popular sovereignty in Muslim-majority countries. They were driven by long-standing grievances against authoritarian governments, both colonial and postcolonial. The only people who were surprised by them are those who, in ignorance of that history, looked at non-democratic post-independence governments in Arab countries and generalized that they represented the preferred or perhaps even requisite form of governance for Arabs or even for Muslims. As Ziad el-Elaimy, one of the leaders of Egypt's 2011 uprisings, put it, "The Egyptian Revolution had begun long before 2011, and [will] continue long after."[8] The same is true of democratization efforts in other Muslim-majority countries. We will therefore argue that, although the Arab Spring did not result—domino-style—in the end of authoritarianism in Muslim-majority countries, democratization did not begin with the Arab Spring and, judging from its history, is bound to continue long after its "winter."

Modernization Theory, Huntington, and the Problem of Seeing "Religion" as the Relevant Variable

Among the reasons the Arab Spring caught Western analysts by surprise is the dominance of modernization theory and its corollary, the secularization hypothesis. Traced to pioneer German sociologist Max Weber (d. 1920) and his characterization of the modern world as "calculating" or rational, modernization theory predicts that as societies industrialize, urbanize, and develop technologically, the appeal of religion—with all its mystery and acceptance of fate—will diminish. Society will "secularize." As happened in Europe, institutionalized religion will be excluded from economic and political affairs; religion will be limited to personal matters.

The privatization of religion—"secularization"—was a result of Europe's process of shifting from authoritarian to democratic governance. But it gradually assumed normativity. Secularization discourse implied that as a society modernizes and democratizes, it *must* secularize. As Danish sociologist Dietrich Jung says, "In its simplistic version, this theory of secularization has been equated with modernization as such, whereby religion and modernity are viewed as being embedded in a zero-sum game."[9] In other words, to the extent that a society is modern and democratic, it will be secular; religion will be confined to the private sphere. To the extent that religion is involved in the public sphere and society is therefore not secular, it can be neither modern nor democratic.

Among the more influential scholars struggling under the weight of the secularization hypothesis was political scientist Samuel Huntington, who famously predicted a clash between Western and Islamo-Confucian civilizations.[10] Huntington actually questions modernization theory, at least insofar as it predicted the inevitable globalization of Europe's model of modernity. He writes, "In the first half of the twentieth century intellectual elites generally assumed that economic and social modernization was leading to the withering away of religion as a significant element in human existence." The emerging society would be "tolerant, rational, pragmatic, progressive, humanistic, and secular."[11] These predictions were incorrect, Huntington says, in view of the "global revival of religion." But rather than revising the theory, Huntington instead generalizes about the "unsecularization of the world." For Huntington, the global religious resurgence is a rejection of modernity.[12] Still bound to modernization theory, he simply excludes societies that are not secular from the ranks of the modern and therefore democratic (or "democratizing").

It is this alleged rejection of democracy that became the focus of Huntington's assumed "clash" between "the West and the rest," as he put it, because embedded in his notion of democracy is secularism and the attendant religious freedom (pluralism) that developed in Europe only with democratization. For Huntington and all those bound by traditional modernization theory, if religion is involved in public life, it will preclude both pluralism and democracy.

These observations reflect Huntington's earlier work on the processes of democratization in which he explained the "democracy deficit" in Muslim-majority countries as due to Islamic societies' lack of the prerequisites for development of democracy. Perhaps not all religions are inimical to religious freedom/pluralism and democracy, Huntington argued, but Islam is. Western Christian societies were able to develop democracy, but Islamic societies would not be able to.

Huntington explained Islamic societies' "democracy deficit" in the context of late 20th-century discussions of evolving global democracy. Following the implosion of the Soviet Union, Francis Fukuyama (Huntington's student) wrote *The End of History and the Last Man* (Free Press, 1992), in which he claimed that history would never again be viewed the same. For nearly half of the 20th century, the conflict between capitalist and communist groups of countries ("blocs")—known as the East-West conflict or the Cold War—had dominated global politics, and those of the United States in particular. It was a "death match" between two archenemies of relatively equal strength; the "Reds" could at any moment take over the "Free World" and end life as we know it. Readiness to deter potential military threats from the Soviet bloc therefore drove US policy and military buildup from the end of World War II until the USSR disbanded in 1991. In the immediate aftermath of that paradigm-shattering development, then-President George H. W. Bush spoke of a "peace dividend"; now that the Soviet Union had been dismantled, Western countries could decrease military spending and use their resources more constructively. Fukuyama attempted to capture the drama of this turn of events. "What we may be witnessing," he said, "is not just the end of the Cold War ... but the end of history as such: that is, the end point of mankind's ideological evolution and the universalization of Western liberal democracy as the final form of human government."[13] In brief, Fukuyama believed that all peoples want the kind of governments in place in Europe and the Americas.[14]

But Huntington disagreed. He singled out as unlikely candidates for democratization Marxist-Leninist regimes, those where Confucianism dominates, and countries influenced by Islam. Why? Because, says Huntington, modern civilization and therefore democracy can only come from a set of values that he describes as uniquely Western: "individualism, liberalism, constitutionalism, human rights, equality, liberty, the rule of law, democracy, free markets, [and] the separation of church and state."[15]

Huntington acknowledges that many of his "democracy-resistant" countries were savaged by Western imperialism and that fascism and communism are also "products of Western civilization." But this does not impact Huntington's characterization of Western values. Regardless of actions by Western powers that defy them, in Huntington's view respect for democracy and human rights remain defining Western values.[16]

Huntington does note a direct correlation between the colonially created states with their non-representative, corrupt postcolonial governments, and the modern revival of Islam as a focus of oppositional discourse. But because he has already assumed that Islam is un- or anti-democratic, he describes Islamist opposition to authoritarianism not as similar to the kind of populist opposition developed in Christian societies but as a substitute for it.[17] Huntington argues that the "general failure of liberal democracy to take hold in Muslim societies . . . has its source at least in part in the inhospitable nature of Islamic culture and society to Western liberal concepts."[18] But failing to take into account the content of Islamist demands, he simply concludes that, unlike Christian societies in post-communist Eastern Europe and the Soviet Union (his third wave of democratization) who "are making progress towards economic development and democratic politics; . . . the prospects in the Muslim republics are bleak."[19]

Opposition to Secularism Does Not Equal Opposition to Democracy: Multiple Democracies

There is, undoubtedly, a "democracy deficit" in most Arab countries. The Regional Bureau for Arab States of the United Nations Development Program (UNDP) and the Arab Fund for Economic and Social Development issued a series of "Arab Human Development" reports beginning in 2002, which identified a "freedom deficit" in Arab countries (along with deficits in women's empowerment and the development of human capabilities or "knowledge"). The Arab Human Development Report (AHDR) of 2002—"Creating Opportunities for Future Generations"—notes that

> There is a substantial lag between Arab countries and other regions in terms of participatory governance. The wave of democracy that transformed governance in most of Latin America and East Asia in the 1980s and Eastern Europe and much of Central Asia in the late 1980s and early 1990s has barely reached the Arab States. This freedom deficit undermines human development and is one of the most painful manifestations of lagging political development. While de jure acceptance of democracy and human rights is enshrined in constitutions, legal codes and government pronouncements, de facto implementation is often neglected and, in some cases, deliberately disregarded.[20]

In fact, the 2002 report ranks Arab countries in the late 1990s at the very bottom in terms of freedom among seven regions (North America, Oceania, Europe, Latin America and the Caribbean, South and East Asia, and Sub-Saharan Africa).

The 2004 report—"Towards Freedom in the Arab World"—focuses on ways "to stimulate a dialogue in Arab societies on how to expand freedom and establish good governance."[21] But unlike Huntington-esque analyses, the AHDR reports avoid essentializing Islam and indeed observe that there are "fundamental principles in Islam which dictate good governance, includ[ing] the realization of justice and equality, the assurance of public freedoms, the right of the nation to appoint and dismiss rulers, and guarantees of all public and private rights for non-Muslims and Muslims alike." Further, the report cites a recent World Values Survey (WVS) in which nine regions were surveyed, including advanced Western countries. Arab respondents were the most likely to agree with the statement that "democracy is better than any other form of governance." Thus, the report states specifically that the democracy deficit "is not cultural in origin." It is not Islam that stands in the way of freedom or democracy, but "political rulers, in power and in opposition, [who] have selectively appropriated Islam to support and perpetuate their oppressive rule."[22] Included in that category are those who attempt to keep Islamists from political involvement. The report recognizes that the most active opponents to authoritarian regimes are Islamists and notes that authoritarian regimes thus suppress the rights of Islamists, claiming that Islamist support for democracy is insincere, a mere ploy to gain power and then eliminate personal and public freedoms. In the view of the authors of the report, then, it is despite Islamic values—not because of them—that Arab countries register low on the democracy scale.

There are, as well, Muslims who reject secularism. For religious Muslims, secularism is not merely the removal of religious coercion from public life, but the removal of moral values from public life. In the words of Muslim Brotherhood ideologue Sayyid Qutb (d. 1966), for example, secularism has resulted in nothing but "troubles, restlessness and fear."[23] Even progressives express concern. Modern Pakistani scholar Fazlur Rahman (d. 1988) equates secularism with atheism and attributes the atrocities of colonialism to the West's secularism. For him it is "the bane of modernity."[24] In the words of contemporary Iranian democracy advocate Abdolkarim Soroush:

> It is amazing that some consider the democratization of the religious government contingent upon the secularization of religion and religious law. . . . Is the religious society not, by nature, plural and pluralistic? . . . Belief is a hundred times more diverse and colorful than disbelief. If the [religious] pluralism of secularism makes it suitable for democracy, the faithful community is a thousand times more suitable for it. . . . We no longer claim that a genuinely religious government can be democratic but that it cannot be otherwise.[25]

But as these statements make clear, what is being rejected is immorality, intolerance, hypocrisy, and specific political agendas—not democracy or even religious pluralism or religious freedom.

Reflecting advances in the understanding of diverse religious paradigms, many scholars today recognize the need to reassess the relationship between religion and modernity—most prominently, anthropologist Talal Asad. He notes with particular clarity the conflict between Western paradigms of privatized ethics and the Islamic paradigm of universal ethics.[26] In the same vein, Jose Casanova describes Western Europe's privatization of religion as a unique phenomenon. It resulted from the specifics of European history and is not universalizable as a template for other communities.[27] Sociologist Rodney Stark famously calls secularization theory "a product of wishful thinking."[28] As a result of the dismantling of the monolithic 20th-century modernization paradigm, many scholars today call for recognition of "multiple modernities."[29] A look at long-term developments in Muslim-majority countries also suggests recognition of "multiple democracies."

Long-Term Developments: The Changing Relationships between Islam and Democracy

Just as there are Muslims who reject secularism, there were, and continue to be, some Muslim ideologues who reject democracy. But these positions must be understood in the broad context of anti-colonial activism. In that context there have been a series of identifiable shifts in attitudes toward the culture of the colonizers, shifts that resulted from specific historical developments. In the late 19th and early 20th centuries, for example, modern science and democratic forms of governance were seen by many reformers as part of a global heritage. While scholars in Islamic civilizations had dominated global cultural and scientific production in the Middle Ages, colonization had made it clear that European scholars had taken the lead. Reformers argued that rejecting European political domination and re-entering the global cultural marketplace required recovering both Islam's lost dynamism and commitment to learning. Reformers such as Persian Jamal al-Din al-Afghani (d. 1897) and Egyptian Muhammad 'Abduh (d. 1905) criticized traditionalists who rejected modern science as a Western product for failing to recognize that Europe's modern science and technology had been developed on the legacy inherited from the medieval Islamic world. At the same time, activists formed political parties demanding democratic reforms. In Persia (known as Iran since 1935), popular protests against a profligate king (1905–1907) led to the establishment of a parliament and constitutional limits to royal authority. In Egypt the Wafd Party, founded in 1919, called for independence from Britain and the establishment of a constitutional government.

But as European colonialism became more entrenched, democratic institutions were weakened and the process of internal critique was compromised. Muslim religious authorities may have fallen into an inflexible traditionalism, but they remained important symbols of communal identity vis-à-vis the European invaders. And that symbolic value increased proportionately as European ways continued to displace traditional life-styles. In this context, the more that reformers criticized the tradition-alist authorities as impediments to development and independence, the more the reformers sounded like the Europeans who justified their impe-rialism by claiming the Muslims were incapable of running their own affairs. As a result, many Muslim reformers actually alienated people in their own societies. In the eyes of people already under the extreme pressure of colonization, these internal criticisms—despite their good intentions—seemed to be betrayals.

This reaction was exacerbated following World War I. Prior to World War I, Britain, France, and pre-Soviet Russia had convinced Arab lead-ers to assist them in defeating their European enemy Germany by rebel-ling against their own rulers and Germany's ally, the Ottoman Turks. In return, Britain promised to recognize Arab independence in Greater Syria (which included the current states of Syria, Lebanon, Israel, Jordan, and the Palestinian West Bank) and Iraq. That promise was violated; Britain took control of Iraq and those portions of Greater Syria now known as Israel, Jordan, and the Palestinian West Bank. France took control of what are now known as Syria and Lebanon. Britain retained its colonial control over Egypt, and France kept its control over Morocco, Tunisia, and Algeria. This betrayal inevitably resulted in a backlash against Europe. In this con-text, Europe's political actions and alien cultural norms were conflated in the minds of a new breed of Muslim reformers who stressed a sharp dis-tinction between European and Islamic culture, the purity and superiority of Islamic values, and the sufficiency of Islam for all human needs.

This new discourse served the dual purpose of appealing to the broadest possible audience in largely undereducated populations and motivating them to become politically involved. Thus, rather than criti-cizing people's passivity and superstitions, as the earlier reformers had done, the more populist post–World War I reformers focused on rais-ing sociopolitical awareness among the masses. As in the American Civil Rights movement, listeners were regaled with accounts of the suf-fering they had endured and encouraged to rise up and assert their rights. At the same time, while earlier activists had stressed the need to recommit to Islam's intellectual and cultural dynamism, the new trend was to stress religious practice as the means to recover Islamic societies' lost strength. As well, people were reminded that Islam was more than mere belief and rituals, as Western Christianity appeared to be. Instead, it was a comprehensive worldview and set of values and principles designed to guide all aspects of life—personal, social, economic, and political.

From the perspective of this politicized Islam (called "Political Islam" or Islamism by scholars), pre–World War II political organization, with its secular orientation, was inappropriate for Muslim societies. The new order would be wholly Islamic. Unlike the earlier political parties, generally populated by educated people from the cities who had often gone to European schools and were comfortable with modern life, postwar reformers represented the majority of people—many of whom were still largely rural or newly urbanized and generally more traditional in outlook. Motivating them to become politically active in order to achieve independence and good governance became a major task of the Islamists. Competing with secular governments with far greater resources, often supplied through close relations with foreign powers, the Islamists demanded that foreign legal systems (which had been imposed by European colonial authorities) and models of government be replaced with authentically Islamic ones.

This is the context in which democracy—identified in populist discourse as Western and therefore not Islamic—was rejected by some ideologues. The founder of the Brotherhood, Hasan al-Banna (d. 1949), respected the West's intellectual freedom and democracy and had no complaints against capitalism as such, and he praised communism's emphasis on social justice. But al-Banna said that Europe's selfish individualism and communism's atheism and tyranny destroy the human spirit.[30] Islam, he taught, provides a comprehensive approach to both social and spiritual well-being, giving rise to the Islamist motto: "Islam is the solution." Muhammad al-Ghazzali, a major intellectual in the early Muslim Brotherhood, described Western imperialism as anti-Islamic cultural aggression. Like the Crusaders of yore, al-Ghazzali said, "The West surely seeks to humiliate us, to occupy our lands and begin destroying Islam by annulling its laws and abolishing its traditions."[31] It was that legacy of domination and disrespect that was being rejected, not democratic governance as such.

Second and Third Waves in the Muslim World

At the end of World War II, most of the Muslim world continued to be under direct or indirect Western imperial control. However, Muslim-majority countries joined others in Asia and Africa in achieving independence by the early 1960s. In almost every country, the first independent government was an elected parliamentary government led by old-style nationalists who represented pre–World War II ideologies and organizations. These basically secularist regimes failed and were generally replaced by authoritarian secular regimes dominated by the military. Some of the new regimes were led by relatively conservative military leaders, like Ibrahim Abboud in Sudan, Muhammad Ayub Khan in Pakistan, and Suharto in Indonesia. In other countries, the new military governments were led by younger officers—like Nasser in Egypt, Ba'th Party military leaders in Syria and Iraq, Abd al-Karim Qasim in Iraq—who worked to define revolutionary ideologies that presented programs of radical social change. In some newly independent states, the military did not assume control, but the civilian leaders established one-party states supported by the military, as happened under Sekou Touré in Guinea and Bourguiba in Tunisia. In Algeria, which achieved independence in 1962 following a costly war, a combination of a tradition of the radical ideology of the Front de Libération Nationale (FLN) with the power of the military under the command of Houari Boumédiène created a one-party military state. In some countries like Malaysia and Senegal, politics came to be dominated by a single party, although within multiparty systems.

While not essentially anti-religious, the new authoritarian regimes, whether conservative or radical, were basically secular in their vision of the role of religion in politics. In most of the Muslim world, the second wave of democratization was brought to an end as a result of a combination of the ineffectiveness of the new secular parliamentary leaders and their replacement by authoritarian military or one-party civilian regimes. In the 1950s and 1960s, the dominant visions were nationalist and secular, rather than religious. Even in the monarchies that had maintained at least formal independence, religion was not the dominant political element. Two monarchies with authentic Islamic identifications, the Zaydi Imamate in Yemen and the Sanusi kingdom in Libya, were overthrown by young military officers in the new radical mode.

An important exception to these developments is Turkey. At the end of World War I, Turkish nationalists led by Mustafa Kemal (later Atatürk) established a one-party republic as the successor to the Ottoman Empire. Turkey participated in the second wave of democratization, but as an established independent state rather than a newly created one. The Kemalist state had been authoritarian in its methods, but at the end of World War II, Kemal's successor, Ismet Inönü, allowed the creation of opposition parties. In a dramatic example of second wave democratization, the opposition Democrat Party (DP) won a major victory in the national elections of 1950, and the previously dominant Republican People's Party (RPP) relinquished control of the government peacefully. However, in 1960, following a series of increasingly violent confrontations between supporters of the two major parties, the Turkish military announced, "Owing to the crisis into which our democracy has fallen, and owing to the recent sad incidents and in order to prevent fratricide, the Turkish armed forces have taken over the administration of the country."[32] Although a multiparty parliamentary system was soon restored, the military assumed the role of independent guardian of secularist democracy and engaged in coups to "restore democracy" in 1971 and 1980. The general attitude of military leadership was frankly described by Çevik Bir, a leader of what came to be called the coup by memorandum of 1997, which forced the resignation of a government. The general said, "In Turkey, we have a marriage of Islam and democracy. . . . The child of this marriage is secularism. Now this child gets sick from time to time. The Turkish Armed Forces is the doctor which saves the child."[33] Turkey's experience represented a partial success for democracy in the final decades of the 20th century but continued a sense of authoritarian secularism as well.

By the 1980s, most of the new secular authoritarian regimes became increasingly repressive and were viewed by growing proportions of their populations as failures. The failure of the secular modernizing regimes to ensure human rights and prosperity increased the appeal of the idea that "Islam is the solution." In the era of what was to become the third wave of democratization, the major opposition to authoritarian rule in the Muslim world was provided by Islamically identified groups, ranging from militant jihadists in Afghanistan to advocates of Islamic ideals of pluralism like Abd al-Rahman Wahid in Indonesia.

The comprehensive vision of an Islamic political society outlined by earlier Islamists like Sayyid Qutb took concrete form in a wide range of movements, although many of the new movements moved away from the abrasive militancy of Qutb. The new era of Political Islam was ushered in by the overthrow of the Shah in Iran and the establishment of the Islamic Republic of Iran in 1978–1979.

Although some groups continued to view democracy, at least in its Western forms, as un-Islamic, most of the significant new groups in the 1980s viewed some form of democracy as appropriate for an Islamic political system. These new manifestations of Political Islam included the Islamic Tendency Movement (Mouvement de la Tendance Islamique; MTI) led by Rashid Ghannouchi in Tunisia, ABIM (Angkatan Belia Islam Malaysia) led by Anwar Ibrahim in Malaysia, and the older Sudanese Muslim Brotherhood organized as the National Islamic Front in Sudan by Hasan Turabi. Each of these groups, and others like them, were willing to participate in democratic politics and included support for democratic principles in their platforms and programs. Even the more rigid ideologues recognized that modern forms of Islamic governance were in the process of being worked out. Sayyid Qutb acknowledged that, saying that Islam calls for flexibility in Islamic governments, rather than a simple return to the past. "The Islamic system has room for scores of models which are compatible with the natural growth of a society and the new needs of the contemporary age."[34] He insisted that government could not be autocratic. It must be based on consultation, and there must be no discrimination based on ethnicity or gender.[35] Qutb's South Asian counterpart Abul A'la Mawdudi also insisted that Islamic governance must be consultative and participatory. All Muslims—not just the elites—have the right to participate in legislation in an Islamic state, and legislation must remain flexible and responsive to the needs of society. But in order to distinguish virtuous Islamic governance from degenerate Western democracy, Mawdudi proposed the term "theo-democracy."[36]

The new Political Islam of the 1980s went beyond this guarded approach. Ghannouchi argued that "it would not be in the interest of Muslims to imagine an incompatibility between democracy and Islam."[37] Turabi affirmed that "an Islamic order of government is essentially a form of representative democracy."[38] Similarly, Anwar Ibrahim states, "It is a moral imperative for Muslims to be fully committed to democratic ideals."[39] By the end of the 1980s, the climax of what people have called the third wave of democratization, movements and groups in a number of Muslim-majority societies were strong supporters of the democratization of their own societies. The third wave did not miss the Muslim world but the results do not present the same dramatic picture as the collapse of the Soviet Union. Instead, what Huntington called the "reverse wave" sometimes caused democratizations to fail relatively quickly. In other cases, democratization simply moved more slowly toward a competitive participatory political system.

Many of the transitions in the third wave involved the overthrow of military dictatorships and one-party authoritarian states that were created in the years following World War II. In the Muslim world in the 1980s and early 1990s, a number of authoritarian regimes were overthrown, with the expectation of having a more democratic state emerging. However, the experience was mixed. In Sudan, the military dictatorship of Ja'far Numayri was overthrown and replaced by a democratic, parliamentary system in 1985. The reverse wave came in 1989, when a military coup placed Umar Hasan Bashir in power. Turabi's organization, the National Islamic Front, participated both in parliamentary politics and in the regime organized by Bashir. In Tunisia, the long rule of the autocrat Habib Bourguiba was brought to an end in 1987 by Zine al-Abidine Ben Ali, who promised a new democratic era for Tunisia. The MTI had been among the prime critics of the old regime but Ben Ali refused to recognize the Nahdah Party formed by the MTI. Ghannouchi went into political exile and Ben Ali re-established one-party autocracy.

Other authoritarian regimes were overthrown with mixed results. The communist government established in Afghanistan as a result of the Soviet invasion in 1979 was defeated by multinational Muslim opposition forces. Following the Soviet withdrawal in 1989 and the collapse of the remaining communist government in 1992, the numerous militias were unable to create a new parliamentary government and power passed to the militant Taliban. In Somalia, the long rule of the military dictator Siyad Barre came to an end when he fled the country in 1991 in the face of numerous armed opposition groups. The collapse of the country into long-term political anarchy followed.

One of the most dramatic failures of democratization in the early 1990s was in Algeria. The FLN regime faced growing opposition in the late 1980s, reaching a climax in 1988 with an explosion of strikes, riots, and demonstrations protesting poor economic conditions, governmental corruption, and repression. The government responded with a political reform program involving a commitment to democratic elections and multiparty politics. In the following months, Islamists emerged as the major national challenger to FLN dominance, and their newly organized party, the Front Islamique du Salut (FIS), won a significant national victory in municipal elections in 1990. This was followed by significant victories in the first stage of the national elections in 1991. In January 1992, the military intervened, invalidating the elections and suppressing FIS. In the following decade, militant groups emerged from the wreckage of the FIS, and by the beginning of the 21st century more than 200,000 people had died in the civil war that followed the military takeover. The military only gradually, and with strong limitations, restored electoral politics.

Two third-wave democratizations in Muslim-majority countries established and maintained competitive multiparty political systems, with tumultuous and often perilous records. In Bangladesh, popular demonstrations in 1990 led to the end of the rule of Hussain Mohammad Ershad, who came to power in a military coup in 1982. Parliamentary elections in 1991 set the pattern of a highly confrontational rivalry between Khaleda Zia (and her Bangladesh Nationalist Party) and Sheikh Hasina Wajid, leader of the Awami League. Because of the high levels of mistrust, "a unique system of interim government (non-party caretaker government) was produced that kept working as a catalyst of power transfer in a democratic way from one government to another."[40] This process has allowed opposition victories in elections since 1991. Albania, the second case, was perhaps the most rigidly authoritarian communist regime in Eastern Europe. When officially imposed atheism was removed, Albania reverted to being a Muslim-majority country. When a multiparty parliamentary order was established in 1990–1991, a two-party system emerged. Although elections were often chaotic, elections were free enough to result in victories by out-of-power parties in the elections of 1992, 1997, 2005, and 2013. Bangladesh and Albania provide important examples of third-wave democratizations that survived, despite many challenges.

Beginning the New Politics of the 21st Century

By the beginning of the 21st century, states and political movements around the world were being transformed by new technologies of communication and the broader impacts of intensified globalization. Religion is increasingly important as the "major world religions are all taking advantage of the opportunities provided by globalization to transform their messages and reach a new global audience."[41] The new technologies are changing the nature of the way movements can mobilize support to the extent that Charles Tilly could argue that old-style social movements could be replaced "as vehicles of popular claim making" by new forms of claim making and new ways of mobilizing expressions of social and political visions.[42] These changes set the framework for movements of democratization in the Muslim world at the beginning of the 21st century.

The events of the Arab Spring in 2011 were seen by some analysts as the coming of a fourth wave of democratization, this time involving Muslim-majority countries.[43] Demonstrations overthrowing the authoritarian regimes in Tunisia, Egypt, Libya, and Yemen; a major civil war in Syria; and demonstrations in many other Arab countries showed the strength of popular support for democratization. However, already by the end of the 1990s, the new politics were visible in a number of places.

Reformasi movements in Southeast Asia were a starting point for a new cycle of democratization. In Indonesia, large demonstrations in 1998 resulted in the overthrow of the authoritarian military regime of Suharto, who had ruled for more than thirty years. The transition created an elected parliament that elected two successive presidents, and then in 2004, a new president was directly elected. The success of the transition to democracy is reflected in the successful transfer of power in the presidency three times.

In Malaysia, the political system was multiparty but the coalition led by the United Malays National Organisation (UMNO) had ruled since Malaysia had gained independence. This dominance was challenged by a *reformasi* movement when the prime minister and head of UMNO, Mahathir Mohammad, fired his deputy prime minister, Anwar Ibrahim, and brought criminal charges against him. The supporters of Anwar joined with other opposition parties to create a major opposition coalition that challenged the UMNO coalition in the 1999 general elections. Although the new opposition did not win, it had success in gaining Malay ethnic and younger voters, and the parties continued to work together as an effective coalition. An observer at the time noted, "The institutionalization of a two-coalition system . . . changes the dynamics of Malaysian politics."[44] In the first decade of the 21st century, this "two-coalition" politics resulted in highly competitive elections and growing power for the opposition coalition. In the 2013 elections, the opposition won a majority of the popular votes but did not yet win a parliamentary majority.

The new politics are visible in Senegal and Turkey. Until 2000, Senegalese politics had been dominated by single major party from the time of independence. Small opposition parties were allowed, like the Senegalese Democratic Party led by Abdoulaye Wade. Wade ran for president four times, losing to the head of the dominant party each time. Then, in 2000, he again challenged Abdou Diouf, who had served as president since 1981, and won. This victory signaled more competitive politics, with Wade serving two terms as president and then losing elections in 2012, followed by a peaceful transition of power.

In Turkey, following military involvement in the resignation of a government in 1997, the Islamically oriented political groups reorganized and some formed the Justice and Development Party (Adalet ve Kalkınma Partisi; AKP), which was "a new style of party"[45] whose populism went beyond the appeal of both the older, more rigid Islamist parties and the secularist parties of the old urban statist elite. The party and its allies won parliamentary majorities in 2002 and subsequent elections, and dominated politics sufficiently to raise fears of "majoritarian" authoritarianism by the second decade of the 21st century. Part of the AKP program was democratic reform to comply with European Union membership guidelines. An important dimension of these reforms was the reduction of the political role of the military. By 2012, an observer could state, "For the first time in the republic's history, Turkey's performance is also totally in civilian hands. The military, once empowered to check civilian politics, is no longer strong enough either to step in or to threaten to take action."[46] During the demonstrations of 2013, there was little indication that the military was prepared to intervene.

Even in the carefully controlled electoral system in the Islamic Republic of Iran, the late 1990s was the time of a major reformist movement. In what analysts regard as a major upset, the reformist candidate for president, Mohammad Khatami, defeated the candidate who had the support of most of the ruling religious establishment in the presidential elections of 1997. Khatami won 70 percent of the vote in elections with an 80 percent turnout of eligible voters. Khatami was an activist supporter of creating an open society and declared, "The essence of Iranian history is the struggle for democracy."[47] Subsequent elections were highly competitive, within the limits set by the system. Popular support for reformist democracy is reflected in the huge demonstrations following the 2009 presidential elections protesting the results which most believed to have been rigged, and also in the surprise victory of the moderate candidate in the first round of the 2013 presidential elections.

The new politics of a possible fourth wave of democratization became globally visible in the events of the Arab Spring and subsequent developments. The year 2011 was a time of mounting protests around the world, with the actions of the Arab Spring leading the way. *Time* magazine named "The Protester" as the Person of the Year. In the global rise of oppositional politics, *Time*, among many others, identified a special role for the new electronic media of communication. "Calling the Arab uprisings Facebook and YouTube and Twitter revolutions is not, it turns out, just glib, wishful American overstatement. In the Middle East and North Africa, in Spain and Greece and New York, social media and smart phones did not replace face-to-face social bonds and confrontation but helped enable and turbocharge them, allowing protesters to mobilize more nimbly and communicate with one another and the wider world more effectively than ever before."[48]

The nature of the 2011 protests tends to confirm Charles Tilly's prediction that social movements of contention would take different forms in the 21st century. In discussing the nature of protests as public performances, Sidney Tarrow noted that in the 21st century, "electronic communication has made some forms of physical performance less effective, while other forms—such as the use of the Internet—have become more so. For example, protests against the stolen Iranian election of 2009 were organized largely through new means of electronic communication—cell phones, the Internet, Facebook, and Twitter."[49] The result is a new type of movement that Manuel Castells calls networked social movements. "Historically, social movements have been dependent on the existence of specific communication mechanisms: rumors, sermons, pamphlets and manifestos, spread from person to person, from the pulpit, from the press, or by whatever means of communication was available. In our time, multimodal, digital networks of horizontal communication are the fastest and most autonomous, interactive, reprogrammable and self-expanding means of communication in history. . . . This is why the networked social movements of the digital age represent a new species of social movement."[50]

The new movements have many dimensions. Throughout the Arab world, and elsewhere in the world of emerging economies, high levels of poverty and economic inequality exist. This deprivation provides a foundation for the strong sense of discontent among the population. The Arab Human Development Reports over the years document the continuing economic problems of Arab societies. However, poverty and economic deprivation are long-standing problems and are often more acute in countries that did not experience major demonstrations in the Arab Spring, and most of the protesters were not from the poorest levels of society. Mohamed Bouazizi, whose self-immolation was the starting point for the Tunisian revolution and the Arab Spring, was not an impoverished peasant; he was a licensed street vendor who was harassed by the police. Khaled Said, who was dragged from an Internet café and beaten to death by Egyptian security police, became a symbol for the rising fervor of opposition in Egypt. He was a middle-class computer repair person. In Tahrir Square in Cairo, the participants were primarily from the urban educated classes, with strong working-class support. In terms of the economic dimensions of the Arab Spring, some argue that the "uprisings were indigenously inspired movements fueled by the rising expectations of a nascent global middle class in the face of opportunity that for too long had been denied."[51]

The new movements were not, however, expressions of class tensions in their societies. Marxist class struggle ideology found little expression in the statements of the protesters. The demands were for an end to authoritarian rule and corruption in government, and greater equality.[52] Whatever might be the specific cause for protest, whether opposition to a military dictator or, as in the protests in Turkey in 2013, the reconstruction of a public park, the new movements have an important economic foundation for discontent but are not part of a self-conscious class struggle.

Younger people were, and are, among the most pressured by economic problems. Even in a relatively strong economy like Tunisia's, the youth unemployment rate was around 25 percent. Throughout the Muslim world, the demographic "youth bulge" is a major factor. In most Muslim countries, the majority of the population is under 30 years of age, with median ages ranging from 31 in Tunisia and Albania to 17–18 in Afghanistan, Yemen, and the Gaza Strip.[53] Although participants in the protests in the Arab Spring and in other protest movements around the world in 2011 came from many different levels of society, young people were central, especially youth with some education and real expectations of upward mobility and freedom. One study of the opposition movements around the world in 2011 concluded, "At the centre of all protest movements is a new sociological type: the graduate with no future."[54] Although urban poor and workers participated, "it was to the 'graduates without a future' that it fell to kick things off. From the rich world to the poor world, it is educated young people whose life chances and illusions are now being shattered. Though their general conditions are still better than those of slum-dwellers and some workers, they have experienced far greater disappointment."[55]

Tawakkol Karman, who received a Nobel Peace Prize for her participation in the Arab Spring in Yemen, identified the movement as "our peaceful popular youth revolution."[56] The youth dimension of the Arab Spring and other protests around the world was central. The new forms of the networked social movements were especially open to encouraging participation by youth. The movements "are organized around informal networks facilitated by new information and communication technologies" most accessible to younger people, and they involve nontraditional and highly theatrical forms of direct action protest in which youth are actively involved. Younger activists are also characteristically drawn to more non-conventional forms of direct action protest, involving "creative, expressive or violent repertoires."[57] Viewing "the activism of 2011 through a national-ist, ethnic or even class lens is to miss its unifying trait—2011 was the year of a global youth revolt."[58]

The youth dimension of Arab Spring is highly visible in the emer-gent pop cultures of protest. Among the most effective articulation of the demands of the demonstrators were the blunt words of rappers. Hip-hop stars like El General in Tunis and Rami Essam in Cairo, and the protest singer Ibrahim Qashoush, who was murdered for singing songs critical of Bashar Assad, the dictator in Syria, in the early days of protests in Syria, provided what some call the "soundtrack of the revolution." The pop cul-ture of the street protests was clearly part of the youth culture in the Arab world from Morocco to Iraq and in many other parts of the Muslim world as well.

Women are also an important element in the Arab Spring move-ments. In general, as one analyst described the broader global move-ments, women are "very numerous as the backbone of movements. After twenty years of modernized labour markets and higher-education access, the 'archetypal' protest leader, organizer, facilitator, spokesper-son now is an educated young woman."[59] Women like Asmaa Mahfouz in Egypt were in the front lines of the early protests and were major voices as bloggers. When *Newsweek* in 2012 published a special study on "150 Women Who Shake the World," at least fifteen of the women listed were participants in some aspect of the Arab Spring.[60] Tawakkol Karman noted the important role of women in the revolution: "Our peaceful popular youth revolution has succeeded in attracting to its ranks and marches hundreds of thousands of women who have ful-filled, and still fulfill, a major noticeable and effective role in its activi-ties, and in leading its demonstrations. . . . Not tens but hundreds of these women have fallen as martyrs or have been wounded for the sake of the victory of the revolution."[61]

In the general non-hierarchical and open frameworks of action in the networks of opposition that developed, patriarchal habits of male domi-nation of organizations as in old-style political parties and associations were limited. This lack of structure made it possible for young people and women to have significant influence in shaping the movements. The new-style movements have been described as leaderless, as a conscious part of their movement. Disappointment with existing leadership is a global phenomenon. "The disaffection is so great, and so pervasive, that allegiances around the world seem to be shifting not to new leaders but to the exact opposite—to leaderless movements like Occupy Wall Street, the Arab Spring, and the Tea Party."[62] In the new movements of democratization, as in the networked social movements in general, key figures were organizers and coordinators rather than more charismatic leaders at the top of an emerging hierarchical command structure. In Egypt, for example, Wael Ghonim was important in organizing a Facebook mobilization for demonstrations but did not emerge as someone in a position of command. He emphasizes his lack of eagerness to assume a leadership command position in the movement which he helped to mobilize. After his Facebook group tried to recruit a major figure like Mohamed ElBaradei to lead the opposition to Mubarak, he and his colleagues concluded, "We did not need a savior; we had to do this ourselves."[63]

In addition to being relatively leaderless in structure, the new movements tend to be non-ideological. Already in the early days of the Arab Spring, analysts like Emad Shahin observed, "It's not the age of ideology anymore." The old competitions between Arabism, socialism, and Islamism were replaced by unifying demands "to end government corruption, institute the rule of law and ease economic suffering."[64] Within this framework, mobilizing people to become engaged became more important than converting people to an ideology of a movement. Wael Ghonim argued that "engagism is more important than activism."[65]

The non-ideological character of the new-style movements means that they may have a very specific demand like the end of the rule of a dictator, but they tend not to have concrete programs and have a variety of demands. Because "demands are multiple and motivations unlimited, they cannot formalize an organization or leadership because their consensus, their togetherness, depends on ad hoc deliberation and protest, not on fulfilling a program built around specific goals: this is both their strength (wide open appeal) and their weakness (how can anything be achieved when the goals to be achieved are undefined?)."[66]

In the new political dynamics of the 21st century, the democratization movements in the Muslim world have a major impact in changing the political orders of their societies. However, the new networked social movements also have distinctive vulnerabilities that open the way for possible reverse waves or unexpected outcomes. Although youth and women were important elements in the movements, when new governments were established, they did not have the same prominent roles. Successful participation in elections requires effective organization and, as a result, old-style groups were better able to compete in the new political arena. Although the success of Islamically identified parties in elections in the aftermath of the Arab Spring surprised many people, that success was based on the widespread grassroots organization of groups like the Muslim Brotherhood in Egypt.

A reverse wave developed in Arab Spring countries, receiving support from people who feared rule by Islamists as well as from groups associated with the old regimes. Democracy can appear to be in trouble when those people are willing to accept the re-establishment of rule by the military, as happened in Egypt in 2013. However, it is no longer possible to speak of the Muslim world as an unlikely participant in democratization developments in the 21st century.

A possible fourth wave of democratization is visible from Senegal to Indonesia, and it is clear that support for democracy is not limited to a small urban elite. A major Gallup research study between 2001 and 2007, conducted in more than thirty-five countries, reported that most Muslims "see no contradiction between democratic values and religious principles."[67] They gave strong support for political freedom and freedom of speech. This support for democratic principles was expressed even before the enthusiasms of the Arab Spring, which confirmed in many ways the Gallup findings. Subsequent polling shows a continued and widespread support for democracy. In 2013 the Pew Research Center published the results of polling done in 2008–2012 in the Muslim world and reported, "Most Muslims around the world express support for democracy."[68]

In the 21st century, political developments throughout the Muslim world show the desire for more democratic governance. Each Muslim-majority country has a distinctive experience and it is difficult to select a few case studies to illustrate the variety of histories. In this volume, we will present seven case studies as a way of opening further discussion on Islam and democracy in the 21st century. Egypt and Tunisia, where the Arab Spring began, provide important examples of the new style of movements in action, with their strengths and weaknesses. Senegal and Indonesia are early manifestations of the new politics in their transformations of military and dominant party rule into functioning democracies. Pakistan allows an analysis of the continuing conflictual relationships between a politically powerful military and supporters of a greater degree of civilian-controlled democracy. Turkey and Iran are the extremes of the spectrum in terms of religion and politics, with Turkey being officially a secular republic and Iran an Islamic republic.

From these studies, it becomes clear that the new politics of the 21st century is a dramatic combination of new types of social movements and a continuation of important elements of the old 20th-century political dynamics. The political power of the military may be transformed in many places but it does not disappear. Youth and women have power and influence that they never had before, but their activism did not cause older patriarchal habits to lose much of their power. New technologies of communication and information have transformed the vocabularies of politics and created new and novel ways of mobilizing popular support, but the old face-to-face methods of institutional and street politics continue to be a necessary part of effective political operation. And the relationship between religion and politics may well have to be re-examined by those who assumed a radical distinction between their spheres of operation. As a result of Europe's history of church support for authoritarian governments, Western liberal democracies developed a separation between political and religious institutions, traditionally manifested in an absence of overt religious claims in political discourse. But the increased presence of religious discourse in US political campaigns over the past two decades suggests that the "wall of separation" is in fact porous; the separation between religion and politics is not as definitive as it once seemed, even in the West. In Muslim-majority countries, on the other hand, Islamic movements tended not to support authoritarian governments. Indeed, the religious leaders often articulated popular political discontent, with frequent reference to Islamic themes. Thus, while in Europe, secular discourse was the vehicle of political opposition to authoritarian governments, in Muslim-majority countries, religious discourse has often expressed populist opposition to authoritarianism. The choice may well not be, then, between religious and democratic political systems, but for some combination of the two.

2

Islam, Democracy, and Turkey's Secular State

TURKEY'S EXPERIMENT WITH democracy and the relationship of religion and the state has had a long, complex, and at times contentious history. For years, Turkey provided the only modern secular (though not completely democratic) state in the Muslim world, believed to be immune from any serious impact from Political Islam. Many believed that Turkey provided the model for Muslim-majority nation-states, adopting in 1928 the secular path necessary for modernization and development. In the late 1980s and early 1990s, Turkey's "Muslim secularism" was promoted by some in the United States and Europe as an antidote to the Islamic "fundamentalist" influences of Iran, Saudi Arabia, or Pakistan.

However, the 1996 election of Dr. Necmettin Erbakan, leader of the Welfare Party (WP), as Turkey's first Islamist prime minister stunned Turkey's secular elite, signaling a seismic political shift: the threat of a retreat from its secular past. Despite the influence and intervention of the military and suppression of the WP and its successor parties, 2002 witnessed the stunning election of the AKP, whose leaders were former members of the WP. Prime Minister Recep Tayyip Erdogan and the AKP's dominance of Turkish politics proved to have lasting power through successive national and local elections. The rigid, authoritarian laic secularism of Ataturk and the dominance of Turkish politics by secular parties and a political culture that restricted the presence and role of religion in politics and society were replaced by a party whose core leaders—many of whom were practicing Muslims but nonetheless committed to democracy, pluralism, and a state secularism—were more in tune with the

Anglo-Saxon than with the more assertive French secularism, since the former provided space for Turkey's Islamic culture and customs.

Origins of Turkey's Secular State

The history of Turkey has its roots in the Ottoman Empire (1299–1922) and with its collapse in 1922, the emergence of modern Turkey. Founded by Osman Bey in northwestern Anatolia in 1299, it became an expansive state, and with the conquest of the Byzantine Empire's capital, Constantinople (Istanbul), by Mehmed II in 1453, it was transformed into an empire. With its capital at Constantinople, it bridged the Eastern and Western worlds for over six centuries. By the mid-1500s, the empire had reached its zenith under Sultan Süleyman (1520–1566). At that time, it was by far the most powerful and largest empire in Europe, viewed and experienced as an infidel enemy and a threat. For centuries, the Christians attempted to keep what seemed like the unstoppable advance of the Ottoman Empire and the Muslims at bay. The Ottoman two-month siege at the gates of Vienna proved a turning point. The Battle of Vienna on September 12, 1683, and defeat of the Ottoman Turks by the Christian army led by Poland's King John Sobieski broke the advance of the Ottoman Empire into Europe. "We came, we saw, and God conquered," wrote Sobieski to Pope Innocent XI.

The historical memory of the Ottoman Muslim threat to Christian Europe and the belief that if Vienna had fallen so would have Europe have remained alive and, some would argue, continue to manifest themselves and affect politics and international affairs. Several examples are the Balkan conflicts; the resistance of some Europeans and countries to Turkish accession to the EU; Islamophobia and fears of a Muslim demographic threat in France, Germany, Austria, and elsewhere; as well as the use of a picture of an Ottoman sultan for the cover of Bernard Lewis' influential article "The Roots of Muslim Rage" in *The Atlantic*, with its allegations of fourteen centuries of jihad in Muslim-Christian history and relations and a modern clash of civilizations.

Islam was the official religion of the Ottomans. Although the Sharia (Islamic law) was its fundamental law, it coexisted with a secular legal system (*kanun*). Thus, Süleyman the Magnificent, the longest-reigning sultan of the Ottoman Empire (1520–1566), was known in the West as "the Magnificent" but in the East as the Lawgiver (*al-Qānūnī*) for his complete reconstruction of the Ottoman legal system. Encompassing much of North Africa, Western Asia, Southeast Europe, the Caucasus, and the Horn of Africa, the empire was a vast multi-ethnic (seventy-five different ethnicities living within its borders) and multi-religious state comprised of large populations of Muslims, Jews, and Christians. The Ottoman system recognized the plurality of religious groups, classifying them into *millets*, or religious communities. Each religious community—Muslim, Christian, and Jewish—was subject to its own religious laws for personal issues such as education. In addition, Süleyman the Magnificent signed a treaty in 1533 with Francis I of France, the first diplomatic alliance of its kind between a Christian and a non-Christian empire, which in its time was denounced in the Christian world as a sacrilegious union or alliance.

The late 19th century and early 20th century saw Ottoman imperial survival in decline, threatened by failed military campaigns and the loss of much of the Balkans and the Middle East, leading ultimately to its defeat and collapse at the end of World War I and to the creation of the modern state of Turkey in the early 1920s by a former Ottoman army officer, Mustafa Kamal (Ataturk, "Father of the Turks"), transforming a portion of the former empire into a modern, secular European-like nation-state.

In contrast to other emerging Muslim states in the first half of the 20th century, modern Turkey was created as a secular state. Unlike countries in the Middle East and North Africa, Turkey's path toward the realization of a secular state was implemented with an early series of sweeping reforms. Mustafa Kemal Ataturk, Turkey's first president, viewed the establishment of a uniquely secular state as a means to ensure the country's social peace and modernization. He disestablished religion by abolishing the Sultanate in 1922 and the Caliphate in 1924, replacing Sharia with a Western-inspired secular legal system and the Ottoman Religious Ministry with the Presidency of Religious Affairs (Diyanet, established in 1924), and closing many religious institutions. That same year, all Sufi (mystic) orders (*tarikats*) were prohibited and a Western-inspired civil code was introduced. In 1928, the article in the constitution that declared that "the state's religion is Islam" was removed, thus breaking the final barrier to the emergence of a republic, whose newfound secularism was enshrined in the 1924 constitution, a single ruling party (Ataturk's Republican People's Party, RPP), and a powerful military.

An urban-based minority ruling elite—civil servants, military, and intellectuals co-opted by the urban and rural rich people, many of whom became rich by grasping the properties of the non-Muslim minority who had to leave the country (Armenians in 1915, and later Greeks)—imposed

Ataturk's secular vision from above. The absence of any strong commitment to democracy could be seen in the gap between Turkey's Kemalist secular elite and the Turkish masses. The principle of democracy was eclipsed by a radical state secularism imposed by a one-party political system. As Nilufer Göle observed, "It [democracy] was absent from the six founding principles [republicanism, nationalism, populism, statism, secularism, and revolutionism/reform] of Turkish republicanism. This ordering was a consequence of the suspicions of the ruling elite that the sovereignty of people would end up in the sovereignty of Islam."[1]

With the death of Ataturk in 1938 and the rise of the Republican People's Party (Turkish: Cumhuriyet Halk Partisi, CHP) under Turkey's new president, Ismet Inonu, the introduction of a multiparty political (limited) democracy in 1946 gave more space to religion. Mosques were built and repaired; the Islamic faculty at Ankara University was reopened; the ban on religious broadcasts was lifted; training programs for imams were reinstated; and religion classes were reintroduced in public schools with parental permission, in part because of fear of the influence of atheistic Soviet socialism. Additionally, Sufi brotherhoods were permitted to function (not legally, but the government turned a blind eye). By 1982, Turkey had the third-largest number of pilgrims making the hajj to Mecca, and by 2013, Turkey had 85,000 mosques and 115,000 imams under the control of Diyanet, with a budget of more than $2.5 billion.[2]

In 1950 the DP came to power in a landslide presidential electorate victory, ushering in a period of political liberalization and greater visibility of Islam, signaling the failure of Kemalism to take root fully in society: "Only the cities and large towns benefited under Kemalism and developed a small class committed to it. The countryside remained virtually untouched by the benefits of modern education, and literacy grew only slowly."[3] The greater visibility of Islam in public life was primarily religio-cultural, not political, and consisted of individuals and groups (intellectuals, Sufi mystics, and cultural organizations) that sought to bring about a religious and moral renewal of society. However different, these movements were critical of Turkish secularism and reaffirmed the centrality of Islam. At the same time, Turkey's new economic development produced a new group of technocrats. They too were modern and educated, but in contrast to the established secular military-bureaucratic elite, Islam had remained a formative influence in their lives.

By the 1960s, rapid industrialization, international economic development, social dislocation, and left-wing politics increased fears of a communist threat, contributing to the reassertion of Islam in Turkish politics. Authors, playwrights, philosophers, and activists emerged and contributed to the formation of an Islamic and conservative cultural and political discourse. They synthesized European and Ottoman sensibilities with a socially (not economically) conservative Islamic perspective, a forerunner of what decades later would become the AKP's Islamic orientation and "conservative democracy."

The Re-emergence of Islam in Turkish Politics

Islamic activism in the 1960s consisted of religiously apolitical and nonpolitical groups. The most prominent movement was that initiated in 1970 by Professor Necmettin Erbakan (1926–2011) in Konya, a city in central Anatolia. An engineer who had trained at Istanbul Technical University and earned a doctorate at Aachen Technical University in Germany, Erbakan combined careers in academia, business, and politics.

Erbakan represented an alternative to the old elite, including disillusioned Anatolian religious businessmen who would emerge as MUSIAD and Anatolian Tigers. Islamically oriented, he was committed to a Turkish nationalism but based upon Ottoman-Islamic traditions—economically and culturally independent of the West, which he associated with decadence and immorality. Like Hasan al-Banna, founder of Egypt's Muslim Brotherhood before him, Erbakan maintained that blind dependence upon the West had robbed Turkey of its identity and strength. As one of his protégés observed: "The European, by making us copy him blindly and without any understanding, trapped us in this monkey's cage and, as a result, forced us to abandon our personality and nobility. That is to say, he was successful in this because he used agents recruited from within, who felt [inferior and] disgusted with themselves, bringing to his knees the Turk who for centuries could not be defeated by the crusades and external blows."[4]

Erbakan was politically active during the 1960s, a time when increased urbanization and industrialization resulted in unemployment, hyperinflation and, concurrently, increased criticisms of Western culture and new questions about the Turkish national identity. In many ways it was an opportune time for a political movement inspired by religious ideals. In 1970, he created the National Order Party (NOP).

The NOP's program emphasized technological innovation, rapid industrialization, and a spiritual and moral renewal of society. It preached material and spiritual salvation to Turks (small businessmen, laborers, young provincial professionals, and intellectuals) who had become the victims of rapid development, import-substitution companies, mass migration to the cities, and the cultural schizophrenia precipitated by modern, urban secular society.

Erbakan's commitment to development, rooted in Turkey's Islamic culture and values, was combined with a call for democratization at a time when many experienced the repression of military rule in 1971. Erbakan and the Islamic parties that he founded and decades later their offshoot, the AKP, persisted in their desire to create a modern, democratic, industrialized, and socially just Turkey.[5]

The National Salvation Party

Banned in 1971 by the military, the NOP was reorganized as the National Salvation Party (NSP) in 1972, again with a platform that combined rapid industrialization and religious/moral reform. The ideology of Erbakan and the NSP was based upon a strong sense of Turkish nationalism, Islamic identity, anti-communism, and anti-Western dependency. The NSP did not directly challenge the legitimacy of the Kemalist state or seek to overthrow it. Rather, it called for religious space within state secularism, specifically that Turkish nationalism and society reaffirm and appropriate the nation's Islamic faith and values.

By the mid-1970s, Erbakan controlled enough seats in parliament to serve as deputy prime minister in three successive governments.[6] Between 1973 and 1980, NSP members and sympathizers found their way into parliament, government offices, education, and business. However, when the military seized power in a coup d'état on September 1980, disbanding parliament and all political parties, military courts arrested and tried Erbakan and the NSP leadership (in contrast to other party leaders), citing (as it would do in subsequent interventions over the years) its defense of Ataturk's secularism against the "threat of radical Islam as embodied by Erbakan's National Salvation Party."[7]

The Welfare Party

In 1983, with the return to civilian and multiparty politics, Erbakan founded a successor to the banned NSP, the Welfare or Prosperity Party

(WP; Turkish: Refah Partisi [RP]). Its name and its economic program—"Just Order"—reflected its mission to create a more socially just society by increasing the country's wealth and assuring a more equitable distribution of resources. Similar to the Kemalists, Turkish Islamists favored a state-centric approach and top-down social engineering. Welfare became a successful modern mass party, the only truly grassroots party in Turkey's history, whose more than four million members were found in major cities as well as the provinces. The WP included laborers, faculty and students, corporate leaders, factory workers, and both men and women, and it represented a diverse spectrum of religious orientations. Its supporters came from the lower-middle and middle classes. The majority were from state secular schools and trained in the sciences, technology, and Western thought. Financial support came from members and overseas workers and supporters, especially those in Germany.[8] However, several Islamic groups such as Nurcus, Suleymancis, and the Gülen movement had stayed away from Erbakan's Islamist parties and voted for center-right parties such as Demirel's True Path and Ozal's Motherland.

Islam and Power-Sharing in the Political Process

Political and social change in the 1980s contributed to the increased profile of Islam in Turkish politics and society. Ironically, the self-described defenders of secularism, the military, and an elected prime minister, Turgut Ozal, a former member of the NSP, were responsible for the new openings. Both the military, under the leadership of General Kenan Evren, and Ozal, after the election of the Motherland Party in 1983, stressed the importance of religious values.

While the presence of religion was expanded, the state controlled the teaching of religion (teachers and the curriculum) and thus the "brand" of Islam (anti- or non-"fundamentalist"; read Islamist) that was taught. Religion was used to counter the influence of the Left (communist/Marxist), strengthen the moral fabric of society, and enhance Turkey's efforts to strengthen its economic ties with and markets in other Muslim-majority countries.

The election of Turgut Ozal and the Motherland Party in May 1983 reinforced the pursuit of a liberalization policy. Like Erbakan, Ozal (1927–1993) was a practicing Muslim, a graduate of the Istanbul Technical

University, and, for a time in the 1970s, a member of the NSP. He too believed that Islam remained an essential part of Turkish culture and identity. Ozal reasserted the importance of Turkey's Islamic heritage as a primary source of Turkish identity, unity, and society, as well as a counter to the influence of the Left within the limits of its secular state. He asserted that an important cause of Turkish "unity and our cohesiveness is the fact that we are all citizens of the Turkish Republic ... Our state is secular. But what holds our nation together, what serves in a most powerful way in our national cohesiveness and what plays the essential role is Islam."[9] Religion was made a compulsory subject in primary and secondary schools and the Imam-Hatip (schools for the training of prayer leaders), enabling their graduates to qualify for admission to university and for jobs in the government and private sector. As a result, many found their way into government, serving in the bureaucracy and in ministries of education and culture.

Welfare's Path to Power: Political Islam, Democracy, and Electoral Politics

The sudden death of Turgut Ozal in 1993 saw a period of transition in which the WP profited from the failures of the state, the internecine battles of Turkey's political leadership, and corrupt and ineffective coalition governments, as well as from the commitment and effectiveness of Welfare's leadership and members. The WP used democracy as a yardstick by which to judge the failure of Turkish secularism to be truly pluralistic and respectful of the rights of all of its citizens, including their freedom of conscience or right to live according to their own religious beliefs. Erbakan maintained that true secularism (separation of religion from the state) should mean not only state autonomy but also religious autonomy. That is, religion also has its autonomy, which is respected by the state and free from government interference. The state should not intervene in the religious sphere by attempting to regulate dress (the right of women to wear a headscarf or, for that matter, men to wear beards) or religious practice.

In 1994, the WP emerged as the leading political party in municipal elections, winning 24.1 percent of the vote, scoring especially well in working-class areas, and electing mayors in twenty-eight municipalities including Istanbul and Ankara, Turkey's capital city. The successes of the WP were due to many factors: the failures of previous governments meant that the WP garnered the support of its members and of a cross-over protest vote from disgruntled voters who would normally support other parties. The vote was at least as much about politics and economics (double- and triple-digit inflation, urban poverty, inadequate social services and healthcare, pollution, congestion, high employment, inadequate housing, crime, corruption) as it was about wholesale support for the WP and its ideology. Indeed, a 1994 survey found that only one-third of the WP's voters voted primarily because it was an Islamic party.[10] Similarly, an ARAS survey conducted shortly after the elections showed that only 16 percent of the WP's voters regarded it as an Islamist organization, and more than 70 percent said that the WP would neither introduce Sharia law nor bring about an Islamic state.[11] Focus on voter issues like employment, pensions, healthcare, housing, and the environment and its indictment of the failures of society, reflected in the WP's slogans of "clean politics" and a "just order," proved effective.

Turkey's Modern Islamist Prime Minister

During Erbakan's brief tenure as prime minister, the WP encouraged the expanded role of religion in society, increasing the number of schools, religious foundations, businesses, banks, social services, and media outlets. Despite the WP's public assurances, both secular Muslims and religious minorities alike, such as Turkey's Alevi Muslim minority (perhaps 20 percent of its 98-percent Muslim population), were skeptical about the WP's commitment to pluralism.

In power, Erbakan proved more pragmatic than some had expected. In order to push back against his critics and also to prevent the possibility of a military intervention, Erbakan extolled the values of democratic order during his inaugural address, emphasizing in particular that he would respect and honor Turkey's laicist path.

Turkey's military has had a long history of influence and intervention in domestic politics, seizing power in 1960–1961, 1971–1973, and 1980–1983. Staunch secularists (some might say militant secularists) have consistently espoused the role of defenders of Kemalism in their political interventions. The military's allergic reaction to any form of religion in public life has been especially evident in its opposition to the right of female students to wear a headscarf (hijab) and to any form of Islamic political activism and participation. Among their common justifications for previous military coups was the claim that the government had betrayed Ataturk's principle of secularism. Thus, the military took every occasion to signal concerns about any compromising of Turkey's secular principles. They instituted a new purge of officers who were suspected of being Islamists (grounds for such a dismissal could be the simple fact that an officer's wife had worn a headscarf or that they had prayed at a mosque). On February 28, 1997, the military's General Staff presented the Erbakan government with a memorandum that contained a set of eighteen demands designed to stem an Islamist threat to the secular state. These included restrictions on the wearing of Islamic dress; measures to prevent Islamists from entering the military or government administration; closer monitoring of financial institutions belonging to religious orders; and a mandate that the Imam-Hatip schools, religious schools that were believed to teach religious propaganda and serve as a training ground for Islamists, be closed because of their anti-secular bias. At the same time, the military demanded that compulsory secular education be increased from five to eight years. These concerns seemed ironic since the schools were started by and funded by the government and subject to state regulation and inspection.[12]

Erbakan and the Welfare Party's brief government proved to be a lightening rod for militant secularists, contributing to the increased polarization of society. As in Algeria, the secularist establishment was willing to compromise Turkey's commitment to democracy to prevent Islamists from participating in politics and society and to preserve their power, privilege, and lifestyle rather than allow voters to choose through free and open elections. Serif Mardin's comparison of this Kemalist attitude to Voltaire's hatred of the Church goes a long way toward understanding the source and living legacy of militant secularism in Turkey.[13]

Erbakan and the WP had to contend with increased pressure from the military, no-confidence votes in parliament, and in May 1997 a petition to the Constitutional Court (the highest court in Turkey) by Turkey's chief prosecutor to ban the WP for violating the Turkish constitution's articles on secularism and pushing the country toward a probable civil war. Finally, the Erbakan-Ciller coalition collapsed when it lost its parliamentary majority due to the resignation of several of Ciller's DYP members. Erbakan submitted his resignation on June 18, 1997. On February 28, 1998, Turkey's Constitutional Court issued an order banning the WP. Erbakan was expelled from parliament and barred from participation in the political process for five years. The WP's assets were seized. Erbakan and a number of other leaders were tried for sedition.

The Virtue (Fazilet) Party

In 1998, former WP members and supporters regrouped and formed the Virtue (Fazilet) Party (VP), the unofficial successor of Welfare. Prime Minister Bülent Ecevit's government, strongly prodded by the military, moved to suppress Islamic organizations or those suspected of ties with them. Twice in the year 2000, Ecevit obtained a government decree enabling him to fire thousands of civil servants suspected of ties to pro-Islamic or separatist groups. On both occasions, Turkey's president refused to sign the measure into law. In June 2001 the Constitutional Court declared the VP an illegal Islamic organization and banned it. The Court cited Turkey's constitution, which enshrines secularism as a cornerstone of the state.

A Split in the Movement

The closure of the VP and ensuing attempt to regroup and move on led to a split in the Erbakan-led Islamic movement—one between the old guard, led by Erbakan, and some younger reformers hoping to establish a new party that would be less controversial and vulnerable to Turkey's secular regime. The new guard of reformists grouped around the charismatic former mayor of Istanbul, Recep Tayyip Erdogan, along with Abdullah Gül and Bülent Arinç. Erdogan's popularity as mayor of Istanbul was based in large part on his administration's efficient and effective running of the municipality and the expansion of its services. The political organization under him coalesced around his vision for the country and the ideological change that he offered—one that was in line with Turkey's republican rules and respected the principles of both democracy and laicism.

The Rise of the AKP

Turkey's Justice and Development Party (AKP) was officially founded in 2001. By November 2002, the AKP won a stunning 34.3 percent of the vote and 363 of the 550 seats in parliamentary elections. The victory, a landslide by all accounts, meant that for the first time in more than a decade, a party had won enough seats in parliament to exercise a clear majority and enjoy a one-party government.

The AKP promised a new social contract—one based on the principles of democracy, human rights, social justice, and underlying ethical and moral principles.[14] The AKP's election strategy focused not on religious ideology or a fusion of politics and religion but instead on "bread-and-butter" issues that resonated across a multiplicity of political, socioeconomic, cultural, and religious divides. Tayyip Erdogan, in a 2003 speech on the emergence of the AKP, expressed the inclusive nature of the party not only in a societal but also in a political sense: "We now witness not a differentiation and polarization of ideologies with sharp and bold lines of division between them, but the formation of new political courses accompanying the pervasiveness of different ideologies. We have before us, therefore, a more colored and multidimensional picture rather than a sharp black-and-white image."[15]

Party Makeup

Indeed, the AKP's election victory was the result of a broad spectrum of voting blocs. Nationalist, conservative, and economically liberal voters came together to elect Erdogan and the AKP. Not only did the AKP win the votes of those registered citizens who were formerly aligned with other parties, but they also won 29 percent of new voters.[16]

How had such a diverse group of voters come to the same conclusion regarding the AKP? First, the AKP limited its message on religious matters and established itself early as a being a proponent of a "conservative democracy" that was not particularly bent on an overarching religious message or the influence of Islam in government policies, but rather was a pragmatic, democratic, and pluralistic party that emphasized the goal of a prosperous future for all Turkish citizens. Erdogan emphasized that "while attaching importance to religion as a social value, we do not think it is right to conduct politics through religion, to attempt to transform government ideologically by using religion, or to resort to organizational activities based on religious symbols. To make religion an instrument of politics and to adopt exclusive approaches to politics in the name of religion harms not only political pluralism but also religion itself. Religion is a sacred and collective value."[17]

The leadership of the AKP included a new generation of practicing Muslim politicians, such as Abdullah Gül, Bülent Arınç, Ali Babacan, and others who possessed a clearly defined Islamic identity; they also had university educations and, as a result of the expansion of education and the media, were more exposed than leaders of the past to European ideas. This engendered a worldview that was built on the overlap of tradition and modernity, one where global discourses were crystallized into the vernacular of well-connected and well-grounded politicians. The result was a hybrid party identity—simultaneously Turkish, Muslim, and Western—and while the party was deeply entrenched in the Turkish-Ottoman tradition, the blending of its identities, religious and political, made the possibilities for its rule less threatening.

Bread-and-Butter Issues

In the immediate years after his election, Erdogan kept many of the promises he made regarding economic improvements. Much of the AKP's early economic success was the result of the fact that it dominated the parliament as a single party. Still, during the period from December 2002 to March 2003, just three months, the party was able to push through more than fifty-four constitutional and statutory amendments that prepared the country for accession to the European Union (EU)—a move that not only boosted the country's profile on the international stage but also led to bounces in markets, increased investments, and a general economic uptick. The move also addressed—at least statutorily—the long-standing discrimination against Kurdish and Christian minorities, though problems persist.[18]

Additionally, the AKP brought about exponential growth in the Turkish GDP, implementing the International Monetary Fund (IMF) stabilization program, which called for privatizing banking and energy sectors, reforming welfare and tax systems, and opening up access to foreign investors. In 2004, inflation sank below 10 percent for the first time in more than three decades (by 2010, Turkey became the sixth largest economy in Europe and gained a seat in the G-20).[19]

As previously mentioned, Erdogan's background as a mayor was also an important factor in his early success as leader of the AKP. Service programs that closed the gap between urban and rural areas of the country were designed and implemented, and metropolitan centers maintained their competitive edge in economic growth and social mobility. Low-cost services, including healthcare coverage, textbook programs, and monthly stipends, aimed to help low-income families move higher up the ladder of social mobility and prosperity.[20]

Foreign Policy

Turkey's foreign policy under the AKP has been multifaceted, which is a reflection of the syncretic nature of the party itself, though a major characteristic of it has been its focus on the West. Turkey's relationship with the United States, for instance, had been rocky since the years of the 1991 Gulf War, yet the AKP government aligned its foreign policy interests with those of the West and the United States and deployed Turkish military forces as part of the International Security Assistance Force (ISAF) mission in Afghanistan in 2001. In the lead-up to the US invasion of Iraq in 2003, however, Erdogan and the Bush administration butted heads on Turkey's involvement. Turkish leadership feared that the war would bring about a surge of instability in the region and on its southern border, which would aggravate its problem with the Kurds.

The AKP had sought to make its relationship with Europe a centerpiece of its foreign policy and established close relations with those countries comprising the EU. Indeed, gaining membership in the EU has come to define, more or less, Turkey's relationship with the continent in recent years. By professing its commitment to implement EU requirements and norms of civilian democracy, the AKP sought to redefine and even limit the role of the military and its allies. Turkish leaders imagine a country defined not so much by its military might as by its strategic geopolitical relations.[21] Yet that has proven to be a difficult path. Popular support in Europe for the inclusion of Turkey into the EU significantly declined in French and Dutch referenda in May 2005, which rejected the possibility of enlarging the Union to receive a new, non-European state. Much of the opposition has been grounded in the perception that Turkey is not culturally a part of Europe. Grappling with its own identity as a result of an increase in the Muslim population, many fear the impact of an Islamist government on the stability of society.[22]

Continued Electoral Success

Five years after its emergence on the political scene in Turkey, the AKP's record was put to the test in the country's sixteenth general election on July 22, 2007. Its near 34 percent of the vote in 2002 jumped to a surprising 46.6 percent of the vote in 2007—an increase of more than 12 percent.

The AKP increased its electoral support in all seven regions of the country and in the five largest cities. In Istanbul, the party received as many votes as all of its opponents combined.[23]

Public opinion surveys reported the most important factor that determined people's vote for the AKP was the economy: 78 percent identified the "economic situation and expectations," 14 percent indicated "democratization," and 11 percent said "the threat to secularism."[24] The economy, not democratization, secularism, or religion, was the primary factor in the election. In the five years before the election, Turkey's GDP grew exponentially with a record spike in foreign investment from $1.2 billion USD to $20 billion per year. In the end, it was the ability of the AKP to get the job done—to provide the necessary leverage that improved the economy, created jobs, and expanded services—that won them the election.

Again in 2011, the AKP scored a stunning win in the general elections, taking 327 seats in the country's parliament and increasing its electoral vote to nearly 50 percent. Its election declaration, "Turkey is Ready, Target is 2023," suggested that the AKP's political horizon would be at least as far as the next twelve years.[25] The AKP brand was, as Menderes Cinar noted, organized around the personal charisma of its leader Recep Tayyip Erdogan, who ran the party's politics and policies.[26]

Ergenekon and an Attempted Military Coup

The rocky relationship between the AKP government and the military came to a head in a series of trials investigating alleged plotting to overthrow the government. On June 12, 2007, after investigations, the prosecutors claimed they had unearthed a series of coup plots against the government. A widespread wave of arrests began, and on January 21, 2008, thirty-one people were arrested following the first Ergenekon indictment.

In 2010, thirty-one members of the military were arrested and jailed on charges of planning to overthrow the Erdogan government. Two years later, in 2012, 330 military officers were convicted of having plotted to overthrow Erdogan's government in 2003 and sentenced to up to twenty years.

In April 2011, over 500 people, including senior military officers, lawyers, journalists, writers, and opposition lawmakers were arrested and nearly 300 formally charged with membership in what prosecutors described as "the Ergenekon terrorist organization," which they claimed had planned assassinations and bomb attacks to stir up unrest and pave the way for a military coup. After almost five years of trials, in mid-March 2013, Turkey's former armed forces chief—along with 275 others (21 defendants were acquitted)—was found guilty and sentenced to life in prison for conspiring to overthrow the government. The Ergenekon case and related legal reforms clipped the wings and unchecked power of the military. However, while many saw a necessary and an important step in bringing the army under civilian control, many others charged that it was a vehicle for the government to suppress its opponents (military, journalists, and politicians). Critics increasingly charged that Erdogan and his government, long regarded as progressive, had become increasingly authoritarian.

It was this shift in perception that brought many onto the streets in 2013. In Gezi Park (discussed below), angry protests against the government brought together an unprecedented coalition from across the political and social spectrum, united in their opposition to the government.

SINCE HIS 2011 general election victory, Erdogan has practically frozen the EU process and stopped democratic reforms. He started criticizing the EU very harshly and kept talking about the Shanghai Cooperation agreement. He and his supporters have started arguing for a Turkish-style presidential system with a very powerful executive without effective checks and balances. (Some of his members of parliament (MPs) called US president Barack Obama a miserable loser since Obama has to cooperate with the Congress.) In 2012, the AKP majority proposed a sixty-item constitutional amendment package to the parliament. This change was trying to create a super-president who would legislate when the parliament was not in session and who would appoint two-thirds of the high court judges. These appointments would be done together with the parliament, but because of the political party laws, the party chairmen, not the party branches, decide about parliamentary candidates. Thus, Erdogan was trying to fuse the executive with the legislative and judiciary. This was rejected by the opposition, so Erdogan could not get three-fifths of the parliamentary majority for a referendum; it required 330 out of 550 votes, and he had 326. But the effort clearly showed his intentions. He repeatedly has said that if his party can get this figure in the 2015 elections, he will change the system into a presidential system.

The Arab Spring

When the revolutions in the Arab world occurred in Egypt and Tunisia, Erdogan and the AKP actively called for the implementation of democracy in places like Egypt and Tunisia. Erdogan had close relations in particular with the Muslim Brotherhood in Egypt and Tunisia's Ennahda and was a popular figure, drawing large crowds. He played a constructive role not only in the region but also with the United States and Europe. Omer Taspinar points out the paradox that the Arab Spring sharpened into relief: the mistaken notion of a "pro-Western" versus "Islamic" divide in Turkish foreign policy. "Turkey's population is almost entirely Muslim, and the AKP, a party with Islamic roots, has won three consecutive elections. Many thus assume that Turkish divergence from the West—'losing' Turkey—is the product of an Islamic revival or Islamization."[27]

Gezi Park Controversy and Charges of Government Corruption

A series of events, including the Gezi Park protests in May–August 2013 and a major corruption scandal in December 2013, fueled by increasing public dissatisfaction and societal polarization, presented a significant challenge to Erdogan and the AKP—one that they had not experienced since coming to power in 2002.

The nationwide protest demonstrations and civil unrest that swept across Turkey were initially triggered on May 28, 2013, by outrage at the violent eviction of sit-in protestors to a government urban development plan for Istanbul's Taksim Gezi Park. The AKP project aimed to develop or remodel Taksim Square, an outdoor space famed for its greenery and cafés, by building a shopping mall and reconstructing an old military barracks into shopping malls and luxury apartments at Gezi Park, adjacent to the square.

While the initial protest was driven by objections to the park's demolition on environmental grounds, it morphed into a broader movement that eventually included those who used the controversy as an avenue to express other grievances against the government: "the young and the old, the secular and the religious, the soccer hooligans and the blind, anarchists, communists, nationalists, Kurds, gays, feminists, and students."[28] They demanded an end to the Gezi Park demolition project, a halt to police violence and brutality, an end to the sale of public spaces to private developers and investors, the right of all Turks to express their complaints against government policies and actions without fear of repression, and increased media and press freedoms.[29] Members of the AKP's secularist opposition wished to emulate the Tamarod and the coup that overthrew the Muslim Brotherhood government in Egypt. Erdogan countered critics and increased tensions, charging that protestors had consumed alcohol even in a mosque and committed other illicit acts, and that the protest was part of an international plot involving the United States, Germany, the United Kingdom, and Israel, which were using the Himzet movement as their puppet. All in all, more than three million of Turkey's eighty million came out into the streets to voice their grievances.

The government's response was defiant. In a televised speech, Erdogan vowed, "Where they gather 10, I will get up and gather 200,000 people. Where they gather 100,000, I will bring together one million from my party."[30] He described his opponents as "looters" and "bums" and warned that his patience had limits.

Amnesty International reported that it had "received consistent and credible reports of demonstrators being beaten by police during arrest and transfer to custody and being denied access to food, water, and toilet facilities for up to 12 hours during the current protests in Istanbul which have taken place for almost three weeks."[31] Eight deaths, more than eight thousand injuries, and nearly five thousand arrests resulted from the conflict.

Though Erdogan had called the police heroes, in an interview on June 20, 2013, the mayor of Istanbul, Kadir Topbaş, announced that seven municipal employees had been removed from office due to accusations that they had burned the tents and belongings of demonstrators camped out in Gezi Park and sought to assuage the public, stating that the government would seek public approval for all future projects.[32]

Despite the unrest in Turkey, as Erdogan had predicted, the AKP won a landslide victory in local elections in March amid corruption allegations, a damaging security leak, and controversial social media bans. Nearly 90 percent of Turkish voters participated, 43 percent of whom voted for his AKP party (higher than the 39 percent the party had received in 2009).[33] The political crisis did not appear to influence a plurality of voters who opened a door for Erdogan's re-election bid in August 2014. Moreover, on July 1, 2014, Erdogan was named the AKP candidate in presidential elections, which he won with 52 percent.

Rather than addressing the concerns through a democratic process— and thereby undermining the charges that he was moving in a direction of authoritarianism—he chose to rely on conspiracy theories and hollow explanations that dismissed the real concerns of the people. He governed solely in the interests of those voters—50 percent—that the AKP secured in the general election. By understanding democracy in a majoritarian sense, Erdogan often pitted one half of the population, which supported him, against the other, effectively forming two large blocs that are at odds. Democracy, however, is more than majoritarian, and tensions in Turkey might well have been resolved had Erdogan understood democracy in a pluralistic sense, recognizing the rights and liberties and empathizing with the concerns of a vastly diverse society comprised of multiple political and social groups.[34]

The AKP Clash with the Gülen Movement

Critics' charges that Prime Minister Erdogan had strayed from the democratization path and increasingly chose the path of authoritarianism were reinforced when after years of coexistence, despite differences, a sharp conflict broke out between the Gülen movement, also known as Hizmet (Service) and the government on December 17, 2013.

Erdogan's AKP government and the Gülen movement share a modernizing Islamic ideology, espousing civil Islam against the political use of religion. Although relations between them had been deteriorating for some time, before the current crisis it was possible to be affiliated with both. Coexistence ended abruptly on December 17. More than fifty pro-AKP figures, including the head of Halkbank, a state-owned bank, and the sons of three cabinet ministers, were taken in for questioning by prosecutors who were alleged to be Gülen's men.

Fethullah Gülen and his Hizmet movement represent a Turkish cosmopolitan Islamic (but more apolitical) movement, operating today in 160 countries with volunteers from many ethnic backgrounds.[35] In Turkey's increasingly politicized context, the group in its early years had walked the fine line between militant secularists and Islamists like the Welfare Party. It emphasized both religion and secular nationalism, modern and religious education—especially science and technology—relations with the West, and relations between Islam and other religions. Gülen and his followers tread carefully, acknowledging the significance of Ataturk, respect for the military, and the dangers of politicized religion. Their message was communicated effectively through their widely circulated newspaper,

Zaman (*Today's Zaman* in English), a network of television stations, and publishing houses.

The Gülen movement specifically stresses the compatibility of Islamic ideas and practices with the market economy, which, along with the spread of democratization, engendered an unprecedented Islamicization of the public sphere with a complex web of business networks and a large media empire.

Throughout the 1980s, the Gülen movement significantly expanded their growing presence in the economic sector through other large holding companies, banks, investment houses, insurance companies, and chain stores.

Gülen's project aimed to advance the goal of creating a new elite, which he called the "golden generation," and he worked to equip them with education and training in the modern sciences and Islamic ethics. Thus, in this light, he moved beyond the realm of leading a purely religious movement and instead spearheaded a social and educational revolution. Their educational projects (the building of schools, universities, and dormitories for tens of thousands of students; book publication and distribution, tutorials; financial aid) proved effective, drawing in future volunteers and exerting a powerful influence on the next generation of professionals. Combining religious, educational, and business interests in Turkey with those abroad, and with the financial help of volunteers from the business community, the Gülen movement created an extensive network of secular schools throughout Turkey and founded more than a thousand elementary, secondary, and high schools in more than 160 countries, mainly in Central Asia, the Balkans, the Caucasus, Pakistan, Afghanistan, Africa, the Middle East, Latin America, the United States, and Europe.[36]

For Gülen, the top-down imposition of dogmatic secularism, as carried out by Ataturk and his followers, created an unnecessary split between Turkish society and the ruling elites. The state, he believed, was responsible for providing internal and external security and stability for its citizens, and while opposed to the implementation of Sharia, for example, for several decades he has championed Anglo-Saxon secularism, democratic pluralism, human rights, and especially individual rights to express one's faith.

Gülen's open criticism of the WP's politicization of Islam drew reproach from WP leaders on both religious and political grounds. Many secularists in the military and intelligentsia remained wary and suspicious of the group, often conflating Gülen's growing following with

the WP and other more politicized groups and regarding all of them as
Islamists. In 1999, Gülen emigrated to America. In self-imposed exile in
his compound in Pennsylvania, he continued to influence Muslims and
non-Muslims around the globe, particularly through his movement's educational agenda. *The Economist*, which profiled Gülen and his movement
in 2008, commented on their extensive reach:

> In the former Soviet south, it fights the "Turkish" corner in areas
> where the cultures of Russia, China and Iran co-exist uneasily.
> "If you meet a polite Central Asian lad who speaks good English
> and Turkish, you know he went to a Gülen school," says a Turkish
> observer. In Kyrgyzstan, for example, the movement runs a univer-
> sity and a dozen high schools, which excel in international contests.
> Even in Pakistan, pupils at Gülen schools learn Turkish songs, as
> well as benefiting from gleaming science labs.[37]

All in all, some 2,000 of the Gülen movement's schools (most private
schools) and institutions operate in 160 countries. After the AKP victory,
Gülen and his Hizmet movement enjoyed a good relationship, though
strained at times, with the government, based on the broader visions of the
AKP and Hizmet's moderately conservative reformist Islamic understanding. That relationship ruptured in late 2013 as tensions mounted between
the two groups, especially with Gülen's strong criticism of Erdogan and
the government's handling of Gezi Park protests. In November, the government announced it would close the *dershane*, a network of private
tutoring schools, about 20 percent of which were run by Gülen's followers,
by 2015.[38] In response, in December, prosecutors and police close to the
movement helped expose a government corruption scandal, which rocked
the AKP with accusations of cronyism, fraud, money laundering, bribery,
and gold smuggling. Eight months before, the national intelligence service had informed the government about the corruption charges. Police
confiscated nearly $20 million, arrested twenty-six, and detained more
than ninety-one overall, including three sons of prominent ministers in
Erdogan's government.[39] Four ministers resigned.

Erdogan charged that the nation's civil servants were staging a "judicial coup."[40] More than forty thousand police officers were reassigned. New
prosecutors have been appointed, and Erdogan never allowed the indictment against his ministers to reach the parliament to be discussed. Media
outlets that were critical, raising questions about the corruption charges,

were shut down; social media sites were blocked. Under proposed legislation that would make it easier for the government to censor the Internet, Turkish officials attempted to control the flow of information that reached the public by arbitrarily blocking websites, collecting personal data from Internet companies, and coercing news sites to remove information that Erdogan and the AKP found objectionable.[41] In early February 2014, the online editor of a popular Gülen movement newspaper, *Today's Zaman*, Mahir Zeynalov, was ordered to leave the country following a series of Tweets that criticized Erdogan.[42] Twitter and YouTube were banned, but this was rescinded by the Constitutional Court.

The economic and political fallout was significant. As tensions flared in the wake of Erdogan's authoritarian drift, the country's financial ranking deteriorated, as did its currency. Fears of a decrease in foreign direct investment rattled financial institutions. The Turkish Central Bank raised interest rates to offset a drop in the lira, the country's official currency, as the concerns of the conservative business class—whose energy and manufacturing companies depended on Turkey's strength in the international market—peaked.[43]

By early 2014, many of those who had hailed the country as a model for other states experiencing political transitions had second thoughts. Turkey's relationship with the EU, which hinges in part on aligning its rule of law with EU structures, risked deterioration, thanks to government "reforms": "The High Council of Judges and Prosecutors, which deals with appointments and promotions, has been put under the de facto authority of the minister of justice, while the judicial police was brought under the control of the police instead of prosecutors. The media no longer have access to police facilities. . . . A highly discretionary new law that, among other things, requires Internet service providers to make web user data available to the authorities was passed in a hurry in parliament and immediately approved by the president, despite widespread criticism to which the president felt compelled to respond."[44]

The increasing public dissatisfaction and the societal polarization created in the aftermath of the Gezi Park protests, and the corruption scandal that broke out in December 2013, were catalysts for new government-proposed legislation in 2013–2014 that would curb academic freedom. The government-controlled Council of Higher Education issued new campus regulations enabling university administrations "to sanction all faculty and students who get engaged in discussions, debates, declarations, and statements that are not 'scientific' in nature."[45] Proposed government legislation transferred tenure and promotion reviews by the independent Inter-University Council to the government-controlled Council of Higher Education and enabled it appoint to board members of private (foundation-funded) universities. The latter undermined the more independent private universities, in particular those affiliated with the Gülen movement.

Conclusion

Although Ataturk created and shaped modern Turkey as a secular state, at the same time, Islam remained strong in non-urban areas, the majority of the country, and in popular piety. Political realities after Ataturk's death produced a more fluid history in which Islam, and Turkish Muslim identity and culture in particular, became more visible in politics and civil society. In the past two decades, Turkey has witnessed the emergence and progressive growth and impact of Political Islam, culminating initially in the electoral successes of the Islamist Welfare Party. The emergence of WP as a key political player precipitated a political crisis and conflict between the military and secular elites and Islamists: "Because secularism did not separate religion and politics, but rather subordinated religion to the political realm, it promoted the politicization of Islam and struggle between secularists and Muslims for control of the state."[46] Despite its critics charges, during its brief period in power, the WP did not impose an Islamic state but created a more democratic Turkey with space for religion and implemented socioeconomic reforms, a more just and equitable society, and an end to corruption and nepotism. The military and many secular elites charged that this violated, or even was an assault on, Turkish secularism. Given their militant secularism, rooted in a 19th-century rationalism, the recourse to religion was viewed as retrogressive, anti-modern, a retreat to the Dark Ages, and a threat to their power and lifestyles.

The AKP's rise to power and stunning success in 2002 demonstrated the ability of former members of an Islamist party (WP) to learn from experience and establish a more diverse and inclusive political party whose economic and social platform and policies rather than an Islamic political agenda attracted widespread support. The military, once a powerful interventionist force, has agreed to the Ergenekon judicial cases, in which many military officers were tried and convicted. Political parties in general, though still strong in their opposition to Erdogan and the AKP, reluctantly accept election results. At the same time, despite many accomplishments and victories in successive elections, Erdogan and the AKP government resorted to an authoritarian-style response when faced with a significant challenge to their authority. The AKP's and Turkey's democratic future is dependent on fostering a more pluralist political culture and values of power sharing, preserving a meaningful system of checks and balances, and strengthening institutional safeguards of checks and balances as well as freedoms that enable the public to protest and avenues to express their discontent without fear of suppression of their rights. At the same time, the military, secular elites, and other opposition are challenged to accept the role of a "loyal opposition" and not use political differences and discontent as an excuse to topple a democratically elected government through military intervention or violence rather than through the electoral process.

3

Iran

CLASSICAL THEMES AND CONTEMPORARY CHALLENGES

AS WE DISCUSSED in Chapter 1, scholars in the 20th century hypoth-esized about democratization, the process by which countries transition from authoritarian to popular forms of governance, with the assump-tion that such a transition was, if not inevitable, at least to be desired. In the context of the Cold War, however, Western (capitalist) governments sometimes feared that too much populism could lead to chaos that could be exploited by Eastern bloc (communist) powers. Caution was urged, therefore, in the promotion of democracy. Some even spoke of the ben-efits of limited democracy, suggesting that allowing a degree of electoral participation—for example, in municipal or provincial councils—could satisfy the urge to self-governance while at the same time allowing an authoritarian national government to maintain ultimate control. Partial democracy could serve as a stabilizing factor in authoritarian govern-ments. Provided those authoritarian governments were solidly in the Western camp, this could prove a capitalist advantage in the East-West competition.[1] Thus, policymakers could shift their analyses from whether or not the country was truly democratic to whether or not its govern-ment could be relied upon to maintain sufficient stability to protect Western financial interests in the country. *Realpolitik* suggested that a semi-democratic authoritarian regime may be more conducive to security than a fully democratic regime dominated by forces averse to the US poli-cies. Better to support an unpopular regime that protects US investments than risk populist governments that may turn against US interests.

At the height of the Cold War, British and US policy toward Iran appears to have been influenced by this line of thinking. It was then that the United States participated in a clandestine operation to overthrow Mohammad Mosaddegh, the first democratically chosen prime minister of Iran, and reinstate the authoritarianism of the king (shah). Though the precise details of this operation continue to be argued by historians, the political impact of this operation has been profound. Indeed, it can be argued that no other single event has had such disastrous regional and global long-range consequences. It led to the 1979 overthrow of the pro-Western shah's regime which, in turn, occasioned Iraq's invasion of Iran. As a result of events during that war, Iraq then invaded Kuwait, leading to the stationing of US troops in Saudi Arabia, which proved to be Osama bin Laden's major grievance against his native country and contributed to the formation of al-Qaeda, whose members attacked the United States in 1993 and again on September 11, 2001. Those attacks sparked the Global War on Terrorism (GWOT), including the invasion of Iraq in 2003, which is the immediate context for the presence of al-Qaeda in the Middle East, and gave rise to the even more brutal ISIS (Islamic State in Iraq and Syria, also known as Islamic State in the Levant [ISIL], Islamic State [IS], and Daish, its Arabic acronym). Yet despite this cascade of militarist interventions and radicalization, Iranians have continued the struggle for Islamic democratic governance.

Shadow of God

Like Egypt, but very much unlike Pakistan, Iran has a long and distinguished history of authoritarian governance.

From the time of the Sasanian Empire of Cyrus the Great in the 3rd century, the ruler of Persia—renamed "Iran" in the 1930s—was considered absolute. The Sasanians were Zoroastrians, and upholding that religion was the king's task. In Zoroastrianism, God is the absolute ruler of the cosmos, the maintainer of order, and the bulwark against chaos and injustice, and the king is his representative. The king of Persia was therefore believed to be more important than any other earthly king; he was the "king of kings"—the *shahanshah*.

Sasanian notions of kingship had an impact on Islamic political thought in the 10th century, when the title *shahanshah* was adopted by some rulers. Persia specialist Said Amir Arjomand notes that in Twelver

Shi`ism, the form of Islam that became dominant in Iran, scholars held religious authority, while kings assumed the absolute political power characteristic of Sasanian Persia.[2] Their task was still to maintain order, as in Zoroastrian times, and in so doing promote justice. Their power was indeed absolute; they controlled the military and there were no effective institutional checks on them. But their authority, as distinct from coercive power, was limited. Religious scholars—referred to as clergy in Shi`i Islam—maintained the exclusive right to interpret Islamic teachings, focused as they are on justice. In that sense, the clergy were in the position of arbitrating whether or not the king was actually carrying out his mandate. That is, they could determine the legitimacy of the ruler. The religious authorities were thus positioned to oppose the king when people experience the opposite of justice: tyranny. As Arjomand puts it, "Tyranny is defective government in which the ruler strives to enslave the servants of God. Just rule, on the other hand, means the rule of the *sacred* law; otherwise the just ruler cannot rule and his subjects cannot prosper."[3] The clergy had no political power and, indeed, were generally averse to political engagement; theirs was the voice only of moral authority. Historian Marshall G. S. Hodgson observes that the Safavid religious scholars "did not accept a status as part of the military regime but preferred to be ranked with the taxable subject population. From that vantage point, they maintained a stance of potential and occasionally actual criticism of the regime." Religious authorities "reached the point of full independence from the . . . state," but the state "ceased to be independent of the [religious authorities]."[4]

This model of kingship served Persia well, particularly during the reign of the great Safavid dynasty, beginning in 1500. That was long after the demise of the classical caliphates and, with them, any thought of global Islamic political unity. Instead, regional dynasties developed, most spectacularly, the Ottomans, headquartered in what would become Turkey but ruling over the Arab Middle East and North Africa. The Ottomans claimed to be the rightful heirs to the last caliphate, the Abbasids; they were therefore officially Sunni. But the Persians valiantly resisted being overtaken by the Ottomans. That resistance was led by the Safavids, who were Turkic but not Sunni. As Shi`ites, they believed leadership of the Muslim community rightly belonged to male descendants of Prophet Muhammad through the line of the Prophet's cousin Ali and his wife, the Prophet's daughter, Fatima. The twelfth "imam" (as the descendants/rulers are called in this tradition) had gone into a state of "occultation" in the 9th century and would reappear only at the end of time, as a Mahdi or "rightly guided" one, and (along with Jesus) usher in a period of peace and justice before the final judgment. Until then, it was up to the Shi`a to follow the law as interpreted by the scholars.

Because Shi`a rejected the legitimacy of Sunni rulers, they were often subjected to persecution, which explains the ferocity of their resistance toward the Ottomans. But the Safavids' Shi`a identity also gave them a basis of legitimacy of their own. After decades of battles, in the mid-16th century the Ottomans and Safavids ultimately accepted a border distinguishing officially Sunni Ottoman sovereign territory from officially Shi`a Safavid territory.[5] The Safavids then set about making sure everyone in their territory was indeed Shi`a, initiating in a period of forced conversions. Today approximately 90 percent of Iranians are Shi`a, with significant minorities of Sunnis and Baha'is, as well as smaller minority communities of Christians, Jews, Zoroastrians, and Hindus, among others.

The high point of Safavid rule was in the 16th and 17th centuries, when Shah Abbas transformed the ancient city of Isfahan into the architectural wonder it remains today. Shah Abbas also brought in Shi`a scholars from throughout the region to establish mosques and schools to develop and propagate Shi`a learning. As important as the scholars were, the king maintained control of the royal court and military and was the ultimate locus of power.

Tribal and other grievances from outside the Safavid court erupted in the 18th century, resulting in the overthrow of the dynasty. Eventually another tribal leader, the Qajar Agha Muhammad Khan, established a new dynasty, with Tehran as its capital. The Qajars did their best to consolidate central control and develop the country's infrastructure and resources. Unfortunately, they did so with the assistance of loans from their northern neighbor Russia and from England, each of whom had serious designs on Persia. Russia was perennially in search of warm-water ports, and the Persian Gulf was profoundly tempting. Russia began efforts to gain control of Persian territory in the early 19th century. The czar had annexed former Persian-held territories of Georgia on the Black Sea and Dagestan on the Caspian Sea in 1796. Beginning in 1804, the two countries battled again for nearly a decade over control of Armenian and Azerbaijani territories (the Caucasus, named for the mountain range between the Black and Caspian Seas). Persia ultimately surrendered, ceding control of the territories to

Russia. The struggle resumed in 1826 when the Qajar shah, struggling in reduced circumstances, attempted to regain the territories. He failed, and he had to pay punishing reparations and allow the Russians to maintain a naval base on Persia's northern border on the Caspian Sea. As well, Russia demanded and received the right to tax-free trade privileges in Persia.

England had at least as much at stake in Persia as Russia did. As an island, obviously, it needed no more ports. But as an island—and a small one, at that—it was dependent upon two things in its competition with other European powers: foreign investments and, in order to enforce its will on those unwilling to cooperate in Britain's foreign investment initiatives, its navy. The Qajar shahs found British investment initiatives slightly less intimidating than those of imperial Russia. The 1872 "Reuter Concession" is a prime example. The British baron Julius de Reuter was granted the rights to develop a broad range of Persian infrastructure and industry, including roads, telegraphs, factories, and mining, for the next five years in return for 40 percent of the profit for the next twenty years. All other profit would go to the baron. Another is the 1890 tobacco concession granted to British Major G. F. Talbot, whereby Talbot was granted sole control over tobacco production and sales, both domestic and foreign, for fifty years in return for £15,000 and 25 percent of net profits. The tobacco concession was so unpopular that it triggered a rebellion, led by religious authorities, the following year.[6] But Persian petroleum became Britain's most desirable investment opportunity. Not only was it valuable on the world market, but the British navy came to rely on that petroleum to fuel its mighty navy. It began the switch from coal to petroleum to fuel its navy in 1912. The new fuel allowed the ships to run faster, longer, and with fewer refueling stops and required less manpower. With Germany demonstrating its own naval prowess, England was determined to secure an absolutely reliable source of petroleum. It did that through the Anglo-Persian Oil Company (APOC), established in 1901. APOC had purchased sole rights to explore, extract, transport, and sell the country's petroleum, natural gas, and other geological resources for sixty years from the Qajar shah who, in return, was to receive £20,000 cash, 20,000 shares, and 16 percent of the annual net profits.[7] (According to historian L. P. Elwell-Sutton, the shah never got his £20,000; instead he was awarded an additional 30,000 shares.[8]) In 1904 oil began to trickle, and in 1908 it began to gush. And APOC became extremely profitable.

Constitutional Revolt 1906

Despite the ancient legacy of Persian authoritarian kingship, the country was among the first in the modern world to institutionalize democratic reforms. Just as the British-owned APOC began to exploit the country's great wealth, Persia itself was going broke. The Qajars' wars with Russia and their development projects had depleted their treasury. They had borrowed heavily from both Britain and Russia, and the country was deeply in debt. The religious authorities had actively opposed foreign involvement in Persia's economy since the late 19th century, ultimately bringing sufficient pressure on the shah to revoke the British monopoly on tobacco exports. The powerful merchant class likewise resented foreign exploitation of Persia's economy and, intellectuals inspired by democratizing movements in Europe and the Ottoman Empire, led popular protests for political reform. In 1906 the Qajar shah finally acceded to demands for a constitution that outlined government by a popularly elected parliament. The constitution also stipulated that the shah would be allowed to appoint a prime minister whose task would be to oversee implementation of parliament's legislation. It called for a senate, as well, half of whose members would be appointed by the shah.

But before the constitution could prove effective, Russia and Britain again interfered. The shah who agreed to the constitution promptly died, and his successor vehemently opposed the new limits on his authority. And newly chosen representatives had little in common and less idea of how to devise legislation that could address Persia's mounting economic and development challenges. As they debated, England and Russia agreed to split the country into regions of influence. With the Anglo-Russian Entente of 1907, Russia assumed northern Persia as its proprietary zone, and Britain assumed dominance over southeastern areas (contiguous to its holdings in the Indian subcontinent; the agreement also allotted Afghanistan to Britain, but that is another story). Between these two areas was a buffer zone, and the two foreign powers agreed not to trespass on each other's newly acquired turf. What is more, they set up militias in each of their zones: the Cossack Brigades in the Russian zone, and the South Persia Rifles in the British zone.

The newly created Persian parliament was powerless against the combined power of Britain and Russia. The incoming shah seized the day, ordered leading constitutionalists arrested, and in 1908 had the Cossack Brigades bomb parliament. When constitutionalists fought back in the northern city of Tabriz, the shah ordered the Cossacks to take control of the city. The following year tribal militias led by constitutionalists attacked Tehran, overthrew the new shah, and replaced him with his young son. The parliament thus reasserted its authority, but only nominally. Britain and Russia maintained control in Persia throughout the fraught period of their alliance against Germany in World War I.

The Pahlavi Coup

The Bolshevik Revolution in 1917 gave Persia's parliament an opportunity to reassert itself. It sought British financial support for developing infrastructure and training and supplying a standing army. But Britain also demanded a continued monopoly on Persian petroleum, including in the provinces formerly controlled by czarist Russia. Wary of more foreign control, many religious authorities and nationalists opposed the agreement.

The tipping point came when, in 1920, revolutionaries in northern Iran attempted to establish a "soviet," with support from the newly formed USSR.[9] Early the following year the leader of the Cossack Brigades, Reza Khan, decided to take action. He led his troops to Tehran, where he effectively took over parliament and appointed a new government. They negotiated with the USSR for the removal of Soviet troops from Persia, Persian control of Russian-built railroad and port facilities, and equal shipping rights on the Caspian Sea. They also rejected British efforts to extend their petroleum monopoly into the former Russian zone. Reza Khan's Cossacks proceeded to quash a number of provincial uprisings against the central government and dismantled the newly established Persian soviet.

Reza Khan's apparent success against foreign intervention and rebellious tribes earned him increasing support among reformers, but especially among the merchant class and traditional nationalists, including members of the religious elite. They supported his self-appointment as minister of war and subsequent assumption of the position of prime minister. In 1925 they supported his assumption of the throne when the parliament deposed the last Qajar shah.[10] Assuming the name of a medieval Persian script, he became the first "Pahlavi" shah.

Reza Shah's ascent to the throne represents one of the two dominant tendencies in Persian politics. As if to reinforce the country's tradition of a strong monarchy, Reza Shah's own military training and personal control of the military predictably resulted in distinct authoritarianism, particularly evident in his social engineering. Not only did he force nomadic herders to adopt a settled, agrarian lifestyle, but in an effort to incorporate women into the public economic sector, he banned the traditional head-covering (chador). He also attempted to regulate religious authority, introducing required exams for licensing religious teachers and bypassing traditional Islamic law—always the province of the religious authorities—by introducing a secular civil code of law. (This, as we shall see, would prove to be a dangerous precedent.) And he attempted to strengthen national identity by mandating "modern" dress, outlawing traditional ethnic and religious sartorial markers of identity. He even changed the name of the country. As of 1935, the country was to be called Iran. And to silence public outcry against such abrupt transformations, Reza Shah banned political parties and silenced media voices critical of his reforms.

In addition, Reza Shah strengthened the central government. He centralized the bureaucracy, instituting direct taxation whose proceeds were then used to finance developments such as a national road system and a railway connecting the Caspian Sea and the Persian Gulf. He modernized the military, introducing national conscription, exponentially increasing the size of military, and vastly increased its hardware through the purchase of ships, tanks, and planes. He also empowered the Ministry of Education, establishing the country's first university, the University of Tehran, in 1924. At the same time, Reza Shah developed the industrial sector, introducing the manufacture of textiles, for example, to reduce the country's dependence on employment in the foreign-controlled petroleum sector.

Reza Shah's monarchy also manifested the tradition of Iran's fierce independence. He attempted to extract the country from the British economic grip, especially in the petroleum sector—a task that would ultimately prove beyond his capabilities. The government began efforts to increase Iran's share in oil revenues almost immediately upon Reza Shah's becoming king. By that time the British government, under First Lord of the Admiralty Winston Churchill, had bought controlling shares of the company. Efforts to increase Iran's share in petroleum profits from 16 percent to 25 percent, reduce the size of the area granted to Britain in 1901, impose a tax on the company's profits, and demand greater transparency in the company's accounting all proved in vain. In 1932, Reza Shah simply cancelled the 1901 agreement, sending Britain to the International Justice Court at The Hague. Reza Shah rescinded his cancellation of the 1901 agreement and managed to forge a new agreement in 1933. The new agreement did decrease the area previously allotted to Britain, but it allowed Britain to jettison the least productive areas, substituted a fixed annual royalty payment for the previous percentage of profits and a fixed annual fee for taxes and duties APOC previously paid, and then extended the whole agreement for another three decades.

Reflecting Iran's increased frustration with both England and Russia, Reza Shah began to look to Germany for technical expertise and development support. As his son Mohammad Reza Shah put it in his 1961 autobiography, "My father had deliberately fostered very close economic and cultural relations with Germany. By 1938 Germany had reached first place in Iran's foreign trade, with Russia (mostly because of her proximity) second." By his account, Germany supplied not only industrial equipment and machinery but engineers, technicians, teachers, and trainers, in addition to pro-Nazi literature for Iran's National Library, radio broadcasts, and an official news agency. The rationale, says Mohammad Reza Shah, was that Germany "had no conspicuous record of imperialism in Iran ... and she was opposed to the two big imperialist powers who had for so long plagued us."[11]

Given the state of German politics at the time, however, this new geopolitical tilt proved to be a colossal strategic blunder. While his own people could be silenced or marginalized, European powers had other options. Following the Nazi invasion of the USSR, British Commonwealth and Soviet troops occupied Iran in order to secure its oil fields and enforce the country's neutrality. Under British and Russian pressure, in September 1941 Reza Shah abdicated in favor of his son Mohammad Reza. Reza Shah was arrested and sent into exile. Once again Persia—now Iran—was divided between British and Russian—now Soviet—spheres of influence. Once again they had a shah who was sympathetic to their interests. And once again Iranians had a king who, supported by foreign powers, was under no pressure to abide by the country's constitutional limits on his power.

Nationalization of Iranian Oil, Operation Ajax, and the Reassertion of Autocracy

Following World War II, Mohammad Reza Shah's Western orientation increased as a result of the USSR's postwar interference in Iran. With Soviet backing, uprisings calling for local empowerment erupted in

Kurdish and Azeri-speaking (non-Persian) areas of northern Iran. At the same time, Iranian nationalists' efforts to wrest control of the country's oil resources from England resumed. The APOC—now AIOC, Anglo-Iranian Oil Company—granted a few more concessions in 1949 but still retained complete control of the management of the company and the lion's share of its profits. Parliament rejected the new agreement but again was powerless to do anything other than vote to reject it as long as the palace-appointed prime minister and senators accepted it.

By that time a number of political movements and parties had been established to promote specific national agendas. (Mohammad Reza Shah had gradually relaxed his father's ban on political parties.) The Tudeh was a communist party established in the early 1940s calling for constitutional limits on royal power, democracy, and national autonomy. In the wake of the overthrow of the aggressive, imperialist czars, it was not unusual for developing countries to look to Russia's communists as effective supporters of the rights of the marginalized and oppressed masses, and Iran's Tudeh Party attracted a large following. Less representative was the Fedayan-e Islam, a shadowy movement foreshadowing militancy that developed later in the 20th century. The Fedayan-e Islam, established in the mid-1940s, called for prohibition of all foreign innovations—including cinema and Western-style clothing—and advocating strict adherence to traditional interpretations of Islamic law. Its primary tool was assassination of public figures it considered pro-West or anti-Islam. Most representative was the mainstream secular National Front, a coalition of several other parties, established in late 1940s by the veteran charismatic politician and leading nationalization advocate Mohammad Mosaddegh, to promote economic and political autonomy and democracy. The nationalization of Iran's oil was at the top of his agenda.[12]

In 1951, with widespread poverty and the gap between Iranian and British standards of living becoming ever more obvious, popular pressure to nationalize oil reached a crescendo. In March the anti-nationalization prime minister was assassinated and, within weeks, parliament voted to nationalize Iran's oil. It was only then that the Shah was forced to appoint Mosaddegh as prime minister after an overwhelming parliamentary vote in his favor. As Mohammad Reza Shah put it in his autobiography, "Parliament overwhelmingly passed a bill, which I fully endorsed, nationalizing the oil industry."[13] The Anglo-Iranian Oil Company now became the National Iranian Oil Company.[14]

It fell to Mosaddegh to implement the nationalization of Iran's oil. Efforts to negotiate with the Anglo-Iranian Oil Company a deal similar to that just concluded by Standard Oil's Arabian-American Oil Company (ARAMCO) and the Saudis for equal shares of profits failed. Britain's appeals to the United Nations Security Council and International Court of Justice also failed.[15] The United States, under the Truman administration, attempted to mediate as well, but these efforts also failed, despite Iran's concession to allow the International Court of Justice to determine compensation for Britain's investment in the company. Rather than negotiate, Britain's response was to pull out their technicians and to convince other countries not to allow its technicians to take their places, to blockade Abadan—the port exporting Iran's oil—making it impossible for Iran to export its oil, and to impose crippling sanctions including freezing Iranian funds held in British banks.

The Shah had supported nationalization, but he did not appreciate the increasing limitation on his power by parliament. Fearing the Shah's interventions, Mosaddegh took measures considered undemocratic by some. The Shah and a close circle of royalists seized upon these measures as proof that Mosaddegh had himself become a dictator—or worse, a communist.

Britain ultimately collaborated with the United States in the clandestine mission to overthrow the government led by Mosaddegh (US code name, Operation Ajax; Britain's code name was Operation Boot). The overthrow may well have been instigated by members of the Iranian military, and Britain clearly had strong motives to support it. But the United States also had vested interests in the Shah's maintaining control of Iran's government. As early as 1949, the Shah had been in high-stakes development contracts with a US engineering consortium, Overseas Consultants Inc., assuring potential investors that he would not allow nationalization of oil.[16] Allen Dulles, then an attorney for the powerful international law firm Sullivan & Cromwell, helped broker the deal. Mosaddegh's coalition refused to support the deal when it came before parliament in 1950, seeing it as a continuation of the pattern of foreign intervention in Iran's economy. Dulles and his brother John Foster Dulles, also an attorney with Sullivan & Cromwell, grew more alarmed when Mosaddegh was elected prime minister in 1951, since their law firm represented the AIOC's bank. By the time Britain presented the plan to overthrow Mosaddegh to US president Eisenhower, John Foster Dulles was secretary of state and his brother Allen was director of CIA.

Both, not surprisingly, strongly encouraged President Eisenhower to support the plan.

The Shah's autobiography deals at length with the Mosaddegh overthrow, describing it as a solely Iranian affair: "I defy anybody to prove that the overturn of Mossadegh [*sic*] was not basically the work of the common people of my country—people whose hearts held a spark of the divine."[17] He says it was essential to protect his dynasty and to protect Iran from an eventual Soviet takeover which he claims Mosaddegh and his supporters were facilitating.[18] He makes no mention of foreign assistance in the operation, presumably because it was secret.

The CIA's own classified account of the affair, written in 1954 by one of the operation's CIA planners, Donald Wilber, appeared in the *New York Times* in April 2000. According to Wilber, Britain's Prime Minister Winston Churchill was desperate to get Iran's oil back under British control and sought US support for the operation. Working with CIA director Allen Dulles, Churchill informed President Eisenhower that Iranian royalists in the military favored a military coup against Mosaddegh's government, and Eisenhower agreed to the plan for the coup. Dulles approved $1 million in unrestricted funds for the operation. Wilber's report claims that CIA operatives set about fomenting chaos and fear that the communists were planning to take over. Operatives posing as Iranian communists threatened members of the religious elite and set off explosives at the home of at least one of them, and, through articles and editorials published by cooperating newspapers, they blamed the bombings on Iran's active communist Tudeh Party and called Mosaddegh's integrity into question, portraying him as inept, autocratic, and responsible for the financial ruin of Iran. (The Shah's autobiography reflects that he believed these claims.) As the plot became apparent and chaos mounted, Mosaddegh undertook countermeasures, organizing a referendum to dismiss parliament.[19] This only helped polarize popular opinion, seeming to confirm carefully planted suspicions that Mosaddegh would allow totalitarian communists to take over. In August 1953 the Shah agreed to dismiss Mosaddegh and appoint the loyal General Fazlollah Zahedi in his place. Mosaddegh loyalists scuffled with pro-Shah loyalists, and initially the plot appeared to have failed. General Zahedi went into hiding and the Shah fled the country.[20] But fears that Mosaddegh had lost his bearings continued to spread. General Zahedi orchestrated a call for jihad against communism. CIA-supported Iranians led crowds attacking pro-Mosaddegh and pro-Tudeh newspapers. Pro-Shah military leaders took control of the streets, key ministries, and communications. The Shah returned from Rome and, with the aid of a $5 million grant from the CIA, was able to consolidate his regime, leaving the vast majority in parliament who had supported nationalization utterly flummoxed.[21]

Mosaddegh was arrested and imprisoned. The AIOC became British Petroleum and agreed to split profits with Iran and to allot US oil companies 40 percent of the company and European companies 20 percent.

The Shah, newly re-empowered, proceeded to enforce unpopular pro-Western policies in Iran, ignoring constitutional limits to his authority. He was supported in those efforts by an efficient and loyal security apparatus, set up by General H. Norman Schwarzkopf (father of the Norman Schwarzkopf Jr., who would direct the US-led Operation Desert Shield against Saddam Hussein in 1991). Those security forces formed the basis of what would become SAVAK, the intelligence forces that terrorized Iranian citizens in the protracted run-up to the 1979 overthrow of the Shah.[22]

Following the failure of the parliament's efforts to assert its authority, the Shah set about strengthening the monarchy. The Shah benignly describes his increased powers: in addition to assuming the power to dismiss parliament and veto its legislation, he says: "As King I appoint the Prime Minister. I also appoint the other ministers, usually with his advice; likewise I sign the decrees appointing governors-general, higher judges, ambassadors, military officers, and certain other officials. I serve as Commander-in-Chief of the armed forces, both declaring war and concluding peace."[23] Political scientist Mehran Kamrava characterizes it differently. He calls it "the era of royal absolutism, which lasted from 1953 until about 1975":

The 1953 coup put an effective end to the independence and powers of the [parliament] and practically every other institution in the state other than the crown. Parliamentary elections became charades that no one, even members of the political establishment, took seriously. For example, provincial governors were authorized to use the rural gendarmeries and the city police to ensure that the government's candidates were elected to office. Parliament again became the rubber stamp it had been under Reza Shah. If, on rare occasions, an unapproved candidate somehow slipped into office, he was duly disqualified and arrested. The crown, and more specifically the person of the shah, became the state.[24]

But Iranians did not forget the 1953 coup. And regardless of who was ultimately responsible for the overthrow of Mosaddegh, Iranians viewed this event through the prism of their troubled relations with Western imperialism. Thus, the United States was perceived as only the most recent Western power attempting to undermine Iran's economic and political autonomy.

1979 Islamic Revolution

Having been reinstated as Iran's monarch, the Shah set about securing his position in a number of ways. With the country's increased oil wealth, he undertook development programs designed to make Iran the dominant power in the Middle East. He vastly increased the size and strength of the military, purchasing the latest weaponry and training from the United States. He undertook land reforms (the "White Revolution," initiated in 1963) designed to improve the lot of peasants and laborers, and he empowered women by granting them the right to vote, thus offsetting the lure of leftists, particularly the pro-Soviet communist Tudeh Party.

However, like his father, in arrogating to himself the right to legislate, not only did he ignore parliament, but he violated the fundamental principle of Islamic political legitimacy: he bypassed the authority of religious scholars to shape legislation. One of those religious authorities in particular—Ayatollah Ruhollah Khomeini—became the voice of opposition to the Shah, who was increasingly perceived as pro-West and irreligious. The ayatollah's opposition enflamed public opinion, leading to sometimes-violent demonstrations. The Shah exiled him but could not silence him. Radio waves and, later, cassette recordings were very effective pre-cyber communication tools for disseminating his populist message.

Ayatollah Khomeini was clearly not the only opponent to the Shah's autocratic ways. More established opposition parties such as the now-banned Tudeh and the National Front continued to operate underground, and militant opposition groups emerged, such as the leftist Mujahideen-e Khalq and the more radical Fedayeen-e Khalq. But these strains of dissent were silenced by the Shah's increasingly vigilant and effective intelligence apparatus. The voice of religious authority, however, even—and perhaps especially—in exile, continued to resonate, even with secularists. Focusing on injustice and the plight of the marginalized and dispossessed, classic themes in Shi`i ideology, the Ayatollah became, by default, the symbol of growing opposition to the Shah.

As opposition grew, the Shah grew increasingly intent on bypassing religious authorities and reasserting the glorious tradition of Persian monarchy. He had already repurposed the "Peacock Throne." That was the name of a dazzling giant jeweled chair built in the 17th century by Shah Jahan, king of Mughal India (the same one who built the Taj Mahal as a mausoleum for his beloved wife Mumtaz Mahal). It took seven years to build; was supported by pillars of gold; and was encrusted with huge diamonds, rubies, emeralds, pearls, and any number of other precious gems, including a mega-ruby that had been donated by a Safavid shah. It was taken as booty by an 18th-century Persian king and came to symbolize the grandeur of the Persian monarchy. Both Reza Shah and Mohammad Reza Shah used later reproductions of the throne in their coronation ceremonies. But Iranians continued to struggle against autocracy, and the clergy increasingly became the channel of their discontent. In a multimillion dollar gambit in 1971, the Shah made one last effort to finesse political authority. Instead of looking to Iran's glorious Islamic past, he staged a massive celebration of 2,500 years of Persian monarchy, going all the way back to pre-Islamic King Cyrus the Great. This could have been the event for which the phrase "over the top" was coined. For a four-day celebration, the Shah had fifty pre-Islamic-themed luxury apartments built for visiting royal guests. They were decorated by Parisian designers; costumes for servants were also designed by French couturiers; cuisine was provided by Maxim's of Paris, all accompanied by the finest French wines, including the priciest French champagne for distinctly un-Islamic toasts.

All this was meant to reinforce the grand Persian imperial heritage. Instead, it further intensified the growing opposition to the apparently megalomaniacal monarch. Ayatollah Khomeini's messages became more pointed, calling for social justice and demanding a new government to implement it.

Khomeini was not a particularly original thinker. But, as historian Ervand Abrahamian has noted, he was an effective communicator of the ideas of other popular ideologues. Chief among them was Ali Shariati (d. 1977). A talented public intellectual and religious activist in the mid-20th century, Shariati had become an active supporter of Mosaddegh. He combined Islamic themes of social justice and care for the dispossessed with charismatic appeals for renewal of Islamic social commitment among

Iran's youth. He was arrested for his activism and then left Iran and went to Paris to continue his studies. Earning a Ph.D. in sociology from the Sorbonne, he returned to Iran imbued with even greater fervor and a new vocabulary of postcolonial struggle against Western exploitation of "the wretched of the earth"—the title of Frantz Fanon's famous work, which Shariati translated into Persian. Returning to Iran in 1964, Shariati continued his teaching and political activism. In packed lecture halls he inspired young Iranians to remember their role as stewards of the earth; to unite their spiritual, social, and political struggles; and to demonstrate their spiritual integrity by working to end tyranny and oppression. That, he stressed, is what is necessary to establish a godly society, and that is what Islam—properly understood—required. His increasing popularity earned him further incarceration. In 1975 he was allowed to leave the country for England, and he died shortly thereafter, reportedly of a heart attack, at age 44.[25]

Shariati's notion of a sociopolitical order reflecting the will of God for justice (*nizam al-tawhid*) clearly echoes not only ancient Persian themes but also key Quranic themes. And it became one of Khomeini's major themes. Another was that of guardianship or governance by religio-legal scholars (*vilayet-i faqih*). This was Khomeini's innovative interpretation of Iraq's Shi`a scholar Mohammad Baqir al-Sadr's (d. 1980) ideas about modern governance, the *wilayet al-ummah*, governance of the people.[26] Both systems rejected authoritarian governance and insisted on elections of popular representatives but called for oversight of the democratic process by religious scholars. In Khomeini's iteration, those with the greatest knowledge of Islam have the responsibility to guide the community in their mundane social and economic lives in order to protect them from injustice, excess, greed, corruption and any number of other base human instincts. It thus went a step further than traditional models wherein the clergy are moral authorities. In Khomeini's new iteration, the clergy would assume political power as well.

Khomeini's *vilayet* was meant to become operational once the people got rid of the tyrannical shah.[27] But details of how it might be implemented were few and of far less importance than the motivational Shariati-esque ideal of demanding justice in the face of tyranny.[28] That ideal is what galvanized diverse strands of social discontent sufficiently for Iranian civilians—against all odds—to drive out the powerful, Western-backed King of Kings Muhammad Reza Pahlavi: "The basis of the dominant political alliances at the end of the Pahlavi period was distaste for the

Shah. . . . In the absence of a viable secular leader, pro-democracy elements and even some leftist elements turned to the leadership that Khomeini represented."[29]

In other words, the 1979 revolution to oust the Pahlavi shah was broadly populist and anti-autocracy. It became the "Islamic Revolution" by default. No one was more surprised than the Iranians that it was successful. The critical events occurred in rapid succession: a protest by religious students in January 1978 was violently dispersed by the police, leaving several students dead.[30] This was followed by spontaneous sympathy protests and more organized demonstrations, culminating in September 1978 in "Black Friday," a mass protest in Tehran, dispersed by the military and resulting in over eighty deaths. Martial law was imposed. The following January saw a mutiny in the air force. The shah appointed a new prime minister and, the next month, left Iran. Unlike his departure during the 1953 overthrow of Mosaddegh, this departure was permanent. On January 17, 1979, Ayatollah Khomeini returned to cheering throngs to take control of the government; on February 11, the remaining troops loyal to the Shah were overwhelmed in street clashes.

The Hostage Crisis and the Iran-Iraq War

Suddenly, Khomeini's novel *vilayet-e faqih*, the rule of the Islamic jurist, had to move from the realm of ideals and become operative. Fortunately, Iran had a functioning bureaucracy that provided continuity in the country's daily functions, and its moribund parliament could be revitalized for legislation. Elections were held for a constituent assembly to revise the 1906 constitution in accordance with the Ayatollah's relatively vague ideal system. The new constitution retained its core democratic elements—most importantly, a popularly elected parliament—but stipulated that ultimately sovereignty rests with God and that the country's Twelver Shi`ite religious establishment are the appropriate "guardians" of that sovereignty. The constitution therefore established a "Supreme Leader," chosen by an "Assembly of [Twelver Shi`a legal] Experts" (popularly elected from a list devised by the religious establishment) who had ultimate authority to appoint six members of the "Guardian Council" (and appoint the head of the judiciary, who will nominate others from which the parliament must elect six additional members), which in turn was tasked with determining the legitimacy of any acts of parliament. The new constitution was approved in late 1979, based on a popular referendum and, not surprisingly, Ayatollah Khomeini was chosen as the Supreme Leader.

But meanwhile, the chaos of revolution took its own problematic routes, first domestically and then internationally. Reflecting the anger of the street that had been building throughout the century but particularly since the reinstatement of the Shah in 1953, one of the first major incidents following the Ayatollah's return to Iran involved a mob scaling the fences surrounding the US embassy in Tehran and berating its occupants for the US role in prolonging the Shah's reign through Operation Ajax in 1953. Iranian authorities took charge of the situation, evicted the trespassers, and restored the embassy to US control.[31] The incident clearly reflected the connection between US interference in Iranian democratic institutions and the ultimately violent events of the Iranian Revolution. But its quick resolution also reflected Iran's and Islam's insistence on the rule of law. However, nine months later, in November 1979, when the United States allowed the ousted Shah to enter the United States for medical treatment, a group of students took to the streets and invaded the embassy. This time the Iranian government declined to interfere, preoccupied as it was by trying to develop a new constitution and bureaucracy in the context of diverse and strongly held ideologies and perhaps distracted as well by the Soviet occupation of Iran's neighbor Afghanistan (December 1979). Given Persia/Iran's history with Russia/USSR's imperial designs, the situation in Afghanistan was indeed worrisome. Immediately the United States froze Iran's not-insignificant assets in the United States, adding not only to an emerging economic crisis but to anti-US sentiment. Efforts by the administration of President Jimmy Carter to resolve the hostage crisis proved unsuccessful, as did a military rescue operation in April 1980.[32]

Yet Khomeini's popular rhetoric of revolution continued unabated. The focus shifted from Iran, whose revolution had been achieved, to "the export of revolution."[33] The Ayatollah encouraged Muslims throughout the region to rise up against their governments, none of which measured up to his standards of Islamic legitimacy. Monarchies and military dictatorships were particular targets, including those with Shi`a minorities, such as Saudi Arabia and Kuwait, and especially those with Shi`a majorities, Bahrain and Iraq.

Ayatollah Khomeini's threatening rhetoric provided Iraq's Saddam Hussein with a rare opportunity to deal with a simmering conflict between the two countries. Traditionally, the Persians had dominated the Gulf (hence, the name "Persian Gulf"), while Iraq, which is Arab, controlled the Shatt—the river created by the confluence of the Tigris and Euphrates as they flow into the Gulf (hence the name Shatt al-Arab). The Shatt is Iraq's only point of access to the Persian Gulf and is therefore critically important for exporting its oil. In 1975, under pressure from the US-backed Shah, Iraq had agreed to allow Iran control of the eastern half of the Shatt.[34] Now, in the post-revolutionary chaos, perhaps Iraq could regain its traditional rights. With the support of the United States, Saddam invaded Iran in September 1980, leading to a brutal and debilitating eight-year war. The war may actually have been instigated by President Carter's national security advisor Zbigniew Brzezinski. Although no official records support the claim, rumors have been widely circulated that Mr. Brzezinski suggested to US ally Saddam that the time was ripe for him to settle Iraq's differences with Iran over the control of the Shatt al-Arab waterway.[35] In any case, there is no doubt that the Iraqi invasion of revolutionary Iran was considered suitable for US foreign policy objectives in the region. Having lost Iran as a main pillar of Western efforts to maintain stable access to Gulf resources, Iraq appeared a likely replacement.

The Iran-Iraq War inflicted untold suffering. Estimates of casualties range well into the hundreds of thousands on both sides. Hostility toward the United States was intensified by its public support of Iraq in the war, including the sale of precursors to chemical weapons that were used against civilian populations. The hostage crisis was eventually resolved, after 444 days, when the United States undertook another clandestine operation—this time allowing the sale of weapons to Iran in return for the release of the hostages.[36]

The Iran hostage crisis therefore was not merely gratuitous anti-Americanism; it was an expression of pent-up anger over decades of economic exploitation and political manipulation. And Ayatollah Khomeini had successfully focused popular discontent on the Shah, associating him with all things un-Islamic: greed, excess, and disregard for the poor and dispossessed. Not only was he un-Islamic, the Ayatollah insisted the Shah was also un-Iranian. He was the tool of Western irreligious imperial powers: "All of our troubles today are caused by America and Israel. Israel itself derives from America; these deputies and ministers that have been imposed upon us derive from America—they are all agents of America, for if they were not, they would rise up in protest."[37]

Recovery and Normalization: Rafsanjani and Khatami

The Iran-Iraq War ended in a stalemate. The ceasefire demanded by UN Security Council Resolution 598, adopted in July 1987, finally took effect in August 1988. It has generally held since then. Almost immediately Iraq was at war again, this time with Kuwait. Under those circumstances, Saddam sought an agreement with Iran in which Saddam accepted reversion to the 1975 mid-Shatt boundary. Iraq has been in constant conflict since then, however, and a formal treaty has yet to be signed clarifying the two countries' borders.

What did become clear with the ceasefire were the challenges now facing Iran. Gone was the euphoria that characterized the Iranian mood immediately upon ousting the autocratic Shah. Iranians had suffered hundreds of thousands of casualties in the Iran-Iraq war, and billions of dollars in property damage caused by waves of urban bombardments.[38] And its new political system was still a work in progress.

Within months of the ceasefire with Iraq, legislators set about revising the 1979 revolutionary constitution. The goal was to clarify legislative and executive authority and streamline the bureaucracy. The new constitution eliminated the office of prime minister and established a council to arbitrate in matters of disagreement between the parliament and the Guardian Council. (The members of this "Expediency Discernment Council" are appointed by the Supreme Leader.) The new constitution was approved in a popular referendum the following year, just as Ayatollah Khomeini died and Akbar Hashemi Rafsanjani was elected as president.

During the lifetime of Ayatollah Khomeini, the office of president was relatively obscure. (Few outside of Iran remember presidents Abolhassan Banisadr and Mohammad-Ali Rajai or that current Supreme Leader Ali Khameini served as president during the 1980s.) But with the death of the first Supreme Leader and implementation of the 1989 constitutional revisions, the president of Iran assumed increased authority.

Akbar Hashemi Rafsanjani was educated as a cleric, studying with Ayatollah Khomeini. But he was from a wealthy landed family, and his focus as president was Iran's economic recovery. The country was literally shell-shocked and its economy in a shambles.[39] Aside from the destruction of the war, Ayatollah Khomeini's government had nationalized the majority of Iran's economy. During his two terms as president, Rafsanjani worked to rebuild, privatize, and modernize, expanding and diversifying Iran's economy. Transportation and communications had to be rebuilt, as did healthcare and education, especially in view of Iran's burgeoning "youth bulge"—over half the population under 30 and rapidly urbanizing.[40]

It was the demands of this new generation that began to drive Iran's politics during the 1990s. Unlike their parents' generations, the younger generations' worldviews were shaped by memories not of autocracy but of war and the limitations on personal freedoms imposed by the clerically led government. Improved communications had provided access to the rest of the world beyond Iran's warring neighbors. Iraq was still under the tyrant Saddam Hussein and, on Iran's eastern border, the Taliban had taken control following the Soviet occupation. Neither was particularly attractive. Many Iranians were increasingly looking toward the West, with its freedoms and opportunities, and anxious to engage with it. These feelings were expressed in the landslide election of Mohammad Khatami as president in 1997.

Running on a platform of comprehensive reform and "Dialogue of Civilizations," Khatami's election showed overwhelming approval of his plan to reintegrate Iran into the family of nations.[41] He acknowledged the history of colonialism as a factor in Iran's isolation, but he called upon Iranians to overcome that legacy, move beyond their current defensive posture, and exercise the freedom of thought and expression necessary for progressive transformation of society. "Transformation and progress require thought," he says, "and thought only flourishes in an atmosphere of freedom. But our history has not allowed human character to grow and to be appreciated, and thus the basic human yearning for thinking and freedom has been unattended at best and negated at worst."[42] Rather than simply following their leaders, Khatami taught, people must be allowed to freely develop knowledge and help guide society collectively.

In a stark departure from standard revolutionary rhetoric, Khatami argued that despite the West's greed and licentiousness, there are positive strengths and achievements in Western society. And modernity is one of them. Modernity involved rejection of "autocratic and whimsical rulers," just like those who continue to plague the Muslim world. He was particularly critical of those who used religion to restrict freedom. No human authority's word should be considered sacred. Once Iranians regain their intellectual freedom, they can work to develop into contributing members of the world community. They can overcome the emotionalism and fanaticism that had come to characterize so much Islamist political rhetoric and constructively engage with the West.

In his inaugural address, Khatami described the ideal society for Iran. Unlike many religious authorities who avoided the term "democracy," associated as it was with the West, Khatami boldly reasserted Iran's democratic heritage. Iran's democracy should respect "social and individual security within the framework of the Constitution." Focusing on the development of civil society, Khatami said Iranians should have "clearly defined rights and duties for citizens and the government." The government should "officially recognize the rights of the people and the nation within the framework of law." Such a government needs "organized political parties, social associations, and an independent free press." This is a society "where the government belongs to the people and is the servant of the people, not their master, and is consequently responsible to the people."[43]

But despite the popularity of reformist President Khatami, his presidency was unable to overcome the entrenched conservative establishment that viewed his reformist agenda as a threat to the stability of the Islamic Republic. In the social sphere, his tenure saw the relaxation of some restrictions, for example on strict codes for women's attire, publishing, and cinema. But the conservatives continued their efforts to control dissent. In 1999 they shut down a reformist newspaper, prompting demonstrations led by student reformers. The security forces then raided student dormitories, resulting in several days of further demonstrations around the country, some of which turned violent. Khatami was powerless to interfere with security matters. He was re-elected in 2001 but voter turnout was low. And then global events intervened again.

9/11, "The Axis of Evil," and the Return of Conservatism: Ahmadinejad

Despite the growing demand for reform and openness, the more conservative members of the clerically dominated government maintained an abiding distrust of the West. For them, Western support of the Shah, Operation Ajax, and Saddam Hussein in the Iran-Iraq war demonstrated that the United States would never allow an independent Iran to prosper. Isolation from the West was the only way to preserve Iran's autonomy. Their fears seemed to be more reasonable in light of the "Global War on

Terrorism" (GWOT) launched by the United States following the 9/11 attacks in New York and Washington, DC, by al-Qaeda. In January 2002, President George W. Bush gave a speech in which he identified three countries as promoters of terrorism and therefore members of a worldwide "axis of evil": North Korea, Iraq, and Iran. The United States had already occupied neighboring Afghanistan. Fears were elevated to crisis level in March 2003 when the US-led forces occupied Iraq. Iraq had nothing to do with 9/11 and its secular government was, in fact, condemned by al-Qaeda. It was easy for Iranian conservatives to see an alarmingly familiar pattern and fear that Iran would be the next victim of what was perceived as US aggression. Within two years Iranian presidential elections replaced the progressive Mohammad Khatami with the provocative, isolationist, and outspokenly anti-American Mahmoud Ahmadinejad.

Running against the veteran former president Rafsanjani who had himself entered the reformist camp, Ahmadinejad represented Iran's non-elites, many of whom had been left out of the country's postwar economic recovery. He called for fairer distribution of the country's oil revenues and effectively compared the marginalization of Iran's poor to the marginalization of Iran by the global community. Still, the election was close and required a runoff.

Ahmadinejad was inexperienced in national governance, and it showed in his policies. His economic policies and efforts to improve the lot of the poor by increasing spending on housing, for example, met with severe criticism as they effectively drove up the price of real estate. He also embarrassed many Iranians with his strident denunciations of Israel and, in particular, his public denial of the Holocaust.[44] Even more pointed, however, was criticism of his human rights record. Reports of violations of women's rights, freedom of expression, and arbitrary arrests circulated, and student protests again began to increase after a slight improvement during Khatami's tenure as president.

Renewal of Reform: Soroush, Kadivar, and the Green Movement

Despite setbacks, reformism in Iran had been consistent from the time of Ali Shariati forward, even with the ascendancy of conservatives, traditionalists, and pragmatists. Among its best-known voices during the 1990s was that of still-active reformer Abdolkarim Soroush. Although

Soroush criticizes Shariati for politicizing Islam, like Shariati, he argues against rigid interpretations of Islamic law. Islamic jurisprudence must remain flexible and dynamic in order to fulfill its mandate to promote social justice. Not only does it have to respond to ever-new developments, it is a human enterprise and therefore eminently fallible. Thus Soroush, like Shariati, argues against privileged positions for any human interpreters, clergy or not. All human beings are endowed with the basic abilities to discern right from wrong. Therefore, democracy—giving voice to the people—is the most suitable form of governance. But democracy does necessarily entail the removal of religious considerations from government's deliberations. Arguing against the secularization hypothesis that religious societies remain incapable of democratization, Soroush says,

> It is amazing that some consider the democratization of the religious government contingent upon the secularization of religion and religious law. Liberal democracy draws inspiration and strength from the authentic axiom that states: human beings are naturally free and unique.... Is the religious society not, by nature, plural and pluralistic? ... Belief is a hundred times more diverse and colorful than disbelief. If the pluralism of secularism makes it suitable for democracy, the faithful community is a thousand times more suitable for it.... We no longer claim that a genuinely religious government can be democratic but that it cannot be otherwise.[45]

The 1997 election of President Khatami took place on the 2nd of the month of Khordad in the Persian calendar. The overall reformist movement associated with his election is known, therefore, as the 2nd of Khordad Front. Neither a party nor even an organized movement, the 2nd of Khordad Front is a broad coalition of supporters of the nonviolent struggle for democracy and human rights, as an expression of authentically Islamic governance. Abdolkarim Soroush is claimed as a progenitor of the movement.

Mohsen Kadivar is another reformer associated with the 2nd of Khordad movement. He became well known during the 1990s. Like his mentor, Ayatollah Montazeri, a dissident cleric, he is a religious scholar but argues against authoritarian clerical rule. No one can be above the law, he insists, including the Supreme Leader. Reflecting the traditional approach to Iranian governance, Kadivar says that religious authorities are meant to study and teach and guide, not govern.[46] Like Soroush, his criticism of clerical rule earned the ire of the government. (They both are in exile and currently teach in the United States.) But Kadivar also argues against "radical secularism"—the removal of religion from the public sphere. He rejects rule by religious authorities through sacrosanct interpretations of scripture, yet he continues to support religious values informing democratic governance.[47]

And there are others, including Mir-Hossein Mousavi. In June 2009, Ahmadinejad was up for re-election. Mousavi, who had served as prime minister during the 1980s, ran against him on a popular reform plat-form. Another popular reformer, Mehdi Karroubi, also ran against Ahmadinejad. Both had strong and energized followings, particularly among students: "The electorate, which had not seen anything quite like this in the thirty-year life of the Islamic Republic, took to the streets in the millions, generating an election euphoria that shook the very foundations of the regime."[48] When the election results were announced in June, and Ahmadinejad was proclaimed the winner, accusations of fraud prolifer-ated and spontaneous demonstrations immediately erupted and spread across the country.[49]

The popular demonstrations were brutally suppressed. Five students were killed in a crackdown at Tehran University two days after election results were announced. This is generally identified as the beginning of Iran's Green Movement, inspired by Mousavi and Karroubi and supported by elderly reformist Ayatollah Hossein Ali Montazeri.[50]

A senior cleric originally designated by Ayatollah Khomeini as his suc-cessor, by late the 1980s Montazeri became critical of the government's conservatism and ruthless suppression of its opponents. His calls for more open government resulted in house arrest by Khomeini's successor Ayatollah Khamenei in 1997. Montazeri was released following public out-cry in 2003. He remained an active voice for democracy and human rights until his death in December 2009. His funeral was massively attended by Green Movement supporters. Security forces moved in, attacking both Karroubi and Mousavi. Violent clashes ensued and continued throughout the month.

Neither Mousavi nor Karroubi was particularly revolutionary as reformists go. They supported political change and democratization but within the framework of the existing constitution of the Islamic Republic of Iran. Associated as a student with Ali Shariati's reform-ist movement, Mousavi was jailed for organizing in demonstrations against the Shah. When the revolution was successful, he supported it and was appointed to official positions by Ayatollah Khomeini, including foreign minister, before being appointed prime minster. However, he had serious disagreements with the conservative then-president Ayatollah Khamenei. Following Ayatollah Khomeini's death and the appointment of Khamenei as Supreme Leader, Mousavi served as advisor to presidents Rafsanjani and Khatami. He then ran for president in 2009 as a centrist candidate but with strong support from reformists, on a simple platform of media openness, control of law enforcement by elected officials, and women's rights. Mehdi Karroubi is a cleric and veteran politician who earned his stripes in the Shah's prisons but became a critic of government control by clerics. He has long advocated the rights of women and ethnic and religious minorities. A candidate in the 2005 elections, he denounced government manipulation of mosques to generate support for the clergy's preferred candidate.

But the results of the 2009 elections seemed clearly fraudulent, especially to the supporters of these two popular candidates. It was their defeat that gave rise to the Green Movement.[51] (Green was the color of Mousavi's campaign posters; it is also the color of Islam, and a symbolic color of hope.) The government crackdown on the spontaneous demonstrations protesting the election results only strengthened the determination of Green Movement supporters.

Following the post-election events of 2009, the government banned public demonstrations and arrested hundreds of politicians, student activists, and journalists known for their reformist views. The Green Movement was silenced—literally. Three days after the election results were announced, Mousavi appeared at a massive rally in Tehran—in which participants, reportedly three million strong, silently protested a fraudulent election.[52] Despite their silence, the government cracked down with force. But silent protests continued, demanding a recount of the presidential election results. "Where is my vote?" was the popular slogan at this time. The Guardian Council's announced partial recount resulted in no changes in election results, and silent protests continued throughout June 2009, although with diminished participation.

Annual commemorative silent protests were held in 2011 and 2012, clearly indicating that despite government controls on expression of popular sentiment, the demand for progressive, civil rights-oriented democratic Islamic governance did not die. Indeed, its residual strength was represented in the election in 2013 of President Hassan Rouhani.

The Struggle Continues: The Arab Spring and Election of Rouhani

Iranians again went to the polls in the summer of 2013. Of 686 aspiring candidates, the Supreme Leader disqualified all but eight, including former president Akbar Hashemi Rafsanjani. Nevertheless, with voter turnout higher than it had been since Khatami's election in 1997, voters chose progressive candidate Hassan Rouhani.[53]

Among Rouhani's priorities was to resolve the nuclear standoff between Iran and the United States. Iran's nuclear program began with President Eisenhower's "Atoms for Peace" program in the 1950s. The United States and European powers continued to support Iran's nuclear power program throughout Shah Mohammad Reza Pahlavi's regime. But foreign support for Iran's nuclear power program largely ceased following the Islamic Revolution of 1979, forcing Iran to find new sources of enriched uranium and develop its own enrichment plants. Iran had signed the Treaty on the Non-Proliferation of Nuclear Weapons (NPT) in 1968 (ratified in 1970) and worked with the International Atomic Energy Association in its enrichment development program. Nevertheless, the United States and other Western powers were concerned that Iran was actually trying to develop nuclear weapons. A 2012 Congressional Research Service report noted that as of August 2012, "Iran had produced an amount of LEU [low-enriched uranium] containing up to 5% uranium-235 which, if further enriched, could theoretically produce enough HEU [highly enriched uranium] for several nuclear weapons." Iran is entitled, as a signatory to the NPT, to develop nuclear power under International Atomic Energy Agency (IAEA) monitoring, which Iran has allowed. But since the 1979 Revolution, the United States has opposed its nuclear power program, alleging that it is a cover for a clandestine nuclear weapons program. As the Congressional Research Service report observes, "Although Iran claims that its nuclear program is exclusively for peaceful purposes, the program has generated considerable concern that Tehran is pursuing a nuclear weapons program."[54]

Based on United States and other Western powers' suspicions that Iran was developing nuclear weapons, despite Iran's protestations to the contrary, Iran was subjected to demands that it cease its enrichment program. When Iran refused to do so, a UN Security Council vote in December 2006 began a series of sanctions, including the freezing of assets of the Islamic Republic of Iran Shipping Lines (UNSC 1929, June 2010).[55]

Immediately upon his election, Rouhani, a former nuclear negotiator himself, appointed seasoned diplomat Javad Zarif to that task. High-level negotiations between the United States, Russia, China, the United Kingdom, France, and Germany ("P5+1") and Iran resulted in a November 2013 interim agreement whereby Iran would temporarily cease and roll back part of its nuclear program and some sanctions would be lifted in return. A framework for negotiating a comprehensive agreement was to follow and discussions regarding the comprehensive remain ongoing, with a new deadline set for July 1, 2015.

While Iran's insistence on its legal right to continue its nuclear energy program may appear as a high priority and even brinksmanship to Western powers, as Rouhani's election demonstrates, Iranians' primary concern is good governance. This was confirmed in a September 2013 Zogby poll which demonstrated that Iranians' primary concerns are domestic: jobs and governmental reform. Nearly one-third ranked employment opportunities as their top priority. Nearly one-quarter put democracy, civil rights, and women's rights in that category. The report revealed only scant concern about Iran's nuclear program.[56] Lifting the sanctions was a priority for President Rouhani because they are a source of Iran's economic challenges. His progress on civil rights and governmental reforms is what Iranians will be watching.

Conclusion

In 2006, political scientists Ali Gheissari and Vali Nasr wrote the following: "A century after the Constitutional Revolution of 1906, Iran is still grappling with how to achieve a democratic state. It is open to question whether Iran is any closer to that goal today than it has been at any other time in the past century."[57] In 2011, in the context of the Arab Spring uprisings, the Green Movement's Mir-Hossein Mousavi claimed: "The starting point of what we are now witnessing on the streets of Tunis, Sanaa, Cairo, Alexandria and Suez can be undoubtedly traced back to days of 15th, 18th and 20th June 2009 when people took to the streets of Tehran in millions shouting 'Where is my vote?' and peacefully demanded to get back their denied rights."[58] Historian Mehran Kamrava echoed both sentiments in 2013: "It was ... feelings of despair and despondency that sparked the Green Movement in Iran in 2009 and the Arab uprisings in 2011. As the second decade of the twenty-first century approaches its midway mark, the Middle East appears to be standing on the precipice of political change once again."[59] But that was before Rouhani's election. Rouhani's election appears to mark a return to the trajectory Iranians began over a century ago, and a confirmation of the progressive orientation expressed in the election of President Khatami less than twenty years ago. As Khatami put it then, Iran is a society "where the government belongs to the people and is the servant of the people, not their master, and is consequently responsible to the people."[60]

It is too early to predict the outcome of Rouhani's efforts to return Iran to its reformist Islamic democratic path. As Kamrava notes, "The establishment of democratic political systems . . . as history teaches us . . . can be prolonged and often fraught with setbacks and difficulties."[61] But as Iran's history teaches us, its decades of efforts, despite the setbacks resulting from regional and global geostrategic complications and both secular and Islamist iterations, will undoubtedly continue.

4

Pakistan

A WORK IN PROGRESS

The Dream of Pakistan

Countries such as Egypt and Iran have long-standing, if diverse, premodern traditions of governance which can influence the struggle for modern democratic institutions. As well, they had modern, secular, and nominally democratic governments established in the postcolonial era, serving as counterpoints to activists' demands for representative, participatory, Islamic governance. By contrast, Pakistan was established in the mid-20th century specifically to be a democracy for Muslims. Starting with a blank slate, South Asia's Muslims would create their new government with no more specific guidelines than those outlined in the Objectives Resolution, adopted by the new country's Constituent Assembly. Among its assertions: "The principles of democracy, freedom, equality, tolerance and social justice, as enunciated by Islam, shall be fully observed."[1] Unfortunately, however, implementing that core resolution has been difficult for a number of reasons. Chief among them is the pervasive role of the military in foreign affairs, abetted by a compliant elite structure of feudal and tribal aristocracy and industrialists. These civilian elites, primarily interested in maintaining the status quo which protects their privileged positions, have acquiesced to the military's preoccupation with national security, thus keeping the country on a war footing throughout its brief history. In efforts to gain support for its policies, Pakistan's feudal-tribal-military industrial complex has manipulated both popular opinion, by focusing on external threats, and religious sentiment, providing privileges for those religious organizations willing to overlook violations of the Objectives Resolution. In the process, the government has drained public coffers of funds necessary for civilian infrastructure and social development. That lack of development, in turn, has fostered discontent often expressed in factionalism and other destabilizing trends that have prompted military intervention and undermined the country's fledgling democracy.

However, this bleak profile may mask more positive trends. Over the past two decades, civil society has demonstrated increasing vigor, with the first-ever completion of a full term for an elected government, and the growing popularity of the first successful new political party since the 1960s—one dedicated to Pakistan's founding Islamic and democratic principles and drawing support from new generations of politically engaged Pakistanis.

THE LAND KNOWN as Pakistan is the home of one of humanity's oldest civilizations. Mohenjo Daro in Pakistan's Sindh province, the center of Indus Valley Civilization and a UNESCO World Heritage Site, was established around 2600 B.C.E. But the state of Pakistan is actually one of the newest on earth, "partitioned" from India by Britain as it ended its more than a century-long domination of the subcontinent.

What became Pakistan began as a desire for autonomy for Muslims living under British rule in India. The "spiritual father" of Pakistan was philosopher-poet Muhammad Iqbal (d. 1938). His plea was expressed at a meeting of the All-India Muslim League in 1930:

> I would like to see the Punjab, North-West Frontier Province, Sindh and Baluchistan amalgamated into a single State. Self-government within the British Empire or without the British Empire, the formation of a consolidated North-West Indian Muslim State appears to me to be the final destiny of Muslims, at least of North-West India.[2]

The political founder of Pakistan was Muhammad Ali Jinnah, a Shi`ite Muslim from Karachi (in Sindh province). Jinnah originally worked with the Indian Congress Party, the party of Gandhi and Nehru, advocating a united India independent of Britain. Disagreements over strategy, in particular, rejection of Jinnah's efforts to secure the Muslim minority's representation in parliament, led Jinnah in 1940 to support the All-India Muslim League's call for separate Muslim and Hindu states within British India.

When England finally had to give up its imperial hold on India, it decided to "partition" the subcontinent into separate Muslim and Hindu countries. Like the partition of Palestine during the same period, the partition of India was extremely inept and virtually guaranteed prolonged instability. Muslim and Hindu populations were intermixed in many areas, so the designation of Muslim-majority population centers of Northwest India and Northeast India as a single Muslim country led to the mass exodus of Hindus to the newly defined Hindu country, India, and a reciprocal mass exodus of Muslims from India to Pakistan. The frantic process involved riots and massacres on all sides, the casualties of which defy the imagination (and statistical certainty).

Like all colonized peoples, Indians had been actively struggling for independence for decades. It was only after World War II, when England's weakened economy made direct colonial control of India no longer feasible, that independence was granted. But the granting was grudging, and in the view of many of the formerly colonized peoples, done in such a way as to provide maximum continued benefit for the departing powers, keeping their former colonies unstable and therefore unlikely to emerge as economic competitors to their former rulers. In addition to the partition of Palestine, the example of France's partition of Syria into contemporary Syria and Lebanon, with consequences we are still witnessing today, is often cited as similar to Britain's partition of India.

Whether instability and civil strife really were the goal of the partition, it could not have been better planned to achieve them. The two parts of Pakistan—West and East—were separated by over 1,000 miles of hostile territory, not to mention different languages and cultures. The name of the new country itself is revealing: Pakistan is an acronym for the regions known as Punjab, Afghania (at the time known as North-West Frontier Province, and now known as Khyber Pukhtunkhwa), Kashmir, Sindh, and Baluchistan. But the British split "Afghania" between India and Afghanistan in 1893—again, with resulting instability and civil strife that we are still experiencing today. Ethnic Afghans (also known as Pashtuns, Pukhtuns, and Pathans) do not recognize the legitimacy of the border which, in any case, runs over 1,500 miles through some of the world's highest mountains and cannot be enforced. Kashmir, a Muslim-majority region, was ruled by a Hindu at the time of partition and not included in Pakistan; it has been the focus of continued hostilities between Pakistan and India and remains disputed territory. And East Pakistan, mainly Bengali, is not even identified in the acronym. Conflicts between the two Pakistans led to bloody civil war that resulted in 1971 in the creation of Bangladesh out of what had been East Pakistan.

Still, Pakistan's "Quaid-i-Azam" (Great Leader) Jinnah had high hopes for the new country. His speech at the opening of the country's first Constituent Assembly in August 1947 expressed ideals still cherished today among Pakistanis:

> You will no doubt agree with me that the first duty of a government is to maintain law and order, so that the life, property and religious beliefs of its subjects are fully protected by the State. . . . Now, if we want to make this great State of Pakistan happy and prosperous, we should wholly and solely concentrate on the well-being of the people, and especially of the masses and the poor. If you will work in co-operation, forgetting the past . . . you are bound to succeed. If you change your past and work together in a spirit that every one of you, no matter to what community he belongs, no matter what relations he had with you in the past, no matter what is his colour, caste, or creed, is first, second, and last a citizen of this State with equal rights, privileges, and obligations, there will be no end to the progress you will make.[3]

Yet today, the United Nations Human Development Report ranks Pakistan, the world's second-largest Muslim country with a population of 180 million, 146th in the world, with nearly 50 percent of its population living in poverty, over 20 percent living on less than $1.25 per day, and the mean number of years of education standing at less than five.[4] Pakistan's economy is extremely fragile. In 2013 the head of the International Monetary Fund (IMF), announcing a multibillion dollar loan, explained that its purpose was "to avoid a full-blown crisis and collapse of the currency."[5] And insurgencies and sectarian violence plague the country. The government has banned sixty organizations engaged in this violence.[6] Human Rights Watch reports the killing of 850 people from Pakistan's Shi`a minority by militant Sunni groups in 2012–2013 alone.[7] Militant Shi`a have reciprocated periodically. Christians have suffered numerous attacks as well, including the killing of eighty-five in the bombing of Peshawar's 130-year-old All Saints Church in September 2013.[8] And the country's Ahmadi minority have been declared non-Muslims and subjected to discrimination and continual harassment (see below).

As in many postcolonial countries, the military became Pakistan's dominant institution by default; it was the most effectively functioning institution left by departing colonial rulers. Being in control of the country's weaponry, the military had little incentive to respond positively to any civilian competitors after the end of colonialism. Yet Pakistan was created specifically to be a democracy, and the military has allowed civilian governments to rule intermittently, so long as they protected the interests of the military.

What are the interests of the military? They are partly economic, of course. The former director of research for Pakistan's navy, Dr. Ayesha Siddiqa, attempted to describe the military's financial stakes in her 2007 *Military Inc.: Inside Pakistan's Military Economy* (Pluto Press). She describes a pattern of involvement in the civilian economy (similar to Egypt's but unlike Tunisia's), including massive real estate holdings, much of it acquired at state expense. In addition, she describes a group of conglomerates—"welfare foundations"—dealing in everything from gas stations, cereal processing plants, and bakeries, to financial institutions, insurance companies, and heavy industry—the latter of which she estimates the military controls one-third. These conglomerates are called welfare foundations because proceeds from them do contribute to the support of retired military personnel. But presumably there are surpluses which, reinvested, allow the foundations' wealth to further increase. The military's wealth is also augmented by billions of dollars in foreign aid. Pakistan ranked third (after Israel and Afghanistan) on the list of US foreign aid recipients in 2012, receiving over $2.1 billion.[9] It ranked fifth (in 2012) in the list of recipients of specifically military aid from the United States (after Afghanistan, Israel, Egypt, and Iraq). Since 2012, Pakistan has received over $26 billion in total US aid.[10] The country also receives significant aid from international organizations such as the IMF and from other countries, including England, China, Saudi Arabia, and the United Arab Emirates.

The financial portfolio of Pakistan's military establishment may be significant, but the institution also has existential concerns. In order to maintain its relevance—or simply because it is the nature of the beast—the military focuses public attention on the need for national security, especially along the country's unstable borders. Thus, the Pakistani military, working directly and indirectly through the national government, has shown a preeminent concern with protecting the country's autonomy by balancing regional powers—India, Afghanistan, Iran, and China—and international superpowers—the United States and USSR/Russia. As Pakistan's hawkish former foreign minister (and then president and, later, prime minister) Zulfikar Ali Bhutto put it in his 1969 *The Myth of Independence*: "Pakistan's security and territorial integrity are more important than economic development. . . . [I]t will have to be assumed that a war waged against Pakistan is capable of becoming a total war. It would be dangerous to plan for less and our plans should, therefore, include the nuclear deterrent."[11]

Focus: National Security

When Pakistan was created in 1947, it had a king, George VI of England. The British monarch remained head of state in Pakistan until 1956, when the country became a parliamentary republic. National hero Liaquat Ali Khan was appointed prime minister by the National Assembly and remained in the position until he was assassinated in 1951. Although there is no official account of the assassin's motive, popular opinion commonly alleges disgruntlement over the division of Kashmir, which was divided between Pakistan and India in an uneasy ceasefire ending their first war in 1948.

In what would become a theme throughout Pakistan's history, popular opinion also suspects US involvement in the assassination, allegedly motivated by Liaquat's cordial relations with the USSR and Pakistan's close ties with Iran. The capitalist United States and communist USSR were locked in competition for global economic dominance. This was the "Cold War," in which each side demanded exclusive loyalty from its allies. Pakistan was expected to choose either the United States or the USSR—not both. Regarding Iran, Western capitalists were horrified over newly elected Prime Minister Mohammed Mosaddegh's plan to nationalize the Anglo-Iranian Oil Company (later to become British Petroleum). Nationalization—the process by which a government takes control of private corporations and property—was viewed by capitalists as theft or, perhaps even worse, communism. The Iranians were therefore viewed as joining the enemy camp in the Cold War, and Pakistan was expected to shun them.

Liaquat was succeeded by a series of prime ministers who led Pakistan into treaties aligning Pakistan with the United States in the Cold War, most notably two that were established by the United States with Western

European support, modeled on the North Atlantic Treaty Organization (NATO). In 1954, SEATO (South East Asia Treaty Organization) was established to protect Southeast Asia from the spread of communist power. In addition to the United States and the United Kingdom, its members included France, Australia, New Zealand, and Pakistan, as well as two actual Southeast Asian countries, the Philippines and Thailand. Other Southeast countries, including Indonesia, Burma, and Cambodia, refused to join, preferring nonalignment; they did not share the West's assumption that nationalism is equivalent to communism or that either is inherently aggressive. The United States persuaded Pakistan to join SEATO, in return for $250 million in aid "so they could quadruple the size of their army."[12] So virtually from the beginning, Pakistan was subject to the vagaries of global geopolitics whose concern was with the country's military capability rather than its domestic socioeconomic development.

Western support for enhancing Pakistan's military capability alarmed India, with whom Pakistan had already fought one war which left border disputes unresolved. Prime Minister Nehru cautioned that the military aid to Pakistan "would weaken the country's nascent democracy, push it toward militarism, and subject it to endless pressures from Washington."[13] (The second pro-West organization joined by Pakistan was CENTO [the Central Treaty Organization; formerly Middle East Treaty Organization, also known as the Baghdad Pact], organized in 1955 to protect the Middle East from communist aggression. Its members were Iraq, Iran, Turkey, Pakistan, and the United Kingdom. Essentially redundant, CENTO provided little benefit to its participants and was defunct by the mid-1970s.)

In 1956 Pakistan ratified its first constitution, allowing it to shed its British monarch and elect its own president. The same year it began efforts to develop nuclear technology, establishing the Pakistan Atomic Energy Commission (PAEC). The United States provided $350,000 toward establishing Pakistan's first nuclear reactor.[14] In 1958, confirming Indian Prime Minister Nehru's concerns, the new constitution was abrogated in a coup that led to nearly fifteen years of military rule, first under Field Marshal Ayub Khan and then General Yahya Khan, and culminating in the civil war that would lead to the creation of Bangladesh out of East Pakistan. Thus began the occultation of the original blueprint for Pakistan. Not only was democracy suspended, but Pakistan's social infrastructure would be sacrificed in favor of extensive and expensive militarization, used with disastrous results in both regional and civil wars.

Pakistan had fought its first war with India in Kashmir, a Muslim-majority state ruled by a Hindu, as noted above. Fearing the state's Hindu ruler would bring Kashmir into newly partitioned Hindu-majority India, Pakistani troops invaded. The UN brokered a ceasefire in 1948 and passed Security Council Resolution 47, calling for a vote to be taken so that Kashmiris could decide their own political future. That vote has never taken place, and Kashmir remains a focus of conflict between the two countries. But it is not the only one.

In 1962, India went to war with China over disputes along those two countries' extensive mountainous borders. Despite US military assistance, India lost territory to China. Pakistan's government felt betrayed by US support for India because of its ongoing conflict with India over Kashmir. Pakistan was further alarmed by a significant military buildup in India. During the Sino-Indian War of 1962, India increased its military spending by one-third; military spending already accounted for one-fifth of its national budget. Following the war, India's military buildup continued.[15]

Zulfikar Ali Bhutto, serving as foreign minister under Field Marshal Ayub Khan, was convinced that India was developing nuclear capability. This was made clear in an interview with Patrick Keatley of the *Manchester Guardian* in March 1965. Bhutto insisted that work had already begun on the project, famously stating that if India did produce a nuclear weapon, Pakistan would have to build or buy one, even if "we should have to eat grass."[16] Ayub and Bhutto visited China the same year and Keatley claims that acquisition of nuclear technology was the chief topic of conversation.

As well, Pakistan was concerned about India's relationship with the powerful Soviet Union. Despite its official nonaligned stance in the Cold War (Indian Prime Minister Nehru was a cofounder of the Non-Aligned Movement), India developed a strong relationship with the USSR. The Soviets publicly supported India's position on the Kashmir dispute with Pakistan, for example, and entered an agreement with India to collaborate on production of MiG-21 fighter jets. As a result, Pakistan was highly suspicious of Soviet intentions in the region, not only on its eastern border with India but also on its western border, in Afghanistan. In the mid-1950s, Afghanistan had begun strengthening its relationship with the Soviet Union. This relationship intensified as the Kabul government showed support for militant Pashtuns along the border with Pakistan. Fearing spillover that would foster insurgency in his own Pashtun border regions—NWFP (the "Afghania" in the country's acronym; now KPK province) and FATA, the Federally Administered Tribal Areas—Pakistan closed its borders with Afghanistan in 1961.

The concern over Soviet intentions in the region both intensified Pakistan's determination to increase its military strength and influenced its tilt toward China, the USSR's regional competitor. Pakistan did not, however, abandon its close relationship with the United States, despite its disappointment over American military support for India in the Sino-Indian war. In 1963 the government established the Pakistan Institute of Nuclear Sciences and Technology (PINSTECH), and in 1965 began construction on Pakistan's first nuclear reactor, supplied by the United States under President Eisenhower's "Atoms for Peace" program. (The program also supplied Iran with its first nuclear training and technology, including reactors.) The US program's goal was to promote the peaceful use of nuclear technology but, as noted, Pakistan had incentives for developing nuclear weaponry, as well.

Pakistan's second war with India soon followed. Anxious to resolve the Kashmir dispute before India's military achieved insurmountable military superiority, Pakistan instigated the conflict by sending irregular troops into Kashmir to incite a rebellion against India. The war ended badly; after thousands of losses on both sides, the UN imposed a ceasefire, the status quo resumed, and resentments continued to seethe.

Foreign Minister Bhutto had encouraged the infiltration to precipitate the war, despite lack of enthusiasm of many in his government. The negative outcome of the war led to conflicts within the government. Following the war, Bhutto, who had been educated in California and Oxford during the days of left-wing student activism, left the Pakistan Muslim League (PML) of Ayub Khan to start his own party, Pakistan People's Party (PPP). The PPP was socialist. Its ideals—social justice and democracy—were very appealing, as was Bhutto's insistence on Pakistan's nonalignment with either the "East" (Soviet bloc) or "West" (the United States and Western Europe) in the Cold War. As it turned out, however, Bhutto's PPP would continue Pakistan's militarization at the expense of socioeconomic development, and it collaborated with both East and West to achieve its goals.

In 1969 General Yahya Khan, who had succeeded Field Marshal Ayub Khan as president, announced the government would allow national elections for the first time. These were held in late 1970. Until that time, West Pakistan had enjoyed political dominance, despite having a slightly smaller population than East Pakistan (at the time, 61 million vs. 67 million, respectively). The elections resulted in a majority of parliamentary seats going to East Pakistan's Awami League (160/300). But Bhutto's newly established PPP received the majority of votes in West Pakistan, and Bhutto refused to recognize the right of the Awami League to form a government. East Pakistani leaders demanded that General Yahya Khan's government accede to results of elections. Yahya postponed the initial meeting of the newly elected National Assembly, whose Awami League majority would have formed a government undoubtedly excluding Bhutto.

Relations with East Pakistan were already tense due to criticism of the government's bungled relief efforts in East Pakistan's catastrophic November 1970 cyclone, which resulted in hundreds of thousands of deaths. By early 1971, mass protests had erupted in East Pakistan against West Pakistan's refusal to allow East Pakistan's Awami League to form the country's national government. In March 1971, West Pakistan launched a military operation to suppress Awami League–led protests, which had developed into calls for Bengal's (East Pakistan's) independence from West Pakistan. By the end of March, East Pakistan had declared independence, leading West Pakistan to launch a punishing war against the Bengalis.

President Richard Nixon and his national security advisor Henry Kissinger had been working on rapprochement with China, with the assistance of its allies in West Pakistan. Nixon feared Soviet involvement in Pakistan's civil war on behalf of East Pakistan, which was receiving assistance from the USSR's ally and Pakistan's foe, India. Nixon's government therefore channeled US assistance to West Pakistan via its Middle Eastern allies Jordan and Iran (the threat of Iran's nationalization of British-controlled petroleum production having been neutralized in a CIA- and MI6-supported coup that unseated Mosaddegh's government).

The war was brutal indeed. On April 6, 1971, US consul general in Dhaka (East Pakistan) Archer Kent Blood sent a now-famous telegram to secretary of state William Rogers. The telegram criticized the US government for failing to "take forceful measures to protect [East Pakistan's] citizens while at the same time bending over backwards to placate the West Pak [sic] dominated government and to lessen likely and deservedly negative international public relations impact against them." Thus, it continued, "our government has evidenced what many will consider moral bankruptcy," and concluded that "the overworked term genocide is applicable."[17] Secretary of State William Rogers, in a phone call to National Security Advisor Kissinger, expressed contempt for "that goddam message," calling it "inexcusable" and "outrageous," and said his office would try to limit its distribution. Kissinger promised to keep it from President

Nixon for a few days.[18] But the bloodshed continued. Claims of casualties vary drastically. Bangladesh claims three million killed; a Pakistani government investigation (Hamoodur Rahman Commission) claims 26,000 civilian deaths. Other estimates range from 300,000 to 500,000 with eight to ten million refugees in India, and from tens to hundreds of thousands of rapes. By any estimate, however, US consul general Blood's memo early in the war does not seem to have been an exaggeration.[19] And the war expanded. Pakistan received weaponry from North Korea. Bengali fighters received weapons and military advising from India, and millions of Bengali civilians sought refuge in India. In December Pakistan launched air strikes on Indian airbases in an attempt to neutralize Indian support for Bengal. Instead, the strikes prompted India to enter the war directly. West Pakistan's forces were no match for the combined Bengali and Indian troops.

Throughout, PPP leader and foreign minister Bhutto presented the campaign against East Pakistan as a heroic effort to save (united) Pakistan, whipping up anti-India sentiment in the process. He delivered an emotional rant before the UNSC laced with anti-India rhetoric on December 15, 1971, saying, "We will fight for a thousand years, if it comes to that."[20] The next day, West Pakistan surrendered. It became Pakistan, while East Pakistan became Bangladesh. Pakistan left behind 90,000 POWs under Indian control and an intensified sense of humiliation following another defeat, as well as increased resentment against India for its support of East Pakistan in the war. Again, the pattern: increased militarization and manipulation of popular opinion to support it, encouraged by a civilian government.

The Die Is Cast

The defeat of West Pakistan appears in retrospect to have been a turning point in Pakistan's troubled history. In the wake of the defeat by India in 1971, Bhutto's insistence on the need to increase Pakistan's military capability, including nuclear weapons, because of the dire threat it faced from hostile neighbors, began to achieve wide support. Two trends began to characterize the new Pakistan. First was the systematic demonization of India. This included presenting them as supporters of Bengali "terrorists" and emphasizing the superiority of Islam over other religions, most notably Hinduism. This demonization would be incorporated into a new curriculum so that future generations would be indoctrinated with a visceral hostility toward India, based on both religious prejudice and limited, one-sided exposure to their own history. As a corollary, the government of Pakistan began catering to conservative Islamist parties' demands for purification of Pakistan from non-Islamic practices. This would create a context for government reliance on them for support, even at the expense of Pakistan's founding inclusive and democratic principles. The effects of these trends can still be felt today.

In December 1971, Zulfikar Ali Bhutto assumed the presidency. In fiery speeches he continued to play on the population's emotions, focusing on their pride and independence. He presented himself as a reformer who implemented policies designed to improve "the lot of the common man, [and] . . . the living standards of workers and peasants."[21] His policies, he said, would improve the economy and address the social inequalities inherent in Pakistani social stratification.[22]

Pakistan had been created with no economic master plan. Wealth was concentrated in a handful of families, large landholders who had been empowered by premodern "feudal" economic systems largely left in place under British colonial rule. In a widely referenced speech in 1968, Dr. Mahbub ul Haq (d. 1998), then chief economist at the Planning Commission of Pakistan, identified the "twenty-two families" who controlled Pakistan's economy, controlling 66 percent of the industrial assets and 87 percent of the banking.[23] Bhutto attempted to redistribute some of this concentrated wealth. Field Marshal Ayub Khan had attempted to limit the size of feudal landholdings, but with minimal effect. In 1972 Bhutto proposed more robust land reforms, further limiting the amounts of land people could own and redistributing land to the poor.[24] As Bhutto put it in his 1973 article in *Foreign Affairs*, "We are as much against the ignorant and tyrannical landlord as we are against the robber barons of industry."[25] "Enterprising and enlightened farmers" would become entrepreneurs. But without sufficient consultation and consensus-building, preparation of the rural poor for transferring their loyalty from traditional elites—"feudals" and tribal chiefs—to the central government, nor providing sufficient compensation to the elites for their diminished status, Bhutto's programs often had an effect opposite to that intended. In fact, his efforts to redistribute power from the large landowners in the provinces caused another level of antagonism whose effects are still being felt today. Especially outside the urban centers, these policies resulted in retrenchment of local identities and mobilization against the central government.

Bhutto also launched annual development plans and instituted a number of rural development programs, based on prevailing socialist models of local sharing and self-sufficiency. However, inflation, inefficiency, and corruption interfered with their success. Ultimately, according to political scientist Saeed Shafqat:

> These policies ran into difficulties of implementation because little effort was made to organize the peasants or create a social environment in which reforms could be implemented. In addition, the entire task of implementing the land reforms was entrusted to bureaucracy—the deputy commissioners and the revenue departments became the primary instruments of implementation. But given their attitudes, social backgrounds, and contacts with the rural elites, effective enforcement of land reforms could not be expected. Consequently, the effectiveness of these land reforms on the rural structures was marginal.[26]

At the same time, Bhutto nationalized basic industries, including iron and steel, heavy engineering and electrical, basic metals, motor vehicles and tractors, chemicals, cement, petrochemicals, and oil and gas refineries.[27] (In 1976 he added cotton, rice, and flour mills to the list of nationalizations.) He also attempted to protect the rights of workers, establishing a minimum wage and the right of labor to strike, be compensated for injuries, and be supported by pensions. Bhutto's plans included free healthcare and education for children as well. Unfortunately, Bhutto did not develop mechanisms to provide financial support for his policies and the government proved inefficient managers of newly nationalized industries. As well, under the threat of further nationalizations, investment in the private sector shrank, further reducing the country's tax base and resulting in increased unemployment. To compensate for reduced employment opportunities in the private sector due to nationalizations, Bhutto encouraged migration of Pakistani labor to the Middle East where, increasingly, petroleum-rich Persian Gulf countries could provide employment. Migrant laborers' remittances, according to Shafqat, increased exponentially during the 1970s, and by 1981 equaled the country's total export earnings and 10 percent of its GNP.[28] While these policies relieved unemployment temporarily, they did little to improve Pakistan's overall economy.[29]

Among Bhutto's policies that did have noticeable impact, however—albeit negative—were those dealing with education. In 1972, in addition to economic nationalizations, Bhutto put Pakistan's schools under government control. The goal of his education policy was to make education universally accessible.[30] However, the policy was implemented without adequate provision for teacher training to staff the schools. Contemporary politician Imran Khan observes, "Perhaps the greatest disaster of Bhutto's years was the nationalization of the school system in 1972, an act which led to the departure of many qualified teachers without adequate teacher-training programmes being put in place beforehand. From then onwards our state school structure declined and generations of Pakistanis have suffered because of his policy."[31]

In 1973 Pakistan's parliament approved a new constitution that established the prime minister as the chief executive of the country and the president as titular head of state. President Bhutto thus became Prime Minister Bhutto. But his continued economic policies produced little in the way of relief for the poor and increased discontent among the rich. And despite the emphasis on revising Pakistan's education, actual spending on education increased only minimally, particularly when compared to military spending. Details about Pakistan's military budget are not made public. Official estimates and averages are matters of dispute among scholars. As Shalini Chawla says, "Only an overall defense budget figure is provided by the government. Estimated military spending is significantly higher as external military assistance in various forms is not included in the official figures of the defence expenditure. Also, several military related expenditures are covered under civil and public administration." Nevertheless, some data are discernible. According to US Country Studies, government expenditure on education in Pakistan in 1960 was only 1.1 percent of the GDP, compared to nearly 6 percent of GDP, over 50 percent of government expenditure, on the military.[32]

As often happens, religious authorities began to channel popular discontent, and Bhutto attempted to mollify them. Religious authorities criticized his socialism as leading Pakistan away from its Islamic roots, despite the 1973 constitution's claims that Islam is the state religion of and that "no law shall be enacted which is repugnant to" the "Injunctions of Islam as laid down in the Holy Quran and Sunnah."[33] In their efforts to encourage a "purely" Islamic Pakistan ("Pakistan" can be translated as "the land of the pure"), some religious authorities had been agitating against Ahmadis, a heterodox Muslim sect. They encouraged boycotts and demonstrations that led to violence, resulting in deaths of dozens of Ahmadis and destruction of many of their mosques, shops, and homes. In what appears to be the beginning of a pattern of manipulating religious sentiment for political gain, Bhutto's government passed a law declaring Ahmadis to be non-Muslims. In 1974 his government amended the constitution, defining Muslims in a way that excluded Ahmadis, leading to increased persecution and further entrenching the most conservative religious leaders among Pakistan's power elites. (Persecution of Ahmadis in Pakistan continues to this day. Eighty-six were massacred during prayer in Lahore 2010, for example, with no record of prosecution of the perpetrators, although it has been overshadowed by persecution of Shi`a Muslims and Christians, as mentioned above.)

Meanwhile, and despite Pakistan's faltering economy, Bhutto continued development of Pakistan's nuclear program. In 1976 his government signed an agreement with France to develop a nuclear reprocessing plant. The United States increasingly suspected that the country's nuclear program had moved beyond Eisenhower's planned "atoms for peace" to Bhutto's plans to develop nuclear weapons for war.[34] US suspicions were not unfounded. Bhutto had authorized the development of nuclear weapons by 1974, retaining A. Q. Khan as his chief scientist.[35] Confirmation of this information emerged publicly in 2004, when A. Q. Khan's network of nuclear proliferation was exposed.[36]

And opposition to Bhutto continued to increase. In March 1977 general elections, the PPP won a majority of seats, but Bhutto's government was accused of vote rigging. Mass protests were organized by opposing parties. In further efforts to curry popular favor by burnishing his Islamic credentials, Bhutto banned the sale of alcohol and gambling for all but non-Muslims. But unrest continued to escalate. In July the military intervened, suppressing protests. Army chief General Zia ul-Haq declared martial law and took control of the government. Bhutto was charged with conspiracy to murder a political opponent, and in March 1978 he was sentenced to death, despite many allegations of flawed legal procedures. After failed appeals, Bhutto was hanged, in April 1979.

As in the case of the assassination of Liaquat in 1951, regardless of the public record, popular opinion sees a US role in Bhutto's death sentence.[37] The United States had been a major supporter of Pakistan since its creation, as noted above, cultivating it as a bulwark against the USSR by including it in the SEATO and CENTO regional alliances. But Bhutto's PPP's nationalizing programs and socialist rhetoric called his Cold War credentials into question, and that made Pakistan's nuclear program all the more problematic for the United States. Reportedly, Bhutto said during his trial that he was being punished by the United States for supporting Pakistan's nuclear program.[38]

Islamization

After Bhutto's death and the assumption of power by another military regime, two regional developments in 1979 transformed the US relationship with Pakistan in fundamental ways. First was the Islamic Revolution in Iran, rendering the United States' former ally Iran a mortal enemy. Ever since the 1953 American- and British-supported overthrow of democratically elected Prime Minister Mosaddegh and consequent elevation of Iran's Shah Mohammad Reza Pahlavi to the position of a foreign-supported autocrat, popular demands for political reform in Iran had been growing. Diverse varieties of reform movements—secular, religious, communist—galvanized around the charismatic religious reformer Ayatollah Ruhollah Khomeini (d. 1989). The Shah had exiled him but popular support continued to grow, ultimately driving the Shah out of Iran. In February 1979, Khomeini returned triumphantly to Iran to take control of the ousted Shah's government and oversee its transformation into the Islamic Republic of Iran.

Perhaps inspired by the Iranians, but certainly to the delight of Pakistan's religious authorities, Zia announced formation of an Islamic system of governance, which he called Nizam-e Mustafa, "system of the Chosen One [Muhammad]." Popularly known as "Islamization," Zia's project would involve establishing a new religious component to Pakistan's judicial system. Sharia courts would be established and have the authority to determine whether laws are "repugnant to Islam"—as the constitution has it.

Among the major elements of Zia's Islamization of Pakistani law, still in effect, was the institutionalization of certain criminal punishments. His government oversaw the replacement of modern judicial punishments such as imprisonment and fines with traditional physical punishments such as the amputation of the right hand for theft and the left foot for robbery. These "judicial amputations" must be performed by physicians, who in fact have systematically refused based on their Hippocratic Oath to abstain from doing harm. For that reason as well as Pakistan's active appeals courts, no judicial amputations have actually taken place to date. But the ordinance has strong symbolic value, as does the ordinance concerning punishment for extramarital sex (*zina*). It calls for whipping unmarried perpetrators and stoning them if they are married to other people. Because of the extremely rigorous requirement for four adult Muslim witnesses to the actual sex act, this ordinance has also been difficult to enforce. It has, however, caused enormous opposition because it effectively punishes rape victims who cannot produce the requisite witnesses.[39] Likewise controversial, although not associated with traditional Islamic norms but rather with British colonial law, is the punishment for blasphemy. Under Zia, the British law was amended to require capital punishment for showing disrespect to Islam, Muhammad, his family, companions, or the Qur'an. As of January 2014, no one has been legally executed for blasphemy: "In every single case the higher courts have acquitted the accused for lack of sufficient evidence."[40] However, as with cases of extramarital sex, the allegations themselves cause enormous suffering and, frequently enough, extrajudicial implementation of punishments.

Zia also built upon the Islamization that had begun under Zulfikar Ali Bhutto, particularly in the realm of education. Bhutto's education policy had called for development of a standard, government-regulated curriculum that included ideological components such as enhancing Pakistani children's social awareness and commitment to Pakistani nationalism.[41] According to Kiran Hashmi, the 1971 defeat of West Pakistan persuaded the government of the need to strengthen commitment to a new national identity.[42] In an effort to meet that need, a "Pakistan Studies" curriculum was introduced in public schools in 1976. The new "Pakistan Studies" curriculum called for by Bhutto's government was not actually implemented until 1981. Hashmi says the Pakistan Studies curriculum was meant to inculcate appreciation of Pakistan's socioeconomic and political challenges, develop consciousness of students' social obligations, and foster patriotism. In 1983 the University Grants Commission directed that national textbooks should aim

> to demonstrate that the basis of Pakistan is not to be founded in racial, linguistic, or geographical factors, but, rather, in the shared experience of a common religion. To get students to know and appreciate the Ideology of Pakistan, and to popularize it with slogans. To guide students toward the ultimate goal of Pakistan—the creation of a completely Islamized State.[43]

Strikingly different from the vision of Pakistan expressed in the 1949 Objectives Resolution and the Quaid-i-Azam's opening speech to the Constituent Assembly, the new focus on an exclusive religious identity was bound to have social and political ramifications. In 1983 Pervez Hoodbhoy and A. H. Nayyar characterized the new state-mandated ideology as "Rewriting the History of Pakistan." They highlighted the problematic nature of describing founding father Muhammad Ali Jinnah—who was Shi`a and, in any case, wore his religious identity lightly—as motivated by orthodox Sunni religious principles, and the reduction of Islam to a set of ritual practices.[44] Later scholars identified other problems. K. K. Aziz's searing 1993 exposé *Murder of History* catalogs myriad inaccuracies in texts approved by the National Review Committee of the Government of Pakistan's Ministry of Education, reflecting not just ideological bias and overall shoddy scholarship, but an insidious political message. Included in his survey of texts in use during the 1980s are blatant efforts to demonize Indians, blaming them for Pakistan's failures.[45] Aside from issues of substandard scholarship, such messages inculcate fear of Indians and support for escalating militarization. Students are taught to take "pride" in being a "fortress." The "Ideology of Pakistan" curriculum embodied the viewpoint of the Jamaat-i-Islami, an exclusively Sunni Islamist party founded in pre-Partition India by Abu'l A`la Mawdudi.[46]

Mawdudi (d. 1979) was opposed to the partition of India, preferring that Muslims reclaim all of India for Islam. But when partition occurred, Mawdudi resettled in Pakistan and set his party to the task of "Islamizing" the state along conservative, specifically Sunni, lines. Initially, his criticism of Pakistan's secular government led to his imprisonment, as did his agitation against the Ahmadis. As we saw, however, by the 1970s the government of Zulfikar Ali Bhutto agreed to some of the Jamaat's demands for conservative Islamic legislation and marginalization of the Ahmadis.

Although it was Bhutto who began the politicization of conservative religious leaders by legislating in accordance with their demands concerning religious orthodoxy, blasphemy, alcohol consumption, and gambling, General Zia ul-Haq adopted the Jamaat-i-Islami's Islamization project wholesale. Jinnah's vision of a pluralist state focusing its energies on Islam's ideals of social justice and religious freedom faded into history; now Pakistan's focus was on implementation of traditional Sunni interpretations of Sharia in a state militarized to defend against the inexorably hostile foe next door. Mawdudi's message appealed to those feeling bereft of the traditional Indian Muslim identity of moral and political superiority; its constant denunciations of Western perfidy and theme of Islamic perfection clearly filled an emotional need. But the message had other important ramifications. With the "Islamization" of formerly pluralistic Pakistan in the 1980s came a privileging of an exclusively Sunni Islamist approach to Islam and concomitant privileging of its proponents, the dominant Islamist parties, as arbiters of political legitimacy. The Jamaat-i-Islami, the oldest of Pakistan's religious parties, is not a terrorist organization nor are its members proponents of terrorism. But the close relationship they developed with the government beginning in the 1970s laid the groundwork for political empowerment of militant Islamist groups in Afghanistan and Pakistan. That empowerment, combined with a failing domestic economy and increased competition for scarce resources among Pakistan's ethnically and religiously diverse population, provides the context for radicalization from which Pakistan is still trying to recover.[47]

Radicalization

The second regional development that would profoundly affect Pakistan in 1979 was the invasion of Afghanistan by the USSR. Despite US concerns about Pakistan's nuclear program under Zulfikar Ali Bhutto, the Soviet invasion transformed Pakistan's new military ruler Zia into America's closest collaborator. The United States, along with allies Saudi Arabia and Egypt, channeled massive support for the Afghan resistance fighters, known as the Mujahideen, through Pakistan's military-dominated intelligence services, the Inter-Services Intelligence (ISI). Money, weapons, and training were supplied to ensure that America's Cold War archenemy would be defeated.

According to Afghan scholar Neamatollah Nojumi, a former member of the Mujahideen, Zia's ISI purposely worked through the Afghan resistance groups that had specifically Islamist orientations and marginalized secular, nationalist, and especially pro-democracy resistance groups.[48] The foreign funding for Islamist militias also allowed them to establish a network of schools ("madrasas") on both sides of the Afghan-Pakistan border, recruiting students from the refugee camps and training them in the basics of conservative Islam, which included stress on their duty to defend Muslims who are under attack—that is, the importance of undertaking jihad. This militant "jihadi" ideology was certainly pertinent during the time of Soviet occupation but would prove problematic following the defeat of the Soviets.[49]

Included among the resistance fighters was Gulbuddin Hekmatyar (b. 1947). Hekmatyar was a leader among Afghan student activists opposed to Soviet influence in the Afghan government during the 1970s, even before the Soviet invasion. He joined a group who styled themselves "Muslim Youth" and vied with other student activists for dominance. Accused at least twice of trying to murder rivals, Hekmatyar took refuge across the border in Pakistan and founded his own Islamic Party (Hezb-e Islami) in 1977. At the time, the Afghan government was attempting to attract support among its willful majority-Pashtun population. Pashtuns naturally resented being split between Afghanistan and Pakistan by the British in 1893, and some advocated creation of a united "Pashtunistan." An autonomous Pashtunistan, if incorporated into Afghanistan, would diminish the population of Pakistan by several million. When the Afghan government expressed support for the idea, therefore, then–Prime Minister Zulfikar Ali Bhutto reacted by supporting anti-Afghan government "student radicals" such as Hekmatyar (himself a Pashtun). Hekmatyar subsequently became a key operative for Pakistan's military/intelligence services. When the USSR invaded Afghanistan in December 1979, Hekmatyar's Hezb-e Islami became the favored conduit for US support as well. (This is the same Hekmatyar whose forces would become one of the most active opponents of post-9/11 US coalition troops in Afghanistan and the US-supported government of Hamid Karzai. His Hezb-e Islami is now designated a terrorist organization by the United States, Canada, United Kingdom, and EU. Also among the US-trained and funded Mujahideen were countless volunteers from around the globe, including Saudi Arabia's Osama bin Laden.)

Many Pakistanis believe that, like Bhutto, the United States actually began supporting Hekmatyar and his "student radicals" before the Soviet invasion, specifically in order to provoke the invasion so that the Soviets could be engaged and defeated militarily. This suspicion is supported by a widely quoted claim made by President Jimmy Carter's national security advisor, Zbigniew Brzezinski, in a 1998 interview with *Le Nouvel Observateur*. In that interview Brzezinski confirmed former CIA director Robert Gates' claim that the United States began supporting the Afghan Mujahideen six months before the Soviets invaded Afghanistan. As Brzezinski put it, "We didn't push the Russians to intervene, but we knowingly increased the probability that they would."[50] In any case, the most conservative Islamist fighters were empowered by the United States and its Arab allies, thanks to Zia's ISI. Millions of Afghans had taken refuge in camps along Pakistan's border with Afghanistan, where ISI-sponsored madrasas became fertile recruiting grounds for fighters. And when the Soviets were defeated and Afghanistan fell into civil war, many of the madrasas along the Pakistan border remained militant—and under the influence of the ISI.

Among Zia's other policies, besides accelerated Islamization, was reversal of Bhutto's nationalization programs. This gained his military government support among the country's economic elites. In 1985, with the support of the United States along with Pakistan's religious and industrial elites, Zia's government approved the 8th Amendment to constitution, which gave the presidency—the position he held—the right to dismiss the prime minister's government. Having thus secured ultimate control over the government, Zia then ended martial law and allowed elections to be held, but without the benefit of political parties. They had been banned. Bhutto's PPP, now led by his daughter, Oxford- and Harvard-trained Benazir, boycotted the elections. PML leader Muhammad Khan Junejo was chosen as prime minister.

An opponent of military governance, Junejo clashed with Zia's government on a number of issues. Most significantly, he supported UN efforts to mediate the withdrawal of Soviet troops from Afghanistan in early 1988. Zia's government opposed the effort, fearing the possibility of a pro-India government in Kabul. Zia preferred to support his proxy Mujahideen fighters to secure a friendly post-Soviet government in Afghanistan. Junejo's government signed the Geneva Accords establishing a timetable for Soviet withdrawal in April. In May, Zia dismissed him and dissolved the national and provincial assemblies, and he continued to support the Mujahideen.

Zia had been useful to the United States in its Cold War struggle to defeat the USSR. But he also kept Pakistan's nuclear program going, allegedly diverting some of the hundreds of millions of US taxpayer dollars being channeled through his government for the anti-Soviet fight to support it. According to Indian counterterrorism expert Bahukutumbi Raman, Zia "collaborated closely" with communist North Korea in efforts to develop Pakistan's nuclear program to weapons grade.[51] Zia also maintained a close relationship with Iran, a country which at the time was engaged in a protracted and devastating war with US-supported Iraq. Concerns were raised to critical levels when US Stinger missiles, sent to help the Afghans defeat the Soviets, were found on an Iranian boat captured in the

Persian Gulf in October 1987. Pakistan and US officials insisted publicly that the Iranians captured the missiles in a border skirmish with Afghan Mujahideen, but suspicions remained strong that the Mujahideen sold them to Iran under instructions from their Pakistani sponsors.[52] This, even as Pakistan was assisting Saudi Arabia in its "Cold War" with Iran; Pakistan positioned some forty thousand troops in Saudi to protect the kingdom in case Iran expanded its war against Iraq. Ayatollah Khomeini had, after all, called for the "export" of his revolutionary Islam.[53] It appears, therefore, that Zia was continuing the effort to guarantee Pakistan's security through military power, attempting to exploit the Soviet-Afghanistan conflict to Pakistan's advantage and at the same time maintain good relations with conflicting regional powers. He may even have thought that Pakistan could negotiate solidarity among opposing Gulf superpowers Iran and Saudi Arabia. But the effort was doomed to failure.

In August 1988, Zia and the US ambassador were among those killed in a suspicious plane crash. Investigations revealed that the plane was indeed sabotaged; bomb fragments were found in the remains. But the investigations have not determined who sabotaged the plane. Zia's daughter, Rubina Salam, reportedly is convinced that the United States, working with anti-Zia elements within the military and in consultation with Benazir Bhutto (whose father had been executed by Zia's government in 1979), had Zia "eliminated." The Soviets had been defeated in Afghanistan, so Zia was no longer needed. What is more, his closeness to Iran and desire to create "an Islamic bloc" led by nuclear-armed Pakistan were entirely unacceptable to the United States. Salam claims that her father was well aware of the US plan to eliminate him and therefore invited the US ambassador and key military figures to travel with him as "insurance." "Everyone in Pakistan knows," she claims.[54]

The mystery of Zia's death remains unsolved. In 1989, journalist Robert D. Kaplan wrote in the *New York Times* that the Soviet KGB secret service is widely believed in the United States to have been responsible for Zia's death. But he also noted that the United States had the most to gain. Without implying that the United States was involved in the assassination, Kaplan does note that Zia's motives in Afghanistan included not just defeating the USSR but creating an Afghanistan strongly allied with Pakistan to provide ballast against Pakistan's perennial enemy (and Soviet ally) India. He therefore channeled support only to those Mujahideen he considered amenable to his vision—those with a religious agenda—effectively prolonging the war in Afghanistan. Meanwhile, Pakistanis themselves suffered the deprivations of an economy focused on war and were increasingly restive under his military rule. His death occasioned elections which brought to power Zulfikar Ali Bhutto's daughter, Benazir, who the United States believed would turn the tide of anti-Americanism in Pakistan.[55]

Benazir was indeed pro-democracy and not overtly anti-American. But she also continued the policies of her father. She continued to support both Pakistan's nuclear weapons program and Islamist militias as part of her geopolitical strategy, and US-Pakistan relations plummeted. US concern with Pakistan's covert nuclear weapons program, which had accelerated after India tested its first nuclear weapon in 1974, became official in 1985. That is when the US Congress passed the Pressler Amendment, requiring annual verification that Pakistan does not have a nuclear weapons program. Lacking such verification, military and economic aid would be cut off. During the Soviet occupation of Afghanistan, Pakistan was considered essential to the US effort to eliminate its Cold War foe; despite clear evidence of Pakistan's nuclear program, the requisite nuclear clearances were forthcoming until the Soviets had been defeated. Then, in August 1990, President George H. W. Bush invoked the Pressler Amendment for the first time. The aid the United States had funneled to Pakistan through Zia's military regime was cut off under Benazir's democratically elected government, seriously harming the country's already-fragile economy. At the same time that the Pressler Amendment was invoked, Benazir's government was dismissed and she and her husband, Asif Ali Zardari, were charged with corruption.

The United States also imposed an embargo on weapons, including twenty-eight fighter jets that Pakistan had purchased from America's General Dynamics and considered essential to defend itself from India. India had conducted a major military exercise along its border with Pakistan in 1987, codenamed Operation Brasstacks. Pakistan inferred that India was planning preemptive strikes on its nuclear installations. All Pakistan's nuclear installations were placed on high alert, and its armed forces were mobilized. Confrontation was averted but the impact of the exercise was to heighten Pakistan's resolve to focus on militarization.[56] And the United States' sanctions and military embargo prompted increased reliance on China in Pakistan's quest for development.

Following Benazir Bhutto's dismissal in 1990, new elections returned a majority for the PML, and its leader Nawaz Sharif became prime minister for the first of his three terms. Nawaz increased Pakistan's reliance on

China, contracting with them to build commercial nuclear power plants in Chashma (the first of which became operative in 2000). B. Raman claims that he also clandestinely continued the relationships forged by Zia with North Korea and Iran. With the cutoff of US weaponry, according to Raman, Pakistan secured Iranian financial support for North Korea to produce copies of US and Russian missiles from old ones in Pakistan's stockpiles.

Sharif also continued Zia's privatization of the economy as well as his Islamization of society through the legal system. As in Zia's time, these policies gained Sharif support among the economic and religious elites. But social pressures mounted. US economic sanctions continued to stifle the economy, and social strife in Karachi between Sindhis and Indian Muslim immigrants—the Muhajirun (sometimes spelled "Mohajiroon"). Never fully integrated into Sindhi society, the Muhajirun had organized into a political party, the MQM (Muttahida Qaumi Movement, formerly Mohajir Qaumi Movement) in the 1980s. Opposed to Sharif's economic and social conservatism, they were powerful enough to dominate the 1990 provincial elections. Social unrest between them and non-Muhajir Sindhis escalated into a period of paralyzing violence in Karachi, the country's economic hub, by 1992. Under allegations of corruption and mismanagement, Sharif resigned in 1993.

New elections once again brought Benazir to the premiership. Despite her image in the United States as a reform-minded feminist, she continued Pakistan's instrumentalization of radical Islamist groups for political gain. Following Soviet withdrawal, Afghanistan had fallen into a brutal civil war, and by Benazir's second term, the Taliban were emerging as a potent force in that war. "Taliban," meaning "students," is the name adopted by the militia headed by a former madrasa teacher in Kandahar, Mullah Omar, a Pashtun. Mullah Omar had developed a close relationship with Pakistan's ISI as it channeled funds through religiously oriented militias to combat the Soviet occupation. Former Mujahideen member Nojumi identifies Mawlana Fazlur Rehman, the leader of Pakistan's organization of conservative religious authorities, the Jamiat Ulema-e-Islam (JUI), as the point person between the ISI and the Taliban. The elder Bhutto had forged strong bonds between the PPP and the JUI in the 1970s as a result of his Islamization program, and the JUI continued its support of Benazir's PPP administration. Aware of Pakistan's ongoing need for stability on its western border, and preference for a friendly regime in Kabul, Mawlana Fazlur Rehman encouraged Benazir to support Mullah

Omar's Taliban in the Afghan civil war.[57] This support ultimately allowed the Taliban to take over Afghanistan in 1996.

Taliban domination of Afghanistan suited Pakistan's geostrategic goals. It now had a compliant neighbor on its western border and access to oil and gas markets in both Central Asia and Iran.[58] It also suited US and Saudi economic interests as companies from both countries sought lucrative contracts to build pipelines across Afghanistan to export that oil and gas.[59] Thus, Nojumi concludes, "favoring the formation of a 'friendly' pro-Pakistan regime in Kabul became the underlying strategy by the Pakistani government toward supporting the exiled Afghan Islamist opposition groups in the 1970s and 1980s and the Taliban in the 1990s."[60]

Benazir also continued Pakistan's policy of collaboration with North Korea for nuclear cooperation and missile delivery systems production, with Iranian support and Chinese assistance. In August 1993, the United States imposed further sanctions on the Kahuta Research Laboratories (KRL), Pakistan's main nuclear weapons facility, in response to its efforts to procure missiles from China.

But again Benazir's economic policies failed. Austerity measures appeared to undercut the PPP's pro-labor stance, and the economy continued to suffer. In 1996 Benazir and her husband Asif Ali Zardari were the target of more corruption charges, and her government was once again dismissed. New elections brought a second term for Nawaz Sharif.

De-escalation Efforts

Sharif had attempted to improve relations with India in his first term and reportedly did so again at the beginning of his second term. He met with India's prime minister, and the two countries' foreign ministers conducted a series of talks aimed at resolving outstanding issues. In 1999 they managed to sign agreements concerning trade and transportation links. But civilian government efforts to improve Pakistan-India relations were stymied by the two countries' military competition. In April 1998, Pakistan carried out a successful test of its own Ghauri missile, capable of delivering nuclear warheads. The next month, India carried out its second test of nuclear weapons, exploding five devices. Within weeks, Pakistan carried out its first tests, detonating five of its own nuclear devices in Baluchistan province.

The dispute over Kashmir also remained a flashpoint between Pakistan and India. One year after Pakistan carried out its nuclear tests, Chairman of the Joint Chiefs of Staff General Pervez Musharraf, working at cross-purposes with the civilian government, ordered Pakistani forces into Kargil in Indian-controlled Kashmir, surprising India's military. India's counteroffensive was reportedly on the verge of failure when US president Bill Clinton intervened, pressuring Pakistan's government to withdraw its troops. The order to withdraw was greatly resented by Pakistan's military.

Conflict between Nawaz Sharif and the military reached crisis proportions in October, when General Musharraf's plane, returning from abroad, was denied permission to land in Karachi, and Sharif announced Musharraf's replacement as military chief. The military mobilized, putting Sharif under house arrest, and Musharraf took over Pakistan's government in yet another military coup.

Musharraf's 1999 coup was initially greeted with relief by many Pakistanis, in hopes it would bring an end to social unrest and corruption, but hopes of reform would soon fade.[61] Sharif was charged with attempted murder and treason but was allowed to go into exile in Saudi Arabia before his trial reached a verdict. In May 2000, the Supreme Court called for the Musharraf government to schedule national elections within seventeen months. Ahead of the appointed deadline, Musharraf declared himself president (June 2001). And global geopolitics would once more impact Pakistan's struggle for democracy.

9/11 and Its Impact on Pakistan

The 9/11 attacks by Arab terrorists operating out of Afghanistan had a profound impact on Pakistan. Pakistan's democratically elected government had once again been ousted by the military. Instead of condemnation, the new military rulers received international support as they became useful for the US-led military response to 9/11. The US government sought and received General President Musharraf's agreement to provide intelligence and logistics support for the invasion of Afghanistan, where Arab-led al-Qaeda had set up headquarters under the protection of the Taliban government. In return, the United States lifted the sanctions that had been imposed on Pakistan under the Pressler Amendment mentioned above, as well as the subsequent Glenn and Symington Amendments, all of which proscribed military and economic aid as a result of Pakistan's nuclear program.[62]

In the face of US support for the military government under Musharraf, Pakistanis felt powerless to re-establish democracy. And again, the infusion of massive US aid into Pakistan made its military government unassailable, despite the unpopularity of the US government and its perceived manipulation of Pakistan for its own advantage. That perception was heightened by the fact that this time around, the United States was using Pakistan to fight warriors it had actually trained and equipped in the first place. As noted above, the Taliban had benefited from US funding and training during the Soviet occupation, and Osama bin Laden himself had been one of the US-allied Arab volunteers in the anti-Soviet jihad.

The fact that Pakistan had been instrumental in training and equipping Afghanistan's Mujahideen and continued to support them in their post-Soviet Taliban iteration put Pakistan in an ambiguous position. It allowed Pakistan to receive enormous US aid but also to continue its support for the Taliban and other militants when and where it suited Pakistan's purposes. Thus, Musharraf played the role assigned for him by the United States in the war against al-Qaeda, delivering countless people into US custody, with or without evidence of guilt. But he also continued a policy of support for Islamist militants in efforts to assure a Pakistan-friendly government in post-Taliban Afghanistan, as well as in efforts to keep India from establishing permanent control in Kashmir.

The US-led war against the very people it had empowered was a decisive factor in the radicalization of Pakistan's Islamist militants. The Taliban, dominated as they are by Pashtuns, could never have been confined to their original turf in Afghanistan, with its highly permeable and unrecognized British-imposed border down the middle of "Pashtunistan." The post-9/11 US-led invasion of Afghanistan drove countless well-trained and well-funded Afghan Taliban to safer ground in Pakistan's Pashtun heartland. There they found refuge and ready recruits to join their fight against this new round of foreign invaders.

Organized Pashtun Islamist militias first became visible in Pakistan in 1992, with the establishment in the Swat region of Khyber-Pakhtunkhwa province (KPK; formerly NWFP, North-West Frontier Province) of the TNSM (Tehrik Nifaz-i-Shariat-i-Muhammadi, "Movement for the Enforcement of Islamic Law"). TNSM leader Sufi Muhammad had been affiliated with the Mawlana Fazlur Rehman's JUI (intermediary between ISI and the Afghan Taliban during the 1990s; see above) but split with them to form his own organization. The TNSM's particular focus was the establishment of Islamic law in Pakistan but, like the JUI, the TNSM continued to support the Taliban in Afghanistan. Sufi Muhammad is therefore sometimes called as "the godfather" of Pakistan's Taliban—although "Taliban" here is used loosely to mean militant, conservative Islamists who support those fighting against the US-led troops in Afghanistan.

In November 2001, US ally General President Musharraf jailed Sufi Muhammad for leading volunteers to fight the US-led troops in Afghanistan.[63] The group was officially banned in 2002 but continued to thrive under the leadership of Sufi Muhammad's son-in-law, Mawlana Fazlullah, known as "Radio Mullah" for his popular radio broadcasts advocating purification of Islamic practice.[64]

Meanwhile, General Musharraf tried to consolidate his hold on the government. In April 2002 he formed a "Grand National Alliance" to support him and held a referendum to provide legitimacy to his self-assigned five-year presidency. But his policy of cooperating with the United States in its punishing war in Afghanistan quickly turned popular opinion against him, especially in Pakistan's Pashtun-dominated tribal areas along the border. In October 2002, Musharraf finally held national elections. The pro-Musharraf faction of the PML (PML-Q) dominated the elections. But a coalition of anti-Musharraf (and anti-US) religious parties formed—the MMA (Muttahida Majlis-e-Amal)—which included Mawlana Fazlur Rehman's JUI. The MMA gained control of the provincial government in the Pashtun homeland, KPK province.

By this time, a new political party had successfully emerged among a new generation of Pakistanis who had lost faith in the revolving governments of the PML, the PPP, and the military. Founded in 1997 by philanthropist and former cricket star Imran Khan, the PTI (Pakistan Tehreek-e-Insaf, "Pakistan Movement for Justice") focused on Pakistan's founding Islamic ideals of democracy and social justice. The PTI was also, and remains, staunchly opposed to the US campaign in Afghanistan. Imran Khan was elected to the National Assembly (Pakistan's national house of representatives) in 2002. With the emergence of PTI, the growing anti-US-led war movement had a voice other than that of militant Islamists.

Anti-Musharraf and anti-US sentiment escalated after the US-led invasion of Iraq in 2003. Increasingly, militant Islamist groups in Pakistan who opposed US-led forces in Afghanistan turned against the government of Pakistan, as well. That is, it was Pakistan's support for the US-led campaign in Afghanistan that gave rise to the Pakistani Taliban which, in turn, brought the US-led "Global War on Terrorism" (GWOT) into

Pakistan, with the introduction of drone strikes in June 2004. Directed against those suspected of being anti-US militants, these strikes terrorized the civilian population, many of whom were its victims. Considered a violation of Pakistan's sovereignty, the drone strikes predictably exacerbated anti-American sentiment in Pakistan overall and further radicalized its militants.

Unrest along Pakistan's western borders spiked, spreading from predominantly Pashtun KPK and the Tribal Areas to Baluchistan, which shares borders with both Afghanistan and Iran. Traditional Baluchistan—like traditional Pashtunistan—is actually split by the western border of Pakistan. The Baluch are ethnically Iranian and many feel more solidarity with Iranian and Afghan Baluch than with Pakistani non-Baluch people, although they share their province with a substantial Pashtun minority—nearly one-third—as well as with far smaller minorities of diverse Punjabis and other minorities. Territorially, Baluchistan is Pakistan's largest, comprising over 40 percent of the country, and its least populated, with less than 5 percent of the country's population. But its natural gas fields—Pakistan's largest—and its copper and gold resources, as well as its 470-mile coastline along the Arabian Sea, make it economically and strategically the country's most valuable province. Discontent with the government of Pakistan had long been expressed in a movement calling for greater autonomy and share in the province's own resources. Rebellions had erupted several times since the creation of Pakistan, most notably from 1973 to 1977. That uprising was brutally suppressed by Zulfikar Ali Bhutto, leaving thousands dead and bitter memories. Discontent again exploded into violence in 2004, augmented by Islamist radicals. In July 2006, Baluch leader Akbar Khan Bugti was killed in a government bombing raid, temporarily suppressing the violence. But bloody conflicts in Pashtun regions among competing militant groups and between militants and government along the border with Afghanistan continued.

The Lawyers' Movement

Lurking behind the growing and diverse strains of unrest in Pakistan was opposition to General Musharraf's government, and 2007 proved to be a pivotal year in the coalescing of that opposition.

The previous year, Musharraf's government had attempted to privatize Pakistan's largest state-owned corporation, Pakistan Steel Mills, awarding it to the highest bidder, a consortium of Russian, Saudi, and Pakistani companies. The Supreme Court, under Chief Justice Iftikhar Chaudhry, nullified the sale, citing irregularities in procedures and raising questions about Pakistani government officials benefiting from the sale of government property. Musharraf's government reciprocated with accusations of improprieties against the chief justice and suspended him. The Supreme Court raised the stakes by investigating hundreds of "missing persons."[65]

Predictably, the Pakistan "street" alleged US involvement in the Supreme Court's decision to nullify the sale of Pakistan Steel Mills. Stories circulated about lawyers receiving large payments for interfering in Russia's (read: "US competitor") involvement in Pakistan's economy. But Lawyers' Movement participants saw it otherwise. Elections were scheduled for 2008 and Musharraf wanted to run. Chaudhry's court was bound to oppose General Musharraf's right to run for election and remain chief of the army. "The military government needed a pliant Chief Justice if Musharraf was to stay in office without removing his uniform," observes Pakistan specialist William Dalrymple.[66]

The lawyers had begun staging public protests in spring, but by May they had been joined by many others, including militant Islamists from the MMA. The MMA's motto when it emerged in elections following the US invasion of Afghanistan was: "It is a war between Islam and the American infidel." Their leader proclaimed in the 2007 protests: "The friend of Bush's is our enemy!"[67]

Opposition to Musharraf reached critical mass in July, when his troops stormed the Lal Masjid (Red Mosque) complex in Islamabad. The mosque-school complex was well known for its anti-US position and allegedly had contacts with the ISI. But its increasingly militant agitation for strictly religious rule within Pakistan—including attacks on businesses deemed irreligious (and abductions of suspected prostitutes)—triggered a military response. Without warning, the government launched a ten-day attack in July 2007 that ended in the deaths of at least seventy-six students, perhaps twice that.

The shock and outrage in Pakistan at the brutality of the attack, added to anger over US drone attacks in Pakistan and Musharraf's interference in the judiciary, resulted in overwhelming pressure against Musharraf's government. Musharraf reinstated Chaudhry as chief justice. In August, news reports began to surface that exiled leader of the PPP Benazir Bhutto was negotiating with the Musharraf government for a return to Pakistan to participate in the elections scheduled for early 2008. In October the government announced a National Reconciliation Ordinance, granting amnesty to all politicians charged with misconduct between 1986 and 1999, and Benazir Bhutto returned to Pakistan. The following month Musharraf resigned his military post and, after a brief and utterly confused state of emergency, prepared to run in the upcoming elections as a civilian.

But the US-led war against terrorism remained intensely unpopular, and opposition continued to organize. In December 2007 charismatic Pashtun leader Baitullah Mehsud, longtime supporter of Afghan Taliban, united a diverse group of militant groups to form the TTP (Tehrik-i Taliban Pakistan), the Pakistan Taliban Movement. Their major concern was no longer next door in Afghanistan; the target was now the government of Pakistan. KPK's pro-(Afghan) Taliban movement, the TNSM (see above), joined the TTP alliance and began taking control of KPK's Swat Valley, imposing its radical interpretation of Islamic justice, including public beheadings and burning girls' schools. The government of Pakistan responded with military attacks in Swat.

In December 2007, Benazir Bhutto was assassinated at a political rally in Rawalpindi. The government suspected TTP's Baitullah Mehsud as the culprit, given Bhutto's public criticisms of "religious extremism." She herself claimed that Musharraf had threatened her.[68] The assassination could just as easily have been perpetrated by members of Karachi's MQM. The MQM is believed to have paramilitary units involved in revenue-raising criminal activities such as kidnapping and extortion, as well as executing of opponents and even party members considered unfaithful to party leadership. Musharraf's National Reconciliation Ordinance resulted in dropping seventy-two criminal charges against MQM leader Altaf Hussain, including thirty-one murder allegations.[69] Benazir's government had implemented "Operation Clean-Up" in 1993–1994 in an effort to neutralize MQM, resulting in bloody confrontations in the streets of Karachi and thousands of deaths and disappearances.[70] MQM therefore certainly had a grudge against her. The Pakistan "street" suggests, of course, that the United States is responsible for Benazir's death; the United States helped negotiate her return to Pakistan, assuming she would be a loyal client, but then they allegedly questioned her loyalty. To date, the only person charged in the case is Musharraf himself, in August 2013.

The Return to Democracy?

The cataclysmic events of 2007 ultimately resolved into a return to democracy in early 2008. Parliamentary elections resulted in a strong majority for Bhutto's PPP and Nawaz Sharif's PML-N. PPP's Yousaf Raza Gillani was named prime minister. Musharraf remained president, until he was impeached and then resigned, in August 2008. Presidential elections then brought the PPP's de facto leader and Benazir Bhutto's widower, Asif Ali Zardari, to the post.

The PPP-led civilian government elected after the death of Benazir Bhutto served the first full five-year term of any democratically elected government in Pakistan's history. The term was not peaceful. Zardari's government continued to support the US-led GWOT, whose drone strikes within Pakistan increased and with them, hostility toward the United States and the Pakistani government allied with it. The Pakistani military launched attacks on suspected militants in Bajaur Agency in FATA, for example, in August 2008, leading to hundreds of deaths and thousands of refugees. The Pakistani Taliban responded with attacks on Pakistan's major weapons factories and the Islamabad Marriott Hotel, killing over fifty people and wounding hundreds more. The government has made periodic efforts to establish ceasefires with various militant groups, while continuing operations against others. In February 2008 Baitullah's TTP announced a ceasefire with the government, for example, and in February 2009, the government reached a ceasefire agreement with TNSM, allowing them to implement their version of Islamic law in Malakand District of KPK.[71] But US drone strikes increased (TTP's Baitullah Mehsud was killed in a drone strike in August 2009), and terror attacks claimed by TTP escalated accordingly: Peshawar's Pearl Continental Hotel 2009 (killing nineteen); military targets such as GHQ in Rawalpindi (2009); Pakistan's naval air base in Karachi (2011); the Kamra air force base and military targets in FATA (2012); and Dera Ismail Khan Central Jail (2013), freeing hundreds of Taliban prisoners.

Despite the ongoing battles with terrorists, the government managed to produce some notable progress in democratic governance. Under PPP leadership, the Public Accounts Committee—constitutionally mandated to oversee public spending—was reactivated following a long period of dormancy. Clearing a ten-year backlog of the ledgers of federally supported development projects, the committee was able to recover billions of rupees previously unaccounted for.[72] Perhaps most significant was the passage of the 18th Amendment in 2010. The amendment trans-ferred numerous ministries and departments to the provinces, respond-ing to provincial demands for greater autonomy. It also repealed the 17th Amendment, passed under Musharraf, which would have allowed him to hold both his position as army chief and the office of president. And it restored the authority of the parliament in the government of Pakistan, reversing the 8th Amendment, passed under Zia ul-Haq, that allowed the president to dismiss the elected parliament at will.

The May 2013 general elections resulted in a strong showing for the PML-N (166 seats), followed by the PPP (45 seats). Another first in Pakistan's democratic history was the strong showing for the "new" party, Imran Khan's PTI (34 seats). This was the first election in which any party other than those of the traditional elites—the PPP and PML—had sig-nificant electoral success. PTI's success represents a quantitative leap in the emergence of political engagement among Pakistan's burgeoning and increasingly youthful urban population.

However, the government continues to cooperate with the US-led GWOT, and militant groups continue to attack it. In the summer and fall of 2014, the TTP carried out devastating attacks on Karachi International Airport as well as ISI offices and police training centers in several cities. As well, the 2013 election results continue to be protested. Imran Khan's PTI insists they were rigged by the PML-N and has presented credible evidence to support that claim.[73] In August 2014 Khan launched a major popular march—the Azadi ("freedom") March—bringing tens of thousands of people to Islamabad to demand the resignation of Nawaz Sharif; new elec-tions; and, more generally, an end to government corruption, an end to cooperation with the US-led war on terror, negotiation with the Taliban, and government commitment to providing healthcare, education, and ade-quate and sustainable power for all Pakistanis.[74] The protests continued throughout the year but have had little impact thus far. Despite widespread popularity with Pakistan's "youth bulge" both at home and abroad, Imran's case has been weakened by its association with another march at the same time, led by Tahir-ul-Qadri. Qadri had founded his own party in 1989, with far less success than Imran Khan. He served in the National Assembly for over a decade but then resigned in 2004 and moved to Canada. When Qadri returned in 2012 to mount his campaign for peaceful reform, suspi-cions were raised about foreign sources of his apparently strong financial support. Although Qadri's march was announced only after the PTI plans gained publicity, his relatively weak popular standing and political record raised questions about PTI's ultimate objectives. More damaging still were accusations by PTI party president Javed Hashmi that Imran Khan had made a deal with the military to unseat the Nawaz government.[75] Imran Khan's supporters reject these allegations and Khan vows to continue PTI's efforts. His calls for an end to support for the US-led GWOT; negotiations with Pakistan's Taliban; normalization of relations with India; and establishment of a corruption-free, civilian-led, progressive, Islam-inspired democracy in Pakistan remain widely popular.

Throughout 2014 Pakistan's PML-led government continued military assaults on militant strongholds. Even as the Sharif government discussed ceasefires with some groups, the military launched Operation Zarb-e-Azb against Pakistani militants in the FATA (June 2014). By September, it claimed to have neutralized terrorist cells in FATA and elsewhere.[76] And on September 14, 2014, the Punjabi Taliban announced that it was abandoning armed struggle in favor of peaceful means to bring about an Islamic state in Pakistan.[77] Hailed as a success for the PML government and military, this is bound to further weaken challenges to the Nawaz government in the near term.

Conclusion: Pakistan's Political Theology

Pakistan was established as a state representing the highest ideals of Islamic life; to its founders there was no question but that it would be a democracy. Without parsing details of some specific kind of democracy that would make Pakistan's identifiably Islamic, and despite periods of military rule, the country is again operating as a democracy. Over the years, it has incorporated a number of identifiably Islamic elements. The government is constitutionally bound to pass no laws that would be "repugnant" to Islam; elements of traditional Islamic law have been incorporated into its legal structure, overseen by Sharia courts; sales of alcohol and gambling have been prohibited; and heterodox Muslims have been declared non-Muslim. Yet reformers of diverse stripes continue to call for Islamic governance. What can that mean?

Among other things, it indicates a broad commitment to the founding objectives of the country and an uneasy awareness that they have yet to be achieved. The abiding suspicion of foreign involvement in Pakistan's troubled history reflects a consensus that simple legislative devices, such as implementation of traditional punishments and prohibition of banned substances, do not an Islamic society make, and that radicalism is not homegrown. Indeed, many Pakistanis see their own militant Taliban and other radicalized groups as the country's greatest threat.[78]

Some of the elements of the 1949 Objectives Resolution have been achieved. The third stipulates that Muslims must be able to live in accordance with the teachings of the Qur'an. On the institutional level, the first objective calls for government through elected representatives; the fifth states that Pakistan shall be a federation; the eighth calls for an independent judiciary; and the ninth demands the country's territorial integrity. Those more practical objectives have been, by and large, achieved. But that leaves three other, more elusive objectives. The second objective calls for, in addition to democracy and freedom, "equality, tolerance, and social justice, as enunciated by Islam" to be "fully observed." The fourth demands that the religious and cultural rights of minorities be protected. And the sixth objective demands that "fundamental rights including equality of status, of opportunity and before law, social, economic and political justice, and freedom of thought, expression, belief, faith, worship and association, subject to law and public morality" shall be guaranteed.[79] It is these more ephemeral objectives that continue to elude Pakistan.

The question in Pakistan, therefore, is not about whether or not Islam and democracy are compatible, or choosing between religious and secular governance, or even whether or not there is a special kind of Islamic democracy. Pakistani anthropologist Naveeda Khan observes that, rather, Pakistan can be seen as a work in progress. She notes that soon after the country's creation, prominent scholar Wilfred Cantwell Smith described Pakistan's formation as a unique challenge. "The Islamic state is the ideal to which Pakistan . . . should aspire. It is the aspiring that has been fundamental; not this or that pattern of the ideal."[80] Smith's observation reflects awareness of classical Islamic political thought, which stipulates no particular formal structure of governance. Instead, it grounds political legitimacy in achievement of the objectives (*maqasid*) of Islamic law. Achieving these objectives, which are indeed reflected in Pakistan's founding documents—preservation of life, religion, family, property, and dignity—is the ultimate challenge of Islamic governance.[81] As Smith summarizes, "The demand that Pakistan should be an Islamic state has been a Muslim way of saying that Pakistan should build for itself a good society."[82]

In Naveeda Khan's view, this challenge shifts the conversation from a vocabulary circumscribed by modernist political terms to a

post-secularist discourse of political theology.[83] Political theology highlights the artificiality of rigid distinctions between religious and secular
concerns: "The concept of political theology provides us a strong orientation to the manner in which theology animates everyday conversations."[84] In stark contrast to Fukuyama's notion of an ultimate political
form that assumes no further need for development, political theology
posits ongoing social aspiration to achieve cherished ideals in functioning political structures. Khan cites Bhrigupati Singh's characterization
of Gandhi's struggle as "modalities of self-making and self-perfecting."[85]
The continued calls for Islamic governance in Pakistan reflect just this
sort of struggle—the struggle to fulfill Pakistan's Islam-inspired objectives of good governances, measured in terms of the well-being of even
the weakest members of society.

5

Indonesia

FROM MILITARY RULE TO DEMOCRACY

Democracy is about listening to the people and taking
concrete action.

JOKO WIDODO

We are committed to ensuring the establishment of
a clean government that conserves democracy and
guarantees people's welfare.

PRABOWO SUBIANTO[1]

IN THE INDONESIAN national elections of 2014, the presidential candidates presented contrasting visions of democracy. The long-established practice of elite leadership providing a "guided democracy" was advocated by a retired general, Prabowo Subianto. In contrast, Joko "Jokowi" Widodo, a municipal and provincial political leader with few ties to the old sociopolitical elite, promoted a more populist, grassroots-based democracy. The election campaign and the contrasting visions and styles of these two men reflected the evolution of democracy in Indonesia during the 21st century.

The election of Joko "Jokowi" Widodo as president marked the fourth successful transfer of presidential leadership through democratic means in Indonesia since the overthrow of the regime of Suharto in 1998. The Indonesian experience in the early years of the 21st century represents an effective transition from a long-standing authoritarian military regime to an electoral democracy. As a result, when the Arab Spring movements began in 2011, some people asked if the "Indonesian model" could provide some guidance for the new governments created by the Arab Spring.[2] In the year following the overthrow of Hosni Mubarak in Egypt, the Indonesian Institute for Peace and Democracy, with the leadership of former Indonesian foreign minister, Hassan Wirajuda, held a series of workshops in Egypt on the processes of democratic transition.

Analysts of democratic transitions debated the relevance of the Indonesian experience for the Arab Spring. Soon after the outbreak of the Arab Spring movements, Thomas Carothers argued that it would be wise "to look to Indonesia as an example of how a democratic transition in a Muslim country can be successful,"[3] while Thomas Pepinsky contended that there "is no Indonesia model for the Arab Spring."[4] In general, both observers and participants in the movements recognized that the "Indonesian context is strikingly different from that of the Arab world context" but that Middle Eastern societies "can benefit from some significant lessons derived from the Indonesian case."[5]

The emergence of the world's third-largest democracy in Indonesia, the world's largest Muslim country, is a major development, whether or not it is considered a "model" for other countries. In examining the "Third Wave" of global democratization in the late 20th century, Samuel Huntington, writing in 1991, asserted that "it is hard to identify any Islamic leader who made a reputation as an advocate and supporter of democracy while in office."[6] Less than a decade later, Indonesian advocates of democracy were leading their country and establishing a democratic system for both electing leaders and the peaceful transfer of power. The process began when the long-standing authoritarian military regime of Suharto came to an end in 1998 as a result of the demonstrations and political pressures of the *reformasi* movement. This movement developed during the 1990s among intellectuals and student groups advocating democratic reforms and thus gained the label of "*reformasi*." When Suharto resigned, the vice president, Bacharuddin Jusuf (B. J.) Habibie, became president and led the transition to a system of democratically elected governance.

The experience of Indonesia provides important insights into the processes of democratization in the contexts of the 21st-century world. While there is no simple single plan of action for successfully creating effective democratic structures, the recent history of Indonesia provides significant examples of how common issues are resolved in the framework of a major political community. This chapter examines how the Indonesian political system developed, noting the interactions among three critical groupings—the modernizing nationalist political elite, the major Islamic organizations, and the Indonesian military. The overthrow of Suharto in 1998 represented a major transition point in the political roles of these elements. The evolution of each of these groupings will be examined and then their roles in each of the national elections since 1998 will be discussed. Within this framework, the presidential election of 2014 will be seen as an occasion in which an emerging political force outside of the long-established elites became visible with the election of Jokowi.

Dynamics of Indonesian Politics

Independent Indonesia was created on the foundations of old political orders that had been partially preserved in the contexts of modern European imperialism and the imperial structures inherited from the time of rule of the region by the Dutch East India Company and then Dutch colonial rule. Dutch policies of indirect rule in some regions preserved parts of the pre-imperialist political elites ruling a series of smaller sultanates, and Islamic organizations like Sufi brotherhoods and religious schools continued to shape the lives of most Indonesians. A long tradition of revolts by Islamic groups and local ethnic groups existed, but organized nationalist opposition to Dutch rule only emerged in the early 20th century. However, it was the new nationalist movement that provided the leadership for the successful opposition to the Dutch, leading to the establishment of independent Indonesia following World War II.

Nationalists announced the establishment of the new independent Republic of Indonesia in 1945. They took advantage of a distinctive opportunity. Like other areas in Southeast Asia, the older Western imperial powers—Britain, France, the Netherlands, and the United States—had been defeated in the region by the Japanese early in World War II, and their imperial role was interrupted or ended. When the Japanese lost the global war, local nationalists in the Dutch East Indies asserted their independence, but they soon faced British and Dutch military forces attempting to re-establish Dutch rule. This "war for independence" ended with Dutch recognition of Indonesian sovereignty in 1949. In addition to the conflict with the old imperialists, the new nationalist government, centered in Java, faced opposition from regional, ethnic, and religious groups unwilling to accept the new government.

By the 1950s, the nationalist government generally succeeded in creating a central state within the framework of the older political boundaries of the Dutch imperial administration in Southeast Asia. However, it continued to face revolts by Muslim opposition groups like Darul Islam, regional separatist groups, and communist militants. During the 1950s, military leaders assumed increasingly important political positions, with the end result being the establishment of the military regime of Suharto in 1966. This complex mixture of elements provided the framework for Indonesian politics since independence. The major groupings that emerged were the civilian nationalist elite, the major Muslim organizations, and the military as a distinctive sociopolitical power group.

In the democratization process in the 21st century, each of these groups continued to play significant roles. The evolution of Indonesian politics shaped the nature of their involvements in post-Suharto politics. To understand the party politics of the new era, it is important to examine how each of these groups evolved as political forces over time.

The nationalists who declared the independence of Indonesia in 1945 came from an important class within Indonesian society. They did not speak for the political culture of the old sultanates that had been preserved by Dutch indirect rule. They did not declare the independence of a precolonial polity. Instead, they proclaimed the independence of the colonial state whose boundaries had been set by the Dutch. "Indonesia" was a modern identity defined by the imperial experience and the challenge faced by the nationalists from the beginning of the nationalist movement was to confirm an Indonesian identity that could take priority over the diverse regional, ethnic, and religious identities within the boundaries of the new state. This challenge continues to be visible in the 21st-century debates about decentralization of government.

With the emphasis on Indonesian unity, religion became an important issue in defining the nature of the state. Since the overwhelming majority of Indonesians are Muslim, some of the activists involved in gaining independence advocated the establishment of a state that would be officially Islamic, while more secular nationalists resisted this option. In the debates in mid-1945 about what the nature of independent Indonesia should be, Sukarno, the recognized leader of the nationalist movement, gave a speech setting forth the Five Principles (Pancasila) that were accepted as the basic foundation for the new state. Pancasila was not a specific program, but represented what Sukarno called, using what he called a "high-sounding term," the " 'Weltanschauung' upon which we should set up the Indonesian State."[7] The Five Principles were humanitarianism, national unity, representative government, social justice, and monotheism. Pancasila continues in the 21st century to be accepted as the foundation principles of the state. In terms of specific policies, monotheism was the most influential of the five principles. Sukarno stated, "Not only should the people of Indonesia have belief in God, but every Indonesian should believe in *his own* particular God."[8] Since 1945, Pancasila has been the answer to the call for establishing an Islamic state in Indonesia. It was and is the position of the nationalists in Indonesia.

This new class represented the people with modern, Western-style educations. Around the world, in the early 20th century, "the intelligentsias were central to the rise of nationalism in the colonial territories."[9] Many of the nationalist groups were also student groups and, especially in the early days of the movements, the leaders as well as the supporters were young. As the movements created organizations, early leaders continued to be prominent and by the middle of the 20th century the major organizations were no longer primarily youth organizations. The leaders of the new independent state were activists with long careers. The most prominent nationalist, for example, was Sukarno. He was about 26 when he participated in the founding of the nationalist organization Perserikatan (later called Partai) Nasional Indonesia (PNI, the Indonesian National Association) in 1927, and 44 when he led the nationalists at the end of World War II.

The young, modern, educated nationalists of the early 20th century became the civilian political establishment in the new country. At independence, this emerging political elite was divided into a number of important factions and interest groups. The diverse groups reflected the long history of nationalist organizations. In the years before and during World War I, a number of organizations were established by the newly emerging educated class. The Budi Utomo (Glorious Endeavour), established by a group of graduates of a major Dutch school in 1908, is often described as the first "nationalist" organization. Like other associations created at the time, the Budi Utomo was consciously not political, emphasizing social reform and indigenous (basically Javanese) culture.

In a remarkable prelude to the politics of independent Indonesia, organizations reflecting the major political tendencies of the modern educated political elite emerged by the end of the 1920s. Sarekat Islam (SI) was established in 1911–1912 to encourage Muslim economic activities in the face of local Chinese economic power. SI soon became involved in broader issues of social reform and began to discuss openly the need for Indonesian self-government. It attracted a large following, especially in Java among the new educated groups, and "became the East Indies' first ever mass-based movement."[10] In this same period, a radical Marxist association was established and many of its followers joined with SI, causing tensions within that organization. The leftists created the Indonesian Communist Party (PKI), and some of the PKI branches led revolts in 1926–1927, which were crushed by the Dutch. Although the organization was suppressed, it continued to have an underground following and re-emerged as a major political force after World War II. The brutal massacre of thousands of communists in 1965–1966, as a part of the overthrow of the ideologically leftist regime of Sukarno, brought an end to the PKI as a political force, but ideologically leftist sentiments continued to be a part of the politics of policy.

The relatively secular early nationalist tendency gained its own organizational identity under a new generation of leaders in the 1920s. Divisions within SI opened the way for younger nationalists to transform student study groups into an explicitly nationalist organization, the Partai Nasional Indonesia (PNI). Leaders of the PNI, like Sukarno and Muhammad Hatta, became the leaders of independent Indonesia in the 1940s, and their families and younger associates continue to be significant in 21st-century politics. Sukarno's daughter, Megawati Sukarnoputri, was, for example, the second elected president following the overthrow of Suharto.

By 1945, a civilian nationalist elite had emerged. It shared a sense of "Indonesian" identity along with a modern Western-style education. Urban professionals were the main proponents of nationalism in those early years, and government policy was, as a result, identified with them and less involved with rural peoples and issues. However, this elite had its internal divisions, and politics was, at least in part, a system of balancing the interests of the various factions and their leaders. These early leaders were mostly Muslim but "their Western schooling and dedication to the cause of Indonesian independence led them to embrace a religiously inclusive nationalism, a doctrine that still enjoys great support in Muslim circles today."[11] This viewpoint provided the basis for continued support for Pancasila. Explicit opposition to religion or advocacy of an anticlerical secularism was not a part of the worldview of this elite, although they did combat the anti-Republic Muslim militants who opposed the new government—and who continued to oppose the central government over the years.

In the late 20th century, this nationalist elite continued to provide the main civilian political voices, with some supporting the guided democracy of Suharto and others advocating alternatives to Suharto's system and gradually becoming a movement of political opposition. In the early 1970s, Suharto allowed three political parties to be organized and participate in carefully controlled elections. Golkar was the major party, representing the government (and the military). One party was created to combine the political activities of the Muslim religious organizations, the United Development Party (PPP; Partai Persatuan Pembangunan), and a second combined the old nationalist PNI with a group of other nationalist or non-Muslim parties into the Indonesian Democratic Party (PDI). By the 1990s, the nationalist opposition began to find a voice in the daughter of Sukarno, Megawati Sukarnoputri. Since she was leader of the PDI, Suharto viewed her as a threat and attempted to exclude her from electoral politics. By 1998 she had become the most prominent political figure in the opposition, and when Suharto resigned, she reorganized her supporters in the PDI as the Indonesian Democratic Party of Struggle (PDI-P; Partai Demokrasi Indonesia Perjuangan), which won the most votes of any party in the parliamentary elections of 1999. The PDI-P shows the continuing significance of the old nationalist elite.

A second major element in Indonesian politics is the power and influence of major Islamic organizations that have deep historical roots but have modern forms of organization. Like the nationalist elite, the new Muslim organizations only have their beginnings in the early 20th century. However, Muslim revolts against Dutch control and movements of Islamic renewal and reform have a long history in the islands of Southeast Asia. By the late 19th century, modern means of transportation, especially steamships, allowed growing numbers of Muslims from the Dutch East Indies to undertake the pilgrimage to Mecca. Often, returning pilgrims (Hajjis) supported movements both of religious renewal and of opposition to Dutch rule.

By the beginning of the 20th century, this Muslim reformism provided foundations for a non-nationalist activism which had reservations about rule over Muslims by non-Muslims but concentrated on reforming heterodox religious practices and local customs that dominated much of Muslim life in Southeast Asian society. This approach was influenced by the developing Islamic modernist movement, especially as articulated by Muhammad 'Abduh in Egypt, and it involved new modes of interpreting religious texts in light of modern history. In 1912, a returning Hajji, Ahmad Dahlan, established what came to be the largest of the modernist associations in Indonesia, the Muhammadiyya. The group "favored a religiously-oriented programme of modernization, concentrated on education and social welfare, and generally did not become involved in political activity."[12]

Religious activists created a number of organizations in the early decades of the 20th century. In the 1920s, more traditionally oriented religious leaders responded to the reformists, and in 1926 they formed a new modern-style organization for the advancement of more religiously conservative positions and programs, the Nahdlatul Ulama (NU). While older traditions of militancy continued to have influence in a variety of areas, like Aceh in northern Sumatra, the NU and the Muhammadiyya soon became the largest Muslim associations in the country, building and maintaining hundreds of mosques and thousands of schools. In contrast to the urban-oriented nationalist elite, they were and are a major presence in rural Indonesia as well as in the cities. Under colonial rule, many Islamically identifiable organizations were created, but they represented a wide range of views and did not represent "a unified Islamic movement that could challenge either the colonial state or the secular nationalist movement."[13]

At the end of World War II, some Muslim leaders tried to establish a broadly based Islamic political party. The Japanese occupation administration had created Masyumi, the Indonesian Consultative Council, and most major Islamic organizations, including both NU and Muhammadiyya, supported the political reorganization of Masyumi. However, the party soon split, with NU withdrawing to establish its own party in 1952. The first general elections in 1955 showed both the strengths and the weakness of politically active Muslims. In that election, almost 44 percent of the votes went to Islamic parties, but the vote was divided, with Masyumi gaining almost 21 percent and NU winning a little more than 18 percent. As Sukarno established his "guided democracy," independent Islamic parties were suppressed. The policy was continued under Suharto, who mandated that all Islamic parties come together in the PPP.

Support for Islamic parties and their political visions was and continues to be strong since independence. In competitive elections, they were not a majority, but were supported by as many as 40 percent of the voters at times. However, radical Islamic parties and programs and advocates of a strict implementation of Sharia never received significant support, although the jihadi militancy of groups like Darul Islam in the early years of independence and Jemaah Islamiyah (JI) established in the 1990s were (and are) important challenges to central government policies.

The major Islamic organizations and parties are not "Islamist," in the sense that that term has come to be used in contemporary political analysis as advocacy for the establishment of a formally defined Islamic state based on implementation of Sharia (as interpreted by medieval scholars). Instead, they emphasize Islamic values as a source of policy. This position is articulated in a debate in the early 1980s by Amien Rais, who later became the head of Muhammadiyya: "I don't think that there is an 'Islamic State' in the Qur'an or in the Sunnah. Therefore, there is no command in Islam to adopt an Islamic state. What is more important is that as long as a state runs on an Islamic ethos, implementing social justice and creating an egalitarian society . . . according to Islam it is already viewed as a good state."[14] Similarly, Abd al-Rahman Wahid, a head of NU, argued that Islam should be an "inspirational base for a national framework of a democratic society."[15] Views like these provide the base for most of the Islamic parties since independence and shape the nature of the involvement of such parties in post-Suharto politics.

Like the nationalist elite, the Muslim organizational elite has real continuity and continuing political power. Abd al-Rahman Wahid, the first president elected by parliament after the overthrow of Suharto, was a grandson of Kiai Haji Hasyim Asy'ari, one of the founders of NU, and his maternal grandfather, Kiai Haji Bisri Syansuri, was also active in the founding of the group. Abd al-Rahman himself had been a chair of NU before entering the politics of the post-Suharto era. The first head of the newly elected parliament, Amien Rais, was head of the Muhammadiyya during the 1990s and was among the leaders of the democratic reform movement. Both of his parents were active leaders within the Muhammadiyya. In the days of colonial nationalism and of the authoritarian military rule, the Muslim organizations had been significant and they continued to be an important part of the political system in the new era of democratic politics.

The third major element in post-independence politics—the military—does not have the same long history as a significant political force. A study of the political role of the military in "new nations" done in the early 1960s noted the origins of the armed forces in more than fifty countries. Indonesia was one of only four countries whose armed forces were created within the framework of a "national liberation" struggle. Most militaries were either continuations of colonial armed forces or armies created after liberation (mostly in sub-Saharan Africa).[16] In terms of political activity, the study noted that "military formations born in the struggle for national liberation have maintained wide political involvements. Each of the four armies created as a force of national liberation has expanded its political role."[17] A study of the Indonesian military at the same time, the early 1960s before the military took direct control of the government in 1966–1967, noted that the Indonesian army "was never a passive professional army and its revolutionary origins and continual operations since 1948 against domestic political rebellions have made its officer corps fully aware of national politics."[18]

From the beginning of independent Indonesia, military commanders were important partners in establishing the new state. They provided support for Sukarno and then in the mid-1960s stepped in to take control of the state when leftist and communist forces appeared to be taking control. Suharto, who became president following the military takeover of government in 1966–1967, had been an important commander in the national liberation army in the 1940s and in the military campaigns suppressing regional and religious revolts in the 1950s. Even before Suharto's coming to power, military officers were active in both politics and economic life.

In the New Order created by Suharto, the military "began to build a new authoritarian system grounded on the so-called 'dwi-fungsi', the double function" of the military in both national security and socioeconomic development.[19] A 1969 law designated a set of seats in the parliament for the military, and officers were important in the leadership of Golkar, Suharto's political party. "Between 1966 and 1998 senior members of the Indonesian military were appointed to legislative and administrative bodies and occupied key positions in the bureaucracy as well as in state-owned corporations."[20] The core of political power in the New Order rested with the armed forces, whose leaders became central to economic and social life as well as to the regular functions of military institutions.

By the 1990s, many high-ranking officers felt marginalized by the prominence of Suharto's family and the group of cronies that surrounded him. The New Order was no longer simply a military regime controlled by the leaders of the armed forces. In addition, the military leadership contained factions which were manipulated by Suharto as a way of controlling the regime and avoiding coups. During the last decade of the 20th century, the major groupings within the military leadership included one that tended to be identified as "nationalist" and more secular and a second that was more Islamically oriented. By 1998, the "nationalists" were led by General Wiranto and the "Islamic" faction by Major General Prabowo. Lieutenant-General Susilo Bambang Yudhoyono led a third pro-reform group that developed soon after Suharto's resignation.[21] It was this factionalized military that faced the demonstrations marking the beginning of *reformasi* in 1998. However, the continuing strength of the military group is reflected in the fact that Yudhoyono was elected president of the new democracy in 2004 (and re-elected in 2009) and that Prabowo was one of the two leading candidates for the presidency in 2014.

At the beginning of the 21st century, the civilian nationalists, the Muslim organizations, and the military remained the most visible powers in the political system of independent Indonesia. They had all participated in the wars of liberation in the middle of the 20th century, and Indonesian politics since that time has involved the interactions of these three socio-political elites. That whole system, whether viewed as a guided democracy or a New Order, experienced an important transition in the late 1990s that shows both strong continuities with the past and a reconfiguration of politics that provides the foundations for Indonesia as the third-largest democracy in the world.

Reshaping Indonesia as a Democracy

The resignation of Suharto in 1998 marks a significant turning point in the political history of independent Indonesia. From its declared independence in 1945 until 1998, Indonesia had only two rulers, both of whom created authoritarian political systems. In the decade and a half following Suharto's resignation, it had five leaders, each of whom came to power by legally defined means rather than coups, with four of them being elected through increasingly democratic procedures and participating in democratically effective transfers of power.

The end of Suharto's long dictatorship surprised many people, both Indonesian and foreign. However, there were strong indications of the weakness of his regime in the late 1990s. Already in 1996 large demonstrations took place when the government attempted to suppress Megawati Sukarnoputri's PDI-P. These protests were put down with a severity that aroused increased opposition. This was followed by national elections in 1997 which were carefully controlled and gave the usual overwhelming majority of votes to Golkar and Suharto. The clear manipulation of the results added strength to the opposition. At the same time as opposition was gaining visibility, the Asian economic crisis put severe pressures on the Indonesian economy and resulted in the collapse of the currency. Suharto was forced to adopt unpopular economic policies, leading to more protests. In early 1998, student demonstrations erupted in many

universities. Their demands were for both economic reform and the resignation of Suharto. By May, as many as 1,200 people were killed in riots.
Suharto resigned, naming the vice president, Bacharuddin Jusuf (B. J.)
Habibie, as his successor. Protests continued as many saw this move as
a simple continuation of the previous regime, but the Indonesian elites
accepted the change as a step in a transition to more democratic rule.

The transition from Suharto to Habibie was the first of six significant
transition points that show the broad trends that are reshaping Indonesia
as a democracy in the 21st century. The second came quickly in 1999, with
the election of Abd al-Rahman Wahid as president, and the third involved
his replacement by Megawati as president. The elections in 2004, 2009,
and 2014 were similarly important in reflecting the ongoing progression
of Indonesian politics. Examining the experiences of the three major
elites in these transitions can provide insight into the continuities and
changes in political life.

The assumption of leadership by Habibie represented a successful
transfer of power without a coup. Many at the time feared that it was
simply a continuation of the old regime without Suharto, but in the year
following Habibie's assumption of the presidency, significant changes
occurred. During his term, the military's position in the legislature was
reduced, and his administration created the legal structure for competitive political parties and elections. He allowed a referendum in East Timor
that resulted in its independence, and began a process of governmental
decentralization. Although the secession of East Timor was associated
with extreme violence and violations of human rights by the armed forces,
it resolved one of the major separatist issues. In 1999 at the end of his
short term as president, it was possible to ask if he was "the man who
overturned much of the repressive legacy of his predecessor and mentor, Suharto, and brought Indonesia galloping toward free elections and a
new era of democracy" or if he was simply moving "before a tidal wave of
reform that swept all the country's politicians along with it."[22] Whatever
the answers to those questions, major changes did take place during his
presidency, and each of the major power groups participated.

Since this was a transition from a military regime, the role of the
armed forces was critical. Suharto's rule "depended on the support of
the Indonesian military; for this reason, the nonintervention of the military was crucial to the country's transition from nondemocratic rule
and the subsequent consolidation of democracy."[23] Leaders within the
military elite provided support for change of regime. General Wiranto,

the commander of the armed forces in the last months of Suharto's rule, was both armed forces commander and Minister of Defense and Security in Habibie's cabinet. He initiated changes in the military structure, separating the police from the military, and was viewed as a supporter of reform, although he was accused of allowing human rights violations by the army in East Timor and in other military operations. In the 1999 presidential elections, he was a vice presidential candidate, but he withdrew from the contest before the final assembly vote. His subsequent candidacies for president (in 2004) and vice president (in 2009) show his continuing participation in the democratic processes. On each occasion, although he was in a position, especially in 1999, to respond to losing in the electoral process by organizing a coup to continue the role of the military in leading a "guided democracy," he chose to accept the results of the elections.

Other military leaders from the 1990s also played important roles in the transition. Yudhoyono was identified as an advocate of ending the *dwi-fungsi* (the double function) of the military and played a role in the depoliticization of the military. He served in the cabinets of the first three post-Suharto presidents and then won the presidency in 2004. Prabowo was not as prominent in the immediate aftermath of Suharto's resignation because of charges of allowing human rights violations by the armed forces. However, he also became active in electoral politics and was a major candidate in the 2014 presidential elections. An important element in the reshaping of Indonesian democracy was the fact that none of these major military leaders attempted to organize coups to restore the political dominance of the military.

Already in the first transition, the involvement of military officers was increasingly as individual political figures rather than as representatives of the military institution. Similarly, there was a civilianization of Golkar, which had been the party of the armed forces under Suharto. In the Habibie presidency, military reformers like Yudhoyono and Wiranto spoke in terms of a "New Paradigm" for the military, which included cutting links to Golkar.[24] As a political party, Golkar quickly took the role of one party among many competing within a relatively free electoral system. Although it included many who continued to have favorable views of Suharto, it tended to lose its identification with the military. In the 1999 and 2004 elections, Wiranto was a Golkar candidate, but neither Yudhoyono nor Prabowo ran as Golkar candidates when they ran for president.

The civilian nationalist elite continued to present a diversity of views. However, by the time of Suharto's resignation, Megawati Sukarnoputri had become the recognized leader of the political opposition to the military regime. Her PDI-P was the best-organized political group in the country and she had broad popular support. In Habibie's transitional regime, Megawati represented the basic nationalist positions, in contrast to the Islamically identified leaders. She had strong support from socially traditional Muslims and non-Muslims as well as the more secular educated elite. She was viewed as the primary alternative to Habibie, and this support resulted in the PDI-P receiving the most votes (34 percent) in the 1999 parliamentary elections. Golkar received 22 percent of the votes, but Habibie withdrew from candidacy in the subsequent presidential election in the parliament.

A number of religiously identified parties emerged in the context of the new political system set in place by Habibie's election reforms. Some were based on older organizations and others were created by people taking advantage of the new political opportunities. Both NU and Muhammadiyya were represented in newly created parties. The Partai Kebangkitan Bangsa (PKB; the National Awakening Party) was organized by Abd al-Rahman Wahid and was supported by NU. The PKB won the most votes (12 percent) among the Muslim organizational parties. Amien Rais of Muhammadiyya led the Partai Amanat Nasional (PAN; National Mandate Party), which was created soon after Suharto's resignation by a *reformasi* consultative group. PAN's grassroots support came from Muhammadiyya members, but "at the national level" it was "an explicitly nonreligious party with a nationalist and populist agenda," with secularists and Christians as well as Muhammadiyya people among its leadership.[25] The party reflected the pluralist modernism of Amien Rais and the Muhammadiyya tradition. PAN received 7 percent of the votes in the 1999 parliamentary elections, which was enough to enable Amien Rais to be elected chair of the People's Consultative Assembly. The PPP was a continuation of the remnant of the party created in the Suharto era with a conservative program, and it won 10 percent of the votes.

Two more explicitly Islamist parties gained small support and a few seats. The Partai Bulan Bintang (PBB; Crescent Star Party) was the organizational successor to the old Masyumi Party, advocating stricter implementation of Sharia (2 percent of the vote). The Justice Party, reorganized in 2002 as the Prosperous Justice Party (PKS; Partai Keadilan Sejahtera), was created out of campus *dakwah* (religious recruitment) movements by leaders familiar with the Muslim Brotherhood in Egypt. It advocated an Islamist program for "the realization of an Islamic-based system based on Sharia."[26] Although it only gained 1 percent of the votes in 1999, it created the foundations for an independent Muslim political organization that was not dependent upon the popularity of a particular leader.

The change following the resignation of Suharto created a transitional period in which each of the three major elites actively participated. The dominant political role of the military was significantly reduced, with the cooperation of reform-minded military leaders. The new political context opened the way for forty-eight parties to participate in the 1999 elections. Most of the parties were built around strong individual personalities. Two basic dividing lines were the distinction between the *reformasi* activists and those who maintained some sympathy for the previous regime and the line between the more Islamically identified groups and more-secular nationalists. The results of the 1999 parliamentary elections reflected these groupings, with Megawati's party receiving about 34 percent of the votes, Golkar about 22 percent, and the combination of the three largest Muslim parties (PKB, PAN, and PPP) receiving about 30 percent.

The second transition in the democratic reshaping of Indonesian politics took place within the context created by the Habibie-led reforms and the 1999 parliamentary elections. After a short period of intense political activity following the 1999 elections, Abd al-Rahman Wahid became president. Although the election process was accompanied by sometimes-violent demonstrations in the streets, the new political system experienced a transfer of power that was defined within the new democratic electoral framework. In the new system, the president was to be elected by the People's Consultative Assembly (MPR), which was a combination of the elected House of People's Representatives (DPR) and additional members designated by the provinces and specially defined social-civic groups. The parliamentary elections resulted in a seemingly fragmented political situation, but it quickly became clear that all of the major parties were willing to construct alliances across the political dividing lines.

The rivalry between Habibie and Megawati opened the way for the smaller parties to play significant political roles in the MPR deliberations. Amien Rais had been one of the most prominent opponents of Suharto, but his party, PAN, did not gain a strong position in the MPR. As a result, he worked to create a coalition that could be an alternative to PDI-P and Golkar. Under his leadership a flexible grouping emerged, the Central Axis (Poros Tengah), which brought together PAN and the Justice Party and a number of the smaller parties. Similarly, Megawati began to create a working relationship with PKB in an alliance between nationalists and a major religious grouping, and reformists in Golkar worked across party lines.[27]

The actual events of the presidential and vice presidential elections in the MPR illustrate the new realities that had already been created in Indonesian politics. In the organization of the parliamentary assemblies, an alliance between the Central Axis and Golkar resulted in Amien Rais being elected Speaker of the MPR, and a major Golkar leader, Akbar Tanjung, as chair of the DPR. This represented cooperation between the dominant party of the Suharto regime and that party's ideological opponent. The presidential election process began with Habibie and Megawati as the strongest candidates, but the first major action of the MPR was to hear and vote on the presidential "accountability speech" presented by Habibie. When the MPR voted to reject this speech, Habibie's candidacy ended and the opponents of Megawati joined with the Central Axis to nominate Abd al-Rahman Wahid, whose PKB had been an ally of Megawati up to that point.

Abd al-Rahman Wahid won the election by a relatively close vote of 373 to 313, and supporters of Megawati engaged in demonstrations throughout the country. However, Megawati and Abd al-Rahman Wahid quickly joined hands and urged calm. The next day, it was Wahid's PKB, not the PDI-P, that nominated Megawati for the vice presidency, which she won in the following day. The result was a new administration that brought together two of the most influential political leaders in the country, bridging the gap between the secular nationalists and at least a major part of the religious political elite.

In this process, the "armed forces delegation played a reactive, almost passive, role, both in the presidential/vice-presidential elections and in the crucial prior elections of the chairs of parliament [DPR] and assembly [MPR]."[28] General Wiranto declined nominations for the vice presidency, first by Golkar and then by a small alliance of parties. He and other important military leaders joined the new administration but they represented reform positions that involved the further depoliticization of the military institutions.

The new president created a cabinet that included a wide range of the major political figures, and it soon became clear that major divisions existed. After less than two years in office, Wahid was removed from office by the MPR and was replaced by his vice president, Megawati. Observers at the time, as well as his fellow Indonesians, had widely differing views about his leadership qualities. One analyst described him as "the charismatic Muslim intellectual and long-time social democratic activist,"[29] while others emphasized his health problems and recent heart attacks, calling him "a frail and nearly blind Muslim cleric" whose physical weakness could result in a stronger leadership role for Megawati.[30]

The presidency created by this second transition of power faced many challenges, and Wahid was viewed as a weak president, prone to making policy mistakes. An analysis listing a dozen problems facing Wahid's presidency sums up the situation by noting that despite Wahid's weak management skills and "erratic leadership style," the "simplest way of explaining the scope of the problems facing President Wahid . . . is that as Indonesia's first democratically elected president he faced the difficult task of overseeing the fraught process of regime change."[31]

Although he was removed from office by the National Assembly, the period of Wahid's presidency, like Habibie's presidency, continued the democratization process. Wahid was not overthrown by a coup or by some kind of populist revolution. Instead, his presidency was ended by the democratically elected assembly, and the transfer of the presidency to Megawati took place within the framework that had been defined by the *reformasi* political processes. Wahid's presidency came to an end in 2001, but the *reformasi* process continued. The political dynamics of his short term in office helped to ensure that the democratization of Indonesian politics was not stopped.

In the politics created by the second transition, again, the nature of the involvement of the major elites evolved. The changing roles of the military elite may be the most significant. Wahid was able to accomplish a number of things that continued the depoliticization of the military. He appointed the first civilian minister of defense in the history of independent Indonesia and initiated a human rights tribunal to examine the actions of the military in East Timor at the time of the independence referendum. He showed the power of the civilian presidency by forcing the resignation of Wiranto, who had been the coordinating minister of politics and security, because of questions of Wiranto's possible involvement in human rights violations by the military. Observers and political leaders concluded that Wahid had "secured a degree of civilian control over the very institution that had guaranteed General Suharto's dictatorial rule."[32]

The experience of Wiranto provides an important indication of the changing dynamics of the politics of democratization. Active-duty officers in the military viewed the recently retired Wiranto "as a civilian who could be appointed and dismissed by the president like any other cabinet member" and there was "no pro-Wiranto armed forces backlash after the fact."[33]

A similar indication of the changing role for the military came in the last months of Wahid's presidency. As it became clear that the MPR was going to act against him and public demonstrations appeared to threaten security, Wahid threatened to declare a state of emergency and call for new elections. This action was seen as indicating his loss of support among the political and military elites, and military leaders indicated that they would not obey orders to impose state-of-emergency restrictions.[34] In some transitions from military to democratic rule in other countries, the military used declarations of states of emergency as opportunities to return to power, but the Indonesian military leaders did not.

In civilian politics during the Wahid period, no majority party emerged. The alliances that had been created for the 1999 presidential elections were fluid. Wahid was ineffective in maintaining the coalition that had elected him. A number of Wahid's political mistakes alienated Megawati and, as vice president and head of the largest parliamentary party, she was increasingly viewed as the best possible alternative.

Older ideological and policy divisions continued, but they tended to be overshadowed by the short-term political goals of the parties and their leaders. The divisions between the *reformasi* advocates and supporters of the previous political order had already been bridged with the alliance between the Central Axis and Golkar in the 1999 political transition. Similarly, the divisions between the more secular nationalists and the more religious groups faded in the early alliances between Megawati and Wahid and with the later support for Megawati from the PPP, who had strongly opposed her in 1999.

Indonesian politics continued to be managed by the three long-standing elites. Possibly the greatest change visible by the time of the Wahid presidency was in the beginnings of the depoliticization of the military. This development paralleled the change in one of the major political organizations, Golkar. Golkar was initially identified as the party of Suharto supporters and the military. However, as the military became separated from political activity, Golkar itself experienced a significant demilitarization. During the Wahid presidency, Golkar came to represent a civilian party that was secular and nationalist and maintained some sympathies for the policies of the guided democracy of Suharto's New Order. It was able to maintain a relatively strong organization at the local level and was different from other major parties in that it was not built around the leadership of a single strong personality.

The old secular nationalist elite continued largely to identify with Megawati but, in political terms, it was not able to expand its base of support beyond the core that had voted for the PDI-P in the 1999 elections. The Islamically identified parties remained divided and, in the end, Wahid received support primarily from his own party and the NU. In this context, the old elites continued to be socially and intellectually identifiable, but their activities and organizations reflected the new fluidity of Indonesian politics.

The removal of Wahid from office in July 2001, followed by his replacement as president by Megawati, is the third major transition in Indonesian contemporary politics. Again, the process of the transfer of power took place within the democratic framework defined by the *reformasi* program. Wahid urged his supporters not to respond with violent demonstrations, and he avoided public confrontations by leaving the country for medical treatment.

Almost immediately after the removal of Wahid, the Assembly elected Hamza Haz as the vice president. This action brought Megawati together with the head of one of her most critical opponents in 1999. Haz was head of the PPP and had campaigned strongly against her, arguing that it was not appropriate for a woman to lead a Muslim country. The PDI-P did not contest his election, and the new government was formed, bringing together the major secular nationalist party and the strongest conservative Islamic party at the top.

The presidency of Megawati resulting from this third transition continued the process of democratizing the Indonesian political system. The presidency and the parliament themselves were reshaped. The MPR approved constitutional amendments that shifted the power to elect the president and vice president from the Assembly to direct national elections, with elections set for 2004. The MPR also redefined the parliament itself, eliminating non-elected members and ending seats designated for the military. The new electoral process was a two-step process, with presidential elections coming after national parliamentary elections. Presidential candidates needed to be nominated by parties or coalitions of parties that had gained 3 percent of the parliamentary seats or 5 percent of votes cast. If a presidential candidate did not receive more than 50 percent of the vote, a runoff election between the two candidates receiving the most votes was required. These changes were more clear steps away from the authoritarian guided democracy of the Suharto era.

Once this new system was defined, competition among major political leaders and groups developed in new ways. Many assumed that Megawati was in the best position to win in a direct general election, given the strength of the PDI-P and her incumbency. However, other major parties began to position themselves for the direct election campaigns, and some new parties were formed in support of possible candidates. The most important of these new groups was the Partai Demokrat (PD) which was "founded in 2001 as a presidential campaign vehicle for General (retired) Susilo Bambang Yudhoyono."[35] Twenty-four parties were qualified to participate in the 2004 parliamentary elections, and seventeen won seats in the new assembly. As a result, coalitions and party alliances continued to be the basic units for political action.

During the Megawati presidency, issues related to the role of Islam in Indonesian politics continued to be debated. Terrorism by extremist Muslim groups, globally and then in Indonesia, became an important concern for her administration. The destruction of the World Trade Center in New York City by al-Qaeda-affiliated terrorists in September 2001, soon after her election as president, raised questions about radical Islamist groups in Indonesia. Indonesian leaders tended to ignore warnings from Asian and Western intelligence agencies that the Jemaah Islamiyah (JI) in Indonesia had operational ties with al-Qaeda. Vice President Hamzah Haz announced that there were no terrorists in Indonesia and publicly demonstrated his support for Abu Bakar Ba'asyir, identified as the spiritual leader of JI.[36] However, this situation changed dramatically in October 2002, when JI-related terrorists exploded bombs in nightclubs in Bali, killing almost two hundred people. Megawati responded quickly with antiterrorist measures for coordinated security and tougher laws regarding the detention of suspects and punishments.

The response to the Bali and subsequent attacks shows an important aspect of the dynamics of the democratization processes in Indonesia. Many people remembered that Suharto had used the military to suppress Islamist activism but "despite fears that a tough approach toward suspected terrorists would provoke an Islamist backlash, none occurred."[37] Instead, leaders of major Muslim organizations and parties condemned the violence and cooperated in efforts to prevent further terrorist acts. These actions emphasized the fact that while the religious groups were strong advocates of Islamic foundations for policy, they were not militant Islamists.

The Muslim but not Islamist nature of the major religious organizations was also clearly expressed in some parliamentary debates. The vice president and his party, the PPP, are advocates of a greater recognition of Sharia by the Indonesian state and introduced legislation in the parliament to give formal recognition to Islamic law. However, both the NU and the Muhammadiyya (and their associated parties) opposed the measure, which was then withdrawn. This incident affirms the continued acceptance of Pancasila as the foundation for policy with regard to religion. In concrete terms, this acceptance is shown in the results of the 2004 elections. The four explicitly Islamist parties won about 20 percent of the vote, while the parties affirming Pancasila (the secular nationalists and Islamic-but-not-Islamist PKB and PAN) won almost 70 percent.[38]

Megawati also faced continued pressure from regional separatist movements. Separatist movements had challenged the central government from the time of independence, and governments had varying degrees of success in reducing conflicts. However, the only region to leave Indonesia and create an independent state was East Timor, which had been allowed to secede following the referendum in the time of Habibie. Megawati's government had some success in reducing regional conflict in Maluku and Sulewasi by negotiations and suppression of Muslim militant groups in those areas. In Aceh, a long-standing separatist movement in the territories of a precolonial sultanate in Sumatra was led by the Free Aceh Movement (GAM; Garakan Aceh Merdeka). Negotiations for regional autonomy proceeded, but during 2003, military conflict resumed. However, this situation was suddenly and cruelly transformed in December 2004, when a major tsunami destroyed much of Aceh (and many other places in Southeast Asia). The rebuilding of society in the region brought government forces and GAM together in a major common effort through the creation of a structure of regional autonomy within the framework of the Indonesian national state.

In the politics created by the third transition, the nature of involvement by the three elites continued to develop. The military continued to play important roles in politics and governance. The counterterror campaigns and the suppression of separatist movements required active military involvement. However, the military leadership did not use these issues to become more directly involved in politics. Political involvement of retired military officers was within the framework of civilian coalition politics. In the first round of the 2004 presidential election, Golkar nominated Wiranto, but Wiranto chose as his vice presidential running mate a brother of Abd al-Rahman Wahid, who was not running because of medical problems. The other former military officer who ran for the presidency was Yudhoyono, who was the candidate of the small Partai Demokrat. In the runoff election, which was between Megawati and Yudhoyono, Golkar leadership gave its support to Megawati, the former *reformasi* rival of the party, rather than supporting Yudhoyono, the retired military officer.

Both the old nationalist elite and the religious organizations remained prominent sources of political leadership, but affiliations and alliances were fluid. A core group of old-style nationalists provided the basic support for Megawati, but many were attracted to the reformist ideas of Yudhoyono, who also gained support from religious groups. The vision of a unified national Indonesia guided by Pancasila principles continued to be the foundation for political action by the nationalists, regardless of which specific candidate, party, or program they supported.

The religious groups were similarly fluid in their alliances while adhering to the ideal of a polity explicitly guided by Islamic principles. The largest groups—NU and Muhammadiyya—interpreted this vision within the framework of Pancasila, and only smaller parties, like the PPP, advocated more explicit recognition of Sharia. By the time of the elections that ended Megawati's presidency, the Islamists divided their support, with the PPP supporting Megawati and the PKS and PBB supporting Yudhoyono. This situation reflects the continuing fluidity of political positions, even among the more ideological Muslim groups. This sets even the political Islamists apart from the extremist militants in the groups like JI.

The first three post-Suharto presidencies provided the frameworks for the reshaping of Indonesia as a democracy. Under the leadership of Habibie, Wahid, and Megawati, the transition from an authoritarian military regime to a popularly elected presidential-parliamentary system took place. One of the most important parts of this era of transition was the successful transfers of power. Each of the three presidents hoped to continue their terms in office but lost their positions through democratic processes. They set an important precedent of accepting loss of position rather than attempting to remain in power by extralegal means. An important part of any democratization process is the acceptance of results of elections by losing candidates, and Habibie, Wahid, and Megawati added to the strength of democratization in Indonesia by their actions.

Both the resulting system and the creative process were remarkably inclusive. Although the Suharto regime was rejected, the party that initially represented that regime, Golkar, was not abolished but became a participating and important political actor. The military as an institution was significantly depoliticized without rejecting former military officers as part of the political leadership. The old civilian nationalist elite continued to be the core of the political system without creating an old-style secular one-party state, and the religious organizational elite was a significant part of political society, even providing an elected president, without trying to impose an Islamist "religiocracy."[39]

Beyond Post-Suharto Politics

The elections in 2004 begin a new era in the post-Suharto political history of Indonesia. The three sets of national elections in 2004, 2009, and 2014 reflect the dynamic development of electoral democracy and they show the continuing transitions of political life. As in the first three post-Suharto transition points, three groupings—the nationalist elites, the religious organizations, and the military—continue to be central. However, in the institutions and modes of action that developed in the years immediately following the end of the Suharto regime, new groups and new patterns of operation among the older groups began to reshape Indonesian politics.

The transition from the presidency of Megawati to Yudhoyono, as a fourth transition following the end of the Suharto regime, can be considered to be the end of "post-Suharto" politics. The dynamism of the *reformasi* movement had succeeded in replacing an authoritarian regime with a regime that was increasingly recognized as the world's third-largest democracy. Freedom House, for example, changed its classification of Indonesia from "partly free" to "free" in its 2006 report.[40] The Suharto regime had consistently been classified as "not free," while the era of post-Suharto *reformasi* (1999–2005) had been recognized as "partly free." The issues and challenges of the *reformasi* era were no longer the major issues in Indonesian politics. The basic questions involved defining institutions and resolving older issues like regional separatism or the political role of Islam within the framework of increasing democratization.

During 2004, Indonesia had three national elections and the results of those elections show the complexity of the new politics. In the first elections, for the parliament, the party that won the largest number of votes and the most parliamentary seats was Golkar (21.58 percent). The results confirmed the success of the party in separating itself from the opposition to the old authoritarianism while maintaining a sense of conservative—and relatively secular—nationalism. It had become an important element in the new politics. The party receiving the second largest number of votes and seats was Megawati's PDI-P. However, the results showed a significant erosion of support, with the party only gaining 18.5 percent of the vote, in contrast to the 34 percent received in the 1999 elections.

Five religious organizational parties that participated in both the 1999 and 2004 elections combined received about the same proportion of the vote in both elections, from 33.8 percent in 1999 to 35.1 percent in 2004. However, a slight shift was visible in the results, with the old larger parties—PKB, PPP, and PAN—receiving a smaller proportion and the reorganized and renamed Prosperous Justice Party (PKS, formerly the Justice Party) jumping from 1 percent to more than 7 percent of the vote.

The major new addition was the Partai Demokrat (PD) of Yudhoyono. The PD received enough votes (7.5 percent) to make it eligible to nominate a presidential candidate. This party was identified with a respected retired general with a reputation for being a reformist. It was nationalist in its appeal and could draw from supporters of the PDI-P and Golkar. Although it had only a small parliamentary delegation, the popularity of its leader gave it an appeal beyond the boundaries of party affiliation.

The subsequent presidential elections in 2004 show the continuing fluidity of political alliances that tended to ignore the older factional divisions of *reformasi* and Suharto's New Order or the secular-religious differences. In the first round of elections, the slates reflect the shifting alliances. As noted above, Golkar nominated a retired general, Wiranto, who chose as his running mate the brother of Abd al-Rahman Wahid, while Megawati chose the head of NU, Hasyim Muzadi. These choices show the importance of the NU/ PKB voters and the willingness to join nationalist with religious blocs. Amien Rais was the PAN candidate, running with a leader of the national farmers' association. The new party, PD, was created around the candidacy of Yudhoyono, who ran with a prominent businessman who was a Golkar leader, but whose candidacy was not supported by Golkar. In the runoff election between Megawati and Yudhoyono, alliances were quickly formed, again reflecting practical political concerns rather than ideological positions. The National Coalition joined Golkar and PPP together with PDI-P to support Megawati, while in the People's Coalition, the Islamic parties of PKS, PBB, and PAN joined the PD in support of Yudhoyono. Although the National Coalition controlled almost half of the seats in parliament, Yudhoyono won the election with more than 60 percent of the votes.

At the beginning of Yudhoyono's presidency, the relations between the opposition, which had substantial control of parliament, and the president were strained, and this constrained what Yudhoyono could do. However, during 2005 a number of developments strengthened the president's position. His vice president, Muhammad Jusuf Kalla, was elected head of Golkar, which brought an end to Megawati's National Coalition. In dealing with the problems created by separatist movements, an agreement was reached with GAM, the separatist organization in Aceh in the wake of the 2004 tsunami that destroyed much of Aceh. By 2006, it was possible to hold district and local elections which were won by GAM leaders, resolving many of the sources of conflict between that region and the central government.

The elections in Aceh can be seen as a part of the trend toward decentralization of government. Laws had been passed initiating significant decentralization already during Habibie's presidency, and the process continued slowly in the following years. In 2005, "nationwide democratic election of local government executives" took place "for the first time in Indonesian history."[41] The development of independent local and regional politics opened the way for people outside of the old elites to gain political power. The GAM victory in Aceh, for example, was viewed on the provincial level as resulting "from deep dissatisfaction with the older parties and their candidates, who were seen as serving the interests of a narrow elite."[42] Locally elected executives could gain national visibility, as is shown by the rise of Joko Widodo from being a mayor to serving as governor of Jakarta and winning the presidency in 2014.

During Yudhoyono's first term as president, he continued to guide some important long-term reforms. One of the major sources of discontent with government was and continues to be high levels of corruption by government officials. All of the post-Suharto presidents campaigned on anti-corruption platforms, but the popular view was that little progress had been made and few important politicians had been convicted. Yudhoyono continued the anti-corruption efforts with some limited success, although corruption remains a major problem. In the first Corruption Perception Index compiled by Transparency International in 1995, Indonesia ranked last, forty-first out of forty-one countries. Over the years there was some small improvement in its ranking. In 2003, Indonesia was 122nd out of 133 countries surveyed, and in 2013 it was 114th out of 177 countries.[43] In every parliamentary and presidential election since 1998, corruption has been a campaign issue.

Greater progress was made during Yudhoyono's first term in the continuing depoliticization of the military. The withdrawal of the armed forces from civilian business operations continued, but at a slow pace. Appointment of reformist officers to high posts in the Armed Forces of Indonesia (TNI) gave some strength to the ongoing, if gradual, transformation of the military's role in state and society.

The growing importance of a new style of politics during Yudhoyono's presidency is at the heart of the fluid coalitions and ongoing reforms. One characteristic of this new style is the changing role of Islam in the political rhetoric and party programs. The various election alliances of leaders and parties reflect a politically effective centrism which was neither secularist nor Islamist. The "centrist tendencies reflect an increasing blend of Islamic values and nationalist convictions in party politics, with Islamic parties becoming more pluralist and previously secular parties opening up to devout Muslim voters."[44] The positions of Yudhoyono's PD are the best example of this "moderate centrist" style which makes it "difficult to discern a consistent ideology in the party's policies."[45] The non-ideological political style can be seen in new movements in many parts of the Muslim world in the 21st century and, in Indonesia, is shaped by the popular acceptance of the pluralism of Pancasila.

A second characteristic of the emerging political style is that the older identification of socio-communal identity with political party identity was weakening. There was a

weakening of an old political pattern known by the Indonesian term of *aliran* (stream), by which ordinary voters identified with various social-cultural groups in Indonesian society. The decline of *aliran*-based voting and the rise of a new model drawing on modern campaigning techniques, the media, image-building, and (to a lesser extent) promises of economic and policy performance was already apparent in 2004. It became even more obvious in 2009.[46]

These changes did not eliminate the influence and power of the old nationalist elite, the religious organizations, and the military, but they did open the possibility for the emergence of new political forces in Indonesian politics along with necessitating new approaches in politics on the part of the old elites. The success of Yudhoyono's PD in 2004 and 2009 reflect these changes, and the election of Joko Widodo in 2014 confirmed them.

The elections of 2009 mark a fifth important transition in Indonesian politics, emphasizing the change from "post-Suharto politics" to an era of new democratization. In 2009, Yudhoyono won a second term in what many people considered a landslide victory. Although he faced well-known and politically powerful opponents, he won more than 60 percent of the popular vote in the first round of the elections, eliminating the need for a runoff election. Although his political party gained the largest number of votes in the 2009 parliamentary elections, it received only about 21 percent. In electing Yudhoyono to a second term, Indonesia was not opening the path for a return to an authoritarian presidency. It was confirming a more stable democratic path, with the expectation that the 2014 elections would involve the election of a new president. Indonesia was confirming the success of the processes of democratization set in motion by the overthrow of Suharto.

The major issues of Yudhoyono's second term involve operational aspects of an increasingly established democratic system, rather than competitions between democratic reformers and opposition to their reforms. In assessing the legacy of Yudhoyono's presidency, Edward Aspinall argued in 2014 that the Yudhoyono decade is "a period of both consolidation of democracy but also one of stasis. Indonesia in these years moved beyond the turbulence of the democratic transition proper (1998–2004), and its new democratic system settled into place."[47]

The legacy of Yudhoyono's second term reflects the greater normality of the major political issues. There were important achievements but overall the results were mixed. The campaign against political corruption continued, and the Corruption Eradication Commission prosecuted and convicted many high-level officials, including leaders in Yudhoyono's own party. However, patronage and corruption were important incentives for elite political participation. "Corrupt payments and 'money politics' have become critical components in the way the political system works."[48] As a result, as measured by Transparency International's Corruption Transparency Index, Indonesia continues to be ranked among those countries with high rates of corruption, while it gets a positive "free" rating from Freedom House. The two aspects of political life may, in the case of Indonesia, be complementary.

Similarly, the emerging centrism on broad issues relating to Islam and politics faced a challenge from the rise of violent attacks on religious minorities by extremists. Groups like the Islamic Defenders' Front (FPI; Front Pembela Islam) and Laskar Jihad (LJ) engaged in vigilante activities and had organized paramilitary forces. Following the overthrow of Suharto, such groups gained greater visibility.[49] During the presidency of Yudhoyono, there were a growing number of attacks on Christians and Muslim minority groups like the Shi`ism and the Ahmadiyah. Actions like a controversial ministerial decree banning the public practice of their faith by Ahmadiyah followers indicated a governmental position of reduced toleration for religious diversity.[50] The Setara Institute, a nongovernmental human rights watchdog group issued a report on the Yudhoyono era and entitled the report *Stagnation on Freedom of Religion*, stating that the title was "representative" for "describing the leadership performance of Susilo Bambang Yudhoyono" who did not make "any achievement in promoting and protecting freedom of religion/belief."[51] In a report on an increase of cases of religious intolerance in 2013, the Institute noted that the "government's slow response was claimed as the cause of increasing cases of intolerance."[52] However, major Muslim leaders, along with the more secular nationalists, condemned the violence and continued to affirm their support for Pancasila and religious freedom.

Military reforms continued under the leadership of the retired reformist general Yudhoyono, but progress was mixed. The ongoing reduction of business and commercial activities by the armed forces was maintained, but military leaders still had strong positions in local affairs in many parts of the country. In terms of national politics, retired military leaders had significant influence, but their importance was related to their actions as competitive civilian politicians rather than as representatives of the military institutions.

By the end of the first decade after the overthrow of Suharto, retired military officers were active in a number of parties and some, like Yudhoyono, were central in the creation of new parties. The identification of the military with Golkar was no longer a political reality. The new parties were not military in orientation and represented a variety of political positions. Gerindra was established as the political vehicle for Prabowo and Hanura for Wiranto. Both presented nationalist ideals and were secular in orientation.

The political activism of retired military officers fit into the broader patterns of political evolution in the contexts of democratization. The centrist style of politics is visible among all three of the old political elite groups—the nationalists, the Muslim organizations, and the military. The emerging political system involved the continuation of a wide diversity of political organizations and identifiable interest groups. The result of the diversity is that no single group has been able to create a clear majority in government (or in societal matters as well), so that the possible difficulties of majoritarian domination do not exist. Despite Yudhoyono's "landslide victory" in 2009, he did not have the parliamentary or partisan base to establish a politically dominant position. All major political forces in Indonesia must engage in political alliances and coalitions to have effective power. As a result, politics involves a constantly shifting "partisan duality" involving the creation of "two broad, internally distinct political groupings,"[53] In this system, there is no "Islamic bloc" or "secular-nationalist bloc" (or singular military lobby). Instead, each of the old elite groupings is divided, opening the way for political alliances across the older sociopolitical boundaries.

The elections of 2014 provide another transition point (the sixth transition mentioned in the introduction) in the dynamic evolution of Indonesian politics. In the parliamentary elections, a wide range of parties competed, with no party winning more than 20 percent. Again, PDI-P of Megawati (about 20 percent) and Golkar (about 15 percent) gained the most votes and parliamentary seats. The party of Yudhoyono (PD) gained about 10 percent of the votes, only half of what it had received in 2009. The religious parties gained a combined total of 32 percent, with the most successful being PKB (9 percent), the party associated with NU, and PAN (7.5 percent), associated with Muhammadiyya. The more strictly Islamist parties won about 15 percent.

The results of the parliamentary elections show the continuing core support by the old-style nationalist elite for Megawati and PDI-P politics, although this support does not provide a base for a majority party. Civilianized Golkar has a similar record of support from a core of supporters. However, by the second decade of the 21st century, this Golkar core of voters is about the same as the core support for the combined smaller Islamist parties (PKS, PPP, PBB).

Yudhoyono's Partai Demokrat (PD) represented a new political element. Although personalities played important roles in all of the parties, the nationalist and religious parties had a programmatic or ideological identity along with the major individual leaders. The PKB, for example, was able to survive the international divisions resulting from the removal of Wahid from the presidency and then later survived the death of Wahid in 2009. The PD was created as a personality-based party and has a pragmatic, centrist identity built around the political abilities of Yudhoyono. Retired generals Prabowo and Wiranto are also the central figures in parties that are more identified with them and their political style than with any programmatic or ideological identity. Their parties competed in the 2009 elections and, at the time, it was noted that the "modest successes of Wiranto and, especially, Prabowo show that authoritarian political actors are not persona non grata in Indonesian democracy."[54]

In 2014, Prabowo's party, Gerindra, won the third-largest number of votes (11.8 percent), and he became the candidate of one of the two coalitions that present nominations in the presidential election. Prabowo is frequently described in terms of his ties with the Suharto regime. He was a major military leader in the 1990s and was a son-in-law of Suharto. He established his own political party when Golkar did not nominate him for president, and in 2009 he was Megawati's running mate in the presidential elections. By 2014 he had become an active participant in the shifting political alliances of the time. As a presidential candidate in that year, he was supported by a wide range of parties, including Golkar and PAN. Prabowo reflects the post-Suharto political realities of Indonesia.

The second major presidential candidate in 2014 was Joko ("Jokowi") Widodo, who reflects the new emerging political realities. He began as an elected city mayor, within the political system created by *reformasi*. He is most frequently described as being distinct among the national political leaders by his lack of any organizational or institutional affiliation with the Suharto regime. He was not even a notable participant in the *reformasi* activities that brought an end to Suharto's rule. The description in *The Economist* reflects a broad consensus: "Jokowi was elected as a new sort of leader for Indonesia: young(ish), pragmatic, approachable and to all appearances untainted by corruption. Propelled by cohorts of younger, technologically sophisticated voters, he rose to prominence not through party ranks but on a record of constituent service and good governance."[55] Shortly after Jokowi's election, Michael Vatikiotis wrote in the *Straits Times*, "The political transition under way as a result of Mr. Joko Widodo's election victory in July is breaking new political ground in Indonesia and showing just how far the country has developed as a democracy in 17 years."[56]

In the new post-2014 era, the older-style elites still have great power but their positions have changed significantly since the overthrow of Suharto. Jokowi could not have been a candidate without the nomination of a major party. He was nominated by Megawati's PDI-P, after she decided not to run again, and was supported by a diverse coalition that included Hanura, the party of retired general Wiranto, who had also decided not to run.

Jokowi's running mate was Jusuf Kalla, who had been vice president during Yudhoyono's first term and was Golkar's unsuccessful candidate for president in 2009. These arrangements show the continuing centrality of the old nationalist elite, as those older leaders adapt to the new generation of Indonesians.

Similarly, the religious organizations have maintained their political positions at least as well as the nationalists. The NU and Muhammadiyya, with their broad infrastructures of schools, mosques, and social facilities throughout the country, remain a social force. Increasingly, Indonesian Muslim scholars and intellectuals are becoming influential in the broader world of Islam.

The political role of the military has been transformed since the days of Suharto. Early in 2013, there were some rumors of coups at a point when Yudhoyono's popularity waned,[57] but they had little credibility. Some in the military continue to think that the military might need to be active in protecting the country from religious extremism and corruption. Juwono Sudarsono, a former defense minister, stated, "The army may have to come forward and make sure that democracy works."[58] However, military leadership has been quite consistently reformist and when former military leaders have become politically active it is as participants in civilian electoral politics.

The 2014 presidential election campaign provided an arena in which the nature of Indonesian democracy was debated. Prabowo and Jokowi did not have significantly visible ideological differences. Instead, the contrasts that they presented were in the type of democracy that they presented and tended to represent. Prabowo presented a style of democratic governance that reflected the long history of management of the state by elites. He argued that "the current form of democracy in Indonesia suffered from a lack of firm leadership" and that it is the elite "who have to change the system and they must."[59] He said that "if he was elected president, he would work with the country's best and brightest minds to realize a better version of democracy for the country."[60] This approach was a call for a return to the spirit if not the structure of the guided democracies of both Suharto and Sukarno.

Jokowi's style of leadership as a mayor and as governor of Jakarta was a more populist approach. He emphasized listening to the people and learning what they wanted and needed. His approach was problem-solving rather than ideological. As governor he "overhauled tax collection in Jakarta, instituted a health-card system for the poor," took "the unusual step of forcing civil servants to come to the office on time," and began many other ambitious improvements in social and economic infrastructure.[61] During the election campaign his "trademark 'blusukan' style of campaigning—impromptu visits to marketplaces, villages and poor urban neighborhoods, where he would meet residents, laugh and joke with them, and talk with them about their lives, their troubles and their aspirations—was deliberately pitched to underline how he differed from typical elite politicians."[62] This style was in sharp contrast to the aristocratic campaign style of Prabowo.

With Jokowi's victory, a new political generation began to emerge in Indonesia. The victory of the populist candidate over the older-style politician reflected the changes in Indonesian society itself in the first decade of the 21st century. In 1998, when Suharto resigned, less than 40 percent of the total population was urban and almost two-thirds was rural. By 2011, the majority of the total population was urban.[63] Similarly, there was a significant growth of an economic middle class with modern urban aspirations and expectations. In 2012, a Bank Indonesia survey estimated that 60.9 percent of the population was middle class.[64] The new urban middle class was creating a public arena for politics and culture quite different from the old public sphere, in which an aristocratic elite could guide the general population. As a result, it is possible to view the elections of 2014 as the climax of the processes of democratization that started with the *reformasi* movement, and also as the beginning of a new era of Indonesian politics.

Conclusion: Possible Lessons

The Indonesian experience of transition from an authoritarian military regime to a functioning democracy is an interesting case study. It may or may not be a model for others, like the Arab Spring movements. However, some aspects of the Indonesian developments can provide informative examples of ways that such democratizing transitions can take place without experiencing what Huntington identified as "reverse waves" in which "countries that had previously made the transition to democracy reverted to nondemocratic rule."[65]

An important part of the democratization experience is the actions of the existing leadership elites in Indonesia. In an analysis in 2014 of the democratization process, Edward Aspinall argues that "one source of the robust democracy is the very broad elite buy-in that it has achieved. Unlike in some countries, most major elite groups support the democratic system. Most aim to participate in its democratic institutions in order to gain influence over policy-making and access to the government's patronage resources."[66] The three elites—the nationalists, the religious organizations, and the military—participated in coalitions and alliances that shaped Indonesia politics after the fall of Suharto.

Old rivalries were bridged over in ways that made continuing democratization possible. Specifically, the old, relatively secular nationalists did not hesitate in the *reformasi* and post-*reformasi* periods to join with major Islamic organizations and even to work with explicitly Islamist groups. Instead, over time, the nationalists utilized the Pancasila traditions to lessen the secularist-religionist tensions that existed in many other countries in the process of democratization.

Similarly, the groupings that were directly identified as Islamic or religious did not insist upon religiocratic policies and were willing to compromise. Abd al-Rahman Wahid, the former head of the largest Islamic association in Indonesia (and possibly in the world) was an active participant in *reformasi* politics. Even conservative Islamists like the PPP found that they could work with more secular nationalists like Megawati.

An additional element of political inclusiveness is the remarkable survival of Golkar, the party which had been the dominating political voice of the authoritarian military regime. The *reformasi* governments did not force the dissolution of the party nor did those governments exclude people who had held office in the Suharto era. There was no "reign of terror" to eliminate the people associated with the old regime. Instead, Golkar was able to transform itself into an effectively competitive party in the new democratic context. The country continued to avail itself of the services of many talented and experienced people that might otherwise have been unavailable.

Finally, the evolving participation of the military was critical to the relative success of the democratization process. Even when presented with the opportunity to resume control through the proclamation of a state of emergency during the presidency of Wahid, they did not do so. Instead, the major military leaders were active themselves in the depoliticization of the armed forces. When military leaders chose to act directly in politics, they did so as retired officers who were civilian participants.

Indonesia might (or might not) be a model for other countries to follow as they pursue democratization. However, Indonesia is an important example of how the transition from authoritarian military rule to democracy can take place without inciting reverse waves or eliminating important groups of people.

6

Senegal

DEMOCRACY AND THE POSTCOLONIAL STATE

> We have shown to the world our democracy is mature.
> I will be president of all Senegalese.
>
> MACKY SALL, winner of the 2012 presidential
> election in Senegal[1]

> Senegal, in a transparent election, has proven once
> again that it is and remains a great democracy,
> a great country.
>
> PRESS SECRETARY OF ABDOULAYE WADE, incumbent
> president defeated in 2012[2]

WHEN SENEGALESE PRESIDENT Abdoulaye Wade called Macky Sall to concede defeat in the 2012 presidenti al elections, people in Senegal and around the world recognized this act as a confirmation of democracy in Senegal. The electoral defeat of an incumbent president and the successful transfer of power to an opposition leader is a clear sign of an effectively functioning democracy. Discussions of democracy in the Muslim world sometimes note the democratic experience of Senegal, usually to identify it, with little explanation, as an exception among Muslim-majority countries. Senegal is also exceptional in being the only country in West Africa, and one of the few in Africa as a whole, that has not experienced direct military rule. From the time of gaining independence in 1960 into the second decade of the 21st century, civilians have ruled Senegal.

Senegal's experience is significant because it has many of the sociopolitical elements that in other countries regularly lead to political instability and authoritarian rule. It is not ethnically homogeneous. The largest ethnic group in the country is the Wolof, with about 43.3 percent of the population. Other major groups include the Pulaar/

Tukulor (23.8 percent), Serer (14.7 percent), and Jola (Diola; 3.7 percent).[3] Similarly, although an overwhelming majority of Senegalese are Muslim (90–95 percent), many Senegalese belong to one of three major Muslim organizations with strong and distinct identities, and there is a small (5 percent) but influential Christian minority. However, ethnic and religious organizational conflicts were not major factors in the evolution of the Senegalese political system in the 20th and 21st centuries, although ethnic and religious identities played, and continue to play, important roles in Senegalese politics.

An urban educated elite is the core of the modern Senegalese state. People in this elite have ethnic and religious identities but tend to be Francophone and relatively secular in attitude. French language provides an effective medium "for the strengthening of ties within the élite, between persons of a range of ethnic and linguistic origins."[4] During the 20th century, this elite developed a sense of a "Senegalese" identity, which by the 21st century became a major part of political life. An Afrobarometer survey from 2008 noted a strong sense of Senegalese identity. The survey posed the following question: "Let us suppose that you had to choose between being a Senegalese and being a _____ (R[espondant]'s Ethnic Group). Which of the following best expresses your feelings?" Only 16 percent responded "I feel only (ethnic group)" or "I feel more (ethnic group) than Senegalese," while 55 percent said "I feel more Senegalese than (ethnic group)" (8 percent) or "I feel only Senegalese" (47 percent).[5] This strong sense of a Senegalese identity did not reduce the attachment to religion, since 95 percent of the respondents also said that religion was "very important" in their lives.[6]

The complex mixture of ethnic, religious, and "national" loyalties provides an important framework for the evolution of politics in Senegal. Major organizations and social groupings shaped the nature of the state as they interacted with each other. The urban civilian elite and leaders of major religious organizations with large rural followings were central to Senegalese sociopolitical history, while ethnic chiefs and military leaders played important but secondary roles. By the time of independence in 1960, each of these groupings had well-established positions and traditions in Senegalese society. In the era of independence, their changing political roles and the evolution of Senegalese democracy can be traced through the history of the major national elections. For this analysis, the evolution of these major groupings will be examined, providing a foundation for the discussion of the development of the Senegalese political system. The elections of 2012 provide a point of summary for the emergence of Senegal as an active Muslim-majority democracy.

The Senegalese Sociopolitical Framework

Political life in the Senegambia region (the area along and between the Senegal and Gambia Rivers) has deep historical roots. A variety of states developed in medieval times, and these states and their economies already were part of global commercial networks by the 15th century. Relations with the Portuguese and then British and French developed and involved the Senegambia in the Atlantic slave trade. By the end of the 18th century, French establishments along the coast became an important part of local political life. The expansion of French influence and control brought both the Senegalese coast and its hinterland into the French Empire by the beginning of the 20th century. French rule ended with Senegalese independence in 1960. French colonial rule created important foundations for the emergence of a democratic political system in the country.

The evolution of Senegal's political system since independence can be traced by looking at the major elections and the presidents (and parliaments) that they brought into office. The first president was Leopold Senghor, who had emerged as the leading political figure during the 1950s. He was elected and re-elected until his voluntary retirement in 1980. The second political era was the presidency of Abdou Diouf, who succeeded Senghor in 1980 and remained president until he lost the elections of 2000. He was defeated by Abdoulaye Wade, who served until he was defeated in elections and replaced by Macky Sall in 2012. The four presidencies reflect the different styles of democratization since the gaining of independence.

Four groupings have helped to shape Senegalese political life—ethnic groups and their chiefs, major religious organizations, the military, and an urban educated elite. Each of these groups has important foundations in the history of the region that became independent Senegal. By the time of independence in 1960, their roles were changing but their traditions set important patterns for their involvement and influence in the political processes of the independence era.

Major ethnic groups like the Wolof and Serer have long histories in the Senegambia region. West Africa had seen the rise and decline of major imperial states of Ghana, Mali, and Songhay, and the rise of smaller polities built by local ethnic warlords and networks of merchants. Already by the 13th and 14th centuries, rulers of Wolof (Jolof) states are noted as important parts of the politics of the region. In the late 15th century, Jolof rulers and merchants established close commercial and diplomatic ties with Portugal. In the context of a dynastic conflict, a Jolof ruler converted to Christianity in 1488 and received Portuguese support. Senegambia, along with much of coastal West Africa, became actively involved in the emerging global trade networks of the era of the "first," pre-Industrial Age, globalization.[7]

In the time before the development of the large-scale Atlantic slave trade of the 17th and 18th centuries, states in the Senegambia region created strong traditions of polities based on ethnic groups and warrior rulers. Particular dynasties rose and fell, but the various ethnic groups continued to provide important foundations for support for rulers of the major states. The slave trade had important economic and societal consequences but it did not destroy the basic pattern of ethnic-warrior states in the region. In the 19th century, an important part of the political history of the region was the interactions between the old ethno-political elites in various smaller states and increasingly activist Muslim organizations and then, later in the century, their relations with expanding French imperialist claims.[8]

As the French established control over Senegal, they worked with many local rulers, incorporating them into the imperial administrative structures. By World War I, in much of western Senegal "the chief had become a professional bureaucrat . . . In effect, the traditional state had been incorporated into the French bureaucratic state"; but that did not mean "that the state ceased to exist or that the chiefs became faceless expressions of the administrator's will."[9]

By the time of independence, the association with the imperialist state undermined the legitimacy of the old ethnic political traditions. An important characteristic of the rise of nationalist sentiments was that nationalist leaders did not emphasize populist appeals to ethnic loyalty or ethnic political traditions. French policy and the experiences of the "chieftaincies" were an important element in the non-politicization of ethnicity in Senegal. Despite the existence of multiple ethnic groups, the political parties that shaped Senegalese politics before and after independence were not defined in ethnic terms. Ethnicity is significant in terms of Senegal's cultural identity, but it has not defined important societal or political cleavages. This situation helps Senegal avoid some of the problems of democracy in ethnically diverse societies.

Muslim organizations are a second major element in the shaping of Senegalese politics. In the era of electoral politics after independence, almost half of the population belonged to the Tijaniyya Tariqa and about 40 percent were Murids. These organizations did not form political parties but their endorsement (or non-endorsement) of candidates was and is influential. Like the ethnic groups, Muslim organizations have long histories in the Senegambia region and have shaped the nature of politics over the centuries.

Muslim merchants came to the region as early as the 10th century, in the networks of the trans-Saharan trade. Within the framework of the ethnic states, Muslim communities developed as important minority groups associated with the political and commercial networks. Itinerant Muslim teachers came to the region along with the merchants and they began the long process of Islamization of societies. At the elite level, rulers blended Islamic and pre-Islamic rituals of governance, and as the broader population became Islamized, a similar popular religious synthesis developed.

The Islamization of rural communities proceeded very slowly and still was continuing in the 20th century. The local teachers, usually called marabouts in discussions of Islam in West Africa, were the keystone of this conversion process. Personal devotional practices and communal rituals developed that combined local religious practices with explicitly Islamic elements. The usual format for this synthesis was the Sufi tariqa (devotional and organizational path) led by a specially respected teacher. Throughout the Muslim world beginning in the 11th century, these tariqas became important social and communal organizations organized as brotherhoods as well as sets of devotional ceremonies.

One of the earliest of these Sufi brotherhoods, the Qadiriyya, had its origins in Iraq in the 11th century, and its devotional traditions spread through informal networks of teachers and scholars throughout the Muslim world. It came to sub-Saharan West Africa by the 15th century and became a major social grouping in the region. The Qadiriyya was not a centrally organized association. Instead, it was a shared identity of different local teachers. In the Senegambia, the order maintained this loosely defined identity and faced the competition from more hierarchically organized (and less widespread) groups in the 19th and 20th centuries. In other areas, Qadiri groups like the jihad movement of Uthman dan Fodio in Nigeria or Ma' al-'Aynayn in Mauritania became politically militant in the 18th and 19th centuries. However, the Senegambian Qadiris were not activist in the various movements of religious renewal and were not especially politically visible, as Qadiris, in the rise of Senegalese nationalism. The Qadiriyya remained an important element in Senegambian society but by the 20th century, other orders were larger and more influential.

By the 17th century, new types of Muslim movements and organizations developed. The expansion and increasing violence of the Atlantic slave trade and the evolution of the warrior states created movements of popular opposition, led by local Muslim teachers. These marabouts were not tied to the state, and their movements were part of a change in the role of Islam in the region. "From being the religion of a minority caste of merchants and courtiers in the royal courts, it was becoming a popular resistance movement against the arbitrary power of the ruling aristocracies and against the noxious effects of the Atlantic trade."[10] This movement became organized in 1673 with the declaration of jihad by Nasr al-Din in southern Mauritania and the Futa Toro region in northern Senegambia. He and his followers succeeded for a time in establishing a self-proclaimed Islamic state, but it was soon defeated by the warrior state rulers. However, his call "for a revival that would operate through new political institutions uniting a Muslim community that would stand above the tribal divisions of the desert and above the political divisions of the Wolof states and Futa Toro"[11] resonated beyond his specific movement. This jihad set in motion a broader movement of militant Muslim activism and jihads seeking to create states that did not compromise with local religious traditions.

For the next two centuries, jihad movements emphasized the divergence between the ethnic-warrior rulers and the new Muslim groups, and they came to provide some of the most important resistance to the expansion of European imperialist rule.[12] During the 18th century, jihads in Futa Jalon and Futa Toro succeeded in establishing Islamically identified states that survived in various forms into the 20th century. Some of the new states created distinctive leadership structures, adopting classical Islamic titles like Imam (which, in local language usage became *Almami*) or Commander of the Faithful (*Amir al-Mu'minin*).

Jihad movements continued into the 19th century throughout West Africa. The jihad of Uthman dan Fodio in Nigeria, declared in 1805, resulted in the establishment of the Sokoto Caliphate, which continues to have an administrative identity in the 21st century. Inspired by dan Fodio, another jihad state was established in the middle Niger valley by Seku Amadu Bari, who declared a jihad in 1818.

In the middle of the century, al-Hajj Umar Tal (c. 1794–1864) linked together the various jihad traditions into a major force that established the largest of the jihad states in West Africa. Al-Hajj Umar came from a family of religious scholars. As a young man he became a member of a new tariqa that was spreading rapidly in Mauritania and the Senegambia region, the Tijaniyya. Founded a few years earlier by Ahmad al-Tijani, an Algerian teacher with a message of Islamic renewal, the new order drew members from the less reformist Qadiriyya and those Muslims who opposed the ethnic-warrior rulers. On a pilgrimage to Mecca in 1828, he was appointed the designated deputy for West Africa of the new Tijaniyya, and in his teachings and work he combined the jihad militancy and the Sufi organization. His military campaigns created a state which survived his death in 1864, but his descendants made peace with the French, who conquered Umar's state by the end of the century. His son Murtada and other leaders "became prominent as chiefs of the order under the French administration,"[13] paralleling the experiences of ethnic chieftains.

While the militant jihad tradition is an important part of the historical memory of Muslims in the Senegambia region, no major jihad movement arose in the area following the end of the Umarian state. The Tijaniyya became the largest organization in the region as a devotional and communal association. An important builder of this non-jihadi Tijaniyya was al-Hajj Malik Sy (1855–1922). After a scholarly Islamic education, he became an itinerant teacher, and on return from pilgrimage to Mecca, he finally established a school in Tivaouane. The school was a major educational and devotional center, and it became the main Tijaniyya center in the region.[14] It continues to be the primary center for the order in the second decade of the 21st century.

The Tijaniyya was already involved in Senegalese politics in the 1930s, but not directly. The leaders provided endorsements for candidates in some of the colonial elections. By the time of the elections following World War II, important Tijani leaders were identified as opposing the Socialist Party. However, the political parties were the organizations of the urban civilian elite rather than being established by the religious organizations. These years set the pattern which has continued into the 21st century, in which the religious organizations exercise political influence by providing popular support for political candidates and parties rather than creating their own political parties.

The major rival of the Tijaniyya was the Muridiyya, an offshoot of the Qadiriyya established late in the 19th century. As the jihads were defeated and the French confirmed control, a young scholarly teacher in the Qadiriyya, Ahmad Bamba (1850–1927), began to develop a large following. The French feared that he would organize a jihad and exiled him. He developed his own distinctive devotional practices and prayers, which became the Muridiyya Tariqa. The number of his followers continued to grow and by the time of its founder's death in 1927, the Muridiyya was a major organization. His tomb in Touba became a major pilgrimage center.

Part of the distinctive character of the new order was that the leadership guided its rural followers into peanut cultivation and the Murids became the major source for a significant export as Senegal's economy developed. During the 20th century, the Muridiyya also attracted significant numbers of urban and middle-class followers. Murids were important in the growing Senegalese diaspora, so that the order had a presence in Western Europe and the United States by the 21st century. As a result, the order has come to represent a cosmopolitan populist force in Senegalese politics.

The Murid leaders did not establish a separate political party. Instead, like the Tijaniyya, they provided endorsements and support for political parties and candidates as electoral politics developed following World War I. A general political framework emerged in which competing groups within the urban political elite found allies in the competing major religious organizations. The Tijaniyya had supported Galandou Diouf, who was elected as the Senegalese deputy in the French National Assembly in 1934 and re-elected in 1936, while Murid leadership gave support to Diouf's rivals. As a result, by World War II, "the political life of Senegal was dominated by two opposing factions: Diouf's partisans who enjoyed the support of the Tijaniyya and the backing of the French authorities, on the one hand; and the Senegalese Socialist Party, headed by Lamine Gueye, which was backed by the Muridist religious group, and which in effect constituted the opposition."[15]

Following World War II, the political scene shifted, with parties being reorganized and new ones developing. The death of Diouf in 1941 opened the way for the socialist party (which was a branch of the French socialist party, the Section Française de l'Internationale Ouviére—SFIO) to win the first postwar elections of deputies to the French National Assembly. In 1948, Leopold Senghor, who had been a major leader in the party, split with Gueye and established the Bloc Démocratique Sénégalaise (BDS) in

1948. The SFIO and the BDS became the major political rivals in the politics of the 1950s.

The cooperation between the parties and the brotherhoods became even more important as rural Senegal began to participate in electoral politics. Politicians regularly visited tariqa leaders and participated in the major Muslim festivals organized by the orders. The fact that Senghor was a Roman Catholic was an issue briefly in early campaigns, but "it was, in fact, the Catholic Senghor who managed to win the support of the most powerful marabous . . . Senghor never ignored the marabous, whose support remained essential."[16] This type of political alliance was essential for political success in independent Senegal.

The major Muslim organizations in Senegal have significance within society and politics. The history of jihads and creation of Islamic states is a part of the history and legacy of Islamic movements in West Africa in general and in Senegal in particular. However, this heritage has not been used to create an Islamist political activism in the politics of independent Senegal. Instead, Islamic traditions have been more inclusive than militant. "It is important not to forget the less spectacular contributions of Muslim teachers who have stuck to more traditional and less 'jihadic' ways. In fact, the overwhelmingly Muslim identity of the [African] savanna region today may be more a product of their efforts . . . This striking Islamization has proceeded despite the destruction of the Islamic states . . . established by jihad in the eighteenth and nineteenth centuries."[17] Mobilizing followers to grow peanuts and participate in modern economic life appears to have been more effective than mobilizing jihads as a foundation for social significance and political influence.

A third grouping shaping Senegalese politics, in addition to ethnic and religious groups, is the military. Its importance, paradoxically, is its relative non-involvement in political developments. In contrast to many of the countries that gained independence following World War II, Senegal has not had any time when the military controlled the state. Military coups have not been a part of Senegalese politics. "Since independence, civil-military relations in Senegal have been proficient and exemplary. The international community has often cited them as a model."[18]

The military were an important part of the early ethnic warrior states. Often the rulers had comparatively large standing armies of slaves and ethnic warriors. The entourage of the rulers and major leaders were usually warriors. As in the Serer states, this group was chosen "originally from the slave class and attached directly to the crown . . . In theory dependent on the Burs [rulers], they were, in fact, independent, powerful, and sometimes unruly . . . every major chief was to some degree the creature of his entourage."[19] The French policies of incorporating the rulers into the administrative system brought an end to the real influence of these entourages and also the military organizations of the rulers.

In terms of military organization, the old warrior courtiers and armies were replaced by French military forces. The French created an African army with European officers and equipment and African soldiers. In West Africa these troops were called *tirailleurs sénégalais* ("Senegalese riflemen"), and the first group was established in 1820. The *tirailleurs* were important in defeating West African jihad states and in the expansion of French control in Dahomey and the Ivory Coast. During World War I, thousands of Senegalese were recruited and served in Europe. Following the war, the French continued to recruit and conscript Senegalese, maintaining an African colonial army that saw service in French colonies around the globe.[20]

During World War II, Senegalese again fought in Europe and elsewhere after French colonial officials in Dakar joined the Free French forces. Leopold Senghor, who became the first president of independent Senegal, joined the French army and was captured by the Germans. Military service created a substantial number of Senegalese with cosmopolitan experience and understanding of global affairs. The active role of the African colonial subjects in the French war effort gave them some political capital in the postwar discussions about the future of the French Empire.

The armed forces of independent Senegal were not a direct institutional continuation of the old French imperial military, but the new military maintained close relations with the French. Senegal gained its independence through negotiations and the evolution of the political system. As a result, its armed forces were not based on a nationalist army of liberation. The Senegalese military did not represent an ideological position of radical liberationism, nor was it simply a continuation of a colonial institution. Because of the long historic participation in the French military, Senegal became independent with a body of experienced soldiers and the new armed forces were professional and basically apolitical from the beginning.

Soon after independence, political and military leaders worked to define civil-military relations in the new country. The tone was set by the relations between the new president, Senghor, and the chief of defense staff, General Jean Alfred Diallo, in 1962. At that time, Prime Minister Mamadou Dia was accused of being a part of a conspiracy for a coup, and the military leadership gave strong support to Senghor. However, beyond that specific event, Senghor and Diallo worked to create an arrangement in which the military could play a constructive role in the development of the country without becoming a political actor. Diallo had been an officer in the French Army Corps of Engineers and had a vision of the armed forces building and modernizing Senegal's infrastructure.[21] Biram Diop argues that the "relationship of these two leaders [Senghor and Diallo] established a fruitful and respectful collaborative basis for civil-military relations and the involvement of the armed forces in development activities. The positive relationship between these two leaders largely shaped the overall good relations that still prevail between civilian authorities and the leadership of the armed forces."[22]

The modern urban educated elite is the fourth and central group in the Senegalese political system. This grouping had its beginnings in the French establishments along the coast in the 18th and early 19th centuries, and their importance grew as French control became more direct in the rural areas. The old educated elite in the cities was part of the broader pattern of Muslim life, with *madrasas* and centers for advanced learning built around communities of scholars of Islamic studies and Sufism. The great devotional centers like Touba and Tivaouanie were also centers of Islamic learning and continue those traditions of learning in the 21st century.

During the 20th century, the expansion of the French educational system provided the foundation for the new urban elite. They were and are from a full spectrum of ethnic groups and were Francophone in their professional lives, although many—especially after independence—spoke Wolof as a lingua franca even if they were not ethnically Wolof.[23] However, this shared language is a hybrid Urban Wolof that "derives from the contact of two worlds, the French and the African, and its use suggests that a speaker maintains a foot in both. Its speakers have been moulded both by indigenous African culture and by Western education. They acknowledge and are proud of their traditional 'roots' but overlay them with a more international or metropolitan set of tastes and values."[24] In many ways, Urban Wolof exemplifies the general character of the Senegalese urban-educated elite in the 21st century and reflects the evolution of that grouping. Beginning as a small Francophone minority, it developed as the voice of a multiethnic and cosmopolitan society. This grouping defined what it meant to be "Senegalese" and shaped Senegalese nationalism.

In the 19th century, this group already had some opportunity for political participation. The French established four urban communes in the Senegambia region. These communes had the vote and had various types of representation in Paris, which by the beginning of the 20th century meant that they had an elected deputy in the National Assembly. In the "first major breakthrough by an African in the French political system," a black African, Blaise Diagne, defeated a field of white and creole candidates to become Senegal's deputy in the National Assembly.[25] Diagne continued to be politically active in both France and Senegal until his death in 1934. He is remembered as an elected black African politician and was cited as part of the Senegalese democratic tradition by Macky Sall soon after his election in 2012.[26] In the first half of the 20th century, the elected Assembly deputies were important leaders in Senegalese politics, and the first president of independent Senegal, Senghor, had served as an influential deputy in Paris. Following World War II, increasing numbers of local, municipal, and national offices were made elective.

The result of this history is that "Senegal came to independence with a long and much-touted history of electoral competition" and could "count a political elite with significant experience in electoral politics."[27] As party-based politics developed in the 1950s leading up to independence, there was remarkably little effort to create ethnic or religious parties and there was little of the tension that existed in other pre-independence countries between "gradualists" and "radicals." The parties reflected the ideological positions and personal orientations of their leaders. Their visions and programs ranged from old-style communism to liberal democratic, with the broad center defined by the emerging leader, Senghor, as African socialism. The fluidity of the political identities of the elite was reflected in the first elections in independent Senegal in 1963, when the major party, Senghor's Union Progréssiste Sénégalaise (UPS), faced an opposition coalition that brought together almost all of the other parties.

The urban political elite has changed over the past century. The small coastal Francophone group that elected Diagne in 1914 has become a cosmopolitan Senegalese core of the political system that integrates major religious organizations, continuing ethnic loyalties, and a nonpolitical military.

Democratization: A Century-Long Process, Not a Revolution

The democracy shown in the Senegalese elections of 2012 was not the result of a revolution like those that brought an end to dictatorships in Eastern Europe or dramatic popular demonstrations like the Arab Spring. The contemporary political system in Senegal is the product of a long history of gradual changes, and democratization was not inevitable. The persistence of the commitment to democratic change in independent Senegal is illustrated by the career of Abdoulaye Wade, who organized an opposition party in 1974 and then competed in every presidential election (1978, 1983, 1988, 1993) until he won in the year 2000, defeating the incumbent president. During that quarter-century, the opposition protested unfair governmental manipulations of elections and maintained a strong critique of the incumbent party leaders, whose party had been in power since independence. The opposition continued to manifest itself through political action rather than revolution or coup. The long-term processes of democratization are reflected in the campaigns and results of a series of elections during the 20th and 21st centuries.

Many discussions of democracy in Senegal mention the 1914 election of Diagne as a deputy in the French National Assembly. That election was not seen as an important new development at the time. Diagne was born in Senegal and had served in colonial offices in a number of places, including Dahomey, French Congo, and French Guinea, and after his election he caucused for a time with the French Socialist Party before joining a group of independents. He was active in shaping laws dealing with the colonies and helped to win recruits in Senegal for the military during World War I. He set a pattern for regular political participation by elected Africans in metropolitan French politics. This pattern was continued through to independence, with Senghor being politically active in Paris as well as West Africa.

The development of political parties in Senegal was shaped by participation in French political parties in the era before World War II. By the late 1940s, a number of parties were organized by Senegalese who were already experienced in party politics. These parties were also shaped by the emergence of regional parties in French West Africa, and issues of regional federalism for the whole of French West Africa were debated. In the debates and coalitions, Senghor emerged as a major voice for Senegal. A critical point came in 1958 when France, in a referendum, gave the West African colonies the choice of full independence or autonomy within a French community. Only Guinea opted for full independence.

The referendum was followed by parliamentary elections in 1959 in which a number of parties participated. However, many of the parties came together in Senghor's UPS, and the party won more than 80 percent of the votes and all of the seats in the new assembly. With independence, the assembly elected Senghor as president as a step toward parliamentary and presidential elections in 1963. In those elections, the non-UPS groups joined together in a coalition, Démocratie et Unité Sénégalaises, which won only about 6 percent of the votes. Senghor ran unopposed for president and his party won 94 percent of the parliamentary votes, setting the stage for a one-party political regime.

Senegal became a one-party state in practice for the next fifteen years. However, in contrast to many of the other new states in Africa at the time, the one-party system never became the official policy. "Although never a de jure single party state, via a combination of Senghor and the UPS's skill in coopting or repressing the opposition and a provision in the 1963 constitution which created a single national constituency with a winner-take-all system for legislative elections, by 1966 only the UPS existed as a legally recognized political party in the country."[28] In this context, the UPS won all parliamentary seats in the elections of 1968 and 1973, and Senghor was unopposed in his re-elections.

The unity of the 1968 elections was not as imposed a unity as was the case in other emerging single-party governments. The UPS list of candidates included a number of leaders and groups that had been in the opposition bloc in 1963. Observers at the time agreed that the results of the election reflected the popular approval of policies of political reconciliation and national unity. In the mid- and late 1960s, a number of important newly independent states that were establishing one-party regimes were taken over by national military leaders. In West Africa at the time, a number of emerging one-party states fell by coup to the control of the military: Upper Volta (Burkina Faso) in 1966, Dahomey (Benin) in 1967, Mali (1968), and even the major Pan-African nationalist leader Nkrumah's one-party state was taken over by the military.

The end of the one-party system came differently in Senegal. During the summer of 1968, after the elections, significant student protest demonstrations occurred, similar in many ways to the protests in Paris and elsewhere during that summer. In addition, economic problems and tensions involving rural development put pressure on the government. The government's long-term response was to initiate some public discussions on issues of policy.

Following the elections of 1973, Senghor began a careful process of incremental reforms leading to a formally multiparty state. In general the process of democratization in Senegal had few dramatic crisis times and involved a steady accumulation of measures and practices that strengthened democratic political life. The history of the national elections between 1973 and 2000 becomes the story of the transformation from a one-party state into a democratic system in which an opposition leader could displace an incumbent leader in an election.

An important event at the beginning of the process is when a former member of the UPS, Abdoulaye Wade, informed Senghor that he would organize an opposition party. With Senghor's agreement, he established the Parti Démocratique Sénégalais (PDS) in 1974. In 1976, legislation defined a three-party system with legally defined ideological identities. The UPS became the Party Socialiste (PS), identified as "democratic socialist" in the center of the political spectrum. The PDS was designated as "liberal democratic" and the Parti Africain de l'Indépendance (PAI) as the Marxist-leftist party. Although leaders of other parties criticized their exclusion, many observers at the time noted that these steps were "enough to make the military regimes and one-party states that predominate elsewhere take notice."[29]

In the next general elections in 1978, the PS and Senghor continued to win huge majorities, but the situation was changed. Many restrictions on the media were removed and the political opposition had greater freedom of action, although many restrictions continued in place. "Despite their limitations, the 1978 elections were clearly a watershed in the move back toward a more competitive system. For the first time since 1963, the opposition was able to contest the PS's hold on power and begin to erode the PS monopoly, if not its dominance."[30]

This erosion of PS dominance can be seen in the voting results in 1978 and the following three elections. In 1978, Wade and the PDS became the most effective opposition, combining its legal opportunity with patient persistence. In the 1978 elections, Wade and his party (in parliamentary elections) won about 18 percent of the vote, with the third legal party, PAI, winning less than 1 percent. In 1983, Wade won about 15 percent; in 1988, he won about 26 percent; and in 1993, he won 32 percent. The trend is remarkable. The PS won 82 percent in 1978, and by 1993, the PS candidate won 58 percent.[31] These trends made the victory of Wade and the PDS in the 2000 elections credible.

A major change following the 1978 elections was the voluntary retirement of Senghor in 1980, with Abdou Diouf named as president. Diouf was a longtime ally of Senghor and leader of the PS, so the transition was smooth. Diouf initiated a number of changes that continued the process of democratization. The limitation on the number of allowable political parties was dropped, and a number of parties were quickly formed. New election laws again increased the openness of the system to opposition participation. The first election in the Diouf presidency in 1983 did not reduce the position of the PS and confirmed Wade as the leader of any effective opposition. For many years, Cheikh Anta Diop, a highly respected intellectual and cultural nationalist, was viewed as the leader with the greatest potential for defeating Senghor in elections. In the new politics of 1983, his party only won one seat in parliament, while Wade maintained his status.

In the 1988 elections, the contest was between the PS and the PDS, and between Diouf and Wade, with other candidates and parties receiving minimal numbers of votes. Although PDS made significant gains, PS still won significant majorities. As happened in 1983, the losing parties protested. In 1988, in the context of the beginnings of the global third wave of democracy, the demonstrations were serious enough that a state of emergency was declared, and opposition leaders were convicted of inciting violence. However, in the aftermath, the leaders were pardoned and Wade joined a government of national unity. Again, major changes were made in the election laws to open the system even more.

The opposition had high hopes in the elections of 1993 but, again, the changes were incremental. The new laws opened the way for new candidates and parties and, in the final results, the PS and Diouf lost ground but still won. In contrast to 1988, Diouf's support went from 73.2 percent to 58.4 percent, while Wade's support went from 25.8 percent to 32 percent, and the six other candidates won almost 10 percent of the vote. Similarly, in the parliamentary elections, four smaller parties gained parliamentary seats and the PDS increased its number of seats by ten, while the SR lost nineteen seats. However, again, there was a high level of disappointment and the level of voter participation was lower than in previous elections, with apparently relatively high rates of nonvoting by younger Senegalese.

Coming out of the 1993 elections, it was noted that "the parties still seem largely committed to the idea that Senegal should be attempting to strengthen and improve its democracy, rather than give up on it." However, in the mid-1990s there were few, except for party enthusiasts, who believed that the long-term process of incremental change would produce the results of the elections in 2000. In that year, after competing in presidential elections for almost a quarter of a century, Abdoulaye Wade was elected president. He defeated the incumbent president Diouf, and the transfer of power by election was accomplished.

No dramatically new development produced these results, which confirmed the democratization process. The continued expansion of the public political arena was not inevitable. Continuing democratization was not a simple linear progress, and the potential for "reverse waves" always existed. However, opposition to the party that had ruled since independence utilized the evolving electoral system to win the election in 2000. "Over the years, Diouf had to give increasingly strong guarantees of transparency and fairness within the electoral institution,"[32] and the result was the possibility that the opposition could and did win.

During the 1990s, the opposition included many different parties and political leaders, but the major contest continued to be between Diouf and Wade and between PS and PDS. However, the new openness can be seen in the 1998 parliamentary elections. The PS won a bare 50 percent of the votes and nine parties in addition to the PS, and PDS won at least one seat in the new parliament. This new political pluralism brought eight candidates to the first round of the presidential elections in 2000, with Abdou Diouf gaining 41 percent of the vote. Although Wade only received 31 percent in the first round, the other opposition candidates supported him in the runoff, in which he won 58 percent of the vote. The defeat of the PS was reinforced in the parliamentary elections in 2001, when the party gained only 17 percent of the vote.

Although Wade and his coalition had clear control of the parliament, the new era involved a major increase in the actual number of parties. In 1997 there were 26 parties, and the number increased to 94 by 2006 and

145 at the end of 2008.[33] The diversity of parties strengthened Wade's position as leader of the country, since he was able to work with a cluster of them to create a coalition as the elections of 2007 approached. Observers and opposition leaders expressed concern about the possible return of a more authoritarian system, but the majority in the country gave support to Wade. He won more than 55 percent of the vote in the first round, defeating a number of prominent older politicians as well as some younger candidates representing a new generation in Senegalese political life. During Wade's second term, many feared that "democratisation since 2000 seems to have reconstructed the erstwhile foundations of dominant party rule, albeit with a different dominant party now in charge."[34]

The fears that democratization was being diverted strengthened when it became clear that Wade intended, in violation of the constitution, to run for a third term in 2012. During 2010 and 2011, demonstrations against Wade sometimes grew violent, but general political activity proceeded in preparations for the elections in which many parties and presidential candidates participated. The actual election had many parallels to the election in 2000. In the first round of the presidential elections, the incumbent, Wade, won the most votes (about 35 percent), but that was a significant loss from his landslide victory in 2007. The second place candidate was Macky Sall (26 percent), and three other candidates receiving about a third of the votes. This forced a runoff election between Wade and Sall, in which the major opposition candidates backed Sall, who received about two-thirds of the votes cast.

It was a significant defeat for Wade and the PDS, who accepted the results with minimal protest. In the following parliamentary elections, the coalition backing Sall won 53 percent of the votes and 119 of the 150 seats. Wade's PDS won a bare 15 percent of the votes, and the old PS ceased to be a significant political force. The elections confirmed the ability of the political system that had evolved over the years to maintain itself as a democracy, now with a new generation of political leaders. Sall was born in 1961, after Senegal gained independence. Four of the eight candidates (including Sall) receiving at least 1 percent of the vote in the first round were born between 1956 and 1965, representing a postcolonial generation of leaders. However, all of them were experienced political leaders—former cabinet ministers and major party leaders—before running for president. Democratization opened the way for new generations of leaders.

One candidate in the election campaign represents a new political dynamic. Youssou N'Dour, a globally well-known popular singer and activist in humanitarian causes, announced his candidacy early in 2012.

He was declared ineligible because of problems with his nomination papers. He supported Sall and was named minister of culture and tourism in Sall's new cabinet. He lost that post in a cabinet reshuffle after about a year. N'Dour (born in 1959) is in the same generation as Sall and is an icon of pop culture in Senegal. He combines traditional African music with popular global genres and won a Grammy Award in 2005. While N'Dour is not active as a party politician, his emergence in politics shows the importance of both the culture and politics of new generations of Senegalese who are part of the global pop-culture world.

Whatever might be the results of policies defined and implemented by the generation brought to political power by the 2012 elections, those elections represent an important transition in the political history of independent Senegal.

Conclusion: Political Dynamics of Senegalese Democracy

Senegal in the first decades of the 21st century is no longer basically a postcolonial state. During the 20th century, the foundations for political action had roots in the experience of the colonial state. Even while under French rule, Senegal began to develop a leadership elite that was experienced in electoral politics and governmental administration. Senghor was both a product of French rule and an important creator of the postcolonial state in Senegal. The history of democratization shows the gradual evolution of Senegalese politics. By the time of the 2012 elections, the state was no longer primarily interacting with the politics of colonialism and old-style nationalism. Strong continuities with the postcolonial politics, of course, existed. Wade, representing the older generation and political style, received significant support, and patterns of political action set during the first half-century of independence continued to be important. In the age of increasingly electronic politics, as seen in the case of N'Dour, and with a new generation of leaders, Senegal no longer fits into the patterns of the old-style postcolonial state. However, like the postcolonial state of Senghor, with its roots in the colonial era, many of the elements of Senegalese politics in the 21st century build on foundations laid during the 20th century.

Three general political developments helped to shape Senegal as a country that has relatively successfully democratized and avoided military dictatorial rule. The relationships between ethnicity and political life are one element, along with a second, the style of political action by major religious organizations. The third is the continuing nonpolitical nature of the military in relationship to state and policy. The foundations for these dynamics were, as have been noted, set during the long history of ethnic, religious, and military groups in the Senegambia region. Their continuing modes of action are important parts of the emerging political styles in Senegal in the era after the postcolonial state in the 21st century. However, old defining societal boundaries between major groupings are being reshaped as new style groupings—like speakers of Urban Wolof—emerge.

Ethnicity continues to be an important element in Senegalese social and cultural life but, even in the more open political arena of the 21st century, no ethnically identified political parties developed. The political activities of ethnic groups involve individual local leaders who act as intermediaries between the general public and the political parties with their urban elite leadership. Although the groups following the political guidance of these intermediaries may be ethnically identifiable, these local leaders do not come together to form ethnic political blocks. Instead, as the research on the elections of 2000 and 2007 by Dominika Koter shows, "politicians express an interest in acquiring intermediaries from across the ethnic spectrum. Likewise, intermediaries also show their willingness to support non-coethnics."[35]

In the 2000 presidential election, there was virtually no distinction among the major candidates in terms of the ethnic identity of their supporters. In the first round of the elections, three candidates (Diouf, Wade, and Niasse) received about 90 percent of the total vote. Using the results of Afrobarometer 2002 survey reports, Koter shows that the "ethnic composition of Abdoulaye Wade's winning electorate is very similar to that of his main rivals. Similarly, his scores among each ethnic group are highly proportional to each group's size [in the general population], with no single group dominating his electorate."[36] In concrete terms, this means that 42 percent of the total votes for Wade came from Wolof supporters, who represent 42–43 percent of the population of Senegal. Similarly, 43 percent of the total votes for Diouf and 42 percent of the votes for Niasse came from Wolof voters. A similar parallel between proportion of the total population and proportion of candidates' votes is in the spread of support from the other major ethnic groups (Pulaar, Serer, Mandinka, and Diola). Each of the three candidates received proportional support from each of the major ethnic groups.[37] This remarkable parallel between the spectrum of support for candidates and the total population emphasizes the effective absence of large ethnic voting blocks and parties in Senegalese politics in the 21st century.

Historically, "early Senegalese political leaders chose not to build their followings by appealing to ethnic interests and identities. As a result, the political parties that contested pre-independence elections did not reflect the ethnic cleavages of Senegalese society."[38] As political parties developed, they began as urban groups led by members of the urban Francophone elite. When the political arena expanded to include rural populations, the parties developed networks of intermediaries who had local ethnic or religious influence among the rural populations. This structure provided a popular support base for the parties in a distinctive way and continues in the 21st century to be a significant feature of Senegalese politics. Koter argues the party-intermediary structure is an important part of the non-ethnic party politics. "Intermediaries change electoral dynamics because unlike individual voters they are in a better position to forge ties with non-coethnic politicians. They have the capacity to produce surprisingly non-ethnic voting patterns in highly ethnic societies."[39] The experience of Senegal supports the conclusion of a broader study of ethnic politics in Africa that "ethnic fractionalization itself does not necessarily result in a lower quality of democracy, but that it is the *politicization* of ethnic differences that impede the development of a higher quality of democracy."[40]

The separatist movement in the Casamance region of Senegal is a possible exception to this non-politicization of ethnicity. The Casamance is the southern region of Senegal, separated from the rest of the country by The Gambia and connected only by a narrow corridor of land at the eastern end of the Gambian enclave. Its southern border is with Guinea-Bissau. When the French brought an end to Portuguese control of the area in the 19th century, they administered it as a separate region and it was integrated into Senegal only at the end of the colonial era.

The majority of the population of Casamance are Diola and the region is the least Islamized part of Senegal. People in the region expected to gain significant autonomy within the country and those expectations became frustrations leading to conflict. The region was marginalized in terms of Senegalese economic development and political influence, and the "Casamance people felt ignored and abandoned by the central authorities."[41] In the 1970s, a Roman Catholic priest in Casamance,

Father Augustin Diamacoune Senghor, spoke of the special character of the Casamance region in popular radio programs and publications. In 1980–1983, student demonstrations and other protests resulted in the jailing of the priest and other activists calling for economic reform and cultural recognition. In the process, the opposition organized the Movement des Forces Démocratiques de la Casamance (MFDC; Movement of Democratic Forces of Casamance), which began the sporadic civil war that continued into the second decade of the 21st century. From time to time ceasefires were signed, but the conflict was not resolved.

Although major support for the MFDC came from the Diola in the Casamance, the movement was not explicitly an ethnic movement so much as it was a movement calling for recognition of the region's autonomy or independence. The MFDC itself was sufficiently divided that it did not present a united front in negotiations with the central government in Dakar. Although there was some resentment against Wolof involvement in Casamance affairs, that resentment tended to be general against "northerners" who were migrating into the region rather than being an explicitly ethnic tension.

Following his election in 2012, Macky Sall set in motion a new initiative which involved negotiations utilizing the international mediation of the Community of Sant'Egidio, a Catholic humanitarian organization. In this process, in April 2014, Salif Sadio, who had led the negotiations and had been viewed as the most prominent hardline leader in the MFDC, announced a ceasefire. He was described as "polishing his image, donating money to a local hospital and holding town hall meetings to update Casamance people on the peace talks" as he exchanged "the rebel underground for mainstream politics."[42] In this apparent post-conflict transition, there was little attention given to creating an ethnic party rather than moving into the general pattern of Senegalese parties.

In general, the nature of ethnicity in Senegal is changing and this reinforces the tendency to avoid ethnic political parties. As urbanization intensifies, the cosmopolitan nature of urban life creates new identities. In Dakar and the other urban centers, Wolof has become the major shared language, but Urban Wolof is a distinctive hybrid language. In this urban context, Wolof becomes "the unmarked or default ethnicity" for people from many different ethnic groups as they become integrated into urban life—a "de-ethnicized identity" using a shared hybrid language.[43] This development does not mean that a homogeneous political culture is emerging but rather that cleavages continue to be non-ethnic in nature.

In the 2012 elections, as in the 2000 elections, there was no ethnic party putting forth a presidential candidate.

In the 21st century, the major religious organizations continued to exercise political influence by providing support for candidates but did not establish their own parties. From time to time, individual religious leaders created small parties, but early attempts did not receive government recognition. In the first decade of the 21st century, five parties with some religious identity were officially registered and competed in elections. Two of these were organized by leaders from the Murids and two were organized by Tijanis. Their programs involved conservative advocacy for greater recognition of Islam in public life, but they were not Islamist in their rhetoric. None of them received significant numbers of votes in the various elections and were not endorsed by the leadership of their brotherhoods.[44]

One party, the Mouvement de la Réforme pour le Développement Social (MRDS; Reform Movement for Social Development), has a more explicitly Islamist-style program. It was organized in 2000 and participated with minimal results in subsequent elections. In the parliamentary elections in 2007 and 2009, it received enough votes so that the party leader, Imam Mbaye Niang, gained a parliamentary seat. Although it is reported to be an Islamist party with some international support,[45] its programs tend to be more socially conservative than radical, and Niang participates actively in various coalitions and political alliances.

There was, however, an increase in Islamist-style advocacy in the late 20th and early 21st centuries, but it tended to be expressed through student movements and other activist groups rather than in overtly political parties. These groups presented critiques of the old political hierarchies and coalitions, some in explicitly Islamist terms, and others arose as reformist groups within the brotherhoods. During the 1990s, "the heretofore virtually unassailable dominance of established Sufism came into question, challenged both by Islamist alternatives and by new movements from within the orders which borrowed from these themes."[46] The major source of support for these developments came from students and other younger Senegalese.

Islam is a continuing significant element in Senegalese politics and culture, but religion's importance takes many different forms. The important political roles of the brotherhoods do not mean that what analysts call "Political Islam" or "Islamism" is a major force. In the 21st century, new ways of expressing religious advocacy continue to reflect the historic inclusive pluralism of Sufi traditions as well as more exclusivist Islamist activism.

Twenty-first-century expressions of identity sometimes are important syntheses, bridging potential cleavages. Global Muslim movements sometimes clash with distinctive local manifestations of religion, but new styles of religious expression may create a combination. The popular music of Youssou N'Dour provides an interesting example. His Grammy-winning album, *Egypt*, combined Senegalese-style subject matter, praising Sufi saints, with Arabic music—as was the case with his earlier album, *Sant*. His "praises of key figures of the black African Sufi tradition are sung in Arabic rhythms . . . , positioning the music squarely in the global Muslim context. Yousou Ndour thus wraps himself in the broader Muslim identity and simultaneously reaffirms the validity of the specific Sufi Muslim heritage."[47] In many ways, the broader trends for Islamic identity in Senegal in the 21st century, as seen in some of the student organizations and movements of reform within the brotherhoods, represent similar lines of development.

Ethnic identities in the contexts of an increasingly urban society also show this tendency for synthesis. The emergence of Urban Wolof as a lingua franca for urban life involves a pluralism that bridges more traditional ethnic cleavages. One example of this is a popular song by Baaba Maal. Maal is a Pulaar speaker who had sung only in Pulaar, but in a significant break with this custom, he switched to Urban Wolof when he sang a very popular song about Dakar, "Ndakaaru." In this, he was presenting "a newly configured urban identity."[48]

In addition to the internal developments, Senegal has important sets of relationships that connect its politics to various aspects of globalization. One important part of Senegal's place in global politics is its active participation in international peacekeeping forces. This global involvement in multilateral forces has been an important part of the mission of the Senegalese military. It has shaped Senegal's foreign policy and emphasized the non-involvement of the military in domestic politics.

An even more important aspect of Senegal's involvement in global relations is the existence of diaspora communities in many different countries. Many in the diasporas continue to have close ties with family in the homeland and send funds back home. In many African countries, remittances from migrants have become an important part of the local economy. In a study of sub-Saharan economies, Senegal was second in terms of remittances as a percentage of GDP, with remittances amounting to

11 percent of Senegal's GDP.[49] The growing Senegalese diaspora "has been politically active not only in funding political parties but also as members of the electorate through Senegal's overseas polling stations."[50] This adds a cosmopolitan and sometimes unpredictable dimension to elections and democratization in the 21st century.

The elections in 2012 provided confirmation of the democratization that has been proceeding in Senegal since independence. While there are many continuities with past politics, the elections brought to office a new political generation. The ethnic and religious groups along with the military and the urban-educated elite continue to shape the Senegalese political system, but each of them operates in new ways in the changing political world of the 21st century.

7

Tunisia

FROM REVOLUTION TO REPUBLIC

Democracy, the return of power to the people is a dangerous undertaking, an adventure filled with risks.

HABIB BOURGUIBA at the Bizerte Congress, 1964

TUNISIA, THE CRADLE of the Arab Spring, was ripe for an uprising long before the events of December 17, 2010, that swept from the coastal town of Sidi Bouzid, across Egypt, Libya, and Syria to Bahrain and Yemen, reflecting deep-seated popular anger and resentment with autocratic Arab leaders. Though Tunisia had only two presidents—Habib Bourguiba and Zine El Abidine Ben Ali—since gaining independence from France in 1956, many Western nations accepted its authoritarian government. A country of a mostly homogenous population with few ethnic, tribal, or religious divisions, it had a liberalized economy; its middle class was not only sizeable but also well educated and productive. Per-capita income was double those of its neighbors, Morocco and Egypt, and higher also than that of Algeria, which benefited from the blessings of oil, a commodity that Tunisia lacked.

But all was not well in the smallest country in North Africa. The Ben Ali regime (1987–2011), deft at image control and maintaining the illusion of a Western secular-Arab synthesis, would soon be challenged by ordinary citizens who were fed up with tacit government bargains, economic imbalance, rampant predatory corruption, crackdowns on political dissenters—Islamists and secularists alike—and a lack of real political participation.

Mohamed Bouazizi, a 26-year-old street vendor, whose act of self-immolation triggered a revolution, was not unique. His suicide was not only an expression of his own tragic plight but also underscored that of Tunisian youth and many other youth in the Arab world. It was a tragic manifestation of marginalized and alienated youth, unemployed or marginally employed despite their education and skills. Protests broke out in underprivileged areas in the South in what is known as the "mining belt." By the second week in January, protests in Tunisia's suburbs spread, fueled by social media networks like Facebook and Twitter, which young demonstrators used to organize and coordinate the mass mobilization of citizens to descend upon the capital city of Tunis.

Despite a progressive facade, Ben Ali's response revealed the true nature of his regime. Security forces, part and parcel of the president's coercive governance, used brutal force against protesters including physical assault, tear gas, and live ammunition. By January 12, human rights groups had confirmed more than thirty deaths—all a result of skirmishes with police.[1] "How can you fire on your own people?" one business owner asked. "If you do that, then there is no return. Now, you are a killer."[2]

Indeed, there was no return. The new year brought a new determination to oust the country's autocratic president. Labor unions, student groups, professional syndicates, and other opposition groups gathered in dozens of cities to demonstrate and organize strikes. As the death toll mounted, Ben Ali retreated, dismissing his interior minister and announcing unprecedented concessions. He vowed not to seek re-election in 2014 and pledged to investigate the government's response. He also vowed to implement more freedoms.[3] But his actions only aggravated the growing crowds who believed that his assurances were disingenuous and simply an attempt to stay in office. When his concessions failed, he imposed states of emergency, dismissed his entire cabinet, and promised legislative elections within six months. But in a final self-inflicted blow to his twenty-three-year-long rule, he deployed the army with a "shoot-to-kill" order—a move that backfired when the chief of staff General Rachid Ben Ammar refused to direct his troops to massacre citizens in the streets. Unable to contain the protests and use the military to crush the uprising, Ben Ali fled the country on January 14, and he eventually settled in Jeddah, Saudi Arabia, to live in exile.[4]

Though Ben Ali was gone, the government with its military, police and security apparatus, dysfunctional bureaucracy, and corrupt officials remained. "The dictator has fallen but not the dictatorship," declared Rachid Ghannouchi, leader of the Islamic opposition party, Ennahda or "Renaissance."[5] His party was one of the many groups that were outlawed and repressed under the reign of Ben Ali. As Nathan Brown observed at the time, the Tunisian regime "squashed out politics" and "no one really knows what's on the menu."[6]

While Rachid Ghannouchi and other Ennahda leaders, who had fled to England and France more than two decades before, were absent during the uprising, they quickly returned to participate in the reconstruction of a "new Tunisia" after Ben Ali was toppled. Despite their absence from Tunisia, they brought impeccable political credentials and credibility. In the words of Mohammed Hedi Ayani, a member of Ennahda: "We were on the frontlines against the regime for years and we paid the price. We suffered all sorts of injustices."[7]

The roots of Ennahda in Tunisia and government suppression and repression date back to the 1960s but the political climate that produced it actually began a decade earlier with Tunisia's independence from France in 1956 and the "father" of the nationalist movement, "Supreme Combatant," and Tunisia's first president, Habib Bourguiba.

Habib Bourguiba: "Supreme Combatant" and President

Habib Bourguiba was a child of the Enlightenment, educated in law and political science in France at the Sorbonne.[8] Bourguiba led Tunisia's independence movement from France with his goal to recreate Tunisia as a modern state modeled on the values and institutions of French colonialism. Bourguiba and his party, the Néo-Destour (ND) Party, were able to mediate that seeming chasm effectively. In April 1956, Bourguiba took over the reins as prime minister, minister of foreign affairs, and minister of defense, and in July 1957, Tunisia became an independent republic with Habib Bourguiba as its first president.[9]

The new president presented himself to his compatriots as someone who could refashion the country and also reform Islam: "Our concern is to return to the religion its dynamic quality."[10] Bourguiba had used religion as a tool for popular political mobilization during the independence struggle. Though he sought to create a strictly secular state, he had previously employed religious language and vocabulary during the fight for independence and took the title al-mujahid al akbar (the grand combatant, the leader of the jihad against the French occupiers).[11] However, in remodeling the Tunisian state throughout the late 1950s and early 1960s,

Bourguiba initiated policies to transform Tunisia into a Western-oriented secular state. Greatly influenced by Ataturk, he declared, "Basically and profoundly, we are with the West."[12]

Bourguiba unified the educational system, eliminating religious schools and integrating the Zaytouna mosque, one of the first and greatest universities in the history of Islam, into a new modern secular university, Université de Tunis, which had a Western-style curriculum.[13] Arabic was replaced by French as the official language of instruction so that the "new generation would not be cut off from technology and modern values" and from government.[14] He also reformed the traditional Islamic law of marriage and divorce with the Personal Status Code of 1956, which significantly improved the legal status and rights of women in Tunisia and later authorized the sale of birth control devices. On July 1, 1965, he passed a law that legalized abortion.[15] At the same time, he prohibited women from wearing the hijab, which he described as an "odious rag," in schools and in public: "We even see civil servants going to work in that odious rag. It has nothing to do with religion."[16] More controversially, in February 1960, he targeted one of the Five Pillars of Islam, declaring that the Ramadan fast could not be justified because it would decrease the economic productivity of the state, comparing his action to a jihad against the enemy: "We have an enemy to conquer—poverty."[17]

While Bourguiba occasionally employed language that was grounded in religion and talked openly about a new "modernist" version of Islam, many religiously minded citizens viewed him not as a religious reformer but rather as a secularist whose faith was superficial. His secular modernist reforms disenfranchised the Arabic-speaking and educated *ulema* and Islamic educational institutions, including graduates of Zaytouna, who were not able to enter local universities where French was the primary language. As Rachid Ghannouchi reflected, "I left for Syria to study there because I belonged to what remained of the Zaytouna School. The Zaytounian graduates had little hope of gaining access to the university; some were recruited by the public offices; others made themselves a place in the Orient."[18] Ghannouchi's experiences first at the University in Cairo, but particularly during his studies in Damascus, would have a profound influence on his life, his perceptions of the West, and, most importantly, his Islamic ideology and activism. Years later, they would lead to his founding of a powerful opposition movement to Tunisia's secular regime.

Rachid al-Ghannouchi

On June 22, 1941, Rachid al-Ghannouchi was born in a province called Gabès in southeastern Tunisia.[19] Ghannouchi's father, Sheikh Muhammad, was a farmer and a devout man. His mother came from a merchant family and had more contact with the outside world than his father; her emphasis on the education of her ten children would produce a professor, a judge, and an Islamic scholar-activist.[20]

Ghannouchi's early education was interrupted when his father withdrew him from primary school to help support his five brothers who were studying in Tunis. He also objected to Ghannouchi's school's Western system of education in French, the language of the colonizers whom he regarded as the enemies of Islam.

Upon the graduation of his brothers, the family's financial situation improved and Ghannouchi resumed his studies at Zaytouna with its traditional Islamic curriculum.[21] During his years in Zaytouna, Ghannouchi was not particularly religious, and at one point, as many teenage students did at the time, he abandoned his daily prayers. He was confused and traumatized by the paradox of the world in which he lived. His formative education within Zaytouna was uncompromisingly traditional and focused on "problems that no longer were ours that had been imposed on us by colonialism and that had become the status quo."[22] After he graduated secondary school, he studied briefly at Zaytouna University's faculty of theology but remained torn between a world of the inadequacy of traditionalism and the new Western-oriented society in which he lived. He left Zaytouna, studying first briefly in Cairo and then Damascus, where he received a bachelor's degree.

Ghannouchi's time at Damascus University (1964–1968) marked a turning point in his life, as it was characterized heavily by his study of Arab politics and history. He was exposed to campus life and bitter student divisions between Ba'athist and Nasserist Arab nationalist movements on the one hand and Muslim Brotherhood–oriented students on the other. The impact of the crushing Arab defeat (the combined forced of Egypt, Syria, and Jordan) by Israel in the Six Day War of 1967 discredited Arab nationalism and, as was true for many Arab youth, Ghannouchi turned to Islam, but an Islamic vision beyond the rigid and lifeless traditional institutions like Zaytouna (he mocked them as "museums"), "an Islam that was alive."[23]

Eventually, my mind rested assured of the wrongfulness of the nationalist way. While my heart was perfectly reassured of Islam, I realized that what I had been following was not the right Islam but a traditional and primitive version of it. The traditional model was not ideological, nor did it represent a comprehensive system. It was a conventional religious sentiment, a set of traditions, customs, and rituals that fell short of representing a civilization or a way of life. I discovered that I was not a true Muslim and therefore I had to take a decision to re-enter Islam.[24]

The Birth of a Movement

In 1968, Ghannouchi went to France intending to obtain a master's degree from the Sorbonne since study in France and mastery of French would help him obtain a good position when he returned to Tunis. Like many others in his generation, studying abroad he found himself immersed in a foreign culture, struggling to retain his faith and identity. He came across a nonpolitical Islamic missionary society founded in Pakistan, whose itinerant missionaries traveled across the world, calling (dawa) Muslims to a more religiously observant lifestyle. The Tabligh provided him with a sense of community, identity, and Islamic activism and purpose. Ghannouchi traveled throughout many parts of France, where he observed and experienced the poor living conditions of North African Muslims, visiting neighborhoods and bars, to bring people back to Islam. In 1969 he became the struggling imam of a small private non-Tabligh storefront mosque, surviving on part-time jobs.

Ghannouchi returned home to visit his family in 1970, having been away for five years. Tunisia was reeling from a failed experiment with a planned socialist economy that had resulted in a depressed economy, unemployment, and strikes. The government turned to political and economic liberalization that also enabled a revivification of Tunisia's Arabic-Islamic identity and heritage. However, Ghannouchi's visit was cut short. His family, fearful that his public criticism of Tunisia's socialist economic policies would result in his arrest and compromise the professional positions of his brothers (a judge and a professor, respectively), convinced him to return to Paris early. Stopping in Tunis, he met some Tablighis who invited him to preach at a mosque and Sheikh

Abd al-Fatah Morou, a lawyer and Islamic activist who nurtured a small grassroots Islamic movement that would soon become a major force in the resurgence of Islam in secular Tunisia. Ghannouchi obtained a teaching position on the philosophy faculty at a secondary, returned to preaching in local mosques, and joined with Morou, whose movement initially focused on social and cultural issues instead of explicit political messages. It offered an Islamic alternative to Western culture: "Our work focused on the development of ideological conscience and consisted essentially of a critique of the Western concepts which dominate the spirit of youth."[25]

A popular teacher and leader, Ghannouchi attracted many young, poor, working-class university students as well as followers from other sectors of society. They then joined forces with the Quranic Preservation Society (QPS), an apolitical cultural and social organization that emphasized piety, morality, and faithfulness to Islam for those who had come to believe that Tunisian society had lost its identity because of an overreliance on the morally bankrupt and corrupt West.[26]

By the late 1970s, Bourguiba's use of the military to crush demonstrations (during the "food riots" of January 1978) and its confrontation with the General Union of Tunisian Workers (UGTT) culminated in a strike and the killing of many workers by Bourguiba's regime. The QPS, including Ghannouchi, became convinced that politics was a reality with which they had to deal: "How could we be that much out of touch with what was actually going on within our own society so that we did not play any role in society?"[27]

The increased visibility of Islam in Muslim politics during the late 1970s, including Iran's Islamic revolution in 1979 and fears of its export, was a challenge for Bourguiba. It threatened his tenure as "President-for-Life," a title appropriated in 1975. He retreated from his campaign against Ramadan and turned to religious scriptures, discourse, and symbols as part of the government's narrative. The official newspaper, El Amal, ran op-eds and features of an explicitly Islamic nature like "The Islamic Origins of Bourguiba's Thought," which appeared with a photograph of the president making a pilgrimage to Mecca.[28]

In 1979, Ghannouchi created the Islamic Association (Jammah al-Islamiyya), which was a political group (though not a political party). The Association reached out to lower- and middle-class families, calling for an end to Bourguiba's one-party system and espousing a vision of Islam that addressed contemporary problems like workers' rights, poverty, wages, and political participation. When Bourguiba liberalized the political apparatus in 1981, the Islamic Association was transformed into a political party, the Islamic Tendency Movement (MTI).

The MTI was not the only Islamic political group to emerge from the early years of the country's religious movement. Other groups included the Islamic Shura Party led by Hassan Ghodbani, the Islamic Progressive Tendency, the Islamic Vanguard, and the Islamic Liberation Party. MTI, however, was the most prominent group but differed with them as a result of Ghannouchi's open commitment to democracy as a viable "system of government and as a method to change."[29] He maintained that democracy and Islam were not incompatible and that it was preferable to live in a secular state where freedoms existed rather than in a strictly religious state with Sharia law where freedoms did not exist:

> [If] by democracy is meant the liberal model of government prevailing in the West, a system under which the people freely choose their representatives and leaders, and in which there is an alternation of power, as well as freedoms and human rights for the public, then the Muslims will find nothing in their religion to oppose democracy, and it is not in their interest to do so anyway.[30]

Despite the MTI's decision to enter officially the political realm, the group was denied a license to operate. Undaunted, it continued to build its movement based on an emphasis of Tunisia's Islamic-Arab identity and values. It found traction among a diverse cross-section of the population: lawyers, bankers, educators, entrepreneurs, union workers, middle-class professionals, and doctors. Its success resulted in growing dissatisfaction and opposition to Bourguiba's repression of dissent and renewed attacks on religion. Tunisian scholar Elbaki Hermassi concluded, "To explain the origin of the MTI one can put forward a reason so obvious that it is rarely taken into account or accorded its full weight. It is that out of all the Arab countries, Tunisia is the only one where the modernist elite deliberately attacked the institutions of Islam and dismantled its infrastructure in the name of systematic reform of the social and cultural order."[31]

Bourguiba cracked down on the MTI two months later, arresting and imprisoning many of its members, including Ghannouchi. The crackdown became a turning point for the Islamist movement in Tunisia. Ghannouchi remained effective during this period, despite his imprisonment, asserting that a violent, Iranian-styled revolution was not the answer. Rather, change, he believed, would be most successful if it came from the bottom up—a slow process that gradually transformed society and used increased political participation and democratic principles to bring about a desired goal: a state that was both Islamic in nature and democratic.[32]

Vitality and growth within the MTI stood in sharp contrast to the Bourguiba government's failures: poor economic conditions, financial mismanagement, and corruption, which led to mounting discontent and bread riots that broke out in 1984. Bourguiba attempted to stave off opposition by claiming that Islamists espoused a "radical fundamentalism" and were linked to an Iranian-style religious revolution. Yet, "despite attempts to link the Islamist movement with Iranian extremism, [the Tunisian government] had not been able to eradicate what Bourguiba routinely and contemptuously described as the vestiges of an outdated religious traditionalism."[33] That year, Ghannouchi was freed from prison, but his release was only temporary. Before long, the initial crackdown on Islamist groups would snowball into a full-blown attack against them and against expressions of religion in the public square.

> The government banned civil servants from praying during work hours and closed mosques it had opened previously to buffer "leftist extremism." Public institutions were ordered not to hire back Islamists who had lost their jobs during the 1981–84 incarceration. Women wearing the veil were barred from the universities and workplaces. Islamist university students were expelled and drafted into the military. Taxi drivers caught wearing neatly trimmed beards—the mark par excellence of the Islamist—or listening to Islamist cassettes had their beards cut and their licenses revoked.[34]

In August 1987, Ghannouchi was arrested again and tried before the state security court, accused of inciting violence and conspiring against the government. Bourguiba's attempt to suppress the MTI and other Islamists was a miscalculation and backfired. The trial aroused sympathies for the MTI and other Islamist groups (including Lebanon's Islamic Jihad) who joined in solidarity with their Tunisian counterparts. When the courts sentenced Ghannouchi to life imprisonment at hard labor, Bourguiba, furious, immediately ordered a new trial, confirming suspicions that he wanted Ghannouchi executed and the MTI eradicated.

Islamist groups, however threatening, were ultimately not the major risk to Bourguiba's reign. Bureaucratic infighting undermined the stability of the president's inner circle. Zine al Abidine Ben Ali, a former general and longtime protégé who had served as the minister of interior and had presided over government crackdowns on Islamist groups like the MTI, sacked and succeeded Prime Minister Mohammed Mzali and his successor, Rached Sfar. Moreover, on November 7, 1987, Ben Ali led a bloodless coup d'état, claiming that the 84-year-old "Supreme Combatant" and "President-for-Life" was senile and incapable of performing his national duties. He took over the reins of power as the country's second president.[35]

The Ben Ali Presidency

The initial months of Ben Ali's arrival on the scene looked promising. He went on a public pilgrimage to Mecca, incorporated religious language into his speeches, reopened the theological faculty at Zaytouna, and announced that the fast of Ramadan would be officially observed. In response to the apparent political liberalization and Ben Ali's requirement that no party could monopolize Islam, MTI agreed to change its name in December 1988 to Hizb ut-Nahda (the Renaissance Party). However, toward the end of 1988, Tunisians soon realized that their new leader was not so new after all.

Ben Ali renamed Bourguiba's ND party the Constitutional Democratic Rally (Rassemblement Constitutionnel Démocratique—RCD), but that did not alter the dominant position of the party within Tunisia's political and social landscape, nor did it mitigate a system of authoritarianism that controlled the electoral process and sought to marginalize any opposition. In April 1989, during the country's first and much-touted multiparty (rather than single-party) presidential elections, the RCD averaged about 1.7 million votes; all of its candidates were elected. Stunningly, despite the fact that they were not granted party status, second place went to independent candidates, backed by Ennahda, who received over 17 percent of the vote, and in urban areas more than 30 percent. Bolstered by their strong showing, party leaders again called on Ben Ali to formally recognize their party and argued that if the government continued down the Bourguiba path and locked them out of political participation, despite their clear public support, they might not be able to control the more radical fringes of their rank and file.[36] Inside Ben Ali's elite circle, some argued that it was time for the president to stop flirting with the Islamists and crush and eliminate them once and for all. A political crackdown seemed imminent, and fearing the outcome, in May 1989, Ghannouchi and key supporters fled from Tunisia to London (others to France), where he lived in self-imposed exile for twenty-one years. He commented at the time:

> All our concessions became of no avail. Not even the relinquishment of the very name of our movement helped. Nor was of any avail the flexibility and moderation that we forced on ourselves to avoid a return to confrontation and to spare our country's resources so that they may not be used except for the purpose of development and in confronting the colossal challenges facing our nation.[37]

Ghannouchi's exit frustrated communications between Ennahda's leadership and its base and set the stage for increased tensions between Ben Ali's government and some members of the movement. Fearing that war in the Gulf would aggravate regional stability and reunify the splintered Ennahda, Ben Ali preemptively struck out at the group, arresting more than two hundred of its members in late December 1990.[38] Three months later, in February 1991, authorities accused Ennahda of being behind an arson attack on the ruling party's offices, and after that, of a plot to overthrow the government entirely. Three months later, in May, security forces in concert with the military claimed to have unearthed a large arsenal of weapons that Islamists had concealed as part of a violent scheme against Ben Ali. Ennahda officially repudiated the attack and the government could not prove that the group was responsible. Human rights organizations criticized the regime for basing their claims about the weapons stash on flimsy evidence. Still, more than three hundred of the party's leaders and supporters were arrested and eventually security forces rounded up thousands of others. For Ben Ali, the event was an opportunity to cripple the group further, and a government campaign to discredit Ennahda eventually led to a split in its leadership. Additionally, between 1990 and 1992, security forces cast a dragnet that hauled in more than eight thousand activists.[39] Late-night searches and raids of homes became commonplace, and stories of forceful interrogation multiplied. At least seven members of Ennahda died in custody, and evidence suggested that their deaths were the result of torture.[40] Two hundred seventy-nine members were tried by a military tribunal and given prison sentences from fifteen years to life.

In addition to the harsh crackdown on Ennahda, Ben Ali created his own personal security apparatus, used to intimidate the press, the judiciary, and any form of potential opposition.[41] Christopher Alexander reported, "Over the past two decades, human rights groups have assembled a very thick brief against the government for a wide range of abuses: prolonged incommunicado detentions; extracting confessions through a variety of methods of torture; surveillance; phone tapping; threats against family members; job dismissals; fabricating prurient stories about personal lives in order to discredit and blackmail; passport confiscations that prevent foreign travel; physical assaults by security officers."[42]

Salafism

Despite the fact that the economy had improved and opposition had been all but exterminated, an increased authoritarian grip, a population that was growing wearier of economic inequality by the day, corruption, and lack of real political participation characterized the first decade of the 21st century, leading up to Tunisia's historic revolution.

Though the emergence of Salafism in Tunisian politics is a recent phenomenon, its origins, diverse manifestations, and orientations date back to the late 19th and early 20th centuries with the arrival of Muhammad 'Abduh's Egyptian Islamic modernist reform in North Africa. The term comes from *salaf,* meaning "forefathers" or the earliest generation of Muslims. In the late 19th century, Muhammad 'Abduh and his disciple Rashid Rida began an intellectual/theological and educational reform movement. It maintained that religion and reason/science are compatible and that Islamic reform required a process of religious reinterpretation (*ijtihad*). The influence of the movement spread to North Africa and to Southeast Asia.

The term "Salafism" (which also includes the similarly minded Wahhabi of Saudi Arabia) today refers to conservative, sometimes called puritanical, movements that may be apolitical or political. "Salafism" within the contemporary Tunisian context refers to a broad spectrum of individuals and movements that are to the right, often far right, of Ennahda. Despite some similarities, their beliefs, rhetoric, and interpretations of Islam and the relationship between religion and politics and tactics often differ significantly. Moreover, within the Salafist movement itself, there are variances.

There are two main strands of Tunisian Salafism: *salafiyya 'almiyya* (often translated as "scientific Salafism" but better understood as "scripturalist Salafism") and *salafiyya jihadiyya*, or jihadi Salafism. Scripturalist Salafists tend to avoid politics. They view it as morally corrupt and instead seek to establish a morally pure caliphate, one in line with their view of God's plan for earth, and one that operates based on the imposition of Sharia law. Democracy is generally perceived as the blasphemous imposition of human rule, as opposed to divine sovereignty or rule.[43] While some scripturalist Salafists have formed a political path (including Mohamed Khouja, leader of the Reform Front), such offshoots tend to be quite small and ineffective. Jihadi Salafists in Tunisia also usually reject political participation, but their approach to changing the dynamics of the government differs from the scripturalists. Jihadi Salafists paint the scripturalists as out of touch and irrelevant and believe that the only way to realize God's will and rule is through direct and deliberate challenge and, when necessary, violent confrontation.[44]

For years, Salafists were silent; they were repressed, driven underground, or forced overseas. Importantly, though, it was during the 2000s that their presence began to be felt in Tunisia. Some Tunisian youth looked online where they found radical Internet preachers. They joined local pockets of Salafist activity and espoused a violent brand of activism against not only the "infidel" forces of the West, but also their own government.

Because Ennahda and other Islamist groups were repressed, the emergence of the Salafists, even if only briefly, proved to be significant as it allowed Ben Ali to advance the narrative of the "Islamist threat" to a greater degree. The 9/11 attacks, the US-led GWOT, and subsequent acts of terrorism in Europe provided a further source of legitimacy rationale for Ben Ali. A strong ally in the United States' quest to root out Muslim extremists, these events allowed him to strengthen his coercive apparatus and justify civil liberties violations which included torture, wiretapping, unwarranted imprisonment, home raids, and intimidation.

In April 2002, al-Qaeda terrorists carried out a violent attack on a synagogue in Djerba. Stefano Torelli notes, "Since the mid-2000s, Tunisians who had fought in Afghanistan, Bosnia, Chechnya and Iraq have linked up with outside jihadists to strengthen a presence in Tunisia, where young men had begun to practice Salafism in order to combat the secular regime of Ben Ali."[45]

Growing Inequity

Despite Tunisia's economic progress, high youth unemployment, income disparity, corruption, and regional inequities were brewing a toxic mix of disillusionment and despair. A drop in the European market demand for Tunisian products compounded this, and thus exports decreased. By 2008 the industrial sector had also contracted.

Though the Tunisian government implemented a reform package in 2010, it did little to address underlying economic and employment problems. It did not, for instance, create jobs for Tunisia's university graduates; some 20 percent were without work. As a result of the economic turmoil in Europe (and in the United States), Tunisian youth could not find work at home, nor were their prospects for work abroad very promising. There was a clear mismatch between the field of specialization and college degree and the actual jobs that existed in the market. Thus, unemployment reached more than 47 percent for graduates with a master's in economics, management, or law, and more than 43 percent for those holding a master's degree in social sciences. Unemployment hovered above 24 percent for those who graduated with a degree in engineering.[46]

The 2010 economic reforms also deepened the gap that existed between the cities and rural areas in terms of economic inequality. This convinced many people, who saw their compatriots in the urban quarters doing just fine, that the government was isolated and focused on city dwellers and did not care about those who existed outside of the metropolises. Neither Ben Ali nor his government was aware of the degree to which such dissatisfaction and desolation existed.[47]

Social inequality was compounded by the corruption of Ben Ali's family. WikiLeaks released a secret cable from the US Embassy in Tunis that exposed the corruption of Ben Ali's family, including the extravagant lifestyle and questionable business deals of First Lady Leila Trabelsi and her son-in-law, Mohamed Sakher El Materi, a 28-year-old business tycoon. In a cable dated July 2009, US ambassador Robert Godec remarked, "The opulence with which El Materi and [his wife] live and their behavior make clear why they and other members of Ben Ali's family are disliked and even hated by some Tunisians. The excesses of the Ben Ali family are growing."[48] The Global Financial Integrity Foundation estimated that the cost of corruption in the country had ballooned over time to about US $1 billion per year.[49] With prescience, the US ambassador warned that Tunisia had a real "problem," that Ben Ali refused to listen to advice, and that "the chorus of complaints is rising."[50]

The Fall of Ben Ali and Birth of a Second Republic?

When Ben Ali realized that the protesters wanted to end his regime, hundreds of security officers were dispersed into the streets and brutally assaulted demonstrators. State security forces, the *mukhabarat*, had in the past used rubber bullets, tear gas, clubs, and even water hoses to quell opposition. But this time, Ben Ali resorted to deadly force. On December 24, they fired real ammunition from the roofs of nearby buildings at protesters in Manzel Bouzayane, killing two people.[51] By the end of January, at least three hundred people were killed and more than seven hundred were wounded.[52]

Social media proved an effective medium of communication and mobilization. Facebook, Twitter, cellphones, and other forms of communication were critical to the early developments of those organizing protests against the government. According to one study, 91 percent of university students in Tunisia maintained a Facebook page and visit it at least once per day, spending 105 minutes there on average.[53] Information about the demonstrations spread quickly, and the government's actions were recorded and spread for the world to see. Responding to this, Ben Ali's regime blocked YouTube, Daily Motion, and other social media sites, and Facebook's chief security officer, Joe Sullivan, confirmed that in December 2010, the Tunisian government attempted to hack into Facebook and steal user passwords but was stopped from doing so.[54] When activists outsmarted the government's strict program of censorship, the government backtracked and announced in January 2011 that the filters had been lifted. The concession and promises of further reforms were too late. On the evening of January 14, Tunisia's leader of twenty-three years gave up the fight and the country was propelled down a pathway toward a second republic.

Where Were the Islamists?

Many wondered in the early days of protests why, as Olivier Roy wrote in the *New York Times*, "there is nothing Islamic about it."[55] The main reason, as discussed earlier in this chapter, was that Ennahda had been excluded from participation in party politics and forced underground, while many of the movement's most influential leaders, like Ghannouchi, were in exile overseas.

Additionally, since the revolt was not primarily about Islam, Tunisians were less concerned about Islam's role in the transition and cared more about a new government, its political institutions, and democratization. Surveys of 1,201 Tunisians and 4,080 Egyptians conducted in October–November 2012, nearly one year after the post-revolutionary elections, indicated that a minority of the population—26 percent in Tunisia and 28 percent in Egypt—believe that Islam should play a governmental role.[56] In Tunisia specifically, only 27 percent of Tunisians who voted for Ennahda in 2011 wanted a close relationship between religion and politics and 32 percent of those polled put economic growth at the top of their priority lists.[57]

Islamists' initial absence and the concerns of Tunisians over non-religious matters did not preclude their re-emergence in politics and stunning victory in elections. This raised many questions, including these two: Why did Ennahda perform so strongly in elections? How could a group that was disconnected from the thrust of the revolution sweep in at the eleventh hour and win? The answer is threefold. First, the ousting of Ben Ali left a vacuum in the capital city's halls of power. After twenty-three years of ruling the country, the president was finally gone and there was not a well-greased system in place to replace him. While many remnants of the "old guard" hoped to (and tried to) remain in place, those that had brought down their country's embattled leader were not going to allow them to remain in power.

Second, Ennahda, though in exile, was not politically dormant. When Ghannouchi returned home to Tunisia in January 2011, the movement was well organized despite its suppression, had charismatic leaders (in particular Ghannouchi), and, most importantly, had a long history as the primary opposition to Bourguiba and Ben Ali and bore the battle scars that gave them popular legitimacy. In the absence of comparably strong political parties and the emergence of so many new but weak parties, they were capable of immediately rising to power.

Finally, Ghannouchi's years in exile provided him with the space to see and reflect, to refine his understanding of secularism and democracy, to study their diverse potential applications in the Arab world and Tunisia in particular, and finally to return home in 2011 with a sense of the direction the country needed to go. Though he vowed not to participate in the presidential elections, his presence represented for Tunisians a prominent reformer and opposition leader who had stood up and suffered for his opposition to Bourghiba and Ben Ali and an Islamic movement markedly different from the images and fear-mongering deployed by Ben Ali and others. It was one that advocated political reforms and a democratic message of political inclusion, pluralism, and freedom.

During the lead-up to the Constituent Assembly election, the Tunisian Higher Election Authority (ISIE) registered more voters across the country, and by the end of August 2011, approximately 4 million out of an estimated 7.5 million eligible voters had registered.[58] On October 23 of that year, the country's first free elections were held since it gained independence in 1956; the occasion also marked the first election in the Arab world since the beginning of the Arab Spring. Ben Ali's former government officials, worried that Ennahda would win the elections, formed several parties including the Al Watan (the Nation), the Justice and Liberty Party, and Al Moubedra (the Initiative). Rachid Ghannouchi countered that the forces of the old regime were "attempting to circumvent the revolution . . . through new parties and behind the scenes by maneuvering powerful figures from Ben Ali's era."[59] Ghannouchi made it clear during the campaign that Ennahda had no intentions of implementing Sharia. His daughter, Soumaya Ghannouchi declared, "We don't believe in a theocracy that imposes a lifestyle or thoughts or ways of life on people; we believe in the right of every Tunisian woman and man to make that choice."[60] Many viewed Ennahda as "more honest than corrupt secularists" and "true to their values."[61]

The election was, by most indicators, a triumph for democracy and nothing short of historic in a region long beset by predetermined results and voter coercion. With a turnout rate of more than 50 percent, the plurality of Tunisians—some 40 percent—cast their ballots for Ennahda. The party was the strongest by far in the legislature and agreed immediately to cooperate with the two runners-up, the Congress for the Republic (CPR) and Ettakatol.

Polling data conducted after the first elections that brought the first Islamist party to power are striking. While many Tunisians believed that religion should inform politics, most reported that they did not seek an active role for religion or for religious officials in public life.[62] For example, 78.4 percent of respondents agreed that "men of religion" should not influence how citizens vote in elections, and only 30.6 percent said that they believed it would be better if Tunisia had more religious officials in office.[63] Moreover, 78.5 percent agreed with the statement that religion is a private matter and it should be separate from social and political life. Some 94 percent said that they believed the revolution would bring about better economic opportunities and an improvement in human rights, and 63 percent said that the primary cause of the uprisings was economic dissatisfaction. Thus, Ennahda's emergence as the victor in the Constituent Assembly elections indicates that Rachid Ghannouchi's vision of Islam as a factor in Tunisian identity, culture, and politics but not the driver, appeared to be consistent with the desires of most Tunisians.

In December, the Ennahda-dominated Assembly elected Moncef Marzouki, physician, human rights activist, and founder of the Congress for the Republic, whose opposition to Ben Ali's abuse of power had resulted in his move to Paris. Both Ghannouchi and Marzouki had a mutual commitment to Tunisian democracy that generally transcended ideological differences and put the country's interests above the interests of their parties. They agreed on maintaining the language of the first article of the 1957 constitution, refraining from mentioning Islamic law: "Tunisia is a free, independent and sovereign state. Its religion is Islam.[64]

The first six months of transition witnessed severe problems that transcended religious and ideological concerns. Tourism was hit hard by the revolution, with revenues dropping by 40 percent and foreign direct investment by 60 percent. There was little economic growth, and unemployment jumped to 20 percent across the board (for university graduates unemployment in 2011 was 25 percent). Complicating matters, Tunisia also lost revenue through remittances as citizens fled the initial violence for Europe and other locations and the government also had to deal with a growing refugee crisis: the Libyan civil war that was raging next door meant that some 150,000 stranded citizens were in need of help along the borders. The coalition government, despite its differences, worked together for the sake of Tunisia's stability.[65]

Domestic politics remained volatile, fueled by secularists and Salafists in particular. On one side of the debate were educated secular elites that insisted on the separation of religion and politics; on the other, a growing segment of youth whose desires for stability led them to an ultraconservative Salafist religious worldview whose militancy sometimes resulted in violence. In late November 2011, hundreds of Salafists clashed with secularists near Tunis in a showdown over segregated university classes and full-face veils (*niqabs*). At Manouba

University, near Tunis, female students wearing *niqabs* were denied entrance to the Faculty of Arts on the basis of their dress, setting off a wave of angry supporters. In June 2012, another flashpoint of conflict between the two groups emerged. Salafists attacked an art gallery in Tunis over an exhibition that they charged insulted Islam. Similarly, in the nearby town of Sousse, a mob attacked a local fine arts shop with firebombs. In Monastir, as well as in Ben Guerdane on the Libyan border, skirmishes erupted between secularists and Salafists.

In February 2013, the shooting death of Chokri Belaid, a 48-year-old secular activist and a fierce critic of Islamists (both Ennahda and Salafists) triggered widespread political unrest and protests. Belaid's death came at a time when relations between the Ennahda-led government and the opposition had deteriorated. Acrimony between secularists and Islamists scuttled a plan by Prime Minister Hamadi Jebali, a member of Ennahda, for a nonpartisan cabinet of technocrats. Jebali hoped to bring calm to the country and form a coalition that would take Tunisia toward elections but he did not consult Ennahda or the secular opposition. Vowing to step down if the plan floundered, he resigned on February 19, 2013. The resignation posed the threat of more volatility. Marzouki urged Ghannouchi to appoint a new prime minister in the wake of Jebali's resignation. Ali Larayedh, the former MTI activist who was imprisoned and tortured for fifteen years (thirteen of which were in isolation) by the regime of Ben Ali, succeeded Jebali. "I almost died several times in the jails of the interior ministry," Larayedh said. "But I mark the difference between that period and now. The revolution came to advance and establish a transitional justice and not to seek vengeance."[66]

Larayedh struggled to keep the coalition together. Despite calls from the secular opposition for the appointment of apolitical technocrats to sensitive state institutions, the government that emerged was made up of the same parties that existed before the assassination of Belaid. There were, however, indications that Ennahda and the coalition government were still operating within the spirit of cooperation, not conflict. Ennahda made a key concession in accepting that ministries such as interior and justice be reserved for independent candidates.

The coalition government faced sharp criticism from those who suggested that the process was playing out too slowly. But few could deny that, despite flashes of progress, conflicts and disagreements remained within established institutions, especially the Constituent Assembly. The polarization between radical Salafists and staunch secularists was trumped by a mainstream that, differences notwithstanding, recognized, even if for some begrudgingly, the importance of collaboration in navigating the challenges ahead. It contrasted sharply with Egypt, where the parliament had been dissolved, the democratically elected president had been deposed by a military-led coup, the Muslim Brotherhood had been banned, and violence and repression had become an everyday occurrence.[67]

A Troubled Transition

In early March 2013, Larayedh unveiled the long-awaited coalition government that had been stalled by the political crisis triggered by the assassination of Belaid. A last-minute deal was reached, however, which allowed a government to take shape and oversee the country's affairs until the end of the year, when elections would be held.

The center-left Ettakatol Party backed the new government, as did the secular Congress for the Republic, a party led by Tunisia's president, Moncef Marzouki. Though Larayedh and his Ennahda associates had hoped to build a broad-based coalition that reflected a more diverse swathe of the population, three parties that were initially invited to participate in the talks pulled out, leaving the task of forming a new government up to Larayedh's Ennahda Party, Ettakatol, and the Congress for the Republic. The inability of the government to include more political parties in the debate underscored the delicate nature of the post–Ben Ali transition. Ennahda made several significant concessions to preserve national unity. Among them, they agreed to hand over key ministries, including the Ministry of the Interior and the Ministry of Justice, to independent candidates.[68] The concessions were an act of good faith on the part of Larayedh, who hoped to avert further instability and strife. The act also set a standard for other states in the region, where similar difficult negotiations often failed to reach resolution as each side refused to cede its position.

The spring of 2013 was a time of troubled transition, characterized by several flashpoint events that underscored growing discontent and animosity between the secular opposition and Ennahda and between Ennahda and hardline Salafists.

The arrest of Amina Sboui (also known as Amina Tyler), a 19-year-old activist who posed topless for FEMEN, a Ukrainian group that stages provocative stunts in order to bring attention to women's issues, launched a national and regional debate about the role of women in post-revolutionary societies. Salafist groups like Ansar al-Sharia complicated the issue. Salafi preacher Alami Adel, head of the Commission for the Promotion of Virtue and Prevention of Vice (enforcers of Islamic law), a nongovernmental civil society organization, suggested that Tyler receive eighty to a hundred public lashings for her act and even argued that death by stoning was the more appropriate consequence.[69]

SALAFISTS WERE COMPRISED of several different groups with varying degrees of militancy. Ennahda initially reached out to Salafists as it did to other groups, due to its commitment to political pluralism, because it saw them as potential allies, and also lest it be vulnerable to Salafist accusations that the government was compromising Islamic faith and values. In its first year, the government registered three Salafist political parties and Hizb ut-Tahrir as it registered many other parties, as well as Salafist charities and schools. In the new climate of freedom of expression, the more extreme Salafi elements also thrived. Salafists unilaterally took over hundreds of mosques (approximately one thousand out of the five thousand mosques in Tunisia), driving out the original imams and worshipers. Many demanded that Sharia be the basis of the constitution, organizing frequent protests against what they perceived as threats to Islam or violations of Islamic culture and practices, and mobilized disaffected factions of the population, including many youth who joined their program of vigilantism, lashing out at artists in particular. Galleries showing contemporary works of art were vandalized in a riot that killed one and injured more than one hundred, and a Sufi shrine was also desecrated.

However, critics exploited the situation, charging that there was little difference between Ennahda and the Salafists or that Ennahda was unable or unwilling to put an end to what had become a serious security issue. Finally, prior to 2014 elections, the Ennahda government moved decisively to take back the mosques seized and occupied by Salafists. Government ministers sought to draw out connections between groups like Ansar al-Sharia and al-Qaeda, considered the most radical of the extremist groups that emerged after the 2011 revolution. Saif Allah Bin Hussein, a former al-Qaeda fighter in Afghanistan, threatened to wage war against the Ennahda-led government, accusing it of policies in breach of Islam.[70]

In the wake of the military coup in Egypt, which deposed Mohamed Morsi and placed him and hundreds of his Muslim Brotherhood colleagues in military custody, Tunisia's ruling party became the only Islamist-led government in the region. Many, including leaders of foreign governments and UN officials, feared that the events in Egypt would have a serious impact on the future and stability of other Arab countries including Tunisia. Prime Minister Larayedh sought to assuage those fears, saying, "Our approach is characterized by consensus and partnership. The possibility of an Egypt scenario is unlikely in Tunisia because I have great confidence in the awareness of Tunisians and their ability to measure the potential of their country."[71] The Tunisian government denounced Egypt's military-led coup and brutal violence and repression in Egypt. Rachid Ghannouchi called on the Muslim Brotherhood to stay in the streets of Egypt until Morsi was freed. When Egyptian security forces opened fire on a Muslim Brotherhood gathering on July 8, he charged, "Putschist forces committed a massacre against peaceful protesters supporting the legitimate President." He called on Egyptians to "reject the coup and support the pro-democratic legitimacy front."[72] Marzouki, the country's secular president, also expressed his displeasure with the chain of events that eventuated in Morsi's toppling, saying that it was a "blow to democracy."[73]

Fomenting Destabilization and Upheaval

Despite concessions from its leaders, the Ennahda-led government continued to face political upheaval, triggered by carefully planned and executed acts of violence and assassinations.

On July 25, secular opposition leader Mohamed Brahmi, a member of the Leftist Popular Front who was critical of Ennahda, was assassinated outside of his home in the Ariana suburb of Tunis, his body riddled with fourteen bullets. The killing was almost identical to that of Chokri Belaid, just six months earlier. Though the assailants escaped on a motorcycle, a report by the Interior Ministry noted that Brahmi was killed with the same gun that was used to kill Belaid. Early indications pointed to Salafist hardliner Boubacar Hakim.[74]

Brahmi's murder prompted massive street protests and fueled secular opposition groups who claimed disingenuously that their charges of possible Ennahda involvement were validated. Augmenting their claim was an attack at Mount Chaambi four days after Brahmi's assassination. Militants ambushed eight Tunisian soldiers on guard near the Algerian border and killed them all. Humans Rights Watch reported a sharp recurrence of violence in the post–Ben Ali period that threatened to undermine rights and reforms: "During the year, assaults were carried out against intellectuals, artists, human rights activists, and journalists by individuals or groups who appeared to be motivated by a religious agenda. While many of the victims filed complaints at police stations immediately after the assaults, the police proved unwilling or unable to find or arrest the alleged attackers."[75] In the wake of Morsi's overthrow, motivated by the killing of figures like Belaid and Brahmi, and a series of bomb blasts that shook urban centers of the country, opposition groups intensified their rhetoric and demonstrations. The animosity between hardline secularists and the Ennahda-led government grew, with many ordinary Tunisians in the middle choosing sides in an increasingly polarized public sphere.

A "Tamarod" (rebellion) group, modeled on the Egyptian organization that helped propel Egypt's military coup, emerged in Tunisia, calling for parliament to be dissolved immediately. After Brahmi's murder, the group issued a statement calling on Tunisians to "occupy the streets until the fall of the government." They added, "We cannot get somewhere with empty words. The best solution is taking the streets over against the authorities who do not know the meaning of protecting citizens."[76] Thousands of Tunisians rallied in the streets, calling on the government to resign. It was a familiar sight. The country's largest labor union, the Tunisian General Labor Union (UGTT), called for a technocratic government to replace the Ennahda-led government, charging that it was incapable of doing its job.[77] Fearing political turmoil, members of the transitional Constituent Assembly began to withdraw their membership, breaking away a critical foundation of the country's stability and institutional capacity. In late August, the secular opposition rejected a proposal for "national dialogue" to address governance and security issues.

Ennahda Resigns

On September 28, 2013, after months of political wrangling, Ennahda withdrew from the government. This marked the second occasion that it chose compromise to curb political instability and safeguard national unity. Ennahda handed over power to an interim caretaker government to guide the country toward parliamentary elections (the new cabinet was sworn in two days after the constitution was approved). In an effort to prevent any one body from becoming too powerful (and thus preserving a critical institution of democracy: checks and balances), the assembly, in which Ennahda held the largest number of seats, remained intact, serving as a check on the new administration.

While some members of Ennahda (and the secular opposition) viewed the resignation as a defeat, Ennahda's decision-makers opted for a less contentious path, one that put the overall political goals of democratic governance and national unity ahead of personal or party ambitions. Rafik Abdessalam, the former foreign minister, said, "It [Ennahda] is being described as the party of concessions. We are not ashamed of these concessions because they are needed by Tunisia and to secure our democratic experience so that Tunisia can reach a safe shore."[78] The decision bore fruit.

Fruits of a Revolution

Tunisia's National Constituent Assembly restructured the government, with Tunisia's industry minister, Mehdi Jomaa, appointed as the interim prime minister and head of the caretaker government.

The process of finalizing the constitution was marked by sharp debate and contentious negotiations throughout the fall and early winter of 2013. The more conservative majority and secular opposition butted heads on more than one occasion, disagreeing over fundamental issues like women's rights and freedoms of speech and religion. As a result a number of articles reflected the twists and turns of diverse interest groups. Article 6, for instance, attempted to appease two very different segments of society: a religious cadre that saw the government as the protector *of* religion, and a staunchly secular contingent that viewed the government as the protector *from* religion.[79] Navigating this sensitive path of disagreement produced an awkwardly worded passage:

> The State is the guardian of religion. It guarantees liberty of conscience and of belief, the free exercise of religious worship and the neutrality of the mosques and of the places of worship from all partisan instrumentalization. The State commits itself to the dissemination of the values of moderation and tolerance and to the protection of the sacred and the prohibition of any offense thereto. It commits itself, equally, to the prohibition of, and the fight against, appeals to Takfir [charges of apostasy] and incitement to violence and hatred.[80]

The imprecise wording allowed for a variety of interpretations and may easily serve as an instrument for judges to advance their personal ideologies within the framework of a legal ruling.[81]

Additionally, some women's rights groups charged that Article 21, which guarantees the "right to life," may be used by some to advance bans on abortions, which are currently legal in the early stages of pregnancy; some also see Article 7, which defines the family as the "nucleus of society," as a possible opening for future limits on divorce.[82]

Despite these concerns, however, on January 26, 2014, three years after demonstrations ousted Ben Ali, Tunisian politicians succeeded in reaching an agreement on the constitution. It was received as a historic success in many domestic and international quarters. While the specific articles would likely be the subject of debate and discussion over the years, the consensus that emerged was a testament to Tunisia's democratic transition following the ouster of Ben Ali: the restructuring of the political process in a way that honored the institutions of democracy and did not allow one group or individual to dominate the process. Whereas Egypt's constitution was shaped to benefit the very people who would eventually come to power, the implementation of the Tunisian constitution ahead of presidential and parliamentary elections was an encouraging sign that the document would form the unshakeable guiding structure that it should in democratic societies.

Central to this process was the involvement of the UGTT and civil society groups, including the employer's union, the Tunisian Bar Association, and the country's Human Rights League. The UGTT was an effective mobilizer, particularly because it served as a platform for such a wide variety of voices and opinions, bringing them together in service of a common goal. The group united citizens from all social classes, embracing doctors, lawyers, bankers, teachers, and laborers. Its leadership, which is nonpartisan, meant that it was better able to bring together a broad spectrum of political parties and ideological orientations. By combining such a diverse group and striking a cooperative balance with the aforementioned civil society groups, the UTGG was a formidable challenge to the government, ultimately forcing it to negotiate.[83] As Sara Chayes writes, "Without the muscular involvement of the General Union of Tunisian Workers (l'Union générale tunisienne du travail, or UGTT)—perhaps the only organization whose power and legitimacy rival the Islamists'—it is unlikely that Tunisia's remarkable political settlement would have come about."[84]

2014 Parliamentary Elections

The year 2014 proved a turning point for Ennahda's political fortunes. In parliamentary elections on October 26, 2014, Nidaa Tounes won 85 seats in the 217-member assembly, ahead of 69 secured by Ennahda. The Nidaa Tounes, a self-styled liberal secular democratic coalition party, like its leader, Beji Caid Essebsi, was composed in large part by Tunisia's traditional, political elite who portrayed themselves as a liberal democratic alternative to Ennahda. They charged that the Ennahda-led government had lacked the political and technocratic knowledge and experience to govern effectively and especially to address its faltering economy and joblessness. Tunisia's media, which had generally consistently opposed Ennahda throughout its governance, portrayed Ennahda as single-handedly responsible for extremist violence and lack of security. Ennahda's loss of political power was finalized with the victory of Nidaa Tounes' Essebsi in the presidential elections on December 21, 2014.

Critics of Nidaa Tounes countered that Ennahda had inherited a stagnant economy and joblessness whose magnitude would take years to resolve. They warned of a return to Bourghiba and Ben Ali's model of one-man governance with its heavy-handed security practices. This concern was reinforced by the technocratic government of Prime Minister Mehdi Jomaa, one of a number of major concessions Ennahda had made to assure national unity and a democratic process. During the previous summer, it had closed more than 155 nongovernmental organizations and approved police roundups of youth as necessary to combat Tunisia's terrorist threat, a precedent that Nidaa Tounes might use to target not only militant Salafists but also its strongest opposition, Ennahda. At the same time, Ennahda's support for the democratic process was evidenced in May 2014 by the passing of an electoral law that rejected voices that demanded the exclusion of Ben Ali officials from serving in the government. Ennahda members had been divided on this issue, but Rachid Ghannouchi (who supported a policy of inclusion, noting the revolution was completed "without revenge") prevailed. Ironically, the exclusion clause would have prevented ex-RCD figures, including Essebsi, from competing in the elections.

After Essebsi's election as president, he initially broke his promise to form a broad coalition (as Ennahda had done following its election), influenced by a illiberal secular leftist current in Nidaa Tounes who were adamant in wanting to exclude Ennahda from governance. In late January 2015, Prime Minister Habib Essid announced a government with twenty-four ministers that excluded Ennahda, the second important political power with sixty-nine seats at the parliament. The exclusion caused a wave of criticism. Faced with the controversy and the fact that Nidaa Tounes was a minority government with less than half the votes necessary to survive a no-confidence vote in parliament, Essid delayed the vote of confidence. On February 2, Essid announced a new Nidaa Tounes-led government whose cabinet members included Ennahda. The Nidaa Tounes party got six ministries and three deputy ministers, while Ennahda got one ministry, the Ministry of Employment, and three deputy ministers, far from the level of Ennahda representation in parliament. Despite this fact, Ghannouchi and the Ennahda leadership supported the government in the parliamentary *vote* of confidence, demonstrating its acceptance of the election results and its commitment to national unity and the democratic process.

Conclusion

Despite significant differences and fierce rivalries in Tunisian politics, in contrast to Egypt's coup or Libya's chaos, Tunisians were able to move along the road to democratization, avoiding its derailment because of its stronger civil society organizations, the military's professionalism, and the responsiveness and significant concessions made by Ghannouchi and Ennahda.

The country's new leadership and government is challenged by major economic problems and high unemployment rates and needs to enact structural reforms and revisions of investment and labor codes, along with exhibiting a commitment to human and civil rights. Violence carried out by political or religious extremists must be dealt with swiftly and effectively under the new laws of the country. Nidaa Tounes and more hardline secularists will continue to be challenged to demonstrate a commitment to political inclusion and not exclusion in its future dealings with Ennahda and other nonviolent Islamists.

At the end of the day, Tunisian politics cannot be perceived as or become a simplistic contest between Islamist and secularist forces that desire a democratic or undemocratic future. The Islamist-secularist divide must give way to a more nuanced understanding of democracy: a system of government that brings together multiple voices and actors, considers the desires of the public, and emphasizes the effectiveness of the democratic process and the well-being of the country instead of ideological differences and repression of dissent. This understanding must include a recognition of the legitimacy of political opposition as long as it is a loyal opposition, an opposition whose ultimate loyalty is to national unity and the equality and prosperity of all.

8

Egypt

FROM DEMOCRATIZATION TO THE RESTORATION OF AUTHORITARIANISM

THE MODERN MUSLIM political experience has too often been one of rulers (kings, military, and ex-military) and regimes that are backed by military and security forces and lack popular legitimacy. Thus, Arab countries have commonly been referred to as security (*mukhabarat*) states. Egypt offers a classic, perhaps even an archetypal, case study of this phenomenon.

Throughout much of its modern history, Egypt was seen as a major power and leader in the Arab world in terms of politics, military strength, religion, education, and culture. It has also been an exemplar of Arab autocracy and authoritarianism, governed by three successive regimes from 1952 to 2011: Gamal Abdel Nasser (1956–1970), Anwar Sadat (1970–1981), and finally Hosni Mubarak (1981–2011), who was overthrown in the Arab Spring uprising. These are of course three very different autocracies with very different records and legacies.

The legitimacy and security of these regimes over the years have been based, in part, on the calculated implementation of an autocratic political system that emphasized top-down rule and the close relationship between the regime and the country's military, police, and other security forces.[1]

While the governments of Nasser and Sadat undoubtedly shaped Egypt's political trajectory in many important though different ways, the sheer length of Mubarak's three-decade-long reign as president crystallized a coercive apparatus that allowed him to perpetuate his rule and severely limit political participation. During his time in office, the electorate never exceeded 6 million—or less that 15 percent of the eligible voters.

In contrast, during the sixteen-month transitional period that followed the 2011 uprising, 62 percent of the population went to the polls and in every one of the elections the Islamist position or candidate won—a dramatic rejection of the politics of the past and an overwhelming display of desire on the part of Egyptians to participate in the political process.[2]

Mubarak's Egypt

Upon assuming office the day after Sadat's assassination in 1981, Hosni Mubarak pledged to support limited presidential terms (he served five six-year terms) and open up Egypt to democracy. He loosened restrictions on freedom of speech and of the press, even allowing critics to critique his administration publicly. Mubarak attempted to discredit extremists by having established religious scholars appear on television to engage, discuss, persuade, or discredit militants and their ideology. Overall, it appeared at the outset that the Mubarak presidency was taking a slightly more liberal turn that that of his predecessor.

The breathing room of the early Mubarak years had an unintended consequence, however, enabling Islamic movements and organizations to grow, expand their institutions, and become part of mainstream society. The Muslim Brotherhood (MB) and other voluntary (philanthropic) Islamic organizations became effective civil society agents of social change. They operated schools, clinics, hospitals, day care, and youth centers; they offered legal aid and provided other social services. Religiously motivated individuals and organizations supported hundreds of Islamic medical complexes in Egypt, ranging from two- to three-room clinics attached to a small mosque to major healthcare centers/hospitals such as the Mustapha Mahmud Islamic Clinic. Their primary concern was the needs of Egypt's poor and middle class. Private (not government-controlled) mosques and financial institutions such as Islamic banks and insurance companies also proliferated. As such they were an alternative set of privately funded institutions and services. They offered an unspoken critique of the failure or inability of the government and public sector to provide adequate services for the masses of the poor and lower middle class.

The mainstreaming of the Muslim Brothers also became evident with their election to leadership in student unions throughout Egypt's universities as well as professional associations of lawyers, doctors, engineers, teachers, and journalists. In September 1992, the Brotherhood won a majority of the board seats in the Bar Association elections, long regarded as a bastion of liberalism, which signaled their growing strength and influence. MB successes reflected the growing number of younger Islamist-oriented professionals, the appeal of the MB to professional classes as the only credible opposition, the indifference of many professionals about voting in association elections, and the ability of a well-organized, highly motivated minority to "get out the vote" and work with purpose and persistence: "Denied access to the political arena, they have made the professional syndicates perhaps the most vibrant institutions of Egyptian civil society."[3]

A Quiet Revolution: Ballots Not Bullets

In the late 1980s and early 1990s, failed economies and mass demonstrations moved governments (Egypt, Algeria, Tunisia, Jordan) to hold elections. Early in its development, the MB had determined that, despite its ability to effect change through social institutions, it had to contest elections if it was to extend its reach and continue to influence society in the way that it hoped.[4] The clearest testimony to the mainstreaming of the MB in society became its changing role in electoral politics. The MB, though technically remaining an illegal organization and thus banned from competing as a political party, participated through alliances with recognized parties. Its members ran for office and secured representation in the People's Assembly (Majlis al-Shaab). As one leader said, "What prompted us to enter the parliamentary elections is the desire to interpret our words into actions."[5] In the 1984 elections, it concluded an alliance with the New Wafd Party and won twelve seats. Three years later in 1987, it formed an "Islamic alliance" with the Socialist Labor Party and the Liberals and increased its parliamentary strength to thirty-two seats. Operating within the political system, moderate activists couched their criticisms and demands within the context of a call for greater democratization, political representation, social justice, and respect for human rights.

The strong performance of Islamist groups in national and municipal elections not only in Egypt but also in Algeria, Sudan, Kuwait, Pakistan, Jordan, Yemen, Malaysia, Turkey, and Lebanon challenged those who insisted that Islamic movements were undemocratic and unattractive to voters.[6] Islamist candidates were elected prime ministers and speakers of parliaments, cabinet ministers, and parliamentarians.

Regime contentions and Western government mantras that Islamist movements were not representative were countered by stunning electoral results. Their electoral performance was all the more surprising since governments controlled the media and access to public political gatherings. Governments regularly restricted or limited the existence or participation of political parties and candidates. Islamist successes at the ballot box threatened many autocrats whose fears of such groups appeared to be confirmed in Algeria by the FIS's electoral sweep of 1991.

While moderate Islamists pursued political challenge through the ballot box, radical violent movements in Assyut, Minya, Cairo, and Alexandria pressed for a violent Islamic revolution. Bent upon destabilizing the Egyptian economy and overthrowing the Mubarak regime, extremists attacked and murdered foreign tourists, Coptic Christians, and government officials as well as bombing banks and government buildings. The deadliest terrorist attack was carried out in Luxor, where more than sixty people—mostly foreigners—were killed in 1997.[7]

The Mubarak government blurred the lines between violent and moderate Islamists, state security and the limits of state authority, the arrest and prosecution of criminals, and repression and massive violation of human rights. It crushed the Gamaa Islamiyya, Egyptian Islamic Jihad, and other radical groups. At the same time, the state used harassment, imprisonment, and torture to curb the growing strength of moderate Islamist movements, in particular the MB. While officially banned from participating as a political party in elections since 1954, the MB continued to operate openly, placing candidates as "independents" in parliamentary elections.

In 1993, the government issued a law that aimed to curb the Brotherhood's electoral success in syndicate professional associations of physicians, lawyers, and engineers in elections. Two year later in 1995, they rounded up hundreds of MB members, trying ninety-five of them in military courts. Additionally, universities where Brothers frequently organized were closely monitored and security apparatuses of the government injected themselves into the students' elections, removing the names of MB candidates from the ballots, thus eradicating any chance they had of success.[8] To counter the prominence of the MB in universities, the government-controlled People's Assembly passed a new educational law that annulled the right of Egyptian professors to elect their faculty deans and allowed the rectors of universities to appoint them instead. Opponents charged that despite the Brotherhood's relative lack of activity or success in university faculties, the law is "one step in the government's attempt to eliminate any possibility of the Islamists capturing any more key positions" and that "if university professors are not to be trusted with electing their own representative, then there is no point in talking about democracy."[9]

The government's "antiterrorism" campaign, which targeted both militants and the Brotherhood, included the use of emergency laws for arbitrary arrest and detention without charge for six months; the arrest of some 21,000 people (the government reported 16,000); torture; and trials in state security or military courts, which excluded the right of appeal, even when the accused were civilians. Scores of death sentences were handed down. Thousands were held without charge and the Arab Human Rights Organization accused the government of routine torture.[10]

At the same time, Mubarak projected a democratic facade to his Western allies. In a 1993 *News Hour* interview on the eve of presidential elections, he declared that Egypt was "very keen on democracy" but then offered a cautious warning to his listeners: "Don't expect that we'll have full democracy overnight. It needs generations."[11]

The Mubarak government's fig-leaf or faux democracy was exposed as he employed a heavy-handed brand of "guided democracy" or "democracy without dissent" and with guaranteed results. In elections plagued by fraud and ballot box stuffing, Egypt's National Democratic Party (NDP) enjoyed a 95 percent majority victory in parliamentary (People's Assembly) elections of 1995. One European Union (EU) official characterized Mubarak's Egypt and its elections as "exceptionally awful."[12] Twice, Egyptian courts forced dissolution of parliament by ruling that election procedures were unconstitutional. After the election in November 1995, which was marred by violent demonstrations in which fifty people were killed, losing candidates went to court to contest the results in more than half of the 444 seats. Fraud, ballot-stuffing, and voter intimidation were all proven. However, the People's Assembly responded that since its members enjoyed parliamentary immunity, only it had the right to expel them. In 1999, Mubarak was re-elected with 94 percent of the vote in a contest that drew only an estimated 10 percent of the population. The credibility of Egypt's electoral reforms was further undermined by the continued arrest of a wide range of government critics from the MB to prominent secular intellectuals. At the time, a US House Foreign Affairs report noted the following:

In May [of 2004] EOHR [Egyptian Organization for Human Rights] reported that it had documented the names of at least 498 Muslim Brotherhood members arrested during the course of peaceful demonstrations staged in Cairo, Sharqiyya, Ismailiyya, Suez, Minya, Bahayyra, Fayyoum, Menoufiyya, Assiut, and Gharbiyya. Charges leveled against members during the year included membership in and revival of a banned organization; obstructing the laws and constitution of the country; inciting the masses against the government; organizing demonstrations critical of the government's policies; and possessing communiqués, booklets and tapes that propagate MB ideology. In November and December the government detained hundreds more MB activists in an apparent effort to limit MB success in the parliamentary elections.[13]

Transition to Multiparty Presidential Elections

Prior to 2005, Mubarak always ran unopposed under an indirect electoral process in which the candidate for president (Mubarak) was nominated by a two-thirds majority of the NDP-controlled People's Assembly and approved by a referendum. However, in February 2005, in the aftermath of large street protests and faced with growing criticism both domestically and internationally regarding limited progress on political liberalization, Mubarak proposed a constitutional amendment initiating direct, multi-candidate presidential elections for the first time. Nevertheless, the pattern of authoritarian control of elections continued. As Human Rights Watch reported: "Plainclothes security agents beat demonstrators, and riot police allowed—and sometimes encouraged—mobs of Mubarak supporters to beat and sexually assault protestors and journalists . . . 'The police and ruling-party assaults on pro-reform advocates yesterday shows just how hollow the Mubarak government's rhetoric of reform really is,' said Joe Stork, deputy Middle East director of Human Rights Watch."[14]

In September 2005, Mubarak was re-elected to his fifth consecutive term, receiving 88.6 percent of the vote from only 21 percent of the electorate (6.9 million out of 32 million eligible voters cast their ballots). Opposition groups, international observers, and the Egyptian Organization of Human Rights criticized the turnout, charging that instances of voter fraud, ballot stuffing, violence, and intimidation discredited the election. Ayman Nour, a former member of the Egyptian parliament and founder of the El-Ghad (Tomorrow) Party, finished a distant second with only 7 percent of the vote in what are widely believed to have been corrupt elections. Nour, the first man to compete in so-called multiparty elections, had been stripped of his parliamentary immunity and arrested on January 29, 2005. He was later released in the wake of global criticism from human rights groups and governments.

After the elections, Ayman Nour was rearrested on allegations of "forgery" and imprisoned for five years. So confidant was the Mubarak government that it allowed some 140 of its candidates to campaign, which produced a stunning electoral result. Muslim Brothers and other Islamist candidates won 40 percent of the vote but 20 percent of the seats in parliament. Despite harassment and imprisonment, the Brotherhood surprisingly emerged as the largest opposition block with an unprecedented eighty-eight seats, or 20 percent of the total vote and close to one-fifth of parliament's seats.

Mubarak increased attempts to downsize and block the MB: postponing local elections in which the Brothers were projected to win seats, arresting student members, closing Brotherhood-owned companies, and conducting frequent detention campaigns of MB members. As *The Economist* concluded,

> That double show of strength prompted the harshest crackdown on the group in Egypt since the 1960s. Not only has the government of President Hosni Mubarak outlawed parties based on religion and fiddled laws to block Brothers from running as independents in future elections. Relentless rounds of arrests, including many of the Brothers' leaders, have crippled the group's organization. Some 250 Muslim Brothers are in Egyptian prisons, including several popular moderates widely regarded as future leaders.[15]

The net result of Mubarak's retreat from any form of liberalization was evident in Egypt's subsequent parliamentary elections on November 28, 2010, which drew domestic and international criticism for the widespread irregularities. The ruling National Democratic Party crushed the opposition, winning nearly 95 percent of the 221 seats settled in the first round while the Brotherhood failed to win a single seat. Committed to reversing their stunning performance success in 2005, the Mubarak government harassed, arrested, and imprisoned MB members and also manipulated the electoral process. Protests spread amidst allegations of fraud, ballot box stuffing, vote buying, illegal campaigning at polling stations, and physical exclusion from polling stations by government security forces and other opposition supporters.

As a result, opposition parties and groups won only 15 of the 504 available seats in the People's Assembly, as opposed to 98 out of 444 seats in the parliament elected in 2005. The MB and New Wafd Party withdrew from runoff elections in protest.

The Arab Spring: Toppling of Mubarak

As discussed in chapter 7, 2011 ushered in an unpredictable series of popular uprisings by pro-democracy movements in the Arab world.

The toppling Zine al-Abidine Ben Ali's regime on January 14, 2011, became the catalyst that sparked Egyptian demonstrations, which erupted only eleven days later. In contrast to Tunisia, a country of 10 million people, where it took twenty-eight days to depose its dictator, pro-democracy activists in Egypt, with its population of 85 million, required only eighteen days to accomplish the same feat. By February 11, Hosni Mubarak was forced to resign in disgrace. The toppling of Ben Ali after his twenty-three-year reign and of Mubarak after his twenty-nine-year rule struck fear in the hearts of many rulers. The events sparked uprisings in Libya, Bahrain, Yemen, and Syria, and inspired protests in Algeria, Morocco, Jordan, and Oman. In Saudi Arabia, the increasingly tense political climate led to the creation of the Ummah Party—the first official (though not sanctioned or recognized by the government) opposition group of its kind since the 1990s, one comprised of Islamists and intellectuals who called for the end of the monarchy and the beginning of representative government; the historic scene also impacted Iran's Islamic Republic, which was shaken by the Green Movement and its presidential elections in 2009.

Egypt's pro-democracy uprising was a popular revolution—a revolt of people, not a well-defined organization with a charismatic leader or defined leadership. Many of the activists and demonstrators were young, well educated, and politically and internationally aware in large part due to mass communications and social media. They were motivated not by the ideologies and slogans of Arab nationalism and socialism or Islamism but by pragmatic issues. As one political chant put it: "Bread, freedom, and social justice."[16] It was broad-based, supported by the secular and religiously minded; young and old; men and women; Muslims and Christians; the poor, middle, and upper classes.

The historic campaign to oust Mubarak represented not only the dawning of a new era in Egyptian and Arab-state politics but also the first real emergence of a new public sphere—one that ran parallel to the state. In this new rhetorical space, which was nurtured by social media tools and online organizing, activists were able to gather, discuss ideas, establish shared perspectives, network with like-minded citizens, and communicate their desires and political beliefs in a way that, under ordinary circumstances, would have landed them in jail. This new climate of communication, combined with decades of grievances, corruption, unkept government promises, and increased authoritarianism, proved to be explosive.

Many in the foreign media dubbed the 2011 Egyptian Revolution as the "Facebook Revolution." Common to both the Tunisian and Egyptian uprisings was the role of youth and social media. Protestors and demonstrations were organized and mobilized through social networking sites, in particular the April 6th Youth Movement Facebook page. Other activists started a "We Are All Khaled Said" page, dedicated to a 28-year-old Egyptian businessman who many believed was the face of the revolt that sprouted in the streets of Cairo. Taken from an Internet café in June 2010 by two plainclothes police officers, he was beaten to death in the hallway of a nearby residential building; human rights advocates said he had evidence of police corruption.[17]

THROUGH THIS PAGE, the April 6 Youth Movement educated youth and contributed to a politically informed civil society. "We Are All Khaled Said," with hundreds of thousands of followers, informed the public about instances of torture and police brutality. Egypt had reached a tipping point of sorts as so many disaffected citizens began to express their grievances against the Mubarak regime. As this new public sphere grew, it would only be a matter of time before the evolution of antigovernment opposition would eventuate in a new and irreversible development.[18]

Though social media was not the cause or basis for the Tahrir Square uprising, activists used new media tools like Facebook, Twitter, and YouTube to organize, discuss, mobilize, build a sense of solidarity, and spread information. After the government attempted to shut down the Internet: "Google and Twitter created mobile phone numbers (one in the U.S., one in Italy, and one in Bahrain) for people to call and report tweets as voicemails. People were then instructed to log-on to Twitter and listen to the tweets rather than read them. This was the first time that prominent search engines worked together to keep information about the uprisings flowing."[19] Here again, the picture of the new public sphere sharpens into relief; communication and coordination—which once took place in coffee shops, mosques, and bookstores—occurred in an environment that was ostensibly out of reach of the government.

As Wael Ghonim, the administrator of the "We Are All Khaled Said" Facebook page and a key organizer of the uprisings, who was imprisoned for twelve days and became the symbol for Egyptian movement, stated in a CNN interview,

> I want to meet Mark Zuckerberg one day and thank him . . . I'm talking on behalf of Egypt. . . . This revolution started online. This revolution started on Facebook. This revolution started . . . in June 2010 when hundreds of thousands of Egyptians started collaborating content. We would post a video on Facebook that would be shared by 60,000 people on their walls within a few hours. I've always said that if you want to liberate a society just give them the Internet.[20]

Like other Arab Spring uprisings in Tunisia and Libya, protesters reclaimed their sense of dignity and respect and were driven by long-standing political and economic grievances: the lack of good governance and accountability, the lack of rule of law and freedoms, large-scale corruption, accumulation of the country's wealth in the hands of the ruling elites, a growing gap between a rich elite minority and the middle class and the poor, high unemployment levels, and a lack of opportunity and a sense of a future.

The MB was not at the forefront of the protest, nor did they speak out publicly or rally supporters, though individual members did join the protests in Tahrir (Liberation) Square. Prominent religious leaders, Muslim and Christian, were initially silent or publicly unsupportive. As pro-democracy activists' signs, placards, statements, and demands demonstrate, protesters espoused Egyptian unity/nationalism, spoke of one Egypt, and sang the Egyptian national anthem. They waved Egyptian flags not Islamist placards.

While Mubarak was forced out, his regime's bureaucratic, military, and judiciary institutions were not. Mubarak was replaced by the interim military transition, the Supreme Council of the Armed Forces (SCAF), which was convened under Mubarak on February 9, 2011, and assumed power the day after the embattled president departed. The increasingly aggressive role of the SCAF during the months after the revolution tempered the initial euphoria of reformers.

If in the past, the question had been "Is Arab culture or Islam compatible with democracy?" the question and concern now became "Are the old guard and entrenched elites (military, courts, police, security, government bureaucrats, and other political and economic elites associated with the Mubarak government) as well as Islamists ready for the transition to democracy?" Celebration of the Arab Spring in Egypt was tempered by fear that it might be hijacked by remnants of the Mubarak regime's institutions. Whatever unity existed among Egyptians during the eighteen days that led up to the ousting of Mubarak soon dissipated once the president fled his post. As Esam Al Amin notes, four active blocs within the Egyptian political theater, each one hoping to obtain advantage over the other, formed transient coalitions and sought to achieve its ambitions: the Islamists, the secularists, the revolutionary youth, and the remnants of the old regime (*fulool*). These fractures were compounded by the fact that the military, which had its own agenda, played these various groups against one another.[21]

Egypt's military rulers moved quickly to assert and extend their power so broadly that a growing number of lawyers and activists questioned their willingness to ultimately submit to civilian authority. At a workshop co-sponsored by the Center for Muslim-Christian Understanding in Istanbul in early October 2011, "The Arab Awakening: Transitioning from Dictatorship to Democracy," an Egyptian activist, as well as activists from Tunisia and elsewhere identified the nature of the threat to a democratic transition: "The Egyptian revolution was peaceful. Whereas the French, American, Russian revolutions ended with thousands getting their heads cut off or killed otherwise, imprisoned, or fired, in Egypt the heads we spared are speaking and working against the revolution—how do we deal with this?" Another activist asked, "Is Egypt transitioning from Mubarak authoritarianism to new military-security regime using a democratic facade?"

Fears that the revolution would result in a new military-security regime were real to many. After all, the military controlled as much as 30 to 40 percent of Egypt's economy and was for years autonomous with little or no governmental oversight or accountability. Many senior military officials used their power and influence to develop vast economic and business interests. Military-owned companies and business interests include ownership of vast amounts of land, buying and selling of real estate, construction companies, farms, high-tech slaughterhouses, nurseries, child care services, cafeteria services, automobile repair and hotel administration, gas stations, domestic cleaning services, chicken and dairy farms, manufacturing food products like pasta and bottled water, pesticides, optical equipment, production of small arms and explosives, exercise equipment, fire engines, and even plastic table covers. There was no regulation regarding accountability or transparency.[22]

BECAUSE THE MILITARY wanted to remain autonomous and refused to allow political groups or parties to interfere in its affairs, it took the necessary measures to ensure that would occur. There were several indicators that raised fears that the revolution would be hijacked by the military, including its reintroduction of an extended emergency law by the SCAF in the name of safeguarding law and order, and its arrest and subsequent military trials of some 12,000 people, 5,000 of whom were held as political prisoners (in October 2012, Egypt's new president Mohamed Morsi pardoned all of the political prisoners detained since the start of the country's revolution, except those who were charged with and convicted of murder).[23]

Although the military had originally pledged in March 2011 to hold the presidential election by September, the generals issued a new timetable that postponed the election until after the parliamentary election (starting on November 28 and lasting until late January 2012). This would then be followed by the formation of a constitutional assembly and the writing and ratification of a new constitution. Supporters of the FJP, on the other hand, feared that if elections were delayed until a constitution was formed, the NDP might slip back into the seat of power and leverage their networks to score a dramatic resurgence.[24] The military's attitude and primary concern about its interests, immunity, and desire to be independent from civilian oversight were compounded by remnants of the Mubarak regime—secular elites (not all by any means) who were intransigent in their opposition to any place for religion in the state. Further complicating the situation were the illiberal democrats, in other words, those Egyptians who advocate democracy but are so worried that its presence would bring to power groups like the Muslim Brotherhood that they often turn to illiberal positions hoping to thwart such a possibility. That fear often led them to support the prolonged presence of military rule; the irony, of course, was that while the democratic process might not guarantee the emergence of a political system built on democratic values, blocking that process out of fear—and in the name of democracy itself—was certain to lead only to an authoritarian outcome.[25]

US secretary of state Hillary Clinton supported the generals' election plan. The *New York Times* reported on the unfolding scene and the position taken by the American government:

> The United States, where concerns run high that early elections could bring unfriendly Islamists to power and further strain relations with Israel, has so far signaled approval of the military's slower approach to handing over authority. In an appearance this week with the Egyptian foreign minister, Secretary of State Hillary Rodham Clinton urged an early end to the emergency law but called the plan for elections "an appropriate timetable."[26]

Clinton's statement seemed to confirm the doubts and fears of many Egyptians that, despite the United States' publicly stated support for Egypt's revolution, self-determination, and democracy, a legacy of support for authoritarian regimes as a sure source of stability and safeguard for American interests and fears that independent elections could bring more independent governments, even Islamists, to power, would result in US interference and intervention. As major Gallup polling reported: two-thirds of Egyptians surveyed thought the United States would try to interfere in Egypt's political future as opposed to letting the people of the country decide alone. A similar number disagreed that the United States was serious about encouraging democratic systems of government in their region. The US position not only reinforced the hand of the Egyptian military but also risked further undermining America's ability to rebuild its credibility and role in the Middle East.[27]

Parliamentary Elections

The SCAF, recognizing the MB's potential electoral power as the country's best-organized and most influential opposition movement, catered to the powerful and wealthy remnants (*fulool*) of Mubarak's

National Democratic Party (NDP) that populate court systems, the military, and intelligence and security services and that manipulated the state-run media outlets to exploit fears of minority Copts, liberals, secularists, and others who were anxious about life under an Islamist-dominated state.[28]

Though the Brotherhood had not been among the early demonstrators in Tahrir Square, they quickly emerged as the key political organization in a state in which they had been the leading opposition. They had done so with a widespread reputation for lack of corruption, effective deliverance of social services, and a willingness to suffer repression and imprisonment as the price for standing up to the Mubarak regime. Their position and that of their political party, the Freedom and Justice Party, established in the aftermath of the revolution, was strengthened by their strong presence throughout the diverse communities they served across Egypt, their experience in previous elections, and the fact that in the year after the overthrow of Mubarak, the non-Islamist activists were unable to unite in an effective political organization of their own.

Gallup pre-election surveys revealed that in the months leading up to parliamentary elections, many Egyptians went from being undecided to supporting the MB and Salafist parties. By December 2011, support for the Freedom and Justice Party jumped to 50 percent and to 31 percent for the ultraconservative al-Nour Party, which was formed by one of the largest Salafist groups in Egypt immediately after the 2011 revolution. At the same time, Gallup's surveys also indicated levels of substantial opposition to Islamist groups. More than four in ten Egyptians did not support the Freedom and Justice Party, and a clear majority (58 percent) did not support the al-Nour Party.[29]

Voters were pragmatic and not ideological. Whatever their religious or ideological bent (Islamist, secularist, etc.), in multiple surveys, Egyptians reported bread-and-butter concerns: inflation, lack of jobs, high unemployment, and worries about the financial security of their families. Few—1 percent or less—mentioned moral decay.[30]

Secular or non-Islamist parties, most of whom did not have the grassroots voter base or provide the social welfare networks and support of the MB and Salafists, were not able to gain any traction. The MB swept to victory in the country's parliamentary elections in January 2012, taking 47 percent of the seats. The MB's Freedom and Justice Party (FJP) won 235 of the 498 seats in the People's Assembly. Their success could be attributed to a number of factors. First and foremost, they were well organized, had dedicated members and experience in elections, and, more than any other party, demonstrated their opposition to the Mubarak regime and willingness to suffer for it. Many nonmembers admired them for their piety and lack of corruption and were beneficiaries of their network of social services. In fact, those characteristics may also explain the sudden popularity of Salafist groups, who, as mentioned above, enjoyed a boost of support just ahead of the parliamentary elections and won a quarter of the vote during the parliamentary elections. Though there exists, undeniably, a percentage within their ranks whose interpretations of Islam as a political guide are militant, many Salafists are popular members of their communities, and ideology aside, are known for their charitable works. They distribute coupons for gas at subsidized prices; kill camels, sheep, and buffalo and distribute the meat to needy families; pay for schoolbooks and medicine; and contribute household gifts to newly married couples.[31]

At the same time, as we have seen, the political system for decades discouraged and restricted the development of a strong independent multiparty system. Most were relatively small and weak. Moreover, in Egypt as in Tunisia, post-Mubarak political freedom meant a proliferation of new parties and candidates with no strong established organizational base and constituency.

The Salafists' participation was a new phenomenon in Egyptian politics. Most were nonpolitical and shunned politics. They were tolerated in Egypt under Mubarak as a counterbalance to the Islamic appeal and more political message of the MB. However, after the 2011 uprising, some began to coalesce around a political message. The Salafist move into the political arena was surprising and threatening for many in Egypt and the West; the emergence of the Salafist al-Nour Party, which took 24 percent of the seats, giving Islamists (MB and Salafists alike) 71 percent of the vote, was even more shocking given the Salafists' political disorganization and lack of central authority. What made many especially worried was the ultraconservative Salafi rhetoric and call for the imposition of Sharia law.

The al-Nour Party, which emerged as the main Salafist party, presented a more accommodating Salafi image. While voters attending Salafist political rallies might have expected bearded *sheikhs* to extol the importance of Islamic law, banning alcohol, restricting women, and the like, many were surprised to hear a powerful and influential embrace of populism that resonated across ideological, religious, and political lines, and struck a chord with those Egyptians who also condemned the liberal Egyptian elite.[32]

Many Salafists were surprised at how well they performed in the parliamentary and presidential elections. Their success invigorated the al-Nour Party and informed a strategy that included regaining these votes while chipping away at the MB's "Islamic credentials" and forming political alliances with diverse groups (but not the MB), including non-Islamists. For example, the MB and the Salafist al-Nour Party agreed on a number of political and economic issues. While the more hardline Salafists espoused an ultraconservative religious ideology and interpretation of Sharia, which they believed should be implemented immediately as law, al-Nour was content to wait years, seeing it as a long-term strategy.

Egyptian Military Attempts a Soft Coup

On June 17, 2012, hours before the second round of presidential elections, the SCAF issued a declaration/charter in their attempt at a military "soft coup" that subverted and delayed democratic transitions under the guise of "protecting" democracy from resurgent Islamist parties that had polled well in elections. Its amendment to the Egyptian constitution gave the SCAF sweeping political and military powers: complete control over its own affairs (including control and continued secrecy around the use of over $1.3 billion in annual military aid from the United States); complete control over its own affairs, including budgetary autonomy as well as the ability to wage war without presidential or parliamentary approval; extraordinary powers of arrest over civilians; immediate assumption of legislative authority; and the further authority to define and limit the executive authority of the president as well as to oversee the writing of Egypt's new constitution.

All of this came only days after the Mubarak carryover and SCAF-influenced Constitutional High Court upheld the SCAF's dissolution of the democratically elected parliament and legitimized the candidacy of General Ahmad Shafiq, a former Mubarak prime minister and the military's (undeclared) presidential candidate. This was despite a political ban issued by the ruling military and enforced by Egypt's Supreme Presidential Election Commission (SPEC), which forbade the candidacy of former regime senior officials for a period of ten years.

The Brotherhood's post-parliamentary performance also undermined its credibility in the eyes of some potential supporters and left them vulnerable to those who opposed them. They reneged on an earlier pledge not to run in presidential elections.[33] When the SPEC disqualified Khayrat al-Shatter, the deputy chairman of the Brotherhood, as the FJP's presidential candidate, they replaced him with Mohamed Morsi rather than reassuring those who feared Islamist-led parliamentary dominance and expanding their political base by supporting another presidential candidate.[34]

Morsi moved aggressively to regain lost ground, reaching out to former rivals/losing candidates to create an anti-Shafiq coalition, appealing especially to other Islamists (including the Salafists). To that end, Morsi received the backing of the al-Nour Party. He strove to garner support from the youth who had been the backbone in Tahrir Square and the streets during the uprising. He pledged to end torture, discrimination, and the detainment of civilians arrested by the army after the revolution. Many decided to support Morsi not because they supported Morsi or the MB but because they supported the revolution and were against the SCAF's attempted soft coup and the possibility of a return to the pre-revolutionary days of the old guard.[35]

The April 6th Ahmed Maher Front (named after the leader of a faction of the April 6th movement) endorsed Morsi, as in the end did the April 6th Democratic Front, which had initially declared that it would boycott the elections. Morsi promised to uphold dignity of all Egyptians, social justice, the constitution, and "the republican system" of government. He promised Christians and women full and equal citizenship and rights if he were elected and that he would appoint a Christian as presidential advisor and even name one Copt as a vice president "if possible." Women would not be required to observe an Islamic dress code in public and would have full access to education and jobs.

General Ahmed Shafiq, on the other hand, appealed for votes as "the law-and-order" candidate. He promised to restore security and put an end to the protests, which many Egyptians believed were harming the economy and their jobs and discouraging foreign companies from investing in the country. In order to broaden his base of support, having previously criticized the uprising and its activists, Shafiq soon changed his tune and praised the "glorious revolution" that ended Mubarak's rule.

Despite the Brotherhood's miscalculations, the overwhelming financial resources mobilized by the SCAF, and "deep-state" (Mubarak regime remnants still occupying strategic positions in government and the state bureaucracy) support for Shafiq, Mohamed Morsi emerged as the winner of the June 16–17, 2012, election runoff. He received more than 13 million votes, while Ahmed Shafiq received more than 12 million; that worked out to just under 52 percent of the vote for Morsi and 48 percent of the vote for Shafiq—a clear indication of just how split the country had become (51 percent of eligible voters turned out).

Post-Presidential Elections

The SCAF continued to insist on retaining the sweeping political and military powers it had granted itself in its unilaterally issued "constitution." The military's assumption of parliament's powers after disbanding it and its formation of a powerful national security council headed by the president but dominated by generals had, in effect, reduced the office and powers of the president substantially.

In the early months, the military appeared to have the upper hand. Although Morsi had indicated he would take his oath of office at the parliament building, he reluctantly acceded to the SCAF's decision that he take his oath at the constitutional court building, in effect symbolically recognizing the court's (a remnant of the Mubarak regime with close ties to the SCAF) decision to dissolve parliament after it ruled that a third of the house had been elected illegally. However, the day before the official oath taking, he symbolically took an oath before tens of thousands of supporters in Cairo's Tahrir Square, declaring "I renounce none of the prerogatives of president . . . You are the source of power and legitimacy . . . There is no place for anyone or any institution . . . above this will."[36]

After Tahrir Square, critics increasingly charged that the military overstepped its boundaries politically, economically, and militarily. They were displeased with the "soft coup," the use of force that led to the killing of protestors, the torturing of civilian detainees and other alleged crimes, and the vast wealth from economic holdings enjoyed by current and retired military officers. There were increasing calls for the generals to be held accountable and put on trial.

Taking advantage of this growing criticism, in August 2012, President Morsi moved to end the tug of war with the SCAF and to assert power to the office of the president and a civilian- (rather than military)-dominated government (the direct reason for removing the generals was the attack on and murder of the Egyptian soldiers at Rafah in early August). Praising the military, he referred to a new generation of military leadership and emphasized their role as one of protectors of the nation rather than rulers of the government. The 76-year-old Tantawi was replaced by the much younger 58-year-old General Abdel-Fattah Al-Sisi, the former head of military intelligence, as defense minister.

President Morsi also annulled the SCAF's declaration/charter in which they assumed legislative and executive powers, control of all laws and the national budget, immunity from any oversight, the authority to veto a declaration of war, and control over the process of writing a permanent constitution.

The president's office went to great lengths to portray Morsi as an independent leader. Morsi came to power with the legacy of decades of suspicions of the Muslim Brothers. Regrettably, he did not do enough to persuade Egyptians that he was the Egyptian president and not "the Muslim Brother president." His rhetoric at times seemed addressed to the Brothers rather than the nation.

The announcement of his presidential team in late August 2012 fell short of both his campaign promises and reiteration after his election to be the president of all Egyptians. Morsi's twenty-one-member presidential team (four senior aides and a seventeen-member council) was dominated by FJP members, as well as four Salafists and other Islamist-leaning appointees. While it included liberals, three women, and two Christians, it failed to deliver on Morsi's campaign pledge to appoint a youth representative, a woman, and a Christian as vice presidents. Moreover, it did not include any members of the revolutionary youth groups that were catalysts for and played prominent roles in the Tahrir Square uprising or members of any political parties other than the FJP and the Salafist al-Nour Party.

The presidential council included a significant number of FJP members. Out of the council's twenty-one seats, individuals associated with either the MB or the FJP filled seven of them. Also on the council was one former member of the MB's Guidance Bureau, its top executive body, three Salafists, two Christians, three women, and one youth under the age of 40.

In late November 2012, amidst public dissatisfaction with Morsi's unkept promises that prompted public protests and the judiciary's dismantling of the lower chamber in parliament and the upper chamber and the second constitution's writing committee), Morsi issued a wide-ranging set of constitutional decrees that further enhanced his power. These included changing the tenure of the prosecutor general (a Mubarak appointee and opponent) from a life term to four years, effective immediately; an article that barred any judicial review of the second chamber of the parliament; and a ban on judicial reviews of all his decisions as president until a constitution was passed. Although Morsi believed that these actions were necessary to safeguard legislative authority and prevent the judiciary from preventing passage of the new constitution, Morsi's unilateral decision backfired and led to widespread opposition.[37]

Morsi did not do enough to dispel critics' charges that the Brothers did not negotiate in good faith; there were numerous instances of agreements reached, as on the constitution, for example, with other political trends. After much bargaining and long hours of discussion some consensus would be reached. Within days, the Brothers would reverse their positions and the negotiations would have to start all over again. In early December 2012, amidst charges that Morsi was leading Egypt down a path toward an authoritarian state with Islamic law, some hundred thousand demonstrators swarmed into the streets of Cairo to deliver a "final warning" to the president. Days later, Morsi agreed to abrogate the controversial measures set forth in the November 22 constitutional decree, which granted him limitless authority to deal with "threats" to the revolution, protected the Islamist-led assembly from the possibility of dissolution, and placed the presidency above oversight.

In contrast to Morsi's base of supporters, many Egyptians were uncomfortable with the constitution and wanted the opportunity to vote for articles that would be included in it, not be forced to accept a doctrine hashed out by a few individuals who shared the president's ideology. Yet as prominent political commentator and former head of Al Jazeera Wadah Khanfar observed, the powerful opposition to Morsi's decision was so deeply rooted in a hatred of Islamists and the MB that those against the constitutional decree committed an unthinkable error: they aligned themselves with remnants of the old regime. "They have allowed their own *Ikhwan*-ophobia to dominate, giving more weight to their hatred of the Islamist forces than their evident love of democracy," Khanfar wrote. "In their desire to topple the Brotherhood—an aim that the liberal leader of the National Salvation Front, Osama Ghazali Harb, admitted last Sunday—they seem prepared to commit the greatest of profanities: to ally themselves with the former regime's forces; they even ignore the violence of the notorious *baltagiya*, or criminal gangs."[38]

After two rounds of voting on December 15 and 22, 2012, some 57 percent and 64 percent, respectively, ratified the new constitution, though voter turnout was considerably low. Of the more than 52 million Egyptians eligible to vote, about one-third (17 million) cast their ballots. During the first round, about 56 percent said "yes," and turnout was slightly higher at 32 percent. There is little doubt that the low turnout was an indication that many were disillusioned with the process and abstained from participating altogether. Additionally, the provinces that voted in the second round were disproportionately rural—areas that are strongholds for the MB and other Islamist groups.

Comparatively, during the first round of votes in Cairo, a city that boasts around 19 million people, 2.3 million voters (out of 6.6 million eligible voters in the capital city) rejected the constitution.[39] (In the 2014 constitutional referendum, held on January 14 and 15, the new constitution was approved by 98.1 percent of voters, with a turnout rate of 38.6 percent [21 of 54 million eligible voters cast ballots]. The Muslim Brotherhood boycotted the election, yet the constitution still received 20 million "yes" votes, nearly double the amount of those received in 2012 under Morsi.[40])

On the second anniversary of the Egyptian revolution, thousands of people came to Tahrir Square to demonstrate. Their presence, though, was not so much a celebration of the ousting of former president Hosni Mubarak as it was a protest against its newly elected president Mohamed Morsi, who had a four-year term and who, under the new constitution, could serve two terms. Morsi's critics called for his resignation and a new presidential election. Interestingly, the MB decided against participating in counterdemonstrations and instead dispersed its members to poor districts of Cairo and other cities to do charitable work for underprivileged families.

As president, Morsi did not remove himself from the shadow of the Murshid (Supreme Guide) of the MB. Many Egyptians believed he was not the real decision-maker. The shadowy presence of Khayrat al-Shatter, an influential senior leader who had been the first choice to run for president but was disqualified, undermined his role in exactly the same way. Moreover, in a country whose modern history and politics had been dominated by autocrats and an authoritarian culture, Morsi seemed to lack the gravitas and advisers to counter those who alleged he was not up to the job of president.

Though many of Egypt's major problems were acute due to the Mubarak legacy and deep state, still critics charged he was not strong enough in defense of Egypt's interests. With the economy in free fall, tourism on the ropes, unemployment still high, investment shriveled, and foreign currency tumbling, clashes that erupted around the country signaled widespread discontent with the economic health of the Egyptian society. Compounding these economic problems were growing frustrations among some segments of society, which alleged that Morsi had moved away from democracy and toward an attempt to control nearly every aspect of the government and public life and that Morsi and/or the Brotherhood was taking the country down the path to an Islamic state.

Morsi denounced the protests as a "counterrevolution" and said that they were being led by "remnants of ousted President Hosni Mubarak's regime to obstruct everything in the country."[41] Members of the National Salvation Front, an alliance of Egyptian political parties that was formed to defeat Morsi's November 22 constitutional declaration, threatened to boycott the parliamentary elections scheduled for the summer of 2013 if a number of conditions were not met, including the creation of a "national salvation" government, a committee of judges to amend the constitution, which it deemed "void," and the dismissal of the prosecutor general appointed by Morsi.[42]

In February 2013, Morsi called for parliamentary elections in April that would finish in late June; the new parliament would be elected and would convene for the first time on July 6, 2013. But, in early March, the Supreme Constitutional Court again intervened. They cancelled the pending elections and ruled that, among other things, Morsi was wrong to declare an election date without seeking the prior approval of his prime minister and cabinet. The court referred the election law to the Supreme Constitutional Court. Morsi appealed the decision.

A Breakdown of Democracy

One of the most important political challenges for Egypt's emerging democracy (its government and opposition) was recognition and adoption of the principle of a "loyal opposition." In contrast to dictatorships and authoritarian regimes, where any opposition is seen as disloyal and to be suppressed or co-opted, opposition to the party in power is bound by loyalty to fundamental national interests and principles.

As a result, despite significant differences, Morsi's government and its opposition failed to work toward a common agenda on economic development, jobs, equality of citizenship, political and religious pluralism, stability and security, freedoms of speech, religion, assembly, women's rights, and religious tolerance. Sectors of the opposition, the military and judiciary in particular, were bent on bringing down the democratically elected government at any cost. Other critics included secularists and illiberal secularists, among them members of the former government and economic elites who wanted military intervention and a restoration of their interests; religiously minded people who didn't want to see religion formally implemented; young Egyptian activists who felt marginalized, excluded, and alienated; and Christians, especially Copts, who at times under previous governments were victims of discrimination and violence and now were even more concerned about "a Muslim Brotherhood government."

Morsi, on the other hand, failed to adequately and effectively demonstrate that "the new Egypt" was a modern and religiously and politically inclusive nation-state where full equality of citizenship exists for all. Failure to be sufficiently inclusive in terms of diverse representation in its appointments and polices left it open to opposition charges that despite some "cosmetic changes" it was a "Muslim Brotherhood government."

Overlooked was the fact that the Morsi government faced formidable sectors of opposition from remnants of the Mubarak regime, the deep state. The Morsi government did not have control over the military, intelligence services, police, judiciary, banking institutions, diplomatic corps (which were staffed by Mubarak holdovers), and other major sectors. For many of Egypt's poor and economically marginalized or unemployed, the economy and Egypt's economic standing remained a disaster. Most importantly, the Egyptian Supreme Constitutional Court, populated by Mubarak-era appointees, was the main instrument used by the military to limit and control any efforts to restructure the state or expand Morsi's power. And indeed the court would later emerge as an ally in the post-coup interim government.

Violent street protests in major Egyptian cities indicated growing discontent with the Egyptian president and his administrations, as Morsi continued down a political path, the optics of which were reminiscent of the Mubarak administration. When Egyptian satirist Bassem Youssef and blogger Alaa Abdel Fattah criticized and lampooned Morsi's policies, his administration sought to silence them.[43] Five anti-Islamist activists were arrested on charges of using social media to incite violence (though no evidence proved that was the case).[44] Ahmed Magdy Youssef explains how the controversy evidenced the way that media outlets in Egypt had couched themselves in the rift formed between the two opposing sides:

Egypt's media outlets have chosen to take sides in the ongoing tragic split. To put it more pointedly, not only the state-owned media avowedly backed the military after Morsi's ouster, but most of the Egyptian privately-owned TV stations and newspapers as well have embraced the military's perspective. It's no secret to say that Egypt's media landscape has never been non-partisan. The Muslim Brotherhood's TV station—Misr 25—and others run by their Islamist allies, in addition to newspapers like Freedom and Justice, official newspaper of the MB's Freedom and Justice Party (FJP), were undoubtedly partisan. Additionally, being perpetually accused of aligning with the regime that rules, state-owned newspapers like Al-Ahram did partly side with Mr. Morsi before the 30-June demonstrations. On the flip side, most of Egypt's privately-owned networks and newspapers were whole-heartedly in the anti-Morsi camp. Their dehumanization and demonization of the Brotherhood's members and other Islamists, not to mention their disparaging of the pro-Morsi protests, has become engrained.[45]

A major turning point occurred when Morsi, reacting to the Mubarak-appointed judiciary's persistent interventions, issued a presidential constitutional decree that neutralized the judicial system and granted him sweeping and unprecedented powers as president. The decree placed Morsi above all oversight, including judicial review of his decisions, until a new constitution was adopted and parliamentary elections were held. The decree introduced a plan to force out members of the Mubarak-era judiciary by lowering the mandatory age of retirement by ten years (from 70 years old to 60 years old). The legislation would have removed more than 3,000 judges. The decree backfired as more than 200,000 people took to the streets in protest and Morsi's justice minister Ahmed Mekky and a number of other presidential advisers as well as the president's advisor for legal affairs, Mohamed Fouad Gadallah. Gadallah, the twelfth presidential advisor to resign over the controversy, was the architect of Morsi's November 2012 constitutional decree.

The country's constitution, which was supposed to be the crowning achievement of the revolution, and the judiciary, which was supposed to guarantee that the historic transition would evolve in a lawful manner, became two of the country's most controversial aspects and causes for division.

Thousands of Morsi supporters and opponents clashed in violent street demonstrations demanding the "cleansing of the judiciary." Morsi's supporters claimed that the judiciary was infused with *fulool*, or remnants of the old Mubarak regime, which were intentionally blocking his initiatives as president. Morsi's opponents argued that Islamists wanted to take over the courts and dismiss secular-minded judges in order to consolidate the MB's power. Indeed, the *fulool* were a major player in the instability, as was the opposition. The two were aligned. Groups that were loyal to Mubarak were still in control of the security apparatus, most of the private media, the judiciary, and also major industries and economic institutions. Their power to influence the objectives of the revolution was still great.[46]

The judiciary, overseen by the Supreme Constitutional Court, ruled against election laws that would have set parliamentary elections into motion; they demanded the return of the country's general prosecutor, a Mubarak appointee replaced by Morsi; and they reversed many attempts to build democratic institutions. In their aim to push back against Morsi's politics and deny his government the opportunity to rule, they rejected, *de facto*, the results of the free election that brought Morsi to power. What emerged was a quandary whereby Egypt's democrats were not necessarily liberals and Egypt's liberals were not necessarily democrats.[47] The MB did not sufficiently demonstrate that they were fully committed to the principles of democracy: pluralism, equal rights for religious minorities, checks and balances, and personal freedoms. The opposition, on the other hand, claimed to support democracy and elections, as long as the elections didn't result in an Islamist-led government.[48]

By late April a new opposition movement, "Tamarod," or "rebellion," emerged with the stated goal to demand presidential elections by gathering 15 million signatures on a petition.[49] A broad-based anti-Morsi campaign grew rapidly, supported by elements of the deep state (military, police, judiciary, and bureaucrats), much of the Mubarak-era public media, secularists, April 6 youth, and some Muslim and Coptic religious leaders. It was heavily financed not only domestically by wealthy Egyptian tycoons, who had prospered under Mubarak and were outraged by the Morsi government's prosecution for corruption, but also and especially by Saudi Arabia and the UAE in particular.

Calls for mass mobilization on June 30th moved from protests to demand government reforms to a call for Morsi to resign. A group of military and security forces, the judiciary, and the bureaucracy transformed a diverse Egyptian movement that had expressed its grievances into a movement to topple the first democratically elected government in Egypt's history. Military intervention and a return to authoritarianism were disguised as a restorative process, one that would ultimately lead to a secular democratic and secure future.[50]

On June 30, 2013, thousands of protestors gathered in Tahrir Square, the site of the protests that ousted Mubarak, and millions more across the country took to the streets in mass protests. Within five hours of the protest's commencement, five of Morsi's cabinet members submitted their resignations. The Egyptian state was collapsing. The Morsi-appointed defense minister and military chief Abdel Fattah Al-Sisi issued a forty-eight-hour ultimatum to the president: reach a compromise or the military would intervene. The following day, Morsi addressed the Egyptian people and announced that he rejected the ultimatum and called on people to support democracy and honor the democratic election that brought him to power. On July 3, Al-Sisi announced that he had suspended the constitution, removed Morsi from power, and nominated the head of the Constitutional Court, Adly Mansour, as the country's interim president, embracing the demands of the opposition and the *fulool*. His move gave Mansour the power to issue constitutional decrees as well as enact legislative authority.

THE INTERIM GOVERNMENT, an illegitimate product of a military-backed coup, proceeded to act very much like the government of Gamal Abdel Nasser in the past, seeking to crush and destroy the Brotherhood. It massacred large numbers of the Brotherhood and other opposition in what some claimed was the largest bloodbath in modern Egyptian history. The security forces deliberately used violence and killing to provoke non-violent pro-Morsi demonstrators to take up arms and fire back, and it has declared its intention to outlaw the MB (as Nasser had, but neither Sadat nor Mubarak did).

The military junta and its appointed government turned to the courts and, arresting Brotherhood leaders on trumped-up charges, blamed the victims of violence for the violence and threatening state security. In fact it was a counterrevolution led by many Mubarak regime appointees, in particular the military and judiciary. The collusion between the military and the courts has been evident from the SCAF's policies, along with the Constitutional Court's invasive decisions such as the dissolution of the FJP and Islamist-dominated parliament as well as the Constitutional Assembly, and has culminated with the appointment of a key anti-Morsi judge and former head of the Supreme Constitutional Court as interim president.

The military and its government did not pursue the democratic process to legitimate their power by using parliamentary and presidential elections to discredit the Brotherhood, unseat and replace a democratically elected government, and establish their own legitimate government. Instead, they put themselves above the rule of law: with a coup, massacres of civilian demonstrators (including many women and children), arrest and illegal detention of thousands of Brotherhood leaders and members, restoration of the dreaded Emergency Law, and resort to trials by a corrupt court system.

Authorities arrested Morsi, along with other senior MB officials, and held them secretly. State media initially reported that arrest warrants had been issued for more than 300 Brotherhood members; the number would soon jump to the thousands. Programs and channels that belonged to the MB or to other Islamist groups as well as independent media like Al Jazeera were suspended and the military surrounded the pro-Morsi demonstrators, cutting off their electricity as well as denying them access to food and water.[51]

The coup that removed Morsi from power elicited strong reactions from many quarters. The African Union suspended its affiliation with Egypt, citing its rules against unconstitutional government changes. But not all of those reactions were so clear. Washington, for one, refused to call the overthrow of a democratically elected Morsi government a coup d'état, despite the fact that interim President Mansour's declaration made it explicitly clear that his authority stemmed from a transfer of power delivered by General Abdul Fatah Al-Sisi, the defense minister. As Khaled Abou Al-Fadl wrote, "By stepping in to remove an unpopular president, the Egyptian Army reaffirmed a despotic tradition in the Middle East: Army officers decide what the country needs, and they always know best."[52]

The ambivalence and reluctance of the United States and EU to strongly condemn the overthrow of Egypt's democratically elected government by a military-led coup seemed to confirm what so many Arabs previously reported in major polling (by Gallup and others), a belief that they were not really interested in supporting the democratic process. Gehad El-Haddad, a spokesman for the MB (later arrested and imprisoned), wrote in a July 8 op-ed for the *Washington Post* that "the Western governments that pretend to be on the sidelines are facilitating this chaos. You cannot call yourself neutral while justifying and financing a military coup against an elected president. News reports have indicated there were five high-level conversations in as many days between the Egyptian government and the Obama administration. Two additional attempts at negotiation involved a European ambassador and an Arab foreign minister. The veneer of ambivalence is thin. And it is unconscionable to try to maintain this pretense in the face of escalating violence against peaceful protesters."[53] Critics charged that the message the Obama administration sent reinforced a widespread belief that when it comes to the Arab world and its aspirations for democratic government, there is a double standard.

In mid-August 2013, the situation in Egypt worsened. In response to Morsi's ousting, supporters of the MB held sit-ins at the Rabaa Al-Adawiya mosque and in Nahda Square. They demanded, among other things, that Morsi be reinstated and that the country's military commanders hand over power. Security forces stormed the two camps, killing scores. While the military-controlled government reported a death toll of 658, other estimates placed it at more than 2,600 with some as high as 5,000 and more than 4,500 injured. The assault was the third time military and security forces had slaughtered Muslim Brotherhood members and their supporters, despite the fact that the country's Interior Ministry had promised a gradual dispersal of demonstrators.

The episode triggered national and international uproar and evidenced what many suspected was a looming reality: Egypt's return to military-led authoritarianism. It prompted the resignation of interim Vice President Mohamed ElBaradei, who criticized the violence and fled the country, as well as tepid and equivocating responses from the United States and EU. President Barack Obama maintained his refusal to label the coup a coup; he condemned the violence on both sides without condemning the fact that the bulk of deaths and casualties were civilians slaughtered by the interim government's military and police. In contrast, Turkey's Prime Minister Recep Tayyip Erdogan called the event a "massacre," and France's François Hollande condemned the "bloody violence" and called for an end to the "repression."[54]

Astonishingly, whereas US president Barack Obama and other world leaders condemned the harsh crackdowns on the MB, US secretary of state John Kerry visited Egypt in early November, shortly before the ban was upheld, and announced that Egypt was on the "right path" to democracy.[55] Later, in an address to the State Department's Overseas Security Council, he stated that the MB had "stolen" the Egyptian Revolution:

And those kids in Tahrir Square, they were not motivated by any religion or ideology. They were motivated by what they saw through this interconnected world, and they wanted a piece of the opportunity and a chance to get an education and have a job and have a future, and not have a corrupt government that deprived them of all of that and more. And they tweeted their ways and Facetimed their ways and talked to each other, and that's what drove that revolution. And then it got stolen by the one single most organized entity in the state, which was the Brotherhood.[56]

An emboldened Al-Sisi and the military implemented additional measures that confirmed the growing authoritarian nature of the interim government. Among them was a military-backed law that banned public meetings of more than ten people without permission and street protests, levying heavy jail sentences and fines for those who expressed their political views in public quarters and issuing mass death sentences.

Coptic Christians in Egypt suffered church, shop, and home burnings, looting, and assaults, in some of the worst sectarian violence in Egypt's history. While many Copts believed that they would fare better in a post-Morsi environment, the failure of the police to intervene left Christian communities, in particular the Coptic Christians who make up approximately 10 percent of Egypt's population, without adequate protections and rights they deserved as equal citizens. MB leadership consistently counseled against violence. However, they were not able to control disaffected Brotherhood members or militant Islamic groups and thugs who exploited Coptic Pope Tawadros II's appearance alongside Al-Sisi as an opportunity to respond to the coup and subsequent massacres carried out in the name of state security.

In March and April 2014, Justice Said Youssef issued a pair of rulings sentencing more than 1,200 people to death—after two trials lasting less than an hour each. Applauded by Egypt's pro-government media, they were condemned by human rights advocates in Egypt and abroad. The April 6 Youth Movement was banned, and human rights organizations criticized court hearings that lasted just minutes, denied the defense the right to speak, and confirmed death sentences for dozens of individuals at a time.[57] The International Union of Muslim Scholars, similarly, spoke out against the alleged torture and illegal detainment of journalists, scholars, youth, women, and even children.[58]

In January 2014, Egypt's new constitution was approved by 98.1 percent of those who voted (voter turnout was only 38.6 percent). It introduced an unparalleled counterterrorism clause that gave the military and security services sweeping and unchecked powers, "a counterterrorism clause that lays the legal foundation for a police state that is a military dictatorship in all but name."[59] Equally problematic, the military was granted the power for eight years to veto the president's selection of Egypt's Defense Minister. In addition to the previous banning of the MB as a terrorist organization, all Islamists in general were marginalized from political life by a ban on political activity based on religion.

Faux Liberals: Liberal Secular Intelligentsia

"Only a dead Islamist is a good Islamist." I shuddered when I read this Facebook message by a young leader of a secular political party. A few days earlier a senior member of that group posted the following: "We will fight with whatever we have, we will arrest as many as we can and we will also kill as many if needed but please don't talk to us about inclusion and reconciliation! Don't talk to us about human rights and Amnesty International reports because frankly we don't give a damn!"[60]

A striking aspect of Egypt's tumultuous ousting of Morsi was the vocal support of individuals in society who identified themselves as liberals. Many were on the front lines of the campaign to oust Mubarak, enthusiastically opposing military rule and demanding the end of an authoritarian state where the president and military were one. During Morsi's tenure, however, that changed. Liberals who loathed the MB and the government's lackadaisical policies not only embraced Morsi's ousting but also welcomed violent crackdowns on the group and hailed the ensuing military. Mohamed ElBaradei, a leading opponent of the Mubarak regime and Egypt's vice president until August 2013, refused to call Morsi's ousting a coup and expressed his support for military efforts to shut down MB media outlets.[61] Similarly, Egyptian feminist Nawaal El-Sadaawi voiced her approval of Morsi's ousting, saying that "democracy is about more than elections."[62]

The failure of so many so-called liberal secular intelligentsia—the sector of society that claims to uphold the values of civil discourse, rationalism, freedom, civic engagement, and democratic principles—to oppose the coup revealed a deep seated illiberal secularism.[63]

The apparent discrepancy between the values of a liberal democracy and Egyptian liberals' support for a military-led coup presumes a single fixed understanding of liberalism. But, as Samer Shehata writes, "Egypt has a dilemma: its politics are dominated by democrats who are not liberals and liberals who are not democrats."[64] The MB participated in democratic elections, but once in office were reluctant to adequately share power. Liberal secular intelligentsia believe in the values of liberalism—equal rights, civil liberties, and the necessity of governing coalitions—but only as long as Islamist groups are kept out of power.

Disillusioned Youth

Young Egyptians were major actors in the protests that led to the toppling of both Hosni Mubarak in 2011 and Mohamed Morsi in 2013. Two-thirds of Egyptians are under the age of 35, and three out of four are under 40. Despite the initial support of many for Morsi's removal, their growing disillusionment and disaffection was evident by their conspicuous absence in the voting for the referendum on the revised constitution, heralded as a show of support for the military takeover. For the first time since the Tahrir Square uprising in 2011, in contrast to six previous national polls, young voters were invisible, choosing not to vote. Many felt marginalized and alienated and were increasingly victims of repression and imprisonment as the police used deadly force in crackdowns against a cross-section of young people—Islamists, liberals, or left-leaning—for organizing anti-government protests. A common epigram—"Gray hairs in the queues, black hairs in the graves"—circulated in Islamist and liberal circles alike, which "contrasted the referendum voters supporting the new government installed by Field Marshall Al-Sisi with the protesters opposing it."[65]

Mohamed Adel, a leader of the April 6 youth movement, expressed his frustration, saying, "We feel now that there is a huge difference between us and the older generation, and I feel they're taking decisions that will drive people toward a very bad place. They have no idea about the reality of the political or social situation."[66] In late April 2014, an Egyptian court banned the activities of the April 6 youth movement, concluding that the group engaged in espionage and defamed Egypt's image abroad. Writing from a prison cell just south of Cairo, the group's founder, Ahmed Maher, imprisoned along with the group's other two founding members, urged activists to tell the world that "the police display brutality every day, and there is no one who can stop them from murdering us in our cells if they want to. Tell them that there is no protection today nor tomorrow, and tell them that whoever is silent about it today will face worse tomorrow."[67] Striking.

The "Election" of a New President

Presidential elections were scheduled for May 26–27, 2014. The expectation and public call by Al-Sisi was for a massive turnout; he expected 40 million voters (80 percent of the electorate) to cast their ballots. However, initial reports indicated an astonishingly low turnout. Reports on voter turnout varied wildly and widely: from 10 percent to the government's High Electoral Commission's 37 percent to estimates as low as 25 percent from many outside observers. Panicking, the government extended the voting period by one day to May 28, which was declared a holiday to encourage voting, and the Justice Ministry threatened to fine those who did not vote $17, a substantial amount for many Egyptians.

The low turnout was humiliating for Al-Sisi and his followers, undercutting the widespread belief that he was the choice of the vast majority of Egyptians. In addition to speculation about possible causes such as the continued downward spiral of the economy, increasing levels of violence, and Al-Sisi's refusal to state his program (he had angrily responded to a query from the media that "I have no program"), the lack of credible political rivals prompted calls by both the MB and the April 6 movement, which played a pivotal role in the January 25 Revolution, for a boycott of the vote, dismissing the polls as a "military election." The absence of broad support saw Al-Sisi supporters among TV commentators desperately shouting and berating their audiences for not voting and Egypt's newspapers like *Al Shorouk* declaring that "the ballot boxes are looking for voters" on its front page; and even those generally supportive of Al-Sisi, such as *Al Masry al Youm*, ran headlines such as "The state is looking for a vote."

Even if a final report of 46 percent, which is contested, is believed, it was a shocking disappointment for Al-Sisi supporters and their expectations and less than the 52 percent participation in former president Mohamed Morsi's election.

Conclusion

If the Arab Spring uprisings stunned both rulers and peoples in the Arab world and raised high expectations of a new dawn with popular sovereignty replacing authoritarian regimes, the path to democratization proved rocky, disappointing, and treacherous.

In 2011 and 2012, Egyptians went to the polls to vote in parliamentary elections and Morsi's Freedom and Justice Party received a plurality of votes; the two major Islamist blocs together received nearly two-thirds of the vote. Then in June 2012, Morsi defeated Ahmed Shafiq by a margin of 52 to 48 percent (more than the margin that Barack Obama received when he defeated Mitt Romney in 2012) to win the presidency.[68] However, the successes of the Brotherhood as an opposition Islamist movement did not translate into effective leadership as a political party (FJP). Morsi failed to adequately reach out early enough to build a strong and diverse political coalition. Instead, the leadership succumbed to a tendency to go it alone in dealing with the military and electoral politics.

A fragile democratic transition was shattered as Egyptian society became polarized to an unprecedented degree with many original Tahrir Square protestors and so-called liberals abandoning democracy, embracing a military-led coup to depose Egypt's first democratically elected president.

Those who championed the ouster now faced the reality that in toppling the Morsi government, they did not usher in a more democratic system but rather restored a military-guided authoritarian government whose repression, violence, and brutality exceeded that of any government in modern Egyptian history. The mass indiscriminate killings committed by Egyptian security forces against demonstrators at Al Nahda and Rabaa Squares were the worst incidents of state violence in the country's modern history. In the guise of a war against terrorism to save the Egyptian state and the spirit of the Tahrir uprising, the MB was outlawed as a terrorist organization and subjected to mass arrests, military trials, and mass death sentences by a corrupt judiciary. Some 21,000 people were jailed (unofficial sources put the number at 40,000); many were beaten, tortured, or held without trial.

The government introduced measures to suppress peaceful opposition and free expression. It banned public protests, required government approval for public meetings, and cracked down on nongovernmental organizations. Democracy activists, secular as well as non-secular, who had been at the heart of the struggle for democracy in 2011 and 2012, were imprisoned; the liberal secular April 6 movement, which initially supported the coup, was banned by an Egyptian court in April 2014. The government took control of the universities, appointing its presidents and arresting university students and schoolchildren accused of "sabotaging" educational facilities. Secret military trials were expanded to include civilians. In a country where most newspapers were no longer independent and supported the government, newspaper editors were pressured to agree not to criticize "state institutions," in particular the army, police, and judiciary.

But what about the future role of religion and of Islamists in the political process? Egyptian identification with Islam has been and remains an important aspect of the country's political process. In recent years, major polling by the Gallup and PEW organizations and others have reported that a majority of Egyptians see religion as an important part of their personal lives and desire a state and society that are consonant with Islamic principles and values.

As in the past under Nasser, Sadat, and Mubarak, Al-Sisi has sought to coopt or control religion and religious institutions. However, Egypt's history provides examples of how the appeal to Islam by autocrats can backfire. Nasser's ostensible eradication of the Brotherhood had two significant effects on Anwar Sadat's presidency. When Sadat came to power and released many of Muslim Brotherhood and others imprisoned for years and tortured, the majority of the MB, ostensibly crushed or eliminated by Gamal Abdel Nasser, re-emerged, rebuilt, and established itself as the major (though unofficial) political opposition party.

It is premature to count the Brotherhood out or discount the emergence of another Islamically oriented political opposition. A radical alternative is also possible. A minority of the younger Islamists imprisoned by Nasser organized or joined militant groups that challenged and eventually assassinated Sadat; and engaged in acts of terrorism in the early years of Mubarak's rule. Al-Sisi's policies have seen an upsurge in militant attacks in Cairo and elsewhere and especially in the Sinai. Some Egyptian youth, MB and others, have turned to ISIS, convinced that with the overthrow of Morsi and the restoration of authoritarianism and repression, ISIS ideology and taking up arms are the only viable option. As a former Muslim Brotherhood youth commented:

> I used to believe in the motto, "Our peacefulness is more powerful than bullets." But when bullets started being directed at us

and we were accused of being terrorists, I started to believe only in force to preserve my beliefs and establish the Islamic State in Egypt.[69]

The euphoria and hopes of Egypt's Arab Spring with the overthrow of Mubarak and Egypt's first democratic elections and then of those who supported the military-led coup have been shattered. The post-coup period saw democratic aspirations wither as Egyptians experienced the most violent use of force and killing by the military in modern Egyptian history, and under President Al-Sisi, the restoration of authoritarianism and repression, release of Hosni Mubarak and on May 16, an Egyptian court condemn Morsi, Egypt's first freely elected president, to death with more than 100 other defendants.

9

Conclusion

IS DEMOCRACY IN trouble or is the world entering the next democratic century? The debate about the future of democracy is global. In these debates, the experiences of the Arab Spring shape the way people view the future of democracy, especially in the Muslim world. The failures of movements that overthrew authoritarian dictators are said to show the current weaknesses of democratization. The successes show the continuing strength of democracy in the Arab world and Muslim world in general.

Tunisia's "Dignity Revolution" (sometimes known as the Jasmine Revolution) in December 2010 raised expectations in some quarters of an "Arab Spring"—a ripple effect from Tunisia leading to widespread democratization not just in the Arab world but in Muslim countries more broadly. While some Western observers expressed shock at the idea, having accepted the Huntington hypothesis that Muslims prefer authoritarianism, many others accepted the developments in Tunisia as inevitable. Tunisians, like most populations under authoritarian regimes, had been agitating for democracy for decades, and soon other countries would follow suit. Indeed, within months other populations rose up against their authoritarian rulers. Egyptians ousted Mubarak, Libyans overthrew Qaddafi, Syrians rose up against the Assad regime, and Yemenis managed to unseat Saleh; several other regional countries launched more limited protests. But by the summer of 2013, the first democratically elected president of Egypt had been ousted in a military coup, Libya had fallen into chaos, Syria had descended into a vicious civil war, and other regional uprisings had been quashed. It seems to many that Tunisia was therefore not the leader of a new wave of democratization in Muslim countries but rather the odd one out, the exception that proves the rule.

Our case studies have demonstrated that these two alternatives—a new wave of democracy is finally coming ashore, or Muslims will never fully democratize—are not sufficient to describe the relationship between the Arab Spring, Islam, and democratization in the 21st century. In fact, democratization has been ongoing in Muslim-majority countries for well over a century and has taken a variety of forms. Significant variables have included whether or not, and the degree to which, a country was colonized; the kind of colonization a country underwent; the strength and nature of the military establishment upon independence; the impact of regional and global geopolitical complications, such as the Cold War and the Global War on Terrorism; and the country's economic development or lack thereof. Some of those who foresaw a ripple effect (if not a tsunami) of democratization after Tunisia's revolution identified demographics—the growing "youth bulge" and increasing empowerment of women—and the role of new social media as critical factors in the Arab Spring revolutions. While these new media certainly played roles in various aspects of the uprising, our research indicates that these were no more determinative than were the telephone, telegraph, audiocassette, and fax machine in earlier political movements. Each innovation has allowed for greater ease of communication and enabled transcendence of traditional class and gender barriers to one degree or another—the creation of a new "public sphere."[1] But the demands for good governance, the rule of law, autonomy, human rights, and improved standards of living have remained constant throughout the modern history of Muslim-majority countries' political movements. They continue to be the pivotal factors in contemporary democratization movements.

The Fukuyama teleological narrative from the 1990s, which asserted that Western-style "liberal democracy remains the only coherent political aspiration that spans different regions and cultures around the globe,"[2] should be avoided. However, we recognize that movements of democratization in the Muslim world did not simply start with the protest movements of the Arab Spring. These movements do not represent "the end of history," but rather are part of the long-term political evolution in the Muslim world. In these histories, there is no single monolithic movement either supporting or opposing democracy. Yet, acknowledging that there are diverse forms of democratic governance, and that Muslims themselves envision democracy differently, major polling by Gallup, PEW, and others—as well as history itself—demonstrate the desire for democratization. In our study, we are not engaged in the arguments of the 1990s, in which people debated whether or not Islam and democracy are compatible. At that time many intellectuals and activists in the Muslim world as well as analysts of what Huntington called the "Third Wave" of democratization agreed with Robin Wright, writing in 1992, when she argued, "The next few years will be as important for democracy's evolution as for Islam's. . . . One of the next major global challenges will be determining whether democracy is adaptable to Eastern countries, including Islamic and Confucian societies, and vice versa."[3]

In the contexts of these debates about the compatibility of Islam and democracy, John Esposito and John Voll wrote (in 1996), "In many areas of the Muslim world, one of the crucial issues defining the political future is the relationship between the forces of Islamic resurgence and the development of democratic political systems."[4] However, their analysis argued that the relationship between Islam and democracy was complex and showed both compatibility and contradiction, depending upon how Islam and democracy were defined. "Like all of the major worldviews and religious traditions, Islam has a full spectrum of potential symbols and concepts for support of absolutism and hierarchy, as well as foundations for liberty and equality."[5]

In the second decade of the 21st century, the relationships between Islam and democracy are in a new phase, reflected in the evolution of the political systems that are studied in this book. There still are some manifestations of the archaic view that Islam and democracy are incompatible, presented by some religious fundamentalists and hard core, old-line secularists, and echoes of the debates of the 1990s can still be heard. However, most Muslims around the world view democracy as desirable and see no conflict with their religious faith. The basic questions now go beyond the simplistic question of "essential" compatibility, and involve the nature of the democratic experiences in the Muslim world. There are few major Muslim organizations or significant political and intellectual leaders who identify themselves as being opposed to all forms of popular and democratic political participation.

The old characterization of virtually all Muslim-majority countries as being authoritarian or without significant movements advocating democracy is no longer viable. Samuel Huntington's assertion that "it is hard to identify any Islamic leader who made a reputation as an advocate and supporter of democracy while in office"[6] may have had some validity in 1991, but it clearly does not describe the situation in the second decade of the 21st century. In a number of Muslim-majority countries, competitive

elections have been held and oppositions have won elections. For most
Muslims in the world, the old question of whether or not Islam and
democracy are compatible is answered. Most believe they are compatible,
and the major issue in the 21st century is how to build democratic systems
and then maintain them. As the developments following the Arab Spring
show, the results are varied and complex.

The political battles are often not between advocates of a religious
state and supporters of a secular state. The struggles, as shown in the
Arab Spring and elsewhere, are between populist participatory democracy
(whether Islamic or secular) and an authoritarian elite-guided "democracy" (whether Islamic or secular). There are both democratic and authoritarian secularists, and also democratic and authoritarian religionists. The
new politics of the 21st century do not involve a "clash of civilizations" as
much as they show a contest between modes of political action. In this
new context, the diversity of experiences in the countries studied in this
book shows that democracy can take many different forms and that it is
not the inevitable "end of history." The seven countries studied in this
book have shown strong support for some form of democracy for well over
a century. In some of them, constitutional movements to limit monarchi-
cal authority go back into the 19th century. While these constitutionalist
groups were not proposing full democracy, like the early constitutionalists
in the United States and Western Europe, they advocated expansion of
popular political participation and restrictions on authoritarian monar-
chical systems. In the Ottoman Empire, Iran, and Egypt, supporters of
constitutional political systems involving some form of representative government (even if with limited power) were significant actors in the political arena by the beginning of the 20th century. In countries under more
direct colonialist control, like British India (as the precursor for Pakistan),
Indonesia, Senegal, and Tunisia, the rise of nationalist activism working
for self-rule also provided important experience for the later democratization movements.

The Ottoman Empire (and then the Republic of Turkey) and Iran took
very different democratization paths, and their experiences show the possible diversity of experiences with democracy in the Muslim world. Both
countries began the modern era as authoritarian monarchies and by the
21st century had become self-identified republics with constitutions, representative legislative bodies, and contested elections. It is likely that the
Ottoman intellectuals and politicians who created the Ottoman constitution in 1876 would find the Turkish Republic as led by President Erdogan

incomprehensible, just as the Ayatollahs and secular intellectuals who led the Iranian Constitutional Revolution in 1905 would be astonished by the 21st-century Islamic Republic of Iran. However, 21st-century states and their early modern ancestors are part of the long set of processes marking the democratization efforts in the modern Muslim world.

As we have discussed, the histories of seven Muslim-majority countries reveal support for some form of democratization for well over a century. During the 19th century, constitutionalist movements had the strongest support in the Ottoman Empire and Iran.

In the case of Turkey, the "Young Ottomans" pressured Sultan Abdul Hamid II in 1876 into establishing a parliament in accordance with a constitution ("basic law," *kanu-i esasi*). Although the constitution remained in effect for only two years, in the early 20th century, the Young Turks (later, the Committee of Union and Progress) pressured the long-reigning Abdul Hamid II into restoring the constitution; Turkey's first multiparty elections were held in 1908. The constitution survived until the end of World War I, when the Allies, occupying the defeated empire's capital, abolished it.

Ataturk's post-Ottoman government followed a militantly secularist path in creating the modern republic of Turkey. However, Kemalism failed to significantly improve the lives of the rural majority and, in suppressing popular religion, was decidedly undemocratic. As a result, in the 1940s parallel to Ataturk's secular republicanism, the election of a new president led to an incremental relaxing of militant secularism. As a part of this evolution of policy, as we noted in Chapter 2, increased public manifestation of religion involved building and repairing mosques, reopening the Islamic faculty at Ankara University, instituting training programs for imams, and reinstating religion classes in public schools. Limited liberalization continued in the 1950s, and a new generation of leaders began to emerge, who, in the context of the Cold War and fears of godless communism, advocated democratic reforms interpreted through religiously conservative lenses. Islam was seen as source of Turkish values.

In 1970 Necmettin Erbakan (d. 2011), modern educated and decidedly Islamically grounded, organized the National Order Party (NOP) to promote modern technology, industrialization, and a religious and moral renewal of society—and democracy. Reacting to this populist challenge, Turkey's military banned the NOP. The NOP promptly renamed itself the NSP, the National Salvation Party, and as such it grew in popularity and electoral performance throughout the 1970s, but once again the military intervened. Suspending Turkey's democracy, the military banned political parties and convicted NSP leaders of threatening secular democracy and replacing it with religious authoritarianism.

In 1983 democracy was restored and the NSP re-emerged as the Welfare Party (WP; in Turkish, Refah Partisi), an avowedly Islamist party. The secularist Motherland Party, led by former Islamist Turgut Ozal (d. 1993), dominated the 1983 elections, running on a platform that included the importance of religious values in Turkey's political and social progress. Ozal and his supporters saw no contradiction between secular democracy and Islamic values. As he put it, "Our state is secular. But what holds our nation together . . . is Islam."[7]

By 1994 the Islamist Welfare Party dominated municipal elections, winning in Istanbul and a majority of other cities across Turkey. It scored a surprise victory in 1995 in general elections. In 1996 Necmettin Erbakan became prime minister, and secular Turkey had its first democratically elected Islamist prime minister. Polls indicated that the determining factors were not ideological or religious so much as economic and political. Welfare's electoral successes polarized society, as did secularists'—including the military's—concerns about the public role of religion. Welfare's coalition government collapsed in 1997 due to pressure from the military, and the party was banned in 1998.

The year 2001 saw the founding of a new Islamist party, the AKP (Justice and Development Party), by a new generation of leaders formerly associated with Erdogan and the Welfare Party. The AKP won a stunning victory in 2002 parliamentary elections. AKP leader Recep Tayyip Erdogan framed the party's platform as "conservative democracy" with an emphasis on pluralism, prosperity, and pragmatism. "To make religion an instrument of politics and to adopt exclusive approaches to politics in the name of religion harms not only political pluralism but also religion itself."[8]

The AKP maintained its dominance in subsequent elections and Turkey enjoyed significant economic and political progress in the early 21st century. However, Turkey's Islamist-led government became the target of critics—both secularist and Islamist—who alleged authoritarianism, particularly in light of Prime Minister Erdogan's efforts to strengthen the presidency (to which he subsequently was elected) relative to the legislative and judiciary branches. This was demonstrated in widespread popular protests in 2013 and the AKP loss of a parliamentary majority in the 2015 elections. On the other hand, many AKP supporters saw it as the protector of Turkey's democracy, vis-à-vis the military and its supporters, and the reason for Turkey's years of economic growth and development. This was demonstrated by the AKP's continued success in national and subsequent presidential elections in July 2014.

Like the Turks (and Russians), Iranians' efforts to establish constitutional limits on the monarchy became effective in the first decade of the 20th century when popular pressure forced the shah (king) to accept a constitution. Yet as would happen in many countries, global geopolitics interfered with popular demands; England and Russia, competing for regional dominance, divided the country into militarized spheres of influence and empowered successive new shahs to ignore parliament. And during the chaotic period of World War I and the Bolshevik Revolution, Iran's social fabric was stretched to the breaking point with various factions asserting autonomy with British or Russian/Soviet support. When national unity was reasserted after World War I and a new monarchy proclaimed, the Turkish model of rapid modernization and radical secularism became the order of the day and, as in Turkey, efforts to impose secular reforms ended up being distinctly undemocratic. Popular protests against what appeared as highly authoritarian social engineering, supported by religious leaders, were suppressed. In addition to this internal suppression of the popular will, Iran was again subjected to foreign manipulation. During World War II, Britain and the Soviet Union again interfered, forcing the shah to abdicate in favor of his son Muhammad Reza Shah. During his reign, foreign control of Iran's resources became a major issue. By mid-20th century, support for nationalization of Iran's petroleum resources had become so widespread that the shah was forced to accept it. Britain struck back, with US support, in the clandestine Operation Ajax, forcing the reversal of nationalization and, with the reinstatement of the shah, effectively neutralizing the country's democratic institutions.

The continued suppression of popular opinion and democratic institutions led to the overthrow of the shah in 1979, the culmination of a movement supported by a broad spectrum of political opposition but distilled into simple condemnations of autocracy and calls for justice by religious leaders. The 1979 Iranian Revolution thus was populist and anti-autocratic in nature; it was Islamic by default. And its conservative policies generated their own share of opposition, supported again by a broad spectrum of society, both secular and religious. That opposition provided a landslide victory to reformist cleric Mohammad Khatami in 1997, running on a platform of freedom of conscience and dialogue with the West. With US-led occupation of Iran's neighbors and the ongoing

Global War on Terrorism, older generations' abiding conservatism and suspicion of the West supported a backlash against reformist efforts throughout the last decade of the 20th century and first decade of the 21st. Yet Iran's reformist strain remains strong. Widely popular reformist candidates were expected to dominate 2009 elections. When the results returned conservative Ahmadinejad to the presidency, protests erupted. Brutal suppression of the protests led to the emergence of the Green Movement. Though legally silenced, the movement and its supporters continue their efforts, often in ingenious ways—including massive protests in which participants maintain strict silence. The popularity of the movement was demonstrated in the 2013 election of reformist cleric Hassan Rouhani. Thus, "a century after the Constitutional Revolution of 1906, Iran is still grappling with how to achieve a democratic state. It is open to question whether Iran is any closer to that goal today than it has been at any other time in the past century."[9] But as in the case of Turkey, the choice is clearly not between religious and democratic governance.

Turkey and Iran took very different democratization paths, but democratization paths they were—and remain. In both, progress involved some rather dramatic transitions. The same is true of Pakistan. Despite the fact that it was created specifically as a democracy, it has struggled with authoritarianism throughout its brief history. Unlike Iran, Pakistan has not been plagued with foreign powers seeking control of its resources, but global geopolitics have definitely affected the country's governance. Since its founding in 1948, Pakistan's government has been dominated by the military, abetted by a compliant elite structure of feudal and tribal aristocracy and industrialists. These civilian elites, primarily interested in maintaining the status quo which protects their privileged positions, have acquiesced to the military's preoccupation with national security, thus keeping the country on a war footing throughout its brief history. In efforts to gain support for its policies, Pakistan's feudal-tribal-military-industrial complex has manipulated both popular opinion, by focusing on threats along its problematic borders, and religious sentiment, providing privileges for those religious organizations willing to overlook interference in the country's democratic institutions. In the process, the government has drained public coffers of funds necessary for civilian infrastructure and social development. That lack of development, in turn, has fostered discontent often expressed in factionalism and other destabilizing trends that have prompted military intervention and undermined the country's fledgling democracy.

Yet for all Pakistan's challenges, its political parties have consistently referred to the democratic ideals outlined in the country's founding Objectives Resolution. The post-9/11 era has seen the military campaigning against the Pakistani Taliban and other militants continue, yet the majority of Pakistanis express dire concern for their country's Islamic and democratic future. Those concerns have been reflected in democratic elections over the past decade. Disputes between the military and civilian governments over the Kashmir conflict resulted in a coup in 1999, in which General Pervez Musharraf ousted and exiled democratically elected Prime Minister Nawaz Sharif. After eight years, increasing radicalization among some regional and sectarian factions, and ultimately the assassination of former Prime Minister Benazir Bhutto, Pakistan returned to democracy with the election of Bhutto's husband Asif Ali Zardari. In 2013, Pakistan experienced its first peaceful turnover of democratic governance through elections. It also experienced a remarkable electoral success for a third party, the Pakistan Tehreek-e-Insaf (PTI). Running on a platform of Islam, social justice, and democracy, PTI gained thirty-four seats in Pakistan's National Assembly.

In the popular jargon of political pundits, Pakistan is a "failed state." But, in fact, Pakistan is a country of some 180 million people, the vast majority of whom are Sunni Muslims who, in the name of Islam, support democratic governance. After decades of militarization and participation in regional conflicts, its economy is a shambles and its infrastructure archaic. But Pakistan remains a state finding its path toward achieving its founding goals. Commitment to those goals is reflected in Pakistanis' dogged determination to return, again and again, to the polls. The 2013 elections reflected a renewed commitment to those goals, and the strong showing by PTI, as noted in Chapter 4, shows a significant increase in the political engagement of Pakistan's youthful urban population. The question in Pakistan, therefore, is not about whether or not Islam and democracy are compatible, or choosing between religious and secular governance, or even whether or not there is a special kind of Islamic democracy. Pakistan has clearly not yet achieved the goals it set for itself over sixty years ago, but it is fatuous to call it a failed state. Rather, as Pakistani anthropologist Naveeda Khan notes, it should be seen as a work in progress toward its goals of "democracy, freedom, equality, tolerance and social justice, as enunciated by Islam."[10]

Indonesia's modern political development appears similar to the experiences of many other countries that gained independence following

World War II. Nationalist movements established governments that were parliamentary in form and these civilian governments relatively soon either created one-party systems or were taken over by military leaders. By the early 21st century, many of these authoritarian regimes faced increasingly strong oppositions which advocated more-participatory democratic politics.

In Indonesia, the nationalist movement led by Sukarno won independence from the Dutch in 1949 and he became the first president. Under his leadership, the state was becoming an authoritarian one-party state when he was overthrown by the military in 1966–1967. The military regime established by General Suharto was a self-proclaimed "New Order" in which authoritarian rule was justified by the rhetoric of "Guided Democracy." By the 1990s, democratic opposition began to emerge as a powerful political force. In 1998 the demonstrations and organized opposition of what came to be called the *reformasi* movement overthrew the military dictatorship in the largest Muslim-majority country—more than a decade before the Arab Spring.

In the decade following the success of *reformasi*, the new democratic system that was established in 1998–1999 successfully evolved, with elections in which opposition candidates and parties could and did win elections. Transfers of power took place with relatively little disturbance or violence. Observers and participants alike viewed the national elections of 2014 as a confirmation of the democratization of the political system.

Although the general outlines of Indonesian history are similar to the histories of many other countries, the successful outcomes of 21st-century democratization in Indonesia are shaped by distinctive features in Indonesian society. Three major groupings interacted in building the Indonesian political system—the modernizing nationalist political elite, the major Islamic organizations, and the Indonesian military. Each of these has historic roots within society and was not simply the creation of the processes of achieving independence.

Both the nationalist elite and the Islamic organizations had well-established institutions and were experienced political actors by the time of independence. This enabled these groupings to maintain organizational frameworks and identities during the long military regime of Suharto. As a result, *reformasi* did not thrust into power groups that had limited experience or organizational coherence.

The two largest Muslim organizations, Muhammadiyya and Nahdlatul Ulama (NU), were reformist groups established early in the 20th century and were politically active but not militantly oppositional in the colonial, Sukarno, and Suharto eras. In the post-Suharto era, leaders from these groups were significant leaders—Amien Rais, of the Muhammadiyya, in the parliament, and Abd al-Rahman Wahid of NU as the first elected president. In the continuing democratization in the 21st century, the Muslim organizations represent significant Muslim voices that are neither militant in program nor fundamentalist in vision.

The nationalist elite also had roots early in the 20th century and the major voice for this group was Megawati Sukarnoputri, the daughter of Sukarno. Like the religious groups, the opposition nationalists were not revolutionaries but rather were and continue to be advocates of democracy. Remarkably, the major military leaders followed this path as well in the new era. Rather than working to re-establish military rule, the most influential military leaders entered politics and became significant civilian politicians.

The ability and willingness of the major political forces to cooperate even as they compete with each other are key to the democratization process in Indonesia. The elections in 2014 were a culmination of many developments, bringing to the office of the presidency Joko Widodo, who represents a new generation of leaders who will determine what the future of democracy will be in their country. In a similar process, national elections in Senegal in 2012 brought a new generation of political leaders to power. As in Indonesia, effective democratization began a decade before the Arab Spring. However, democratization was a longer and more gradual process in Senegal, with roots in electoral politics even in the colonial era a century before. By the time of independence in 1960, the Senegalese nationalist-urban elite was experienced in parliamentary politics. This elite worked effectively with leaders of mass religious organizations and ethnic leaders in a political system in which no specifically ethnic or major religious political parties developed. One distinctive feature of the political history of Senegal since independence is that it never experienced military rule.

Following independence a *de facto* one-party system emerged under the leadership of Leopold Senghor, the first president. However, already in the 1970s, Senghor opened the way for multiparty, competitive elections, especially after he voluntarily retired in 1980. Abdoulaye Wade established a major opposition party in 1974. Wade and his party contested national elections in 1978, 1983, 1988, and 1993, gradually winning growing support over the years. After competing for a quarter of a century, Wade and his party won the national elections in 2000 and took power in a peaceful transition. Throughout that period, there were times of popular demonstrations and protests, but there was little support for overthrow of the state, from either civilian radicals or the military. In the first decade of the 21st century, multiparty political activity flourished and Wade won re-election in 2007. However, he raised concerns about a return to a one-party state when he announced that he would compete in the 2012 presidential elections for an unconstitutional third term as president. Many different opposition parties contested the parliamentary and presidential elections, but in the presidential runoff election, they joined together in support of Macky Sall, who was elected. Wade accepted the election results, confirming the continuation of democratization in Senegal.

Senegalese democracy is remarkable because Senegal has significant ethnic and religious diversity, which in many other countries has resulted in some form of authoritarian rule or significant political instability. In Senegal, the ethnic diversity has not prevented the emergence of a concurrent strong sense of Senegalese national identity. This national identification began as a characteristic of the urban Francophone elite but by the 21st century was characteristic of most Senegalese in an increasingly urbanized society. The new trans-ethnic feeling is often expressed in a new Urban Wolof, which is the common lingua franca of life in the public square.

Two large Muslim organizations—the Tijaniyya and the Muridiyya—have political significance. These groups have roots in 19th-century Islamic developments and were important voices for the general public in the days of French rule. Most Senegalese are associated with one or the other of these brotherhoods and have historically looked to their leaders for guidance in political as well as religious affairs. However, the brotherhoods provided support for the urban political elite rather than creating their own political parties. In this way, they helped to bring the rural and non-elite Senegalese into the political arena.

In the 21st century, some smaller, more activist groups established political parties, but their more Islamist views won little public support. As is the case in Indonesia, the largest Muslim organizations affirm Islamic ideals and beliefs but are not "Islamist" in either their programs or their modes of operation.

The cooperation between the urban political elite and the leaders of religious and ethnic groups was and continues to be an important part of the long-term democratization process in Senegal. The elections of 2012 confirmed the commitment of both the Senegalese political elite and the general public to democracy.

In light of these narratives, it is indeed amazing that so many observers were surprised—even "shocked"—by the "Arab Spring" developments. They are very much a part of the ongoing, if erratic, process of political recovery of Muslim-majority countries whose development had been stunted by decades of foreign control.

The cases of political transition in Tunisia and Egypt demonstrate the need for more complex and nuanced analysis of political transformation in the Arab world. They underscore the importance of analyzing individual countries within their contexts rather than utilizing a few ahistorical, extreme scenarios that paint the Arab world as an enclave of authoritarianism and chaos. In Egypt, a lack of compromise among the political elite has led to an exclusive system in which the winners are exercising unchecked authority over the very foundations of their country's political and economic institutions. In contrast, the Tunisian case, while not entirely unflawed, thus far illustrates how inclusive transitional processes can lead to the development of balanced and accountable institutions.

As noted in Chapter 7, Tunisia, where the Arab Spring began, showed signs of opposition to authoritarian rule long before the events of December 17, 2010. Since independence from France in 1956, it had had only two presidents, both dictators. Both regimes were characterized by authoritarianism, failed economies, high unemployment, corruption, maldistribution of the country's relatively significant resources (oil and gas), and a lack of civil and political liberties. Those were the primary reasons for the uprising.

When the uprising proved successful, driving dictator Ben Ali into exile, the Islamist Nahda (Renaissance) Party won the first-ever free elections in Tunisia—upsetting the model of Islamic opposition to democracy constructed by Western observers. While undoubtedly there are Islamists who consider democracy a tool of godless Western imperialists, Nahda has consistently advocated democratic reforms. Soon after the country's first postcolonial ruler, the radically secularist Habib Bourguiba, declared himself "President for Life" in 1975, scholar-activist Rached Ghannouchi established the Islamic Association, which became the Islamic Tendency Movement (MTI) in 1981, during a period of brief liberalization in Tunisia. Within months, a government crackdown landed Ghannouchi and other MTI members in jail.

Bourguiba was replaced by his protégé Zine al-Abidine Ben Ali in 1987, but nothing improved for Tunisians. In an effort to undermine MTI, Ben Ali declared that no single party could represent Islam; MTI thus became Hizb ut-Nahda (The Renaissance Party). Sham elections in 1989 resulted in victories for all the government party candidates. Al-Nahda's very strong showing, despite not being allowed party status, resulted in another crackdown, sending Ghannouchi and many key supporters into exile.

But suppression of pro-democracy activists, Islamist or secularist, did not mitigate social discontent. As the economy continued to worsen and corruption ran rampant, antigovernment pressure reached a boiling point in 2010. The "Arab Spring" riots, led by generally non-ideological urban youth, ultimately forced Ben Ali to resign. Returning from exile, al-Nahda leaders ran the most effective campaign and dominated the elections. Since that time, the party has faced off against radical Salafist violence and formed coalitions with secularist parties. In September 2013, in the wake of terrorist attacks and mounting secularist concerns about Islamist governance, Nahda ultimately withdrew from the government in order to preserve national unity. In January 2014, Tunisians approved the painstakingly negotiated constitution.

The year 2014 proved a turning point for Ennahda's political fortunes. Nidaa Tounes won parliamentary and then the presidential elections.

Ironically, Ghannouchi's overriding his party's wishes and not allowing a law to be passed in May 2014 forbidding former members of Ben Ali's government and the RCD from running enabled the Nidaa Tounes parliamentary victory and Essebsi's candidacy and presidential victory.

Tunisia provides a fascinating case study of contemporary concerns about Islamic groups' involvement in government in the wake of the rise of international terrorism. Despite its repeated disavowals of theocracy, fears continued. The party demonstrated its absolute commitment to democratic governance by withdrawing from the coalition it had created.

As discussed previously, the Nidaa Tounes failed to demonstrate its stated commitment to political inclusion in its dealings with Ennahda and other nonviolent Islamists as well as leftists, to pursue a path of political inclusiveness and compromise and foster national unity to build a democratic future as Ghannouchi and Ennahda had done.

The secularist-Islamist divide must give way to a system of government that brings together multiple voices and actors, considers the desires of the public, and emphasizes the effectiveness of the democratic process and the well-being of the country instead of ideological differences and repression of dissent. This understanding of democracy must include a recognition of the legitimacy of political opposition as long as it is a loyal opposition, an opposition whose ultimate loyalty is to national unity and the equality and prosperity of all.

The impact of manipulation of fears of terrorism was even more dramatic in the case of Egypt. It was only in 1952 that Egyptians took back control of their government. But that independence was achieved through a military coup that would lead to a line of military dictators.

Egypt's independence movement included the world's first Islamist organization, the Muslim Brotherhood. The Brotherhood actively supported Gamal Abdel Nasser and other military officers in the July 23, 1952, coup with the expectation that it and the Brotherhood's agenda would be included in government. When that failed to happen, relations between Nasser and the Brotherhood became increasingly polarized.

In January 1954, Nasser's government banned political parties, declared the Brotherhood dissolved, and had Brotherhood leaders arrested. Following Nasser's death in 1970, this pattern would repeat itself through the military-dominated regimes of Anwar Sadat (1970–1981) and Hosni Mubarak (1981–2011). Despite being banned, the Brotherhood continued to provide social services—including education and healthcare—to social sectors underserved by the government and, as a result, their popularity continued to spread. Beginning in the 1980s and throughout the 1990s, members of the Brotherhood entered political alliances with legal parties, gaining representation in parliament and leadership in a number of the country's labor and professional organizations.

By the time of the Tunisian uprising in 2010, many Egyptians after decades of Mubarak's authoritarian rule, repression, and massive violation of human rights, and amidst a failed economy, high unemployment, poor social services, and widespread corruption proved ready to take to the streets in protest. In early 2011, spontaneous demonstrations exploded throughout the country. An underemployed "youth bulge" played major roles, influenced by the example of Tunisia's uprising and social media, in getting people to fill the streets. And the unprovoked beating death of young computer programmer by the police in an Alexandria Internet café provided a focal point for popular outrage. But the uprising, as we showed in Chapter 8, was a popular revolution with broad-based support from all sectors of society, secular and religious, male and female, Muslim and Christian, poor and rich.

The Muslim Brotherhood did not lead the uprising against Mubarak. But when it was successful, they were the best-organized and most visible organization throughout the country. They were therefore poised to dominate the country's first-ever free elections. However, they were in no position to replace the country's entrenched and military-dominated bureaucracy. As we argued in Chapter 8, if the basic question in the past was, "Is Arab culture or Islam compatible with democracy?" the Arab Spring question became, "Are the old guard and entrenched elites (military, courts, police, security, government bureaucrats, and other political and economic elites) as well as Islamists ready for the transition to democracy?"

It was this residual elite structure—the *fulool*, "the remnants"— that proved the undoing of Egypt's first democracy. As the military and Mubarak-appointed judiciary sought to undermine the newly elected government, Morsi's government clumsily attempted to protect itself with measures designed to enhance presidential powers. These measures were highlighted by members of the old guard, who supported a new "rebellion"—*tamarod*. Also ostensibly youth-led, the well-financed Tamarod fanned fears of radical Islam and imposition of archaic Islamic legal strictures. Criminal gangs—the notorious *baltagiya*—wreaked havoc in the streets, and an effective communications campaign attributed its atrocities to the Brotherhood. Radicalized Muslims attacked Christian minorities—these, too, were attributed to the Muslim Brotherhood. Panic overcame the country, precluding any sort of economic recovery, much less further rounds of elections. By the first-year anniversary of Morsi's election, the streets were full again, this time demanding his ouster. With support from the UAE and Saudi Arabia, Morsi's defense minister General Abdel Fattah al-Sisi demanded Morsi compromise with the military. Morsi refused, the military declared the constitution no longer in effect, and al-Sisi appointed himself head of an interim government and rounded up the usual suspects. Morsi and thousands of Muslim Brotherhood members were arrested, and hundreds were sentenced to death. Opposing media voices were silenced, and opposition demonstrations were brutally suppressed, leading to hundreds of deaths. Christian support for al-Sisi's counter-coup further inflamed radicals, leading to more attacks on Christians—again, attributed to the Muslim Brotherhood and Islamists more generally. The Muslim Brotherhood was declared not just illegal but officially a terrorist organization—and not just in Egypt. Syria, Saudi Arabia, and the UAE all designated the group a terrorist organization.

And once more, highly questionable elections confirmed the presidency of a military leader. The sentencing, in May 2015, of Morsi, the democratically elected president to death confirmed the restoration of old-style military authoritarianism.

The Muslim Brotherhood's political acumen in Egypt's first-ever and highly contested experiment with democratic governance was sorely lacking. But its support for democracy and rejection of violence is well established. As the list of supporters of the banning of the Muslim Brotherhood strongly suggests, it is precisely the Brotherhood's demand for democratic governance that troubles them, rather than any concerns about conservative Islamic law or terrorism. Yet again, the example of Egypt demonstrates that the question of the compatibility of Islam and democracy is hardly the issue.

The question of the future of democracy in the 21st century is a global one. All major cultural traditions have substantive modern histories of both authoritarianism and democracy. Some, like David Held, note that globally "there are clear tendencies which are combining to weaken democracy and accountability within and beyond the nation-state."[11] Francis Fukuyama, in analyzing developments after "the end of history," argued that the "third wave [of democracy] crested after the late 1990s, however, and a 'democratic recession' emerged in the first decade of the twentieth century."[12] Others speak of the 21st century as the century of democracy.[13]

The political history of major Muslim-majority countries adds important dimensions to these debates about the nature and future of democracy. However, the alternatives are generally either authoritarian or democratic rather than "religious" or secular. The issue of whether or not a particular religious tradition like Catholicism or Eastern Orthodox Christianity or Islam is compatible with democracy is part of another era of political history.

In this volume we have examined the experience of seven distinctive Muslim-majority countries and found that Islam and democratic governance are far from incompatible, but democratization is a work in progress. While there have been significant setbacks in Egypt and elsewhere, one needs to remember that the processes of democratization are often long term and complex. The annual reports by Freedom House show the ebb and flow of support for freedom and democracy around the world. These reports show that by the late 1990s there was a significant global shift to electoral democracies, but that in the first years of the 21st century, there was a reduction in democratic freedoms. In its 2015 report on the global situation in 2014, Freedom House stated, "For the ninth consecutive year, *Freedom in the World*, Freedom House's annual report on the condition of global political rights and civil liberties, showed an overall decline. Indeed, acceptance of democracy as the world's dominant form of government—and of an international system built on democratic ideals—is under greater threat than at any point in the last 25 years."[14]

In this context of global change, the record of the Muslim-majority countries studied in this book is somewhat different. In the second decade of the 21st century, six of the seven countries had competitive elections in 2013–2014, with Egypt being the only exception. While these elections may not be a fourth wave of democracy, they show the long-term commitment of the majority of the world's Muslims to democracy. The basic question is not if Islam is compatible with democracy. Most Muslims have already answered that question affirmatively. The question now is what forms a democratic state can take in a Muslim-majority society. The variety of visions and programs from North and West Africa to Southeast Asia shows that Muslims are actively engaged in this task.

Notes

CHAPTER 1

1. Gregory Gause, "Why Middle East Studies Missed the Arab Spring: The Myth of Authoritarian Stability." *Foreign Affairs* 94:4 (July–August 2011): 81–90.
2. *New York Times*, September 18, 2011.
3. *New York Times*, June 23, 2012.
4. Samuel Huntington, *The Third Wave: Decmocratization in the Late Twentieth Century*. Norman: University of Oklahoma Press, 1991.
5. See, for example, Stephen R. Grand, "Starting in Egypt: The Fourth Wave of Democratization?" *Brookings Opinion*, February 10, 2011. www.brookings.edu/research/opinions/2011/02/10-egypt-democracy-grand. Accessed June 2, 2012. Also, in the massive demonstrations that characterized the uprisings, large numbers of people participated in new types of activism in the public arena. For some, the Arab Spring became the "Facebook Revolution," attributing its success to the power of contemporary social media to create a new public sphere. "Yet little of this participatory mobilization from civil society seems effectively to connect with formal structures and institutional processes" (see Seyla Benhabib et al., *The Democratic Disconnect: Citizenship and Accountability in the Transatlantic Community*. Washington, DC: Transatlantic Academy, 2013, p. vii). The result was that many of the protesters did not organize effectively for participation in the standard election processes and felt cheated when they lost elections. Some felt that this represented a weakness of democracy (leading to domination by the majority) and became willing to accept non-democratic alternatives.
6. http://www.pewglobal.org/2012/05/08/egyptians-remain-optimistic-embrace-democracy-and-religion-in-political-life/. Accessed September 23, 2014.

7. Ahmet T. Kuru, "Authoritarianism and Democracy in Muslim Countries: Rentier States and Regional Diffusion." *Political Science Quarterly* 129 (November 3, 2014): 399–427.

8. Paraphrased by Robert F. Worth, "The Pillars of Arab Despotism." *New York Review of Books*, October 9, 2014. http://www.nybooks.com/articles/archives /2014/oct/09/pillars-arab-despotism/?utm_medium=email&utm_campaign= NYR+Nudging+Seneca+Scotland+Ilham+Tothi&utm_content=NYR+Nudging +Seneca+Scotland+Ilham+Tothi+CID_0bacd6600269faa9b53916a21a97f4d5& utm_source=Email%20marketing%20software. Accessed September 23, 2014.

9. Dietrich Jung, *Orientalists, Islamists and the Global Public Sphere*. Sheffield, UK, and Oakville, CT: Equinox, 2011, p. 44.

10. Samuel P. Huntington, "The Clash of Civilizations?" *Foreign Affairs* (Summer 1993); *The Clash of Civilizations and the Remaking of World Order*. New York: Simon & Schuster Paperbacks, 1996.

11. Ibid., p. 95.

12. Ibid., pp. 96–97.

13. Francis Fukuyama, *The End of History and the Last Man*. New York: Free Press, 1992, p. 31.

14. Those "liberal democracies" evolved from monarchies, where power had been limited to rulers and major landowners, often with the support of local religious authorities. Gradually, "Enlightenment" ideas became popular: human beings are endowed by nature (or their creator) with freedom and the ability to order their own lives. They should be able to exercise their freedom collectively, using their wits to determine how to organize society and delegating authority to representatives of their own choosing to carry out their collective will. European monarchies were replaced and democratic rights were achieved gradually, sometimes through bloody revolutions like those of the United States and France. Antidemocratic institutions such as the Roman Catholic Church were excluded from politics, and voting rights were extended from select male elites to the general population. (In the United States, women were granted the right to vote in 1920; in France, it was 1944. African-American men were granted the right to vote in 1870, and obstacles to exercising those rights were prohibited in 1965.)

    In Europe and some of its former colonies, one country after another established liberal democracies of various forms throughout the 18th, 19th, and 20th centuries. The totalitarian Soviet Union had been the major obstacle in preventing communities and states under its control from achieving that goal. In Fukuyama's view, with the USSR was out of the way, all countries could progress toward that goal. They could democratize. Even countries that had not been under Soviet control or influence would democratize.

15. Huntington identifies Western civilization as distinctly modern civilization. Modern civilization is characterized by "broad processes . . . that have been

going on since the eighteenth century." They include "industrialization, urbanization, increasing levels of literacy, education, wealth, and social mobilization, and more complex and diversified occupational structures" (1996, 68). And he insists that the West's modern civilization is unique among other civilizations that might become modern (1996, 69).

16. In a logical paradox worthy of Monty Python, Huntington concludes his discussion of the West's "but nots" with the following claim: "Double standards in practice are the unavoidable price of universal standards of principle."

17. Huntington, *The Clash of Civilizations and the Remaking of World Order*, pp. 111–114.

18. Ibid., p. 114.

19. Ibid., p. 29.

20. *Arab Human Development Report [AHDR] 2002: Creating Opportunities for Future Generations*. New York: United Nations Development Programme, Regional Bureau for Arab States, 2002, p. 2.

21. *AHDR 2004: Towards Freedom in the Arab World*. New York: United Nations Development Programme, Regional Bureau for Arab States, 2005, p. 1.

22. Ibid., pp. 1–12.

23. Syed Qutb, *Islam: The True Religion*. Tr. Ravi Ahmad Fedai. Karachi: International Islamic Publishers, 1981, pp. 25–26.

24. Fazlur Rahman, *Islam and Modernity: Transformation of an Intellectual Tradition*. Chicago: University of Chicago Press, 1982, p. 15.

25. Mahmoud Sadri and Ahmad Sadri, trs. and eds., *Reason, Freedom, and Democracy in Islam: Essential Writings of Abdolkarim Soroush*. Oxford: Oxford University Press, 2000, pp. 144–145.

26. Talal Asad, *Formations of the Secular: Christianity, Islam, Modernity*. Stanford, CA: Stanford University Press, 2003, p. 209ff.

27. Jose Casanova, "Civil Society and Religion: Retrospective Reflections on Catholicism and Prospect Reflections on Islam." *Social Research* 68:4 (2001): 1040–1080.

28. Rodney Stark, "Secularization, R.I.P." *Sociology of Religion* 60:3 (1999): 269.

29. In his article by that title, sociologist Shmuel Noah Eisenstadt, for example, sees Western modernity as only one among many possible approaches (S. N. Eisenstadt, "Multiple Modernities." *Daedalus* 129:1 (2000): 1–29. See also Ulrich Beck, Anthony Giddens, and Scott Lash, *Reflexive Modernization: Politics, Tradition, and Aesthetics in the Modern Social Order*. Palo Alto, CA: Stanford University Press, 1994). Explicitly challenging both Durkheim and Weber, Eisenstadt says that while "family life, economic and political structures, urbanization, modern education, mass communication, and individualistic orientations" undoubtedly change with modernization, "the ways in which these arenas were defined and organized varied greatly … giving rise to multiple institutional and ideological patterns" (2000, 2). This diversity was a function

of "specific cultural premises, traditions, and historical experiences." Even though in many non-Western societies, distinctively modern movements articulated anti-Western or even anti-modern themes, Eisenstadt acknowledges the right to be called modern.

That is because, he claims, there is a "common core" of modernity that even anti-Western/anti-modern movements can share with traditional Western modernity. Among other things, Eisenstadt claims, modernity involves changing notions of human agency (2000, 3; citing Björn Wittrock) and a reciprocal decline in "the unquestioned legitimacy of a divinely preordained social order" (2000, 4; citing James D. Faubion). Specifically, human beings are viewed as free agents, "emancipat[ed] from the fetters of traditional political and cultural authority" (2000, 5). "This project of modernity entailed a very strong emphasis on the autonomous participation of members of society in the constitution of the social and political order, on the autonomous access of all members of the society to these orders and to their centers," he says (2000, 5). Further, among the diversities of these diversely modern communities are "multiple interpretations of the common good" (2000, 5). It is upon notions of the common good that emancipated modern individuals choose to order their societies.

Eisenstadt also identifies other pertinent aspects common among diverse modernities: "the restructuring of the center-periphery relations as the principal focus of political dynamics in modern societies" and "a distinctive mode of constructing the boundaries of collectivities and collective identities" (2000, 6). New collective identities are emerging across the globe, Eisenstadt observes, and have "contested the hegemony of the older homogenizing programs, claiming their own autonomous place in central institutional arenas—educational programs, public communications, media outlets. They have been increasingly successful in positing far-reaching claims to the redefinition of citizenship and the rights and entitlements connected with it" (2000, 18).

Eisenstadt provides a number of examples of groups who share the above characteristics but differ on details, including perspectives on the ultimate goals for society. They therefore constitute diverse modernities. As he concludes, "The undeniable trend at the end of the twentieth century is the growing diversification of the understanding of modernity, of the basic cultural agendas of different modern societies—far beyond the homogenic and hegemonic visions of modernity prevalent in the 1950s" (2000, 24). Unfortunately, to the extent that Eisenstadt addresses Muslim movements in his analysis, he focuses only on radicalized Islamist movements, which he calls "fundamentalist" and likens to communists, appropriating modernity for their own totalizing agenda. He focuses on the ideologically motivated utopian, exclusivist, and militant groups and foresees continued confrontation on a global scale. There is no acknowledgement of ongoing democratization in Muslim-majority countries.

30. See Richard P. Mitchell, *The Society of the Muslim Brothers*. New York: Oxford University Press, 1969, reprinted 1993, pp. 225–226.

31. Muhammad al-Ghazzali, *Our Beginning in Wisdom*. Trans. Isma'il R. el Faruqi. Washington, DC: American Council of Learned Societies, 1953, p. 15.

32. Quoted in Walter F. Weiker, *The Turkish Revolution, 1960–1961*. Washington, DC: Brookings Institution, 1963, p. 20.

33. Quoted in GerassiMos KarabeliAs, "The Military Institution, Atatürk's Principles, and Turkey's Sisyphean Quest for Democracy." *Middle Eastern Studies* 45:1 (2009): 62.

34. Yvonne Y. Haddad, "Sayyid Qutb: Ideologue of Islamic Revival." In *Voices of Resurgent Islam*. Ed. John L. Esposito. New York: Oxford University Press, 1983, p. 71.

35. Sayyid Qutb Shaheed, *This Religion of Islam [hadha 'd-din]*. Kuwait: International Islamic Federation of Student Organizations, 1988, pp. 49–64.

36. See Abul A'la Mawdudi, *Islamic Law and Constitution*. Ed. and trans. Khurshid Ahmad. Lahore: Islamic Publications, 1967, pp. 158, 172.

37. Quoted in Azzam S. Tamimi, *Rachid Ghannouchi: A Democrat within Islamism*. New York: Oxford University Press, 2001, p. 90.

38. Hassan Turabi, "The Islamic State." In *Voices of Resurgent Islam*. Ed. John L. Esposito. New York: Oxford University Press, 1983, p. 244.

39. "An Ode to Democracy Delivered by Anwar Ibrahim." *UQ News Online*, The University of Queensland, Australia, July 27, 2006. www.uq.edu.au/news/ article/2006/07/ode-democracy-delivered-anwar-ibrahim. Accessed March 18, 2015.

40. Abul Kalam Azad and Charles Crothers, "Bangladesh: An Umpired Democracy." *Journal of Social and Development Sciences* 3:6 (June 2012): 203.

41. Scott M. Thomas, "A Globalized God: Religion's Growing Influence in International Politics." *Foreign Affairs* 89:6 (November–December 2010): 101.

42. Charles Tilly and Lesley J. Wood, *Social Movements 1768–2012*. 3rd ed. Boulder: Paradigm, 2013, p. 154.

43. See, for example, Stephen R. Grand, "Starting in Egypt: The Fourth Wave of Democratization?" *Brookings Opinion*, February 10, 2011. www.brookings.edu/ research/opinions/2011/02/10-egypt-democracy-grand. Accessed June 2, 2012.

44. John Funston, "Malaysia's Tenth Elections: Status Quo, 'Reformasi' or Islamization?" *Contemporary Southeast Asia* 22:1 (April 2000): 57.

45. Jenny B. White, *Islamist Mobilization in Turkey: A Study in Vernacular Politics*. Seattle: University of Washington Press, 2002, p. 274.

46. Ömer Taşpınar, "Turkey: The New Model." *Brookings/Woodrow Wilson Center Paper*, April 2012. www.brookings.edu/research/papers/2012/04 /24-turkey-new-model-taspinar. Accessed July 30, 2013.

47. Quoted in Ervand Abrahamian, *A History of Modern Iran*. Cambridge, UK: Cambridge University Press, 2008, p. 186.

48. Kurt Andersen, "The Protester." *Time* 178:25 (December 26, 2011–January 2, 2012): 82.

49. Sidney G. Tarrow, *Power in Movement: Social Movements and Contentious Politics.* Revised and updated 3rd ed. Cambridge, UK: Cambridge University Press, 2011, pp. 98–99.

50. Manuel Castells, *Networks of Outrage and Hope: Social Movements in the Internet Age.* Cambridge, UK: Polity Press, 2012, p. 15.

51. Brian P. Klein, "The Crisis of the Global Middle Class: Part I." *Briefing, World Politics Review,* August 6, 2012. www.worldpoliticsreview.com/aticles/ print/12231. Accessed July 31, 2013.

52. See, for example, the statement by a prominent Egyptian protester in Wael Ghonim, "In Bleak Cairo, a Call for Optimism." *New York Times,* November 29, 2011.

53. CIA World Factbook. www.cia.gov/library/publications/the-world-factbook.

54. Paul Mason, *Why It's Still Kicking Off Everywhere: The New Global Revolutions.* 2nd ed. London: Verso, 2013, p. 66.

55. Ibid., p. 72.

56. Tawakkol Karman, "Nobel Lecture." December 10, 2011. www.nobelprize.org/ nobel_prizes/peace/laureates/2011/karman-lecture_en.html. Accessed August 2, 2013.

57. Carles Feixa, Inês Pereira, and Jeffrey S. Juris, "Global Citizenship and the 'New, New' Social Movements: Iberian Connections." *Young: Nordic Journal of Youth Research* 17:4 (2009): 427.

58. Siv Malik, Jack Senker, and Adam Gabbatt, "Arab Spring Anniversary: How a Lost Generation Found Its Voice." *Guardian,* December 16, 2011. Accessed July 31, 2013.

59. Mason, *Why It's Still Kicking Off Everywhere,* p. 272.

60. "150 Women Who Shake the World." *Newsweek,* March 5, 2012, pp. 50–63. www.newsweek.com/150-women-who-shake-world-66131.

61. Karman, "Nobel Lecture." December 10, 2011.

62. Andrea Ovans, "When No One's in Charge." *Harvard Business Review,* May 2012. http://hbr.org/2012/05/when-no-ones-in-charge/ar/I. Accessed August 1, 2013.

63. Wael Ghonim, *Revolution 2.0: The Power of the People Is Greater Than the People in Power.* Boston: Houghton Mifflin, 2012, p. 57.

64. Michael Slackman, "In Mideast Activism, a New Tilt Away from Ideology." *New York Times,* January 23, 2011.

65. Quoting a speech at Harvard University. Micah L. Sifry, "Wael Ghonim: Why 'Engagism' Is More Valuable Than Activism." http://techpresident.com/ news/21794/wael-ghonim-why-engagism-more valuable-activism. Accessed February 20, 2012.

66. Castells, *Networks of Outrage and Hope,* p. 227.

67. John L. Esposito and Dalia Mogahed, *Who Speaks for Islam? What a Billion Muslims Really Think.* New York: Gallup Press, 2008, p. 63.

68. The Pew Forum on Religion & Public Life, "The World's Muslims: Religion, Politics and Society." Washington, DC: Pew Research Center, April 30, 2013, p. 3 2.

CHAPTER 2

1. Nilufer Gole, "Authoritarian Secularism and Islamist Politics." In *Civil Society in the Middle East.* Vol. 2. Ed. Augustus Richard Norton. Leiden: E. J. Brill, 1996, p. 20.

2. Ihsan Yilmaz, "Homo LASTus and Lausannian Muslim: Two Paradoxical Social-Engineering Projects to Construct the Best and the Good Citizen in the Kemalist Panopticon." *TJP Turkish Journal of Politics* 4:2 (Winter 2013): 116.

3. Feroz Ahmad, "Turkey." *The Oxford Encyclopedia of the Modern Islamic World.* Vol. 4. Ed. John L. Esposito. Oxford: Oxford University Press, 2009, p. 244.

4. Feroz Ahmad, "Political Islam in Modern Turkey." *Middle East Studies* 27:1 (1991): 14–15.

5. Ibid., p. 15.

6. Binnaz Toprak, "Refah Partisi." *The Oxford Encyclopedia of the Modern Islamic World.* Vol. 3. Ed. John L. Esposito. Oxford: Oxford University Press, 2009, p. 414.

7. Ertugrul Kürkçü, "The Crisis of the Turkish State." *Middle East Report* (April–June 1996): 3.

8. For a fuller discussion, see M. Hakan Yavuz, "Political Islam and the Welfare Party in Turkey." *Journal of Comparative Politics* 30:1 (October 1997): 63–82.

9. David Kushner, "Self-Perception and Identity in Contemporary Turkey." *Journal of Contemporary History* 32 (1997): 230.

10. Metin Heper, "Islam and Democracy in Turkey: Towards a Reconciliation?" *Middle East Journal* 51 (1997): 35.

11. For an excellent analysis of the ARAS survey and general attitudes of Turkish citizens regarding the political process and questions of Islam and democracy, see M. Hakun Yavuz, *Islamic Political Identity in Turkey.* Oxford: Oxford University Press, 2003. p. 220.

12. Kelly Couturier, "Anti-Secularism Eclipses Insurgency as Army's No. 1 Concern." *Washington Post*, April 5, 1997, A-22.

13. For a discussion of this phenomenon, see Serif Mardin, "Ideology and Religion in the Turkish Revolution." *International Journal of Middle East Studies* 2 (1971): 197–211, especially pp. 208–209.

14. M. Hakun Yafuz, *Islamic Political Identity in Turkey*, p. 256.

15. Quoted in Hakan Yavuz, ed., *The Emergence of a New Turkey.* Salt Lake City: University of Utah Press, 2006, p. 334.

16. Yavuz, *Islamic Political Identity in Turkey*, p. 258.

17. Quoted in Yavuz, *The Emergence of a New Turkey*, p. 336.

18. Kamal Karakas, 2014 Turkey Report, 31. http://www.sgi-network.org/docs/2014/country/SGI2014_Turkey.pdf.

19. For a detailed study of the AKP's economic policies, see Marcie J Patton, "The Economic Policies of Turkey's AKP Government: Rabbits from a Hat?" *The Middle East Journal* 60:3 (Summer 2006): 513–536.

20. Ibrahim Kalin, "Political Islam in Turkey." In *Oxford Handbook of Islam and Politics*, ch. 28. Ed. John L. Esposto and Emad Shahin. New York: Oxford University Press, 2013, pp. 430–431.

21. Yavuz, *Secularism and Muslim Democracy in Turkey*, p. 204.

22. Angel Rabasa and F. Stephen Larrabee, *The Rise of Political Islam in Turkey*. Washington, DC: RAND National Research Defense Institute, 2008, p. 77.

23. Ibid., p. 49.

24. Ibid., p. 256.

25. Menderes Cinar, "The Electoral Success of the AKP: Cause for Hope and Despair." *Insight Turkey* 13:4 (2011): 478.

26. Ibid.

27. Omer Taspinar, "Turkey: An Interested Party." In Kenneth Pollack, Daniel Byman, et al., *The Arab Awakening*. Washington, DC: Brookings Institution, 2011, p. 268.

28. Victor Kotsev, "How the Protests Will Impact Turkey at Home and Abroad." *Atlantic*, June 2, 2013. http://www.theatlantic.com/international/archive/2013/06/how-the-protests-will-impact-turkey-at-home-and-abroad/276456/.

29. Fidel Martinez, "Turkish Protesters Release a List of Demands." *Daily Dot*, June 4, 2013. www.dailydot.com/news/occupy-gezi-turkish-protest-taksim-demands/.

30. "Erdogan: For Every 100,000 Protesters, I Will Bring out a Million from My Party." *Haaretz*, June 1, 2013. http://www.haaretz.com/news/middle-east/1.527188.

31. "Turkey: End the Incommunicado Detention of Istanbul Protesters." Amnesty International, June 16, 2013. http://www.amnestyusa.org/news/news-item/turkey-end-the-incommunicado-detention-of-istanbul-protesters.

32. "Istanbul Mayor: We Will Now Ask Even for Bus Stops." *Hurriyet Daily News*, June 20, 2013, http://www.hurriyetdailynews.com/istanbul-mayor-to-ask-residents-about-all-future-projects.aspx?pageID=238&nID=49153&NewsCatID=341.

33. "Turkey Elections: Test of Erdogan's Rule?" *Al Jazeera*, April 1, 2014. http://www.aljazeera.com/programmes/insidestory/2014/03/turkey-elections-test-erdogans-rule-2014331161154603492.html.

34. Burak Kadercan, "Turkey's Gezi Park Episode Is Far from Over." openDemocracy, August 11, 2013. http://www.opendemocracy.net/burak-kadercan/turkey%E2%80%99s-gezi-park-episode-is-far-from-over.

35. For more on Nurcu political activism, see M. Hakan Yavuz, "Print-Based Islamic Discourse and Modernity: The Nur Movement." In *Third International Symposium on Bediuzzaman Said Nursi.* Vol. 2. Istanbul: Sozler, 1995, pp. 324–350.

36. Sencer Ayata, "Patronage, Party, the State: The Politicization of Islam in Turkey." *Middle East Journal* 50:1 (Winter 1996): 51.

37. "Global Muslim Networks: How Far They Have Traveled." *Economist*, March 6, 2008. http://www.economist.com/node/10808408?story_id=10808408. Accessed February 7, 2013.

38. "Turkish Government Determined to Close Private Tutoring Schools." *Hurriyet Daily News*, November 5, 2013. http://www.hurriyetdailynews.com/turkish-government-determined-to-close-private-tutoring-schools.aspx?PageI D=238&NID=57375&NewsCatID=338.

39. Bayram Balci, "What Are the Consequences of the Split between Erdogan and Gülen on Turkey's Foreign Policy?" *Foreign Policy Journal*, January 17, 2014. http://www.foreignpolicyjournal.com/2014/01/17/what-are-the-consequences-of-the-split-between-erdogan-and-gulen-on-turkeys-foreign-policy/.

40. Kharunya Paramaguru, "Turkey: Police Chiefs Fired after High-Profile Bribery Arrests." *Time*, December 18, 2013. http://world.time.com/2013/12/18/turkish-police-chiefs-fired-after-high-profile-bribery-arrests/

41. Tim Arango and Ceylan Yeginsu, "Amid Flow of Leaks, Turkey Moves to Crimp Internet." *New York Times*, February 6, 2014. http://www.nytimes.com/2014/02/07/world/europe/amid-flow-of-leaks-turkey-moves-to-crimp-internet.html.

42. Humeyra Pamuk and Dasha Afanasieva, "Turkish Paper Says Journalists Expelled for Criticizing Erdogan." *Reuters*, February 7, 2014. http://www.reuters.com/article/2014/02/07/us-turkey-media-idUSBREA1614520140207.

43. Marc Pierini, "How Far Backward Is Turkey Sliding?" Carnegie Europe, March 3, 2014. http://carnegieeurope.eu/2014/03/03/how-far-backward-is-turkey-sliding/h29v.

44. Ibid.

45. A. Kahir Yildirim, "The Slow Death of Turkish Higher Education." *Al Jazeera*, July 10, 2014. http://www.aljazeera.com/indepth/opinion/2014/07/turkish-higher-education-reform-20147106282924991.html

46. Hakan Yavuz, "Political Islam and the Welfare (Refah) Party in Turkey." *Comparative Politics* 30:1 (October 1997): 65.

CHAPTER 3

1. See Larry Diamond, "Thinking About Hybrid Regimes." *Journal of Democracy* 13:2 (2002): 21–35; Andres Schedle, "The Menus of Manipulation." *Journal of Democracy* 13:2 (2002): 36–50; Nicolas van de Walle, "Africa's Range of

Regimes." *Journal of Democracy* 13:2 (2002): 66–80; Andreas Schedler, "The Logic of Authoritarianism." In *Electoral Authoritarianism: The Dynamics of Unfree Competition*. Ed. A. Schedule. Boulder, CO: Lynne Rienner, 2006; Steven Levitsky and Lucan Way, "The Rise of Competitive Authoritarianism." *Journal of Democracy* 13:2 (2002): 51–65; and *Competitive Authoritarianism: Hybrid Regimes After the Cold War*. Cambridge: Cambridge University Press, 2010. See also Jennifer Gandhi and Adam Przeworski, "Authoritarian Institutions and the Survival of Autocracy." *Comparative Political Studies* 40 (2007): 1279–1301; Ellen Lust-Okar, "Legislative Elections in Hegemonic Authoritarian Regimes: Competitive Clientelism and Resistance to Democracy." *Democratization by Elections*. Ed. S. I. Lindberg. Baltimore: Johns Hopkins University Press, 2009; Beatriz Magaloni, "Credible Power-Sharing and the Longevity of Authoritarian Rule." *Comparative Political Studies* 41 (2008): 715–741. This approach to foreign policy then descended into an argument as to whether authoritarian regimes or totalitarian regimes are more reliable guardians of US interests. Former US ambassador to the United Nations Jeane Kirkpatrick gained notoriety for distinguishing between totalitarian communist states and merely authoritarian pro-Western regimes. The totalitarian regimes were more stable in her view, and thus more dangerous to US interests, because they could more effectively influence their neighbors. They should therefore be opposed, even if that opposition entailed supporting authoritarian regimes—provided they are pro-Western, of course. This "Kirkpatrick Doctrine" was influential in the Reagan administration's support of non-democratic but anti-communist governments in Latin America, for example, and its support for the Contras' revolution against the socialist Sandinista-dominated government of Nicaragua in the 1980s.

2. See Said Amir Arjomand, "The Shadow of God on Earth: The Ethos of Persian Patrimonialism." In *The Shadow of God and the Hidden Imam: Religion, Political Order, and Societal change in Shi'ite Iran from the Beginning to 1890*. Chicago: University of Chicago Press, 1984.

3. Ibid., p. 97; italics added.

4. Marshall G. S. Hodgson, *The Venture of Islam*. Vol. 3, *The Gunpowder Empires and Modern Times*. Chicago: University of Chicago Press, 1974, pp. 35, 57.

5. Interestingly, the Treaty of Amasya, distinguishing Ottoman from Safavid lands, was signed in 1555, the same year that the Holy Roman Emperor and a group of Germanic princes signed the Peace of Augsburg, meant to stop the wars between Catholic and Lutheran Christians.

6. The arrangement was so unpopular that the king, Nasir al-Din Shah, was forced to cancel it after one year. See Nikki Keddie, *Religion and Rebellion in Iran; The Tobacco Protest of 1892–92*. London: Frank Cass, 1966, p. 5.

7. See Daniel Yergin, *The Prize: The Epic Quest for Oil, Money, and Power*. New York, London, Toronto, Sydney: Free Press, 2008, p. 121.

8. L. P. Elwell-Sutton, *Persian Oil: A Study in Power Politics*. London: Lawrence and Wishart Ltd., 1955, p. 15.

9. See Cosroe Chaqueri, *The Soviet Socialist Republic of Iran, 1920–21*. Pittsburgh: University of Pittsburgh Press, 1994.

10. See Ali Gheissari and Vali Nasr, *Democracy in Iran: History and the Quest for Liberty*. New York: Oxford University Press, 2006, p. 38.

11. Mohammed Reza Shah Pahlavi, *Mission for My Country*. London: Hutchinson & Co. Ltd., 1961, p. 66. Curiously, the shah contradicts himself two pages later, stating, "It was well known that as part of their so-called Rosenberg Plan the Nazis were aiming at the conquest of the Middle East as far as the Persian Gulf."

12. See Chrisopher de Bellaigue, *Patriot of Persia: Muhammad Mossadegh and a Tragic Anglo-American Coup*. New York: Harper, 2012.

13. Mohammed Reza Shah Pahlavi, *Mission for My Country*, p. 90.

14. See "Anglo-Persian Oil Company." In *Encyclopaedia Iranica*. www.iranicaonline.org/articles/anglo-persian-oil-company. Accessed October 3, 2014.

15. See Alan Ford, *The Anglo-Iranian Oil Dispute of 1951–1952*. Berkeley: University of California Press, 1954.

16. See Mohammed Reza Shah, *Mission for My Country*, p. 139. See also Stephen Kinzer, *The Brothers*. New York: Henry Holt, 2013. Kindle Edition, location 2042–2052.

17. Ibid., p. 58.

18. Ibid., p. 97.

19. For an excellent discussion of the factors contributing to Mosaddegh's countermeasures, including the economic crisis caused by the British blockade and blocked efforts to resolve the issue through international law, see Ervand Abrahamian, *The Coup: 1953, the CIA, and the Roots of Modern U.S.-Iranian Relations*. New York, London: The New Press, 2013.

20. Or, as he puts it, "[F]ollowing a pre-arranged plan, the Queen and I had left Teheran before learning of the revolution's success. . . . I had decided upon this move because I believed that it would force Mossadegh and his henchmen to show their real allegiances and thereby it would help crystallize Persian public opinion." Mohammed Reza Shah, *Mission for My Country*, p. 104.

21. See Steven Kinzer, *All the Shah's Men: An American Coup and the Roots of Middle East Terror*. New York: John Wiley & Sons, 2003.

22. See Palash Ghosh, "Iran's Feared SAVAK: Norman Schwarzkopf's Father Had Greater Impact on Middle East Affairs." *International Business Times*, December 28, 2012. http:ww.ibtimes.com/irans-feared-savak-norman-schwarzkopf's-father-had-greater-impact-middle-east-affairs-976502. Accessed September 27, 2014.

23. Mohammed Reza Shah, *Mission for My Country*, p. 171.

24. Mehran Kamrava, *The Modern Middle East: A Political History since the First World War.* 3rd ed. Berkeley, Los Angeles, London: University of California Press, 2013, p. 145.

25. See Ali Rahnema, *An Islamic Utopian: A Political Biography of Ali Shariati.* London: I.B. Tauris, 1998.

26. See Chibli Mallat, "Muhammad Baqir as-Sadr." In Ali Rahnema, *Pioneers of Islamic Revival.* London: Zed Books, 1994.

27. See Said Amir Arjomand, *Turban for the Crown: The Islamic Revolution in Iran.* New York: Oxford University Press, 1988.

28. See Mansor Moaddel, *Class, Politics, and Ideology in the Iranian Revolution.* New York: Columbia University Press, 1993.

29. Ali Gheissari and Vali Nasr, *Democracy in Iran: History and the Quest for Liberty.* New York: Oxford University Press, 2006, pp. 65–66.

30. See Charles Kurzman, "The Qum Protests and the Coming of the Iranian Revolution, 1975 and 1978." *Social Science History* 27:3 (Fall 2003): 187–325. http://www.unc.edu/~kurzman/cv/Kurzman_Qum_Protests.pdf. Accessed October 4, 2014.

31. Mehran Kamrava, *The Modern Middle East: A Political History since the First World War.* 3rd ed. Berkeley, Los Angeles, London: University of California Press, 2013, pp. 157–158.

32. See Paul Ryan, *The Iranian Rescue Mission: Why It Failed.* Annapolis, MD: Naval Institute Press, 1985.

33. See Hafizullah Emadi, "Exporting Iran's Revolution: The Radicalization of the Shiite Movement in Afghanistan." *Middle Eastern Studies* 31:1 (January 1995): 1–12.

34. The "Algiers Agreement." See F. Gregory Gauss III, *International Relations of the Persian Gulf.* Cambridge: Cambridge University Press, 2009, pp. 37–39.

35. See Said K. Aburish, "Secrets of His Life and Leadership." *Frontline.* http://www.pbs.org/wgbh/pages/frontline/shows/saddam/interviews/aburish.html. Accessed October 23, 2014. See also Howard Teicher and Gayle Radley Teicher, *Twin Pillars to Desert Storm: America's Flawed Vision in the Middle East from Nixon to Bush.* New York: William Morrow and Company, Inc., 1993: "Brzezinski maintained that with the right combination of blandishments, Iraq could be weaned away from Moscow. Encouraged by the suppression of the Iraqi Communist party, and perhaps believing that Iraq could, like Egypt after the October 1973 War, also be convinced to turn toward Washington, Brzezinski concluded that Iraq was poised to succeed Iran as the principal pillar of stability in the Persian Gulf. . . . Indeed, in April, Brzezinski stated on national television that he saw no fundamental incompatibility of interests between the United States and Iraq" (pp. 62–63).

36. See US Congress, "Report of the Congressional Committees Investigating the Iran-Contra Affair." Washington, DC: US Government Printing Office, 1987.

37. Imam Khomeini, *Islam and Revolution: Writings and Declarations of Imam Khomeini*. Tr. and annotated by H. Algar. London: KPI, 1985, pp. 187, 210–211.

38. See Dilip Hiro, *The Longest War: The Iran-Iraq Military Conflict*. New York: Routledge, 1991.

39. See Jahangir Amuzegar, *Iran's Economy under the Islamic Republic*. London: I.B. Tauris, 1993.

40. See Hooshang Amirahmadi, *Revolution and Economic Transition: The Iranian Experience*. Albany: State University of New York Press, 1990.

41. Statement by H. E. Seyyed Mohammad Khatami, President of the Islamic Republic of Iran and Chairman of the Eighth Session of the Islamic Summit Conference, Tehran, December 9, 1997. http://www.undp.org/missions/iran/new.html.

42. Khatami, *Islam, Liberty and Development*, p. 11.

43. Khatami, *Hope and Challenge: The Iranian President Speaks*. Binghamton, NY: Institute of Global Cultural Studies, Binghamton University, 1997, pp. 77–78.

44. In December 2006 Ahmadinejad's government sponsored "The International Conference on Review of the Holocaust: Global Vision" in Tehran, which was seen as profoundly anti-Semitic. See Nazila Fathi, "Holocaust Deniers and Skeptics Gather in Iran." *New York Times*, December 11, 2006. http://www.nytimes.com/2006/12/11/world/middleeast/11cnd-iran.html?_r=0. Accessed October 5, 2014.

45. Mahmoud Sadri and Ahmad Sadri, trs. and eds., *Reason, Freedom, & Democracy in Islam: Essential Writings of `Abdolkarim Soroush*. Oxford: Oxford University Press, 2000, pp. 144–145.

46. See Robin Wright, *Dreams and Shadows: The Future of the Middle East*. New York: Penguin Press, 2008, p. 296.

47. See Mohsen Kadivar, "Wilayat al-Faqih and Democracy." In *Islam, the State, and Political Authority: Medieval Issues and Modern Concerns*. Ed. Asma Afsaruddin. New York: Palgrave Macmillan, 2011. See also http://en.kadivar.com/wilayat-al-faqih-and-democracy/. Accessed October 5, 2014. There are many others, such as journalist Saeed Hajjarian, who are also strongly associated with the 2nd of Khordad movement. An ardent opponent of the shah, Hajjarian participated in the takeover of the US embassy following his overthrow and joined the intelligence services soon thereafter. In that capacity he discovered the ferocity of the regime's opposition to dissent, allegedly leaking stories of the disappearances and murders of dozens of dissidents throughout the 1990s. He became an outspoken reformist and served as an advisor to President Khatami. In 2000 he was the victim of an assassination attempt. He argued that the control of government by religious authorities inevitably secularized them. In order to preserve religion's essential advisory and informative role, its spokespeople must not be involved in the quotidian power struggles of political activism. See

F. Khosrokhavar, "The New Intellectuals in Iran." *Social Compass* 51:2 (2004): 191–202. http://scp.sagepub.com/content/51/2/191. Accessed October 5, 2014.

48. Mehran Kamrava, *The Modern Middle East: A Political History since the First World War.* 3rd ed. Berkeley, Los Angeles, London: University of California Press, 2013, p. 166.

49. See Nader Hashemi, "Renegotiating Iran's Post-revolutionary Social Contract: The Green Movement and the Struggle for Democracy in the Islamic Republic." In Rex Brynen, Pete W. Moore, Bassel F. Salloukh, and Maire-Joelle Zahar, eds., *Beyond the Arab Spring: Authoritarianism and Democratization in the Arab World.* Boulder, CO: Lynne Rienner Publishers, 2012, pp. 191–222.

50. See Negin Nabavi, ed., *Iran: From Theocracy to the Green Movement.* New York: Palgrave Macmillan, 2012.

51. See Hamid Dabashi, *The Green Movement in Iran.* Piscataway, NJ: Transaction Publishers, 2011.

52. See Afshin Salimpour, "Turmoil Follows Silent Protest," *Frontline,* June 16, 2009. http://www.pbs.org/wgbh/pages/frontline/tehranbureau/2009/06/turmoil-follows-silent-protest.html. Accessed October 23, 2014.

53. See Jessica T. Mathews, "Iran: A Good Deal Now in Danger." *New York Review of Books,* February 20, 2014. http://www.nybooks.com/articles/archives/2014/feb/20/iran-good-deal-now-danger/. Accessed October 23, 2014.

54. Paul K. Kerr, "Iran's Nuclear Program: Status." Congressional Research Service, October 17, 2012. http://fas.org/sgp/crs/nuke/RL34544.pdf. Accessed October 23, 2014.

55. See "Citing Iran's Failure to Clairfy Nuclear Ambitions, UN Imposes Additional Sanctions." UN News Centre, June 9, 2010. http://www.un.org/apps/news/story.asp?NewsID=34970&Cr=iran&Cr1=#. Accessed October 23, 2014.

56. Zogby Research Services, LLC, "Iranian Attitudes, September 2013." http://www.zogbyresearchservices.com/blog/2013/12/6/zrs-releases-september-2013-iran-poll. Accessed October 23, 2014.

57. Gheissari and Nasr, *Democracy in Iran,* p. 158. See also Nader Hashemi, "Religious Disputation and Democratic Constitutionalism: The Enduring Legacy of the Constitutional Revolution on the Struggle for Democracy in Iran." *Constellations* 17:1 (2010): 50–60.

58. Mir Hossein Musavi, January 29, 2011, facebook.com/mousavi, as noted by Charles Kurzman, "The Arab Spring: Ideals of the Iranian Green Movement, Methods of the Iranian Revolution." *International Journal of Middle East Studies* 44 (2012): 162.

59. Kamrava, *The Modern Middle East,* p. 405.

60. Mohammad Khatami, *Hope and Challenge: The Iranian President Speaks.* Binghamton, NY: Institute of Global Cultural Studies, Binghamton University, 1997, pp. 77–78.

61. Kamrava, *The Modern Middle East,* p. 405.

CHAPTER 4

1. Pakistan Objectives Resolution. http://www.pakistani.org/pakistan/constitution/annex.html. Accessed July 18, 2014.

2. http://www.columbia.edu/itc/mealac/pritchett/00islamlinks/txt_iqbal_1930.htm. Accessed July 18, 2014.

3. http://www.columbia.edu/itc/mealac/pritchett/00islamlinks/txt_jinnah_assembly_1947.html. Accessed July 18, 2014.

4. http://hdr.undp.org/en/countries/profiles/PAK. Accessed July 18, 2014.

5. "Pakistan Gets $6.6 Billion Loan from IMF," IMF Survey, September 4, 2013. See Pervez Hoodbhoy and Zia Mian, "Nuclear Thinking in Pakistan." Asia Pacific Leadership Network for Nuclear Non-Proliferation/Center for Nuclear Non-Proliferation and Disarmament. February 2014. http://www.princeton.edu/sgs/faculty-staff/zia-mian/Hoodbhoy-Mian-Changing-Nuclear-Thinking.pdf. Accessed July 2, 2014.

6. Tariq Butt, "60 Banned Organisations Identified by New NISP." *International News*, March 30, 2014. http://www.thenews.com.pk/Todays-News-2-235921-60-banned-organisations-identified-by-new-NISP. Accessed September 13, 2014.

7. Phelim Kine, "Pakistan's Shia under Attack." *Diplomat*, July 5, 2014.

8. Jon Boone, "Pakistan Church Bomb: Christians Mourn 85 Killed in Peshawar Suicide Attack." *Guardian*, September 23, 2013.

9. http://abcnews.go.com/Politics/OTUS/fullpage/top-10-us-foreign-aid-recipients-17534761. Accessed July 19, 2014. Cf "Aid to Pakistan by the Numbers." Center for Global Development. http://www.cgdev.org/page/aid-pakistan-numbers.

10. http://www.pbs.org/newshour/spc/multimedia/military-spending/. Accessed July 19, 2014; Susan B. Epstein and K. Alan Kronstadt, "Pakistan: U.S. Foreign Assistance." Congressional Research Service, July 1, 2013. www.fas.org/sgp/crs/row/R41856.pdf.

11. Zulfiqar Ali Bhutto, *The Myth of Independence*. Karachi: Oxford University Press, 1969, pp. 152–153.

12. Stephen Kinzer, *The Brothers: John Foster Dulles, Allen Dulles, and Their Secret World War*. New York: Henry Holt and Company/Times Books, 2013. Kindle loc. 3509–3518.

13. Kinzer, *Brothers*, Kindle loc. 3518–3529.

14. George Perkovich, *India's Nuclear Bomb: The Impact on Global Proliferation*. Berkeley and Los Angeles: University of California Press, 1999, p. 48.

15. See Patrick J. Killen, "Nehru Given Mandate to Drive Out the Chinese," *Times-News* (Hendersonville, SC), October 14, 1962. Compare w/Robert S. Allen and Paul

Scott, "India Beefs Up Military Might." *Sarasota Herald-Tribune*, May 17, 1962. See also George Perkovich, *India's Nuclear Bomb: The Impact on Global Proliferation.* Berkeley and Los Angeles: University of California Press, 1999, p. 107.

16. Patrick Keatley, "The Brown Bomb." *Manchester Guardian*, March 11, 1965.

17. http://history.state.gov/historicaldocuments/frus1969-76v11/d19. Accessed July 17, 2014.

18. http://history.state.gov/historicaldocuments/frus1969-76v11/d20. Accessed July 17, 2014. Consul General Blood was recalled from his position.

19. Henry Kissinger acknowledged the "brutal military repression" in a discussion of the memo in his 1979 memoir *The White House Years*: "There was some merit to the charge of moral insensitivity." (New York: Little, Brown and Company, 1979, p. 854).

20. http://gulhayat.com/Zulfiqaralibhutto.asp. Accessed July 17, 2014.

21. Z. A. Bhutto, "Pakistan Builds Anew." *Foreign Affairs* 3 (April 1973): 543. http://www.foreignaffairs.com/articles/24423/zulfikar-ali-bhutto/pakistan-builds-anew.

22. Although Pakistan is a Muslim country, and Islam rejects class stratification of any kind, vestiges of India's age-old caste system are ubiquitous in Pakistan in slightly modified form. Large landowning elites claim superiority based on descent from the original 8th-century Arab conquerors or else the great medieval Mughal rulers, or, in the case of Pashtuns, simply being Pashtuns. Lower on the scale are wealthy industrialists who made fortunes despite not being landed, and lower still are small landowners, then shopkeepers and tradespeople. The lowest ranks of the social scale are occupied by servants and laborers of diverse kinds. Christians are often in this rank. See, e.g., H. A. Rose, *A Glossary of the Tribes and Castes of the Punjab and North-West Frontier Province.* New Delhi: Nirmal Publishers, 1997.

23. *Economist*, http://www.economist.com/node/169653.

24. See Ronald J. Herring, "Zulfiqar Ali Bhutto and the 'Eradication of Feudalism" in Pakistan." *Comparative Studies in Society and History* 21:4 (October 1979): 551.

25. Omar Noman, *Pakistan: Political and Economic History Since 1947.* London: Routledge, 2013, p. 93.

26. Saeed Shafqat, "Public Policy and Reform in Pakistan 1971–77: An Analysis of Zulfikar Ali Bhutto's Socio-Economic Policies." *Journal of South Asian and Middle Eastern Affairs* 11:3 (Spring 1988): 48 (37–56).

27. Ibid., p. 41.

28. Ibid., p. 44.

29. In fact, Pakistan sank deeper into debt. In 1975 alone, the Asian Development Bank (ADB) lent Pakistan over $200 million for various development projects. *Asian Development Bank Annual Report 1975.*

30. "The Education Policy: 1972–1980." Islamabad: Ministry of Education, Government of Pakistan, 1972.

31. Imran Khan, *Pakistan: A Personal History*. London, Toronto, etc.: Bantam Books, 2013, p. 75.

32. Shalini Chawla, "Trends in Pakistan's Defence Spending." Manekshaw Paper #5, New Delhi: KW Publishers and Centre for Land Warfare Studies, 2008. http://www.claws.in/administrator/uploaded_files/1233139340Manekshaw %20Paper%205.pdf. Accessed July 4, 2014.

33. The Constitution of Pakistan. http://www.pakistani.org/pakistan/constitution/ part9.html. Accessed July 17, 2014.

34. See Shirin Tahir-Kheli, *India, Pakistan, and the United States: Breaking with the Past*. Washington, DC: Council on Foreign Relations, 1997.

35. Feroz Khan, *Eating Grass: The Making of the Pakistani Bomb*. Palo Alto, CA: Stanford Security Studies, November 7, 2012.

36. See Jeremy Bernstein, "He Changed History." *New York Review of Books*, April 9, 2009. http://www.nybooks.com/articles/archives/2009/apr/09/he-changed-history/. Accessed September 16, 2014.

37. See, e.g., "CIA Sent Bhutto to the Gallows." http://sixhour.com/cia_sent%20 bhutto_to_the_gallows.htm. Accessed July 5, 2014.

38. Reported by zeenews.india.com per public litigation lawyer Mohammad Azhar Siddique, who claims to have inspected reports of Bhutto's murder case. From the report:

> "I was told in August, 1976 by Dr. Henry Kissinger (the then Secretary of State) that if you (Bhutto) do not cancel, modify or postpone the Reprocessing Plant Agreement, we will make a horrible example from you. For my country's sake, for the sake of people of Pakistan, I did not succumb to that black-mailing and threats," *The News* quoted Bhutto as having stated before the full bench of the Lahore High Court, which ultimately awarded him the death sentence. (http://zeenews.india.com/news/south-asia/zulfikar-bhutto-had-blamed-us-for-his-horrible-fate_698531.html. Accessed July 4, 2014)

39. See Charles H. Kennedy, "Islamic Legal Reform and the Status of Women in Pakistan." *Journal of Islamic Studies* 2:1 (1991): 45–55.

40. Mumtaz Ahmad, "The Politics and Theology of Blasphemy Laws in Pakistan." Unpublished lecture delivered at University of Calgary, Edmonton, January 30, 2014.

41. D. E. Jones and Rodney W. Jones, "Nationalizing Education in Pakistan: Teachers' Education and the Peoples' Party." *Pacific Affairs* 50:4 (Winter 1977–1978): 581.

42. Kiran Hashmi, "An Analytical Study on Issues, Challenges and Reforms in the Pakistan Studies Curriculum of Secondary Level." *International Journal of Social Sciences and Education* 1:3 (July 2011): 210–222, which cites Saifur Rehman Ullah, "The Impact of Culture Conflict on Identity with an Emphasis on Pakistan." Ph.D. dissertation, University of Punjab, Lahore, 1973.

43. University Grants Commission directive, Islamabad: Mutalliyah-i-Pakistan, Alama Iqbal Open University, 1983, p. xi.

44. Pervez Hoodbhoy and A. H. Nayyar, "Rewriting the History of Pakistan." In *Islam, Politics, and the State*. Ed. Asghar Khan. London: Zed Press, 1985, pp. 164–177. http://www.sacw.net/HateEducation/1985HoodbhoyNayyar060220 05.html. Accessed July 17, 2014.

45. Khursheed Kamal Aziz, *The Murder of History: A Critique of History Textbooks Used in Pakistan*. Lahore: Vanguard, 1993, pp. 164–177. For example, fourth-year students were taught that when Muslims ruled India, they "treated the non-Muslims very well. Yet the non-Muslims nursed in their hearts an enmity against the Muslims. When the British invaded the area the non-Muslims sided with them and against the Muslims. So the British conquered the whole country" (p. 15). Aziz points out that when the British entered the areas that became Pakistan, there were relatively few non-Muslims and that, in any case, there are no records of non-Muslims siding with the British. On the other hand, there are records of Muslims siding with the British to help defeat Muslims from rival tribes. Aziz points out that fifth-graders were taught about this history under the following textbook headings: "Differences in Muslim and Hindu Civilizations, Need for the Creation of an Independent State, The Ideology of Pakistan, and India's Evil Designs against Pakistan" (p. 19). They are reminded of what they had been taught in prior grades about Hindus gladly siding with the British invaders to "suppress" the Muslims of India. The 1971 civil war that resulted in the creation of Bangladesh is presented counterfactually: "India engineered riots in East Pakistan through her agents and then invaded it from all four sides. Thus Pakistan was forced to fight another war with India" (p. 19). After rehearsing the story about India fomenting the 1971 civil war, the lesson concludes, "All of us should receive military training and be prepared to fight the enemy" (p. 21). In a passage Aziz describes as a "real gem," the text claims that prior to the 1947 Partition, India "was a part of our country" (p. 24). Eighth-graders are again primed to feel extreme pride in Pakistan. After enemies had "tried to damage the country in every possible way," including the "conspiracy" that resulted in the separation of Bangladesh from Pakistan, "now Pakistan has become so strong that the Islamic countries consider it as the fortress of Islam and God willing soon Pakistan will be counted among the countries of the first rank in the world" (p. 38).

46. Hoodbhoy and Nayyar point out that the phrase "Ideology of Pakistan" was first introduced in the Jamaati-i-Islami's manifesto, in 1951: "Nobody should indulge in anything repugnant to the Ideology of Pakistan. Any effort towards turning this country into a secular state or implanting herein any foreign ideology amounts to an attack on the very existence of Pakistan." Pervez Hoodbhoy and A. H. Nayyar, "Rewriting the History of Pakistan." In Asghar Khan, ed., *Islam, Politics, and the State*. London: Zed Press, 1985. http://www.sacw.net/Hat eEducation/1985HoodbhoyNayyar06022005.html. Accessed July 17, 2014.

47. For an overview of the Pakistan Studies curriculum and its impact, see Tariq Rahman, *Denizens of Alien Worlds: A Study of Education, Inequality and Polarization in Pakistan*. Karachi: Oxford University Press, 2004.

48. See Neamatollah Nojumi, "The Rise and Fall of the Taliban." In *The Taliban and the Crisis of Afghanistan*. Ed. Robert D. Crews and Amin Tarzi. Cambridge, MA: Harvard University Press, 2008.

49. See Ahmed Rashid, *Taliban: Militant Islam, Oil and Fundamentalists in Central Asia*. New Haven, CT: Yale University Press, 2000, p. 106.

50. "Les revelations d'un ancient conseilleur de Carter. 'Oui, la CIA est entrée en Afghanistan avant les Russes.'" *Le Nouvel Observateur* (Paris), January 15–21, 1998. Trans. by William Blum and David N. Gibbs. In David N. Gibbs, "Afghanistan: The Soviet Invasion in Retrospect." *International Politics* 37:2 (2000): 241. http://dgibbs.faculty.arizona.edu/sites/dgibbs.faculty.arizona.edu/files/afghan-ip.pdf. Accessed July 6, 2014.

51. See B. Raman, "The Pakistan-North Korea Nexus." *Rediff Special*, April 8, 2003. http://www.rediff.com/news/2003/apr/08spec.htm. Accessed July 21, 2014.

52. "Ahmed Rashid, "Pakistan after Reagan." MERIP MER155. http://www.merip.org/mer/mer155/pakistan-after-reagan. Accessed July 6, 2014. The Iran-Iraq War itself may well have been instigated by US president Carter's national security advisor Zbigniew Brzezinski. Although no official records support the claim, both the Pakistani and Arab "streets" widely believe that Mr. Brzezinski suggested to US ally Saddam Hussein following the 1979 Iranian Revolution that the time was ripe for him to settle Iraq's differences with Iran over the control of the Shatt al-Arab waterway, over which the two countries had been squabbling for years. US credibility was not helped by the fact that it publicly supported Iraq in the war but clandestinely sold weapons to Iran as well, even as it condemned Pakistan for allowing its Stinger missiles to end up in the hands of Iranians. See US Congress, "Report of the Congressional Committees Investigating the Iran-Contra Affair." Washington, DC: US Government Printing Office, 1987.

53. See Said Amir Arjomand, *Turban for the Crown: The Islamic Revolution in Iran*. New York: Oxford University Press, 1988.

54. "You can ask any Pakistani and he will tell you who the people involved (in the murder) were." Reported in interview by Khalid Hasan, "US Eliminated My Father, Charges Zia's Daughter." *Fact* 9 (May 2004). http://www.fact.com.pk/archives/may/feng/zia.htm. Accessed July 7, 2014.

55. Robert D. Kaplan, "How Zia's Death Helped the U.S." *New York Times*, August 23, 1989. http://www.nytimes.com/1989/08/23/opinion/how-zia-s-death-helped-the-us.html. Accessed July 4, 2014.

56. The de-escalation is sometimes attributed to "cricket diplomacy." See Rone Tempest, "War Talk Evaporates on First Pitch: Zia's Cricket Diplomacy Gets High Score in India." *Los Angeles Times*, February 23, 1987. http://articles.

latimes.com/1987-02-23/news/mn-3286_1_cricket-fans. Accessed September 16, 2014.

57. Nojumi also contends that Benazir appointed Interior Minister General Nasirullah Babar, a Pashtun who had been appointed by Benazir's father to support Afghan insurgents against the Afghan regime in the 1970s, to oversee Pakistani training and support for the Taliban. Nojumi, "The Rise and Fall of the Taliban," p. 101.

58. See Jan H. Kalicki, "Caspian Energy at the Crossroads." *Foreign Affairs* 80:5 (Sept.–Oct. 2001): 120–134.

59. See Nojumi, "The Rise and Fall of the Taliban," p. 102.

60. Ibid., p. 103.

61. See Rory McCarthy, "Sharif Family Alone against the Military." *Manchester Guardian*, March 31, 2000. http://www.theguardian.com/world/2000/apr/01/pakistan.rorymccarthy. Accessed July 23, 2014.

62. See Touqir Hussain, "U.S-Pakistan Engagement: The War on Terrorism and Beyond." United States Institute of Peace Special Report No. 145, July 2005. http://www.usip.org/events/us-pakistan-engagement-the-war-terrorism-and-beyond. Accessed September 14, 2014.

63. See "Top Pakistani Militant Released." *BBC*, April 21, 2008. http://news.bbc.co.uk/2/hi/south_asia/7359523.stm. Accessed July 24, 2014.

64. For an in-depth analysis of popular Pashtun preachers' sermons, see Sam Robinson, *Islamic Sermons in North West Pakistan: Harnessing the Power of Heaven and Hell*. Ph.D. thesis, University of Birmingham, Department of Theology and Religion, 2011.

65. Asma Jahangir, Pakistani human rights lawyer and participant in what came to be called the "Lawyers' Movement," estimates that there were around 600 unsolved "disappearances" between 2002 and 2007, many of them in the restive areas along the border with Afghanistan and Iran. Suspicions that the missing were the victims of the government's extrajudicial methods of dealing with its enemies ran high. See William Dalrymple, "Days of Rage: Challenges for the Nation's Future." *New Yorker*, July 23, 2007, p. 7. http://www.newyorker.com/reporting/2007/07/23/daysoof-rage. Accessed July 19, 2007.

66. Dalrymple, "Days of Rage," p. 3.

67. Ibid., p. 2.

68. See Carlotta Gall, "What Pakistan Knew about Bin Laden." *New York Times Magazine*, March 19, 2014. http://www.nytimes.com/2014/03/23/magazine/what-pakistan-knew-about-bin-laden.html?_r=0. Accessed September 16, 2014.

69. http://www.theguardian.com/world/2013/jul/29/altaf-hussain-mqm-leader-pakistan-london. Many Pakistanis accuse the British government of protecting Altaf Hussain because they use his party members as a source of intelligence on Taliban activities in Karachi. See http://www.theguardian.com/

world/2013/jul/29/altaf-hussain-mqm-leader-pakistan-london. Altaf Hussain was granted British citizenship in 2002.

70. See Vazira Fazila-Yacoobali, "The Battlefields of Karachi: Ethnicity, Violence and the State." *Journal of the International Institute* 4:2 (Fall 1996). http://quod. lib.umich.edu/j/jii/4750978.0004.108/--battlefields-of-karachi-ethnicity-violen ce-and-the-state?rgn=main;view=fulltext. Accessed September 16, 2014.

71. "Pakistan Agrees Sharia Law Deal." BBC, February 16, 2009. http://news.bbc. co.uk/2/hi/south_asia/7891955.stm. Accessed July 24, 2014.

72. Personal communication with committee co-chairperson, May 21, 2014.

73. See, e.g., "Election Rigging: Imran Khan Presents 2000-Page White Paper." *Express Tribune with the International New York Times*, August 21, 2013. http:// tribune.com.pk/story/593204/election-rigging-imran-khan-presents-2000-p age-white-paper/. Accessed September 14, 2014.

74. For years, Pakistanis have suffered with insufficient power and endured power outages, known as "load shedding," for several hours each day. As of May 2014, power was cut to areas outside the capital for at least 12 hours per day. As well, fuel for cars and trucks is in short supply. Many cars have converted to CNG (compressed natural gas), but it is available only on certain days of the week, leading to long lines at fuel stations, with many lining up the evening before 6 a.m. station openings. Pakistan has numerous rivers and dams and thus high potential for hydroelectric power.

75. "Imran Khan Said We Cannot Move Forward without Army: Javed Hashmi." *Dunya News*, September 15, 2014. http://dunyanews.tv/index.php/en/Pakista n/234977-Imran-Khan-said-we-cannot-move-forward-without-Arm. Accessed September 14, 2014.

76. See Daniele Grassi, "The State of Terrorism in Pakistan." *Diplomat*, September 8, 2014. http://thediplomat.com/2014/09/the-state-of-terrorism-in-pakistan/. Accessed September 14, 2014.

77. Zahir Shah Sherazi, "Punjabi Taliban Call Off Armed Struggle in Pakistan." *Dawn*, September 15, 2014. dawn/news/1131738/punjabi-taliban-call-off-ar med-struggle-in-pakistan. Accessed September 14, 2014.

78. Hoodbhoy and Mian report that "the army has lost more soldiers to terror- ism than in the four wars against India." Pervez Hoodbhoy and Zia Mian, "Changing Nuclear Thinking in Pakistan." Asia Pacific Leadership Network for Nuclear Non-Proliferation/Center for Nuclear Non-Proliferation and Disarmament. February 2014. http://www.princeton.edu/sgs/faculty-staff/ zia-mian/Hoodbhoy-Mian-Changing-Nuclear-Thinking.pdf. Accessed July 2, 2014.

79. The Objectives Resolution. http://www.pakistani.org/pakistan/constitution/ annex.html. Accessed October 18, 2014.

80. Wilfred Cantwell Smith, *Islam in Modern History*. Princeton, NJ: Princeton University Press, 1957, p. 238.

81. See Tamara Sonn, "Elements of Government in Classical Islam." In *Islamic Democratic Discourse: Theory, Debates, and Philosophical Perspectives*. Ed. M. A. Muqtedar Khan. New York: Lexington Books/Rowman and Littlefield, 2006, pp. 21–36.

82. Smith, *Islam in Modern History*, p. 239.

83. See Naveeda Khan, *Muslim Becoming: Aspiration and Skepticism in Pakistan*. Durham, NC: Duke University Press, 2012, p. 11.

84. Ibid., p. 11.

85. See Bhrigupati Singh, "Inhabiting Civil Disobedience." In *Political Theologies: Public Religion in a Post-Secular World*. Ed. H. de Vries and L. Sullivan. New York: Fordham University Press, 2006.

CHAPTER 5

1. "Presidential Debate Highlights Democracy." *Jakarta Post*, June 9, 2014. www.thejakartapost.com. Accessed August 27, 2014.

2. James B. Hoesterey, "Is Indonesia a Model for the Arab Spring? Islam, Democracy, and Diplomacy." *Review of Middle East Studies* 47:2 (Winter 2013): 157–165.

3. Thomas Carothers, "Egypt and Indonesia." *New Republic*, February 2, 2011. www.newrepublic.com/article/world/82650/egypt-and-indonesia. Accessed November 5, 2014.

4. Thomas Pepinsky, "There Is No Indonesia Model for the Arab Spring." *Foreign Policy, Democracy Lab*, February 27, 2013. www.foreignpolicy.com/articles/2013/02/27/there_is_no_indonesia_model_for_the_arab_spring. Accessed November 5, 2014.

5. Giora Eliraz, "Reflections on the Post-Arab Spring Landscape by Sailing in Thoughts to Indonesia," Middle East Institute, October 20, 2014. www.mei.edu/content/map/reflections-post-arab-spring-landscape-sailing-thoughts-in-donesia. Accessed November 5, 2014.

6. Samuel P. Huntington, *The Third Wave: Democratization in the Late Twentieth Century*. Norman: University of Oklahoma Press, 1991, p. 298.

7. *"Lahirnja Pantjasila" (The Birth of Pantjasila): President Soekarno's Speech*. 2nd English ed. Jakarta: Ministry of Information, Republic of Indonesia, 1952, p. 16.

8. Ibid., p. 28. Emphasis in the original.

9. Benedict Anderson, *Imagined Communities*. Revised ed. London: Verso, 1991, p. 116.

10. Robert W. Hefner, "South-East Asia from 1910." In *The New Cambridge History of Islam*. Vol. 5, *The Islamic World in the Age of Western Dominance*. Ed. Francis Robinson. Cambridge, UK: Cambridge University Press, 2010, p. 604.

11. Hefner, "South-East Asia from 1910," p. 605.

12. Paul Kratoska and Ben Batson, "Nationalism and Modernist Reform." In *The Cambridge History of Southeast Asia. Vol. 3, From c. 1800 to the 1930s.* Ed. Nicholas Tarling. Cambridge, UK: Cambridge University Press, 1999, p. 266.

13. Greg Fealy, Virginia Hooker, and Sally White, "Indonesia." In *Voices of Islam in Southeast Asia.* Ed. Greg Fealy and Virginia Hooker. Singapore: Institute of Southeast Asian Studies, 2006, p. 44.

14. Fealy and Hooker, *Voices*, "Amien Rais, Mohamad Roem and Nurcholish Madjid," p. 225.

15. Quoted in Robert W. Hefner, "Islamization and Democratization in Indonesia." In *Islam in an Era of Nation-States.* Ed. Robert W. Hefner and Patricia Horvatich. Honolulu: University of Hawai'i Press, 1997, p. 101.

16. Morris Janowitz, *The Military in the Political Development of New Nations.* Chicago: University of Chicago Press, 1964. pp. 10–11, 13–15. The three others with national liberation struggle origins are Burma, Algeria, and Israel.

17. Ibid., p. 15.

18. Daniel S. Lev, "The Political Role of the Army in Indonesia." *Pacific Affairs* 36:4 (Winter 1963–1964): 349.

19. Francesco Montessoro, *Reform and Modernization of the Indonesian Forces.* ISPI Analysis No. 268. Milan: Istituto per gli Studi di Politica Internazionale, July 2014, p. 2.

20. Ibid., p. 1.

21. Leo Suryadinata, "A Year of Upheaval and Uncertainty: The Fall of Soeharto and Rise of Habibie." *Southeast Asian Affairs* 1999: 116.

22. Seth Mydans, "Indonesia Changed, But Who Deserves the Credit?" *New York Times*, June 13, 1999.

23. Siddarth Chandra and Douglas Kammen, "Generating Reforms and Reforming Generations: Military Politics in Indonesia's Democratic Transition and Consolidation." *World Politics* 55:1 (October 2002): 125.

24. Damien Kingsbury, "The Reform of the Indonesian Armed Forces." *Contemporary Southeast Asia* 22:2 (August 2000): 308–309.

25. R. William Liddle, "Indonesia in 1999: Democracy Restored." *Asian Survey* 40:1 (January–February 2000): 35.

26. Kikue Hamayotsu, "The Political Rise of the Prosperous Justice Party in Post-authoritarian Indonesia." *Asian Survey* 51:5 (September–October 2011): 975.

27. Details of the political negotiations involved in the 1999 parliamentary elections and then the MPR elections of the president and vice president are clearly presented and analyzed in Eric C. Thompson, "Indonesia in Transition: The 1999 Presidential Elections." *NBR Briefing No. 9* (December 1999). www.nbr.org/publications/briefing/pdf/brief9.pdf. Accessed November 18, 2014.

28. Liddle, "Indonesia in 1999," p. 36.

29. Ibid., p. 34.

30. Keith B. Richburg, "Vice President Megawati," *Washington Post*, October 22, 1999, A-25.
31. Greg Barton, *Abdurrahman Wahid: Muslim Democrat, Indonesian President.* Sydney: University of New South Wales Press, 2002, p. 374.
32. Chandra and Kammen, "Generating Reforms," p. 103.
33. R. William Liddle, "Indonesia in 2000: A Shaky Start for Democracy." *Asian Survey* 41:1 (January–February 2001): 211.
34. See, for example, news coverage at the time indicating the military leaders' position. Seth Mydans, "Indonesia's President Threatens Parliament over Its Efforts to Remove Him." *New York Times*, July 10, 2001.
35. R. William Liddle and Saiful Mujani, "Indonesia in 2004: The Rise of Susilo Bambang Yudhoyono." *Asian Survey* 45:1 (January–February 2005): 120.
36. Michael S. Malley, "Indonesia in 2002: The Rising Cost of Inaction." *Asian Survey* 43:1 (January–February 2003): 136–137.
37. Ibid., p. 138.
38. Liddle and Murjani, "Indonesia in 2004," p. 121.
39. This neologism is more accurate as a description of the Islamist programs and visions than the more commonly used term "theocracy." What is meant by a religiocracy is the dominance of religious leaders and scholars in the defining and shaping of governmental policy, whether or not those leaders actually hold any formal political office.
40. www.freedomhouse.org/report/freedom-world/2006/indonesia
41. R. Michael Liddle and Saiful Mujani, "Indonesia in 2005: A New Multiparty Presidential Democracy." *Asian Survey* 46:1 (January–February 2006): 136.
42. "Indonesia: How GAM Won in Aceh." *Asia Briefing No. 61* (March 22, 2007). Jakarta/Brussels, p. 1.
43. The figures come from the reports of the annual indices at www.transparency.org.
44. Marcus Mietzner, "Indonesia in 2009: Electoral Contestation and Economic Resilience." *Asian Survey* 50:1 (January–February 2010): 187.
45. Nadia Bulkin, "Indonesia's Political Parties." *Resource Page*, October 24, 2013. Carnegie Endowment for International Peace. http://carnegieendowment.org/2013/10/24/indonesia-political-parties.
46. Edward Aspinall, "Indonesia in 2009: Democratic Triumphs and Trials." *Southeast Asian Affairs* 2010: 107.
47. Edward Aspinall, "Democratic Deepening in Indonesia: Challenges for the New Administration." *Strategic Review (The Indonesian Journal of Leadership, Policy and World Affairs)*, October–December 2014. www.sr-indonesia.com/in-the-journal/view/democratic-deepening-in-indonesia-challenges-for-the-new-administration.

48. Ibid.

49. Greg Fealy, "Islamic Radicalism in Indonesia: The Faltering Revival?" *Southeast Asian Affairs* 2004: 104–121.

50. Ehito Kimura, "Indonesia in 2010." *Asian Survey* 51:1 (January–February 2011): 190.

51. "Stagnation on Freedom of Religion." Setara Institute for Democracy and Peace, November 20, 2014. http://setara-institute.org/en/stagnasi-kebebesan-beragama.

52. "Religious Intolerance Increases in Indonesia Watchdog Says." Setara Institute for Democracy and Peace, January 18, 2014. http://setara-institute.org/en/english-religious-intolerance-increases-in-indonesia-watchdog-says/.

53. Using the terminology of Damien Kingsbury, "Indonesia in 2007: Unmet Expectations, Despite Improvement." *Asian Survey* 48:1 (January–February 2008): 39.

54. Aspinall, "Indonesia in 2009," p. 121.

55. "Indonesian Politics: The Empire Strikes Back," *Economist*, October 4, 2014, p. 45.

56. Michael Vatikiotis, "Indonesia and Jokowi: Right Place, Right Time." *Straits Times*, November 21, 2014. www.straitstimes.com/news/opinion/more-opinion-stories/story/indonesia-and-jokowi-right-place-right-time-20141121.

57. Geoffrey C. Gunn, "Indonesia in 2013: Oligarchs, Political Tribes, and Populists." *Asian Survey* 54:1 (January–February 2014): 49.

58. Michael Vatikiotis, "Indonesian Democracy's 'Guiding Hand.'" *New York Times*, February 21, 2014. www.nytimes.com/2014/02/22/opinion/indonesian-democracys-guiding-hand.html.

59. "RI Suffers from Weak State: Prabowo." *Jakarta Post*, May 31, 2013. www.thejakartapost.com/news/2013/05/31/ri-suffers-from-weak-state-prabowo.html.

60. Margareth S. Aritonang, "Prabowo Wants 'Guided Democracy' if Elected." *Jakarta Post*, December 19, 2012. www.thejakartapost.com/news/2012/12/19/prabowo-wants-guided-democracy-if-elected.html.

61. A. Lin Neumann, "As the Yudhoyono Era Ends, Sweeping Changes Are in Store." *Strategic Review (The Indonesian Journal of Leadership, Politics and World Affairs)*, January 13, 2014. www.sr-indonesia.com/web-exclusives/view/as-the-yudhoyono-era-ends-sweeping-changes-are-in-store.

62. Aspinall, "Democratic Deepening in Indonesia."

63. These figures are drawn from the relevant *Britannica Book of the Year.*

64. Geoffery Gunn, "Indonesia in 2012: An Electoral Democracy in Full Spate." *Asian Survey* 53:1 (January–February 2013): 119.

65. Huntington, *The Third Wave*, p. 16.

66. Aspinall, "Democratic Deepening in Indonesia."

CHAPTER 6

1. Afua Hirsch and Sheriff Bojang, Jr., "Senegalese President Admits Defeat in Election." *Guardian*, March 26, 2012. www.theguardian.com/world/2012/mar/26/senegalese-president-admits-defeat-election.
2. Adam Nossiter, "A Turbulence-Free Election in Senegal." *New York Times*, March 2, 2012. www.nytimes.com/2012/03/26/world/africa/president-concedes-race-in-senegal.html.
3. Population estimates vary greatly but these figures, drawn from the CIA *World Factbook*, give a sense of the proportions. No group is a majority in the country.
4. Donal Cruise O'Brien, "The Shadow Politics of Wolofisation." *Journal of Modern African Studies* 36:1 (March 1998): 30.
5. Afrobarometer, *Summary of Results: Round 4. Afrobarometer Survey in Senegal.* Compiled by Michigan State University. p. 73. www.afrobarometer.org.
6. Ibid., p. 78.
7. See the general analysis in David Northrup, *Africa's Discovery of Europe, 1450–1850.* 2nd ed. New York: Oxford University Press, 2009, Chapters 2–4.
8. See, for example, the description of politics in the Senegambia in J. F. Ade Ajayi, ed., *Africa in the Nineteenth Century until the 1880s, General History of Africa VI.* Abridged edition. Paris: UNESCO, 1998, pp. 252–255.
9. Martin A. Klein, "The Evolution of the 'Chefferie' in Senegal." In *Nations by Design: Institution-Building in Africa.* Ed. Arnold Rivkin. New York: Anchor Books, 1968, p. 204.
10. B. A. Ogot, ed., *Africa from the Sixteenth to the Eighteenth Century, General History of Africa V.* Abridged edition. Paris: UNESCO, 1999, p. 141.
11. Philip D. Curtin, "Jihad in West Africa: Early Phases and Inter-relations in Mauritania and Senegal." *Journal of African History* 12:1 (1971): 14.
12. A helpful summary of the history of these movements can be found in David Robinson, "Revolutions in the Western Sudan." In *The History of Islam in Africa.* Ed. Nehemia Levtzion and Randall L. Pouwels. Athens: Ohio University Press, 2000, pp. 131–152.
13. Jamil M. Abun-Nasr, *The Tijaniyya: A Sufi Order in the Modern World.* London: Oxford University Press, 1965, p. 142.
14. See Ibid., pp. 143–150.
15. Ibid., pp. 147–148.
16. Lucy C. Behrman, *Muslim Brotherhoods and Politics in Senegal.* Cambridge, MA: Harvard University Press, 1970, pp. 88–89.
17. Robinson, "Revolutions in the Western Sudan," p. 144.
18. Biram Diop, "Civil-Military Relations in Senegal." In *Military Engagement: Influencing Armed Forces Worldwide to Support Democratic Transitions.* Vol. 2, *Regional and Country Studies.* Washington, DC: Brookings Institution Press, 2013, p. 236.

19. Martin A. Klein, *Islam and Imperialism in Senegal: Sine-Saloum 1847–1914*. Stanford: Stanford University Press, 1968, p. 9.
20. For development of the tirailleurs as discussed here, see Patrick Manning, *Francophone Sub-Saharan Africa, 1880–1995*. 2nd ed. Cambridge, UK: Cambridge University Press, 1998, pp. 63, 66–67, 79.
21. Diop, "Civil-Military Relations in Senegal," p. 238.
22. Ibid., pp. 238–239.
23. Cruise O'Brien, "The Shadow Politics of Wolofisation," pp. 25–46.
24. Leigh Swigart, "Cultural Creolisation and Language Use in Post-colonial Africa: The Case of Senegal." *Africa: Journal of the International African Institute* 64:2 (1994): 180.
25. Manning, *Francophone Sub-Saharan Africa*, pp. 78–79.
26. "Africa's Turn: A Conversation with Macky Sall." *Foreign Affairs* 92:5 (September–October 2013): 2.
27. Leonard A. Villalón, "Democratizing a (Quasi) Democracy: The Senegalese Elections of 1993." *African Affairs* 93:371 (April 1994): 167.
28. Ibid., p. 168.
29. John Darnton, "Multiparty System Is Being Revived in Senegal." *New York Times*, July 17, 1976.
30. Villalón, "Democratizing a (Quasi) Democracy," p. 169.
31. The election results are from African Elections Database, Elections in Senegal. http://africanelections.tripod.com/sn.html.
32. Tarik Dahou and Vincent Foucher, "Senegal since 2000: Rebuilding Hegemony in a Global Age." In *Turning Points in African Democracy*. Ed. Abdul Raufu Mustapha and Lindsay Whitfield. Woodbridge, Suffolk: James Curry, 2009, p. 15.
33. Christof Hartmann, "Senegal's Party System: The Limits of Formal Regulation." *Democratization* 17:4 (2010): 772.
34. Dahou and Founcher, p. 15.
35. Dominika Koter, "King Makers: Local Leaders and Ethnic Politics in Africa." *World Politics* 65:2 (April 2013): 212.
36. Ibid., p. 217.
37. See Table 2 in Ibid., p. 218.
38. Kristen Angela Harkness, "The Origins of African Civil-Military Relations: Ethnic Armies and the Development of Coup Traps." PhD diss., Princeton University, 2012, p. 181.
39. Koter, "King Makers," p. 226.
40. Robert A. Dowd and Michael Driessen, "Ethnically Dominated Party Systems and the Quality of Democracy: Evidence from Sub-Saharan Africa." *Afrobarometer Working Paper No. 92* (2008): 11. Emphasis in text.
41. Aïssatou Fall, *Understanding the Casamance Conflict: A Background*. KAIPTC Monograph No. 7 (2010), p. 13. Africa Portal Library. www.africaportal.org/dspace/articles/understanding-casamance-conflict-background.

42. J. C., "Senegal's Casamance Region: The Next Hot Place to Go on Hols?" Baobab: Africa. *Economist,* May 7, 2014. www.economist.com/node/21601806/print.

43. Fiona McLaughlin, "Dakar Wolof and the Configuration of an Urban Identity." *Journal of African Cultural Studies* 14:2 (December 2001): 158, 170.

44. The names and brief histories of these parties are provided in Hartmann, "Senegal's Party System," pp. 777–779.

45. Hartmann, "Senegal's Party System," p. 779.

46. Leonardo A. Villalón, "ASR Focus: Islamism in West Africa—Senegal." *African Studies Review* 47:2 (September 2004): 65.

47. Ibid., p. 70.

48. McLaughlin, "Dakar Wolof," pp. 154, 158.

49. Kim Yi Dionne, Kris L. Inman, and Gabriella R. Montinola, "Another Resource Curse? The Impact of Remittances on Political Participation." *Afrobarometer Working Paper No. 145* (January 2014): 8.

50. US Agency for International Development, *Democracy, Human Rights, and Governance Assessment of Senegal, Final Report.* January 2013, p. 36.

CHAPTER 7

1. David D. Kirkpatrick, "Tunisian Protests Spread to Capital." *New York Times,* January 12, 2011. http://www.nytimes.com/2011/01/13/world/africa/13tunisia. html?_r=0. Accessed February 19, 2013.

2. Ibid.

3. Esam Al-Amin, *The Arab Awakening: Understanding Transformations and Revolutions in the Middle East.* Washington, DC: American Educational Trust, 2013, p. 27.

4. Ibid., p. 28.

5. As quoted in ibid., p. 31.

6. Naseema Noor, "Tunisia: The Revolution That Started It All." *International Affairs Review,* January 31, 2011. http://www.iar-gwu.org/node/257. Accessed February 26, 2013.

7. "Islamists Speaking Out after Tunisia's 'Jasmine Revolution.'" *Times of Malta,* January 28, 2011. http://www.timesofmalta.com/articles/view/20110128/world/ islamists-speaking-out-after-tunisia-s-jasmine-revolution.347471. Accessed February 26, 2013.

8. Marion Boulby, "The Islamic Challenge: Tunisia since Independence." *Third World Quarterly* 10:2 (1998): 591.

9. Ibid.

10. M. Tessler, "Political Change and Islamic Revival in Tunisia." *Maghreb Review* 5 (1980): 11.

11. Boulby, "The Islamic Challenge," p. 592.

12. "Tunisia: Neighbor's Duty." *Time,* December 2, 1957, p. 2.

13. Ibid.
14. Abdelkader Zghal, "The Reactivation of Tradition in a Post-traditional Society." *Daedalus* 102:1 (1973): 231.
15. Ibid., p. 230.
16. Ibid.
17. Boulby, "The Islamic Challenge," p. 594.
18. Ibid., p. 593.
19. Azzam S. Tamimi, *Rachid Ghannouchi: A Democrat within Islamism.* Oxford: Oxford University Press, 2001, p. 3.
20. John L. Esposito and John O. Voll, *Makers of Contemporary Islam.* Oxford: Oxford University Press, 2001, p. 93.
21. Ibid.
22. As quoted in Tamimi, *Rachid Ghannouchi*, p. 11.
23. As quoted in Esposito and Voll, *Makers of Contemporary Islam*, p. 95.
24. As quoted in Tamimi, *Rachid Ghannouchi*, p. 21.
25. As quoted in Boulby, "The Islamic Challenge," p. 599.
26. Christopher Alexander, "Opportunities, Organizations, and Ideas: Islamists and Workers in Tunisia and Algeria." *International Journal of Middle East Studies* 32 (2000): 466.
27. As quoted in Esposito and Voll, *Makers of Contemporary Islam*, p. 99.
28. Boulby, "The Islamic Challenge," p. 601.
29. Tamimi, *Rachid Ghannouchi*, p. 105.
30. As quoted in Esposito and Voll, *Makers of Contemporary Islam*, p. 114.
31. As quoted in Boulby, "The Islamic Challenge," p. 591.
32. John L. Esposito, *The Islamic Threat: Myth or Reality?* New York: Oxford University Press, 1999, p. 167.
33. Dirk Vanderwalle, "Ben Ali's New Tunisia." *Field Staff Reports: Africa/Middle East, 1989–90*, p. 8.
34. L. G. Jones, "Portrait of Rachid al-Ghannouchi." *Middle East Report* 153 (July–August 1988): 22.
35. Ibid.
36. Christopher Alexander, *Tunisia: Stability and Reform in the Modern Maghreb.* New York: Routledge, 2010, p. 58.
37. As quoted in Tamimi, *Rachid Ghannouchi*, p. 69.
38. Alexander, *Tunisia*, p. 60.
39. Ibid.
40. Tamimi, *Rachid Ghannouchi*, p. 70.
41. Alexander, *Tunisia*, p. 64.
42. Ibid.
43. Monica Marks, "Who Are Tunisia's Salafis?" *Foreign Policy*, September 28, 2012. http://mideast.foreignpolicy.com/posts/2012/09/28/who_are_tunisia_s_ salafis. Accessed March 10, 2013.

44. Ibid.
45. Stefano Torelli, Fabio Merone, and Francesco Cavatorta, "Salafism in Tunisia: Challenges and Opportunities for Democratization." *Middle East Policy* 19:4 (2012): 143.
46. Ibid.
47. Mohamed A. El-Khawas, "Tunisia's Jasmine Revolution: Causes and Impact." *Mediterranean Quarterly* 23:4 (2012): 7.
48. Ibid., p. 8.
49. African Development Bank.
50. El-Khawas, "Tunisia's Jasmine Revolution," p. 8.
51. Peter J. Schraeder and Hamadi Redissi, "Ben Ali's Fall." *Journal of Democracy* 22:3 (2011): 10.
52. Ibid., p. 11.
53. Ibid.
54. Ibid.
55. Olivier Roy, "Where Were the Tunisian Islamists?" *New York Times*, January 28, 2011.
56. Lindsay Benstead, Ellen M. Lust, Dhafer Malouche, Gamal Soltan, and Jakob Wichmann, "Islamists Aren't the Obstacle." *Foreign Policy*, February 14, 2013. http://www.foreignaffairs.com/articles/138940/lindsay-benstead-ellen-m-lust-dhafer-malouche-gamal-soltan-and-j/islamists-arent-the-obstacle?page=show. Accessed March 11, 2013.
57. Ibid.
58. Ibid.
59. Roula Khalad and David Gardner, "Islamist Leader Warns on Tunisian Democracy." *Financial Times*, June 22, 2011.
60. El-Khawas, "Tunisia's Jasmine Revolution," p. 18.
61. HDS Greenway, "Analysis: Tunisia's Democracy Has a Head Start." *Global Post*, October 11, 2011. www.globalpost.com/print/5677609. Accessed March 12, 2013.
62. Michael Robbins and Mark Tessler, "Tunisians Voted for Jobs, Not Islam." *Foreign Policy*, December 7, 2011. http://mideast.foreignpolicy.com/posts/2011/12/07/tunisians_voted_for_jobs_not_islam.
63. Ibid.
64. John Thorne, "Tunisia Debate Turns Personal: 'Pray More and Turn Down that Metallica.'" *Christian Science Monitor*, April 19, 2012. http://www.csmonitor.com/World/Middle-East/2012/0419/Tunisia-debate-turns-personal-Pray-more-and-turn-down-that-Metallica. Accessed March 12, 2013.
65. Anne Wolf and Raphael Lefevre, "Tunisia: A Revolution at Risk." *Guardian*, April 18, 2012. www.guardian.co.uk/commentisfree/2012/apr/18/Tunisia-revolution-at-risk/print.

66. "Ali Larayedh, Moderate Islamist Set to Head New Tunisia Government." *Business Recorder*, March 9, 2013. http://www.brecorder.com/general-news/172/1161320/. Accessed March 11, 2013.

67. Benstead, et al., "Islamists Aren't the Obstacle."

68. "Tunisia Unveils New Coalition Government." *Al Jazeera*, March 8, 2013. http://www.aljazeera.com/news/africa/2013/03/2013381546957967.html.

69. Emily Greenhouse, "Tunisian Feminist Amina Tyler's Topless Photos: How to Provoke National Unrest on Facebook." *New Yorker*, April 8, 2013. http://www.newyorker.com/online/blogs/elements/2013/04/amina-tyler-topless-photos-tunisia-activism.html.

70. "Tunisia's Salafists: A Growing Concern." *Economist*, May 22, 2013. http://www.economist.com/blogs/pomegranate/2013/05/tunisia-s-salafists.

71. Tarek Amara, "Tunisia's Islamist PM Says Egypt Scenario Unlikely to Happen There." *Yahoo News*, July 2, 2013.

72. Vivienne Walt, "After Morsi's Ouster in Egypt, Tunisia's Islamists Fear a Similar Fate." *Time*, July 16, 2013. http://world.time.com/2013/07/16/after-morsis-ouster-in-egypt-tunisias-islamists-fear-a-similar-fate/#ixzz2ZJ88iUGE.

73. In Dilip Hiro, "Egyptian Coup Splits Middle East." *Yale Global*, July 11, 2013. http://yaleglobal.yale.edu/content/egyptian-coup-splits-middle-east.

74. "Tunisian Opposition Figures 'Shot by Same Gun.'" *Al Jazeera*, July 27, 2013. http://www.aljazeera.com/news/africa/2013/07/201372611531821363.html.

75. "Tunisia: Slow Reform Pace Undermines Rights." *Human Rights Watch*, February 6, 2013. http://www.hrw.org/news/2013/02/06/tunisia-slow-reform-pace-undermines-rights.

76. Rachel Shabi, "Tunisians Must Be Wary of Going Down the Same Road as Egypt." *Guardian*, July 26, 2013. http://www.theguardian.com/commentisfree/2013/jul/26/tunisia-wary-route-egypt.

77. "Tunisia's Biggest Union Urges Islamist-Led Government to Quit." *Reuters*, July 30, 2013. http://www.reuters.com/article/2013/07/30/us-tunisia-protests-idUSBRE96T0MW20130730.

78. Carlotta Gall, "Islamist Party in Tunisia To Step Down." *New York Times*, September 28, 2013.

79. Amna Guellali, "The Problem with Tunisia's New Constitution." *Human Rights Watch*, February 3, 2014. http://www.hrw.org/news/2014/02/03/problem-tunisia-s-new-constitution.

80. Constitution of the Republic of Tunisia, Article 6. Unofficial Translation by the Jasmine Foundation. http://www.jasmine-foundation.org/doc/unofficial_english_translation_of_tunisian_constitution_final_ed.pdf.

81. Guellali, "The Problem with Tunisia's New Constitution."

82. Sarah Mersch, "Tunisia's Compromise Constitution." Carnegie Endowment for International Peace, January 21, 2014. http://carnegieendowment.org/sada/2014/01/21/tunisia-s-compromise-constitution/gyze.

83. Mohamed Kerrou, "Tunisia's Historic Step toward Democracy." Carnegie Middle East Center, April 22, 2014. http://carnegie-mec.org/2014/04/17/tunisia-s-historic-step-toward-democracy/h8sv#.

84. Sara Chayes, "How a Leftist Labor Union Helped Force Tunisia's Political Settlement." Carnegie Endowment for International Peace, March 27, 2014. http://carnegieendowment.org/2014/03/27/how-leftist-labor-union-helped-force-tunisia-s-political-settlement/h61o.

CHAPTER 8

1. Hamdy A. Hassan, "Civil Society in Egypt under the Mubarak Regime." *Afro Asian Journal of Social Sciences* 2:22 (2011): 1.

2. Essam el-Amin, "Showdown in Egypt." *CounterPunch*, November 30, 2012. www.counterpunch.org/2012/11/30/showdown-in-egypt/. Accessed January 15, 2013.

3. Raymond William Baker, "Invidious Comparisons: Realism, Postmodern Globalism, and Centrist Islamic Movements in Egypt." In *Political Islam: Revolution, Radicalism or Reform?* Ed. John L. Esposito Cairo: The American University in Cairo Press, 1997, p. 124.

4. John L. Esposito and James P. Piscatori, "Democratization and Islam." *Middle East Journal* 45:3 (1991): 429.

5. Comments of Abd al-Rahman al-Faramawi in al-Anba', May 3, 1987.

6. John L. Esposito, *Unholy War? Terror in the Name of Islam.* Oxford: Oxford University Press, 2002, p. 148.

7. Samer Shehata, "Egypt: The Founders." In "The Islamists Are Coming." Woodrow Wilson Center. http://theislamistsarecoming.wilsoncenter.org/islamists/node/23181/#the_founders. Accessed January 22, 2013.

8. Hesham el-Hawadi, "Mubarak and the Islamists: Why Did the 'Honeymoon' End?" *Middle East Journal* 59:1 (2005): 74.

9. "Professors Can Not Choose." *Middle East Times*, June 6–12, 1992, p. 1.

10. Amnesty International, "Time for Justice: Egypt's Corrosive System of Detention." London, 2011.

11. Larisa Epatko, "Mubarak in 1993: Egypt 'Keen' on Democracy, but It Takes Time." *PBS NewsHour*, February 4, 2011. http://www.pbs.org/newshour/rundown/2011/02/mubarak-on-democracy.html. Accessed January 24, 2013.

12. As quoted in "Arab Autocracy Forever?" *Economist*, June 5, 1997. http://www.economist.com/node/90481.

13. House Foreign Affairs Committee, "Near East and Africa." Hearing Transcript 1794. Available online at http://democrats.foreignaffairs.house.gov/archives/109/26464.004.PDF.

14. "Egypt: Calls for Reform Met with Brutality." *Human Rights Watch*, May 26, 2005. http://www.hrw.org/news/2005/05/25/egypt-calls-reform-met-brutality.

15. "The Muslim Brothers: Appease or Oppose?" *Economist*, October 8, 2009. http://www.economist.com/node/14587812.

16. Mariz Tadros, "Where's the 'Bread, Freedom and Social Justice' a Year after Egypt's Revolution?" *Guardian*, January 25, 2012. http://www.the-guardian.com/global-development/poverty-matters/2012/jan/25/egypt-bread-freedom-social-justice.

17. Jennifer Preston, "Facebook and YouTube Fuel the Egyptian Protests." *New York Times*, February 5, 2011. http://www.nytimes.com/2011/02/06/world/middleeast/06face.html?_r=2&ref=facebookinc&. Accessed January 25, 2013.

18. Kira Baiasu, "Social Media: A Force for Political Change in Egypt." The New Middle East Blog, by Eric Davis, professor of political science and former director of the Center for Middle Eastern Studies at Rutgers University, New Brunswick, NJ, April 13, 2011. http://new-middle-east.blogspot.com/2011/04/social-media-force-for-political-change.html. Accessed June 27, 2012.

19. Rateb Joudeh, "Egypt: Social Network Revolt with New Twists." *Ria Novosti*, January 2, 2011. http://en.rian.ru/analysis/20110201/162405989.html. Accessed July 11, 2012.

20. Catharine Smith, "Egypt's Facebook Revolution: Wael Ghonim Thanks the Social Network." *Huffington Post*, February 11, 2011. http://www.huffington-post.com/2011/02/11/egypt-facebook-revolution-wael-ghonim_n_822078.html

21. Esam El Amin, "Showdown in Egypt." *CounterPunch*, November 30, 2012. http://www.counterpunch.org/2012/11/30/showdown-in-egypt/.

22. Zeinab Abul-Magd, "The Army and the Economy in Egypt." *Jadaliyya*, December 23, 2011. http://www.jadaliyya.com/pages/index/3732/the-army-and-the-economy-in-egypt.

23. "Egypt's Mursi Pardons Political Prisoners." *Reuters*, October 8, 2012. http://www.reuters.com/article/2012/10/08/us-egypt-president-pardon-idUSBRE89711K20121008. Accessed January 26, 2012.

24. Michele Dunne, "Egypt: Elections or Constitution First?" Carnegie Endowment for International Peace, June 21, 2011. http://carnegieendowment.org/2011/06/21/egypt-elections-or-constitution-first/7f.

25. Marina Ottoway, "Egypt's Democracy: Between the Military, Islamists, and the Illiberal Democrats." Carnegie Endowment for International Peace, November 3, 2011. http://www.carnegieendowment.org/2011/11/03/egypt-s-democracy-between-military-islamists-and-illiberal-democrats/6lzl#.

26. Ibid.

27. Dalia Mogahed and Mohammed Younis, "Egyptians Oppose U.S. Aid to Political Groups in Their Country." June 8, 2011. http://www.gallup.com/poll/147953/egyptians-oppose-aid-political-groups-country.aspx.

28. John L. Esposito and Shamil Idris, "Egyptian Military Seizes Power: Is This Democracy?" *Huffington Post*, June 19, 2012. http://www.huffingtonpost.com/john-l-esposito/egyptian-militarys-seizes_b_1608590.html.

29. H. A. Hellyer, "Egyptians Shifted to Islamist Parties as Elections Neared." Gallup World Polling, January 24, 2012. http://www.gallup.com/poll/152168/egyptians-shifted-islamist-parties-elections-neared.aspx.

30. Ibid.

31. Jenny Cuffe, "Salafism: Why Ultra-Conservative Islam Is Finding Support in Post-revolution Egypt." *BBC News*, October 16, 2012. http://www.bbc.co.uk/news/world-middle-east-19914763.

32. David D. Kirkpatrick, "Salafists in Egypt Have More Than Just Religious Appeal." *New York Times*, December 10, 2011. http://www.nytimes.com/2011/12/11/world/middleeast/salafis-in-egypt-have-more-than-just-religious-appeal.html?pagewanted=all&_r=0.

33. John L. Esposito and Shamil Idris, "Egyptian Military Seizes Power."

34. Ibid.

35. Nathan C. Lean, "Egypt Elections: After Court Ruling, The Real Concern Is Not the Muslim Brotherhood." *Christian Science Monitor*, June 15, 2012. http://www.csmonitor.com/Commentary/Opinion/2012/0615/Egypt-elections-After-court-ruling-the-real-concern-is-not-the-Muslim-Brotherhood.

36. "Morsi Takes Oath of Office." *Brunei Times*, July 1, 2012. http://www.bt.com.bn/news-world/2012/07/01/morsi-takes-oath-office.

37. Wadah Kanfar, "In a Polarized Egypt, the Thugs and the Remnants Return to Centre Stage." *Guardian*, December 11, 2012. http://www.guardian.co.uk/commentisfree/2012/dec/12/polarised-egypt-thugs-islamists-morsi.

38. Ibid.

39. Juan Cole, "Egypt's Controversial Fundamentalist Constitution Meets Low Turnout." December 23, 2012. http://www.juancole.com/2012/12/controversial-fundamentalist-constitution.html.

40. "Egypt Constitution Gets 98.1 % 'Yes' Vote." *Associated Press*, January 18, 2014. http://www.cbc.ca/news/world/egypt-constitution-gets-98-1-yes-vote-1.2502021

41. Aya Batrawy and Maryam Rizk, "Anti-Morsi Rallies Mark Two Year Anniversary of Egypt Uprising." *CTV News*, January 25, 2013. http://www.ctvnews.ca/world/anti-morsi-rallies-mark-two-year-anniversary-of-egypt-uprising-1.1128996.

42. "Egypt Opposition Threatens Morsi with Boycott of Parliamentary Polls." *Middle East Online*, January 26, 2013. http://www.middle-east-online.com/english/?id=56653.

43. Mike Giglio, "Crackdown in Egypt: Bassem Youssef and Alaa Abdel Fattah Face Charges." *Daily Beast*, April 3, 2013. http://www.thedailybeast.

com/articles/2013/04/03/crackdown-in-egypt-bassem-youssef-and-alaa-abdel-fattah-face-charges.html.

44. David Kirkpatrick and May El Sheikh, "Arrest of Anti-Islamist Figures Is Ordered in Egypt." *New York Times*, March 23, 2013. http://www.nytimes.com/2013/03/26/world/middleeast/in-egypt-arrest-of-5-anti-islamist-figures-sought.html.

45. Ahmed Magdy Youssef, "In Egypt's Media: Two Camps, One Loser." *Media Politics in Perspective*, July 16, 2013. http://mediapoliticsinperspective.wordpress.com/2013/07/16/in-egypts-media-two-camps-one-loser/.

46. Ibid.

47. Samer Shehata, "In Egypt, Democrats vs. Liberals." *New York Times*, July 2, 2013. http://www.nytimes.com/2013/07/03/opinion/in-egypt-democrats-vs-liberals.html?_r=0.

48. Ibid.

49. Esam Al Amin, " In Egypt, the Military Is Supreme." *CounterPunch*, July 5, 2013. http://www.counterpunch.org/2013/07/05/in-egypt-the-military-is-supreme/.

50. Ibid.

51. Ibid.

52. Khaled Abou Al-Fadl, "The Perils of a 'People's Coup.'" *New York Times*, July 7, 2013. http://www.nytimes.com/2013/07/08/opinion/the-perils-of-a-peoples-coup.html?ref=opinion&_r=0.

53. Gehad El-Haddad, "In Egypt, a Violent Step Backward." *Washington Post*, July 8, 2013. http://www.washingtonpost.com/opinions/in-egypt-a-violent-step-backward/2013/07/08/8d5c2802-e7f7-11e2-a301-ea5a8116d211_story.html.

54. David Kirkpatrick, "Death Toll in Egypt Clashes Climb to 525." *New York Times*, August 16, 2013. http://www.nytimes.com/2013/08/16/world/middleeast/egypt.html?pagewanted=all.

55. Michael R. Gordon, "Egyptians Following Right Path, Kerry Says." *New York Times*, November 4, 2013. http://www.nytimes.com/2013/11/04/world/middleeast/kerry-egypt-visit.html.

56. Robert Mackey, "Egypt's Revolution Was 'Stolen' by Muslim Brotherhood, Kerry Says." *New York Times*, November 20, 2013. http://thelede.blogs.nytimes.com/2013/11/20/egypts-revolution-was-stolen-by-the-muslim-brotherhood-kerry-says/.

57. "Egypt Unfair Trial, Death Sentences Make Mockery of Justice." Amnesty International, April 28, 2014. http://www.amnesty.org/en/news/egypt-unfair-trial-death-sentences-make-mockery-justice-2014-04-28.

58. "Muslim Scholars Slam Arbitrary Arrests and Torture in Egypt." *Memo: Middle East Monitor*, April 23, 2014. https://www.middleeastmonitor.com/news/africa/11051-muslim-scholars-slam-arbitrary-arrests-and-torture-in-egypt.

59. Mara Revkin, "Worse Than Mubarak." *Foreign Affairs*, February 11, 2014. http://www.foreignaffairs.com/articles/140729/mara-revkin/worse-than-mubarak?nocache=1.

60. Ronald Meinardus, "Why Western Liberals Have Problems Understanding Egypt." *Daily News Egypt*, February 9, 2014. http://www.dailynewsegypt.com/2014/02/09/western-liberals-problems-understanding-egypt/.

61. John Judis, "Egypt's Liberals Are in Denial." *New Republic*, July 16, 2013. http://www.newrepublic.com/article/113885/egypts-liberals-denial#.

62. Ibid.

63. Khaled Abou El Fadl, "The Collapse of Legitimacy: How Egypt's Secular Intelligentsia Betrayed the Revolution." July 11, 2013. http://www.abc.net.au/religion/articles/2013/07/11/3800817.htm.

64. Samer Shehata, "In Egypt Democrats vs. Liberals." *New York Times*, July 2, 2013. http://www.nytimes.com/2013/07/03/opinion/in-egypt-democrats-vs-liberals.html.

65. David Kirkpatrick and Mayy El Sheikh, "In Egypt, a Chasm Grows between Young and Old." *New York Times*, February 16, 2014. http://www.nytimes.com/2014/02/17/world/middleeast/a-chasm-grows-between-young-and-old-in-egypt.html.

66. Ingy Hassieb, "Egypt's Youth Feel Disenfranchised after Revolution." *Los Angeles Times*, May 28, 2013. http://articles.latimes.com/2013/may/28/world/la-fg-egypt-youth-disillusionment-20130529.

67. "Egypt: Lift Ban on Youth Opposition Group." *Human Rights Watch*, April 30, 2014. http://www.hrw.org/news/2014/04/30/egypt-lift-ban-youth-opposition-group.

68. Ibid.

69. Ayah Aman, "Egypt's youth turn to Islamic State." *AlMonitor*, November. 4, 2014. http://www.al-monitor.com/pulse/originals/2014/11/egypt-youth-turn-to-islamic-state-peaceful-brotherhood.html#.

CHAPTER 9

1. John O. Voll, "Epilogue: Islam and the New Public Sphere." In *Engaging with a Legacy: Nehemia Levtzion (1935–2003)*. Ed. E. Ann McDougall. London: Routledge, 2013, pp. 348–359.

2. Francis Fukuyama, *The End of History and the Last Man*. New York: Macmillan Free Press, 1992, p. xiii.

3. Robin Wright, "Islam, Democracy and the West." *Foreign Affairs* 71:3 (Summer 1992): 145.

4. John L. Esposito and John O. Voll, *Islam and Democracy*. New York: Oxford University Press, 1996, p. 3.

5. Ibid., 7.

6. Samuel P. Huntington, *The Third Wave: Democratization in the Late Twentieth Century*. Norman: University of Oklahoma Press, 1991, p. 298.

7. Quoted in David Kushner, "Self-Perception and Identity in Contemporary Turkey." *Journal of Contemporary History* 32:2 (April 1997): 230.

8. Recep Tayyip Erdogan, "Conservative Democracy and the Globalization of Freedom." (Speech at the American Enterprise Institute, January 29, 2004.) In *The Emergence of a New Turkey: Democracy and the AK Parti*, Appendix 1. Ed. M. Hakan Yavuz. Salt Lake City: University of Utah Press, 2006, p. 336.

9. Gheissari and Nasr, *Democracy in Iran*, p. 158. See also Nader Hashemi, "Religious Disputation and Democratic Constitutionalism: The Enduring Legacy of the Constitutional Revolution on the Struggle for Democracy in Iran." *Constellations* 17:1 (2010): 50–60.

10. Naveeda Khan, *Muslim Becoming: Aspiration and Skepticism in Pakistan.* Durham, NC: Duke University Press, 2012, p. 11.

11. David Held, *Models of Democracy.* 3rd ed. Stanford: Stanford University Press, 2006, p. 304.

12. Francis Fukuyama, *The Origins of Political Order.* New York: Farrar, Straus and Giroux, 2011, p. 4.

13. Larry Diamond, "The Next Democratic Century." *Current History* 99 (January 2014): 8–11.

14. Arch Puddington, "Discarding Democracy: A Return to the Iron Fist." *Freedom in the World 2015.* Washington, DC: Freedom House, 2015, p. 1.

Index